Reimagining Reference
in the 21st Century

Edited by David A. Tyckoson and John G. Dove

Charleston Insights in
Library, Archival, and Information Sciences

Purdue University Press
West Lafayette, Indiana

Copyright 2015 by Purdue University. All rights reserved.

Cataloging-in-Publication data on file at the Library of Congress.

Reimagining Reference in the 21st Century

Contents

Foreword   i
Joseph Janes (University of Washington)

About the Book   v

Introduction   1
*David A. Tyckoson (California State University, Fresno)
and John G. Dove (Former CEO of Credo Reference)*

PART 1: SKILLS AND SERVICES

**1 Participatory Approaches to
Building Community-Centered Libraries**   19
*Anastasia Diamond-Ortiz (Cleveland Public Library) and
Buffy J. Hamilton (Norcross High School Media Center)*

2 Guiding Learners: Information Literacy   41
Alesia McManus (Howard Community College, Maryland)

3 The Reference Interview Revisited   61
M. Kathleen Kern (University of Illinois at Urbana-Champaign)

4 Readers' Advisory Services as Reference Services   75
Jessica E. Moyer (University of Wisconsin-Milwaukee)

PART 2: CONTENT AND INFORMATION SOURCES

5   Reference Publishing in the 21st Century:
Lead, Follow, or Get Out of the Way   **89**
Rolf Janke (Mission Bell Media)

6   Wikipedia, User-Generated Content,
and the Future of Reference Sources   **103**
Phoebe Ayers (Wikimedia Foundation and University of California, Davis)

PART 3: TOOLS AND TECHNOLOGIES

7   Discovery Tools   **121**
Michael Courtney (Indiana University)

8   Collaborative Virtual Reference: Past, Present
and Future Trends   **133**
Kris Johnson (AskColorado/AskAcademic Virtual Reference Cooperative)

9   The Value of Reference Services:
Using Assessment to Chart the Future   **149**
Amanda Clay Powers (Mississippi State University)

INNOVATION IN ACTION: STUDIES AND EXAMPLES

A   Alienation, Acceptance, or Ambiguity?:
A Qualitative Study of Librarian and Staff Perceptions
of Reference Service Change   **163**
*Mara H. Sansolo (Pasco-Hernando State College, Florida) and
Kaya van Beynen (University of South Florida St. Petersburg)*

B   Meet Your Personal Librarian   **173**
Martha Adkins (University of San Diego)

C Roving Reference 181
   Madeline Cohen and Kevin Saw (Lehman College, City University of New York)

D On-Call Reference 191
   Krista Schmidt (West Carolina University)

E Peer Reference Tutoring 199
   Michelle Twait (Gustavus Adolphus College, Minnesota)

F A Single Service Point 207
   Diane Hunter and Mary E. Anderson (University of Missouri-Kansas City)

G Community Outreach Through LibGuides 215
   Mandi Goodsett (Georgia Southwestern State University) and
   Kirstin Dougan (University of Illinois at Urbana-Champaign)

H 24/7 Global Virtual Reference Cooperation:
   The Case of QuestionPoint 223
   Susan McGlamery (OCLC QuestionPoint)

I Serving the "Somewhere Out There" Patron:
   The View From the Digital Cooperative Reference Desk 231
   Nicolette Warisse Sosulski (Portage District Library, Michigan)

J Integration of Library Resources Into the
   Course Management System 243
   Janet Pinkley (California State University, Channel Islands) and
   Margaret Driscoll (University of California, Santa Barbara)

K Negotiating Space for the Library: Embedding Library
   Resources and Services Into a University Learning
   Management System 253
   Jolanda-Pieta van Arnhem and James Williams (College of Charleston)

L   Boosting User Engagement With Online Social Tools   265
       Georgina Parsons (Brunel University London, United Kingdom)

M   You Have a Question, So Tweet Me Maybe:
A Study in Using Twitter for Reference   271
       Amanda L. Folk (University of Pittsburgh at Greensburg)

N   Embedding LibraryThing for Libraries
in the Online Library Catalog   279
       Amanda Viana (Norton Public Library, Massachussetts)

O   CrowdAsk: Crowdsourcing Reference and Library Help   285
       Ilana Stonebraker and Tao Zhang (Purdue University)

P   The *Guide to Reference*:
A Solution for Teaching Reference Sources   295
       Denise Beaubien Bennett (University of Florida)

Q   Reference to Patrons With Disabilities   303
       Michael Saar, (Lamar University, Texas)

R   Discovery Service: Goals, Evaluation, and
Implementation of OhioLINK Academic Consortium   317
       Ron Burns (EBSCO) and Theda Schwing (OhioLINK)

S   OCLC and Discovery   327
       John McCullough (OCLC)

T   Discovery and the Digital Reference Desk   335
       Andrew Nagy (ProQuest)

U   Reference: An Architect's View   339
       Rayford W. Law (Rayford W. Law Architecture+Planning)

**V Addressing User Intent:
Analyzing Usage Logs to Optimize Search Results   351**
   Christine Stohn (Ex Libris)

W Educating Reference Librarians for First-Day Success   361
   Elizabeth Mahoney and Christinger Tomer (University of Pittsburgh)

Where Do We Go From Here?   371
   *David A. Tyckoson (California State University, Fresno)
   and John G. Dove (Former CEO of Credo Reference)*

About the Contributors   379

Index   389

Foreword: Exactly the Same and Completely Different

Joseph Janes, University of Washington

"Reference," to be honest, has always been a problematic word for me. Let's be clear: I'm fine with the concept. When I went to graduate school lo these eons ago, I fully intended to be a reference librarian, spending my professional life and career digging out hard-to-find answers to challenging questions for a grateful populace, trusty *World Almanac, American Heritage Dictionary,* and *Encyclopaedia Britannica* by my side, along with the more exotic sources like the *Essay and General Literature Index* and *Famous First Facts*. The one time I got to enter the sanctum sanctorum of a busy public library telephone answer service, and beheld the six-foot-tall lazy susan stacked with the tools of the trade, I could feel a thin trickle of drool forming in the corner of my mouth.

The word, though, the name of the service, always left me a bit cold. Yes, I know it denotes the ability we have to "refer" people to the right information or source, and yes, it's been plastered on every service desk and millions of bookmarks for about a hundred years, but let's face it, that name (a) doesn't actually denote the nuanced, complex, and sophisticated nature of the work, and (b) means precisely zero to your average person.

However, we soldiered on, and when the Internet came to stay, many of us were faced with the once-in-a-lifetime challenge of translating this familiar service into that domain. Which we did, by using and adapting email, web forms, video, instant messaging, text, and chat, proving that everything old is new again, revisiting the discussions around providing reference service by mail correspondence, telephone, and even teletype each in their turn.

Throughout much of this, over the last twenty years or so, I've been teaching courses to prepare students to fulfill this function in a variety of settings. The titles of the courses and the settings and the sources have evolved, as have the delivery mechanisms. I was cleaning out some old files the other day and found some of my old class notes and was startled to see just how dramatically some topics have changed.[1] On the other hand, there are a number of larger principles, dare one say truisms, which have stayed constant or even deepened over the years:

Method over material. I stole this from Isadore Gilbert Mudge, perhaps one of the first academic reference librarians worthy of the name, who established much of what we think of as reference practice in her time at Columbia and in compiling early versions of the *Guide to Reference Books*. This phrase captures the importance and centrality of process, even and perhaps especially in the face of new, changing, and dying sources, and the fact that she coined this about a hundred years ago is pretty darned impressive.

Content over containers. I don't know if OCLC coined this in their 2003 report, but it rang a bell then and still does today. Simply put, lots of the time, people don't really give a fig what format information comes in; they just want it, which partially explains why streaming music and television are soundly thrashing discs (except vinyl, which is having its own renaissance) and, well, television. Pay attention to the what, and the how-represented will often follow.

Memory and imagination. Another blatant theft, this time from Eva Miller, a friend and former student, who used it in a keynote address once and rang another bell. That's really what reference work is, isn't it? Remembering a source you know or suspect has the answer, and if not, imagining what one might look like. I don't know that there's a specialized dictionary of geological terms, but I can sure picture it.

The au courant question for the last few years for the faux-information-sophisticate set has been, "What do we need a library for, when everything's on Google?" We all have our private answers to that one—preferably delivered after counting backward from ten in Latin to avoid bloodshed—but in the context of reference, I can rattle off a bunch for you: We know multiple ways of searching; in fact, try to stop us. We know information and information sources, and which ones are trustworthy, authoritative, and worth the trouble. We can use Google in ways that will make your eyes spin. We know when to *stop* searching. I could go on. For the record, if somebody had demonstrated Google to any decent reference librarian twenty years ago, she would have fallen on her knees in awe and admiration and thought of a dozen ways her service could be improved using a magical tool like that. Living in the future has its advantages.

So here we are, yet again, wrestling with this concept, this service, this mindset, and this function that we treasure so much and that can have such a transformative effect on individuals and their communities. Still challenging, still changing, still a little fraught, and also well worth continually reinventing and reworking. Reference work helps. It's an essential part of libraries and librarianship, and lots of other places, too. It fits in the gaps, making information systems work, making them more human and humane—and beware anything calling itself a "library" that doesn't offer some kind of personal service component. Because it isn't.

There are some wonderful people and ideas represented in the rest of this volume, gathered so ably by my good friends Dave and John, and I'm honored to have been asked to kick off the discussion here. Let me leave you with two final aphorisms: *Yesterday and tomorrow.* I'm a particular fan of history, including the history of the library and the profession of librarianship. A lot has been learned over the decades, about information resources and how to evaluate them, about search technique and how to adapt it to changing tools and conditions, about information needs and how to pry them out of people's heads, about information services and how to design them to best help a community, and about how all these pieces work together. Much of that is time- and situation-dependent and thus of little ongoing use, and there's also a lot that's well worth preserving, adapting, transforming, and moving forward, as good reference librarians always do.

Then, finally, the catchphrase that I cooked up with my dear students and colleagues at the Internet Public Library way back in 1995, when they were building from the ground up the first general-purpose, globally available, question-answering service and, incidentally, forging new plans and models of service provision. The more they worked and built and the more they compared what they were creating with what was then familiar at the time, the more it became clear that reference work in this new and still largely unknown environment was: *Exactly the same and completely different.*

So whatever we call it, and however and wherever it's done and by whom, using whatever tools and resources, "reference" work goes on, because people have questions and need help, and that's what we're here to do. What follows in the rest of this book should spur lots of discussions and ideas and deep thinking about where—and what—that critical and pivotal service could and should be, going forward. All my best wishes to you all as you endeavor your way through what follows here and beyond.

Seattle, Washington
August 2014

NOTES

1. I also found, *mirable dictu*, the final examination from the reference course I took in 1980, complete with the question I completely muffed, asking for a person's address, and after working my way through *Who's Who, American Men and Women of Science, Current Biography,* and other equally fruitless ideas, I came up empty, only to discover later that he was in the local phone book. A valuable lesson, though my face still gets hot when I think about this. But I digress.

About the Book

This book is part of a series of books that focus on the practical aspects of contemporary librarianship. The purpose of this title is to take a look at some of the things that currently are happening in reference service. This work contains nine chapters on major themes in reference, from the reference interview to reference publishing, collaborative virtual reference, and assessment. These nine chapters review the history, recent developments, and factors influencing each topic—with an eye toward how those activities will change in the coming years. None of us knows for sure what that future will be like—but we all know that it will be both similar to and very different from what we are doing today.

The chapters are supplemented with examples and case studies of some of the things that are happening in libraries today. These examples are provided so that the reader can see the current range of different ideas implemented and actions taken to improve reference services. Topics range from measuring attitudes toward change to the use of new tools (such as Twitter and LibraryThing), the implementation of discovery services, and changes in service patterns. These examples are not intended to imply that all libraries must adopt such services and tools, but to highlight the various options that librarians have available to them for enhancing reference services.

The contents of this work focus on the practical rather than the theoretical. The papers included are not intended to be comprehensive research studies and thus do not contain extensive bibliographies on their respective topics. What they do instead is to present ideas of how librarians are changing their reference services to meet ever-changing demands. This book should be used to develop ideas for your library and its programs and services—not as a basis for dissertation research.

One important aspect of this book is that it contains voices from all segments of the library community. The editors intentionally sought out contributors from public libraries, academic libraries (including community colleges), publishers, and vendors. Edited by a reference librarian and a vendor, we attempted to include contributions that reflect the varying issues faced by people in all segments of the field of librarianship.

About the Series

The Charleston Conference and its related venues for discourse provide a unique forum for discussion of issues of mutual interest across traditional divides between librarians, publishers, and vendors. Discussion is often "ahead of the curve," anticipating as well as reflecting the most important trends. The Series will focus on significant topics in library, archival, and information science, presenting the issues in a relatively jargonfree way that is accessible to all types of information professionals. Most volumes will be edited collections. A typical volume will present an overview of issues by an expert volume editor and then thematic chapters. Reflecting the pragmatic tone of the series, chapters will often include case studies that describe lessons learned and suggest best practices.

Introduction to *Reimagining Reference in the 21st Century*

David A. Tyckoson, California State University, Fresno, and John G. Dove, Former CEO of Credo Reference

What's wrong with reference? For decades, librarians and library administrators have been asking some variation of that question. Bill Miller eloquently began the debate thirty years ago, expressing concerns about the pressures and demands being place upon public services, many by reference librarians themselves. Jerry Campbell shook the conceptual foundations of reference in his scathing critique in 1992, concluding that using high(er) paid reference librarians to interact with users was no longer necessary. David Tyckoson tried to update and answer some of Miller's questions a decade and a half later. An entire Rethinking Reference movement arose from these discussions, resulting in many conferences, articles, and books on the topic. And we have been rethinking, reinventing, and now reimagining reference ever since.

How did we reach this point? And how do we move on? Is reference still a useful component of library services? If so, how will it serve users? If not, how will it evolve into something else that is relevant? Or should reference service just die off, leaving users to more modern methods of assistance? This book attempts to answer some of these questions. It looks at reference from several perspectives, from the traditional (reference interview, information literacy, and readers' advisory) to the contemporary (assessment and collaborative virtual reference) to the view from vendors (discovery systems, reference publishing, and Wikipedia). These various perspectives are highlighted with examples of innovative practices (embedding librarians in course software, moving public services to a single service point, and using a variety of social media).

To understand the future of reference, we must understand its past. Imagine a world where:

- The amount of information is proliferating dramatically.
- Many people do not have access to or cannot afford to purchase information themselves.
- Libraries are seeing ever increasing usage.

If that sounds familiar, it should—that was the state of society in the 19th century when the idea for reference service was first conceived. The idea of the free public library was exploding, with any community that saw itself as cultured establishing a library to demonstrate that fact. The new public libraries provided free access to information for everyone in the community—and the community responded by visiting those libraries in droves. However, there was a basic problem—many people in those communities had no idea how to use a library.

As a result, Samuel Green made his now-famous speech at the first meeting of the American Library Association—later published in the first volume of the *American Library Journal* (now *Library Journal*)—that is commonly attributed as the beginning of reference service. In that paper, Green presents a variety of examples of how librarians could provide direct assistance to users. Those examples fall into four categories:

- Teaching people how to use the library
- Answering information queries
- Recommending resources
- Promoting the library within the community

Those same functions are still happening today, almost 150 years after Green first articulated them. We still teach users how to find and evaluate information; we still help them answer questions; we still recommend resources; and we still promote the library to our community. The tools that we use and the way that we communicate with people in our communities have changed drastically, but the functions themselves have remained constant. While access to information is now faster and easier than ever, the need for reference service has not gone away.

To better understand why reference is still with us, we need to step back and look at the role that libraries play in our communities. First, we

THE LIBRARY COUNSELLOR

For centuries, libraries have been complex and mystifying places. As the volume of knowledge to be organized has increased over time, the ability to identify and retrieve that knowledge has become more difficult. This is not a new phenomenon, as documented by the statement below from the *Report of the Committee appointed by the Board of Overseers of Harvard College to examine the Library* (1868). The handwritten notes—written by Ralph Waldo Emerson—are included in the Harvard University Archives.

> No library is perfect until it has within its walls, besides men of that method & dispatch & general providence & activity which the conservation & the circulation of books requires,—a master of bibliography,—and we must add certain moral qualifications: And whilst the Committee are not prepared at this day to recommend the addition to the University of a new chair, of a Professor of Books,—they would be glad to secure to it the contemplated advantage in some form.
>
> The first use of a college library is to be irresistibly attractive to young men. In daily experience it is not so. Young men go in & then go out of it repelled by the multitude of books which only speak to them of their ignorance,—their very multitude concealing from the gazing youth the one or the few volumes which are there waiting for him with the very information & leading he wants. Would some kind scholar take pity on his sincere curiosity, & by a little discreet [blank] guide him to the class of works & presently to the precise author who has written as for him alone. Could not a gentleman be found to occupy a desk in Gore Hall as the *Library Counsellor*, to whom the Librarian could refer inquiries on authors & subjects?

> We are aware that such selection would be a delicate point,—easy to miss,—& that it requires a man of sympathy, a lover of books & of readers of books, to fulfil the design. Everyone of us has probably known such persons, but it will commonly happen that they are of such condition or pre-engagements as not to be thought of as candidates.
>
> The suggestion was made in conversation at the last meeting of the Committee but found such favor that it was directed to be embodied in the Report.
>
> For the Committee.
> R. W. Emerson.
> October 24, 1868.

need to remind ourselves that most libraries were established to serve the people of very specific communities. Academic libraries serve the faculty, staff, and students of a specific college or university. Public libraries serve the residents of a specific geographic region, usually a city or county. Law libraries serve the employees of a specific law firm. Hospital libraries serve the physicians, nurses, and patients of that specific hospital. School libraries serve the students and teachers of a specific school. Libraries are not independent organizations that exist in isolation, but are organizations that exist to assist the members of their parent community.

The relationship of the library to the community is key in understanding and evaluating the role of the library. To paraphrase the late Thomas P. "Tip" O'Neill, all librarianship is local. Everything that we do in our libraries, including which services we provide, what materials we put in our collections, and what social media we use, must be evaluated by how well it serves our parent community. If we serve our community well, we will be respected and supported by that community. If we do not serve our parent community well, we will be neglected and marginalized by that community. Each decision that we make must be evaluated in terms of how it benefits our specific community.

What this means is that there is rarely one magical answer to any given problem. Just because a library serving another community makes a certain decision does not mean that the same decision is relevant for a different library. Each library needs to determine what is best for its local community and not feel compelled to adopt a decision from another community just because others are doing it. There is no one-size-fits-all solution to any library issue.

While each community is unique, there are obviously many similarities between communities, and libraries have long worked together to share resources and services. Interlibrary loan is a time-honored way for libraries to share collections, dating back at least a century in practice. Shared cataloging is another standard practice, where one library creates a catalog record for an item and others use and modify that record for their own needs. Cooperative reference allows staff in one location to answer questions for patrons in another location, whether those questions are asked via telephone, email, chat, or through the postal service. We have much to share—and learn—from each other (for example, in Chapter 8 Kris Johnson writes about the development of cooperative virtual reference). However, each lesson needs to be evaluated within the context of the local community.

So what exactly do reference librarians do to meet the needs of their community? The answer is very simple—they help. They instruct community members on methods for finding valid information. They answer information queries. They recommend resources. By doing so, they promote the library within the community. In short, reference librarians today are doing the same thing that they did back in the 1870s. In Chapter 1 of this book, Anastasia Diamond-Ortiz and Buffy J. Hamilton talk about how libraries can engage their local community by becoming community-centered libraries.

However, the tools with which we currently operate are almost entirely different. In the 19th century, the best tools were the library catalog and *Poole's Index to Periodical Literature*. Of course, everything was in print form—and if it was not at the library, it was not available. The only way to communicate with users was in person at the library or by letter through the mail. In today's electronic and networked environment, we have a plethora of information sources and communication methods. Email, chat, instant messaging, text messaging, and telephone are available pretty much anytime and anywhere in most of our communities. The Internet brings the most comprehensive collection of human knowledge ever created directly into the homes of most of our community members. In the 19th century, discovering information was a major part of the problem. Today, filtering and evaluating all that is discovered is the larger issue.

The popular image of the reference librarian is of someone who answers factual questions and can quickly and accurately provide obscure facts, serving like a walking encyclopedia. What are the names of Santa's reindeer? What is the population of Corfu? Does the king of the Watusi tribe drive a car?

As intriguing as that definition may be of a reference librarian, it was never really the case. Most questions that reference librarians get asked do not have single factual answers. Even in the 1950s, factual questions were never the majority of questions asked. Today, they are almost nonexistent. Instead, we get questions like: Is global warming real? Would a change in immigration policy be good for the country or the state? What is the relationship between fast food and diabetes? Should the United States adopt an English-only language policy? None of the those questions has a single factual answer; they all have many potential answers, depending on what any individual user is really looking for. The librarian is not someone who spits out facts, but someone who counsels the user on the most effective process to find the information that they desire. We recommend sources and search strategies much more than we give out answers—and this has always been the role of the reference librarian. Whether referring to the Encyclopaedia Britannica, Pubmed, Google, or Wikipedia, we suggest strategies much more than we provide answers.

In the 19th century, information was a relatively rare commodity. Print was the only format available and was beyond the budget of most households. Since users had to rely on the library as a primary place to get information, that meant that the library maintained many factual books—dictionaries, directories, almanacs, and encyclopedias—that would answer community needs. Now that such information is available everywhere on the Internet, the need for libraries to collect those kinds of sources has been greatly reduced. Reference books were once the revered and elite members of the library collection, given special status in location policy (usually front and center—and always near the librarians), circulation (noncirculating, so that they would always be available to users who came into the library), and revision (updated regularly so that users and librarians would have access to current information). Reference became a niche market for publishers—and a profitable one. In most library collections, reference books were considered essential. Although priced out of reach for most households, they were almost required purchases for libraries. Everyone had to have an updated encyclopedia, statistical compendium, almanac, and directory. Reference became a specialized publishing industry, with companies like Oxford, Gale, Macmillan, and World Book building their entire market strategy on the fact that libraries bought their products on a regular basis.

Today, it must be very difficult to be a reference publisher. Besides the fact that most people look things up on the Internet—and often find what they need there—they now need to compete against free, open-source works such as Wikipedia. In its short period of existence, Wikipedia has become the most consulted reference tool in human history, and people use it because they typically find what they are looking for in it. It is current, complete, and mostly accurate. For anyone desiring a summary or brief history of a topic, Wikipedia is a great resource. It is updated as events happen, rather than the next time an edition is printed. It is not a definitive source on most topics, but it makes a great starting point for just about any topic. It links to other resources, often including government, association, or other authoritative sources. It is free, always available, and written in just about any human language that a user can read. It includes many images, sounds, and other multimedia features.

A good definition or explanation of any of the myriad terms or topics that might be used to answer a factual question are available free on the web from multiple sources today, so the business of producing a commercially viable reference product is increasingly challenging. Companies like Gale have sought to be inclusive of other publishers' reference content in order to create a viable online reference offering. Credo Reference has added additional reference-related services to its general reference database and continues to grow in popularity. In Chapters 5 and 6, Rolf Janke writes about how the publishing industry is reacting to this changing environment and Phoebe Ayers talks about how user-generated content supports reference work through Wikipedia and other open-source tools.

Whether consulting published reference works or crowdsourced tools like Wikipedia, reference librarians have always relied upon external information sources when assisting users. In most cases, the librarian offers a recommendation to the user—what is often referred to as readers' advisory. Readers' advisory originally implied recommending fiction for pleasure reading. A reader who liked an author such as James Patterson would want to find other authors who wrote with the same style, character types, geographic location, time period, or plot construction. Librarians have been making these kinds of recommendations for over a century. However, the idea of recommendation has become a much bigger part of society—and one that users expect to see pretty much everywhere they look. Amazon tells you that shoppers who bought one book also bought other similar titles. Pandora streams music that is similar to what you like and allows you to modify the profile as the music is playing. Netflix recommends films based on your past viewing habits. People view recommendations as a standard component of their lives, and they expect it at the library as well.

When librarians recommend one website over another, we are providing readers' advisory (or maybe browser's advisory). When we recommend one database over another, we are providing readers' advisory (or perhaps searcher's advisory). When we recommend one journal's articles over another's, we are providing readers' advisory. Every time a librarian recommends one source over others—or in addition to others—we are providing readers' advisory services to our users. Since most questions do not have factual answers, we do a lot of recommending of books, databases, websites, and other resources. This is a common practice in every kind of library, even though we do not always call it readers' advisory. In Chapter 4, Jessica E. Moyer talks about the impact of readers' advisory and its value as a service.

We have developed a wide range of communication tools that allow our users to contact us, including the telephone, email, text messaging, instant messaging, and chat. We have created cooperative reference service projects that allow users to get help from librarians anywhere and anytime. OCLC's QuestionPoint service is the most well-known, but other systems also are available. AskColorado, Maryland AskUsNow!, and Ohio's KnowItNow24x7 are all examples of groups of libraries who have banded together to offer their users cooperative virtual reference services. In Chapter 8, Kris Johnson discusses the development of and benefits from cooperative virtual reference services. Communication tools for reaching librarians have proliferated, but how we communicate remains a constant.

At the heart of all reference and readers' advisory services is our ability to find out what our users need. Unfortunately, most users do not ask for what they really want. In some cases, they do not even know what they really want but just have a vague idea of an information need. They frequently have a general idea of a topic that they want to find information about, such as global warming. Their interest may be internally motivated (e.g., due to an inherent curiosity, finding more about something that they have read or seen in the media, or from a personal problem) or it may be externally motivated (e.g., from a school assignment or for a project at work). Through open- and closed-ended questioning, the librarian helps the user figure out what specific aspects of the subject she will search for and which tools to search in. With guidance from the librarian, the user moves from the very general question—perhaps about global warming—to the very specific question—such as whether climate change is altering rainfall patterns in the American West and how these rainfall patterns are affecting crop production for fruits and vegetables. The librarian must have the skills to help the user shape the information need, assisting this person in defining ever more precisely what it is that he wants to find. This process traditionally has been called the reference interview, and M. Kathleen Kern reviews it in Chapter 3.

Whether occurring face-to-face at a service point, over the telephone, or online via email, chat, or instant messaging, the reference interview is where direct human contact occurs during the reference process. Every reference interview is different, because every reference interview is personalized to meet the needs of each individual user. The psychology of having to ask for help inhibits many users from even asking in the first place. Users are often reluctant to ask for assistance and see the need for help as a sign of their personal failure. Many users believe that everything that they might ever want to know is on the Internet and that they should be able to access it through Google, Wikipedia, and other search tools. When they cannot find information on their own, they blame themselves for that failure. They then either give up or come to the reference librarian for help, beginning the transaction by saying something like, "I know that I should be able to find this myself, but . . . " or "I've been searching for this for an hour . . ." or "I am sorry to bother you, but . . ."

Each of those questions—and all of the others similar to it that librarians hear every day—are indicators that users find the search for information complicated, frustrating, and difficult. To help mitigate those problems, most libraries have programs to help their users improve their information literacy skills. Librarians at most colleges and universities offer instruction sessions, workshops, and even for-credit courses that focus on search techniques in specific disciplines. Public libraries offer classes on computer skills, search techniques, and evaluating search results. All of these activities are part of the effort to build better information literacy skills within our communities, as Alesia McManus describes in Chapter 2 on guiding learners toward information literacy.

Are all of these activities worthwhile? Should libraries invest in tools to support users? Should those expensive librarians spend their time interacting with users? Should libraries continue to purchase reference sources, or should those funds be spent in other areas? These are questions that all libraries must ask. In order to be relevant to our communities, we need to find out what we are doing that is working—and what is not. This is where assessment comes into the discussion. Assessment is a growing aspect of librarianship, because through assessment we learn what we are doing well and where we are not living up to expectations. Assessment comes in many sizes and flavors—from measuring usage of the print reference collection to determining the impact that libraries have on student success. One of the largest assessment projects is ACRL's Value of Academic Libraries initiative, which is developing tools that academic libraries can use to show their value to the university. Amanda Clay Powers reviews library assessment programs in Chapter 9.

What makes reference services—and libraries in general—somewhat unique in society today is the direct human contact that users have with professional library staff. At click of a web link, dial of a phone, or a simple walk up to a reference desk, anyone in the community is able to receive the services of the library, customized to their specific needs. The librarian will help the user solve problems large and small, from getting authoritative information to support them through a medical issue, suggesting a new book to read or film to watch, finding a known information source, citing a source in APA or MLA style, or figuring out how to print. The librarian provides that assistance without an appointment, at no direct cost, and with assurances that the question and sources will not be shared with other people or companies. This makes libraries a human place, which is why users tend to return to them. The library is a place where members of the community get human help—and most community members value that type of assistance very highly.

Even as we start to look for ways in which our personalized services can be scaled up to the 24/7, anytime/anywhere access to the library, the principles that have been established in the face-to-face world should be squarely placed on the design agenda for the development of the online presence and the technologies that support us. That the American Library Association's Reference and User Services Association is now teaching courses in user-centered design is a reflection that reference librarians need to be able to play a role in creating and building the structure of our users' online world. And products such as search engines, discovery tools, online catalogs, and browsing aids need to be able to accept input from the individual libraries that use them, so that they, too, can live up to the requirement that all librarianship is local.

Do you remember the world that influenced the start of reference service? The world where the volume of information expanded dramatically, where people often could not afford to purchase the information themselves, and where use of libraries rose dramatically? That world is as much ours as it was Samuel Green's. The tools that we use today are completely different, but the needs of our users remain. And the library is there to help meet those needs in a very personal and individual way. A library that is integrated into the community remains a place where members of that community get the assistance that they need when they need it. It is because of the personal service that librarians provide—which we still call reference service—that libraries and reference will not disappear, but will remain relevant to our communities today and for the foreseeable future. As we reimagine reference in this book, as we develop new tools and techniques to discover information and to deliver services, and as we continue to meet the needs of our own communities, reference librarians will continue to provide the direct, personal, and truly human service they have been known for in the past.

The title of this book is *Reimagining Reference in the 21st Century*, and it is loaded with reimagined reference ideas that are happening in libraries right now. The examples that we include here document the ever changing nature of reference service. Reference has never been a static concept, nor is it likely to become one. New tools, new information sources, and new user populations have been part of the evolving nature of reference service for at least a century, and it will continue to give us news opportunities throughout the next one. S. R. Ranganathan's fifth law of library science—the library is a growing organism—is as true today as it was when he first wrote it in 1931. Successful libraries evolve and change. Unsuccessful libraries remain static and risk fading into irrelevance.

What will the future of reimagined reference look like? None of us knows for sure, but we expect it to resemble something like this:

- *Reimagined reference will serve new user communities.* As our local community changes, so will the collections and services available for our users. We will provide materials and services in new languages, matching the needs of the latest immigrants to our community. We will teach information skills to new groups of people, helping them to become information literate and independent. We will interact with a wider segment of our local community, wherever they may be located at the time. We will offer programming that reaches all people in our community who are not currently library users. We will draw more users into the library—some physically, many virtually. We will teach them how to find and evaluate information, making the library and its services a useful component of their daily lives.
- *Reimagined reference will use new tools.* Not too long ago, the majority of reference work was done face-to-face. Users would come to a library to get help and the librarians would work with them in person to provide assistance. The librarian was able to direct the user to appropriate information sources, all of which were printed materials used in the library building. However, even in reference's early days, librarians responded to queries from remote users by answering questions in the mail. Over time, new communication tools (such as the telegraph and telephone) allowed the librarian to connect with users who were located outside the library building. With the advent of electronic computers and telecommunications networks, we now converse instantly with users anywhere. Today, we rely on chat or instant messenger, email, and the telephone to communicate with our users. Some libraries are also using Skype and other video teleconferencing methods. In the future, newer and even better communication tools will be developed and adapted by libraries. Today's libraries would look like a scene from a science fiction

novel to librarians of the 1950s—and the libraries of the 2050s will look like science fiction to us. Our tools will continue to change and improve, and we will adapt those that best benefit the users in our local communities.

- *Reimagined reference will use new information sources.* Traditionally, reference librarians have relied upon commercially published sources for answering reference questions. We built reference collections and restricted circulation of reference materials so that the sources that we needed to help users would be there when we wanted them. When we had users with questions, we took them to those reference collections in search of a source that met their needs. Finding information was difficult. When those sources first moved online, they were in subscription databases where the searching was powerful but access was restricted by subscription costs. After the invention of the Internet, access became universal and cost became negligible, opening up the world of information to everyone. Today, reference librarians rarely use books except in very specialized situations. Through the Internet, reference librarians and library users have access to more information than any library contained at any time in human history. Finding is not the problem—evaluating the sources found to identify the best and most reliable is the difficult part. And with social media, the publication of reference sources has also become part of the public domain. Wikipedia is the most consulted reference work of all time, and it is constantly growing and changing as contributors add and edit its content. While it is difficult to imagine that even better information sources are on the horizon, new tools will be developed that will make our present information sources seem quaint. And when they are developed, they will be incorporated into the reimagined vision of reference.
- *Reimagined reference will remain personal and professional.* Through all of the changes in our communication tools, our information sources, and our community members, reference librarians continue to provide an individual and human-scale service to our users. The reference librarian is the library's connection between the contents of the library and the people who use it. The reference librarian identifies the specific needs of each user and matches the sources provided to those needs. The essential skill required is the ability to communicate with users in such a way that they are willing to inform us of their needs—what we traditionally called the reference interview. Whether that interview takes place in person, on the phone, via instant messenger,

or using some as yet undeveloped communication medium, the successful reference librarian is the one who can provide personal service that meets the unique needs of each library user. Librarians are skilled at asking the right questions to get the user to expand on his or her need while not making them feel defensive or stupid by having to ask for help. Over time, a good reference librarian develops relationships with community members who come back again and again when they need additional information.

- *Reimagined reference will be customized to each individual library.* Not only are user needs of one library different than another's, but more importantly the content available to each library may differ widely. To be effective, reimagined reference needs to promote those library resources that are available and relevant to that particular library's users.
- *Reimagined reference will be evaluated by its impact on users.* What is truly important about reference is its impact on each and every individual user. Success is not to be measured in the numbers of questions asked, the accuracy of answers given, the availability of information sources, or the speed of a response, but on how well the service fits the specific needs of each individual user. Reference is a very personal service, where the user who needs help receives it in a personal, professional, and private manner. What makes reference important is not the sources that we have access to or the type of technology that we use, but the human connection that is made between the librarian and the user. In today's do-it-yourself society, there are few institutions in which someone can receive individualized service from a professional at no direct cost and without requiring an appointment—yet that remains the case in most libraries. Reference librarians humanize the world of information, and it is that humanity that our users will value the most. A reimagined reference service will have new tools, new information sources, and new users, but it will continue to provide personalized and professional assistance. In a society in which we have less and less direct human contact, reference librarians will continue to offer such a service, thus bettering the lives of the people in their community.

REFERENCES

Campbell, J. D. (1992). Shaking the conceptual foundations of reference: A perspective. *Reference Services Review, 20*(4), 29–35. http://dx.doi.org/10.1108/eb049164

Emerson, R. W. (1868). *Report of the Committee appointed by the Board of Overseers of Harvard College to examine the Library*. Harvard University Archives, USll 10.6.3 Volume XI.

Green, S. S. (1876). Personal relations between librarians and readers. *Library Journal, 1,* 74–81.

Miller, W. (1984). What's wrong with reference: Coping with success and failure at the reference desk. *American Libraries, 15*(5), 303–306, 321–322.

Ranganathan, S. R. (1931). *The five laws of library science*. London: Edward Goldston.

Tyckoson, D. A. (1999). What's right with reference. *American Libraries, 30*(5), 57–63.

REIMAGINING REFERENCE THROUGH THE YEARS

Reference has been rethought, reengineered, reinvented, reborn, and reimagined on a rather frequent basis. This book is just the latest in a long line of attempts to redefine the function and role of reference services. The books listed below provide a chronological review of reference revision over the last fifteen years. Readers of *Reimagining Reference* will also be interested in these previous discussions.

Miller, R. K., Meier, C., and Moorefield-Lang, H. (2012). *Rethinking reference and instruction with tablets*. Chicago: ALATechSource.

Mulac, C. (2012). *Fundamentals of reference*. Chicago: American Library Association.

Bopp, R. E., & Smith, L. C. (2011). *Reference and information services: An introduction* (4th ed.). Santa Barbara, CA: Libraries Unlimited.

Murphy, S. A. (2011). *The librarian as information consultant: Transforming reference for the Information Age*. Chicago: American Library Association.

Zabel, D. (2011). *Reference reborn: Breathing new life into public services librarianship*. Santa Barbara, CA: Libraries Unlimited.

Radford, M. L., & Lanke, R. D. (2010). *Reference renaissance: Current and future trends*. New York: Neal-Schuman Publishers.

Cassell, K. A., & Hiremath, U. (2009). *Reference and information services in the 21st century: An introduction* (2nd ed.). New York: Neal-Schuman Publishers.

Lankes, R. D. (2008). *Virtual reference service: From competencies to assessment.* New York: Neal-Schuman Publishers.

Steiner, S. K., & Madden, M. L. (2008). *The desk and beyond: Next generation reference services.* Chicago: Association of College and Research Libraries.

Anderson, B., & Webb, P. T. (2006). *New directions in reference.* New York: Haworth Information Press.

Connor, E. (2006). *An introduction to reference services in academic libraries.* New York: Haworth Information Press.

Lankes, R. D. (2004). *The virtual reference experience: Integrating theory into practice.* New York: Neal-Schuman Publishers.

Janes, J. (2003). *Introduction to reference work in the digital age.* New York: Neal-Schuman Publishers.

Lipow, A. G. (2003). *The virtual reference librarian's handbook.* New York: Neal-Schuman Publishers.

Sarkodie-Mensah, K. (2003). *Managing the twenty-first century reference department: Challenges and prospects.* Binghamton, NY: Haworth Information Press.

Hales-Mabry, C. (2001). *Doing the work of reference: Practical tips for excelling as a reference librarian.* Binghamton, NY: Haworth Information Press.

Whitlatch, J. B. (2000). *Evaluating reference services: A practical guide.* Chicago: American Library Association.

Thomsen, E. (1999). *Rethinking reference: The reference librarian's practical guide for surviving constant change.* New York: Neal-Schuman Publishers.

Part 1

SKILLS AND SERVICES

1 | Participatory Approaches to Building Community-Centered Libraries

Anastasia Diamond-Ortiz, Cleveland Public Library, and Buffy J. Hamilton, Norcross High School Media Center

Participatory librarianship is a lens that posits learning as the primary mission of libraries. Every aspect of the library program comes back to Dr. David Lankes's mantra, "It's all about learning . . . there isn't a part of the library that isn't about learning. Learning is a collaborative conversation" (Lankes, 2012). This framework emphasizes inquiry, promotes shared decision making and ownership of the library vision and program, and honors knowledge construction and content creation by learning communities. If a library is truly embracing this approach to librarianship then libraries should not only support and facilitate learning communities, but those learning communities should also be an essential part of how libraries identify points of need, service, collection, learning spaces, and learning experiences for all users. They also should be an essential voice in assessing the impact of the library on the larger community. A participatory framework of librarianship can position a library to operate from a proactive stance rather than a reactive mode to the needs, wishes, and aspirations of its community, and in turn, embed the library as an essential thread in the fabric of its community.

A library that embodies participatory culture and learning, believes in:

1. Multiple access points to artistic expression and civic engagement
2. Strong support for creating and sharing
3. Fluidity in the roles of novices and experts
4. A sense of connectedness and community
5. Patron contributions matter and will be visible in library services, programming, and learning spaces (Jenkins, 2006)

How might libraries embody this culture of learning and practice with its community members in reenvisioning library experiences and what libraries perceive as reference services? How might libraries cultivate a culture of staff participation in rethinking what library organization and hierarchy to more authentically distribute staff expertise that can result in more effective and innovative library programming and services? What are the possibilities when libraries become shared spaces, places of collaborative learning, and codesigned learning experiences that meet the information-seeking needs of its local community? How might a participatory stance might make libraries not only more accessible, but also become transformative experiences and spaces that address issues of equity and empowerment in communities? In her e-book, *The Participatory Museum*, Nina Simon asserts that scaffolded design of participatory experiences is essential for institutions to craft a culture of participatory learning.

> How can cultural institutions use participatory techniques not just to give visitors a voice, but to develop experiences that are more valuable and compelling for everyone? This is not a question of intention or desire; it's a question of design. Whether the goal is to promote dialogue or creative expression, shared learning or co-creative work, the design process starts with a simple question: which tool or technique will produce the desired participatory experience?" (Simon, 2010)

Whether structured or more open-ended (Simon, 2010), participatory learning experiences in libraries can provide communities the means and opportunities for artistic expression, collaborative problem solving, individual agency, crowdsourced knowledge, or engagement with a network of community mentors. The design drivers of participatory learning and culture are essential to transforming libraries into hubs for lifelong learning and civic engagement that offer multiple and diverse pathways of learning through different modalities.

GUIDEPOSTS FOR PARTICIPATORY DESIGN FROM THE PAST: CHILDREN'S LIBRARIANS OF CLEVELAND PUBLIC LIBRARY

While this new emphasis on participatory learning may seem like a radical shift, the Cleveland Public Library reflects this approach in its early history during the first three decades of the 20th century. Library clubs, which were initially organized around reading interests in the late 1800s and early

1900s, provided children opportunities to explore interests and engage in inquiry with their peers; these clubs were facilitated by children's librarians as well as community members who served as mentors to help children engage in "multiple activities to stimulate minds, inspire imaginations, and have some fun" (Wieland, 2013). At their height, some 40,000 children were participating in library clubs, and 95 volunteers served the clubs. Some clubs were supported by community organizations, such as the Natural History Museum and the Cleveland Museum of Art.

The clubs were organic in nature, with some lasting only a few weeks while others were sustained over long periods of time, including some that reorganized over periods of five to ten years. The clubs included a diverse range of groups, including those who belonged to gangs as well as children of various ethnicities. Some clubs included both boys and girls, while others were primarily one gender. Clubs met at various times of the day and intervals; a club for working adolescents even met at night to accommodate the needs of teens who held day jobs to support their families. Some clubs took field trips, staged productions of plays, and donated their crafts, such as rag dolls and quilts, to others in need throughout the community.

Interests of the clubs included music, languages, art, knitting, aviation, model airplane building, nature, science, drama and plays, electricity, gardening, poetry, stamps, sports, debate, travel, and crafts. The clubs not only provided entry points to hands-on exploration of an area of interest, but they also were a real-world springboard to books and informational materials. The library clubs reflected the qualities of participatory culture and what James Gee today calls affinity spaces: "locations where groups of people are drawn together because of a shared, strong interest or engagement in a common activity . . . affinity spaces encourage the sharing of knowledge or participation in a specific area, and informal learning is a common outcome" ("Affinity space," 2013).

These clubs are historically significant because they embody the principles of participatory learning: clubs were learning communities formed around patron interests; librarians, mentors, and patrons were colearners. Many clubs provided opportunities for participants to share their knowledge or creations with a larger community; and the clubs contributed to a sense of belonging for children and teens whose needs and interests were at the center of this medium for interest-driven learning that provided fun, enrichment, and education. Children's librarians had the professional freedom and agency to help establish, facilitate, and design learning experiences for these clubs with input from the children.

MUSEUM PARTICIPATORY PRACTICES AS INSPIRATION FOR LIBRARIES IDENTIFYING COMMUNITY NEEDS

How might we begin to more concretely envision what participatory practices could look like in a library? As institutions of lifelong learning, how do we begin to place more emphasis on building relationships and trust with the people of our communities to frame the library as space for experiences? Our colleagues in the world of museums are leading the way in participatory practices in two ways. First, many museums are framing patron engagement through a lens of participatory culture, and consequently, their educational and community programming reflects this approach. Second, many museums are embracing participatory engagement with staff, volunteers, and interns. The participatory experiences and opportunities that museums scaffold then become rich, interpretative narratives of learning that embed the community's voices.

Museums are deeply engaged in exploring the ways they might partner "directly with artists and the community to develop new forms of engagement that extend the boundaries of what is possible" (Murawski, 2013, October 14). What would libraries look like today if librarians, like the children's librarians of the Cleveland Public Library in the early part of the 20th century, were to partner more directly with individuals and groups in their communities to reimagine the possibilities of library experiences? How might libraries flourish as hubs of civic, artistic, social, and economic engagement with this approach?

These participatory practices, while seemingly simple, can be a powerful means for identifying community needs and then making those needs visible in library services and programming. While traditional approaches to library services are top-down and designed to provide everyone an "equal" experience of quality, participatory approaches are messier. A library that takes a participatory stance on designing library experiences "supports multi-directional content experiences. The institution serves as a 'platform' that connects different users who act as content creators, distributors, consumers, critics, and collaborators. This means the institution cannot guarantee the consistency of visitor experiences. Instead, the institution provides opportunities for diverse visitor co-produced experiences" (Simon, 2010). Art museums have embraced what is known as *social practice*, a participatory art form in which "practitioners freely blur the lines among object making, performance, political activism, community organizing, environmentalism and investigative journalism, creating a deeply participatory art that often flourishes outside the gallery and museum system" (Kennedy, 2013). A more participatory approach to librarianship and libraries could foster similar experiences with greater impact outside of the library and in the community.

CHANGING THE LIBRARY LANDSCAPE WITH DATA: CONNECTING WITH COMMUNITY NEEDS

The rhetoric about the changing nature of library service and particularly reference service permeates much of the recent professional scholarship and conference content, addressing both the internal and external work of libraries. Regardless of the library type, the expectation is that all libraries will be responsive to changes in information needs and provide access, reference service, and assistance to enable a greater understanding of new information sources. There have been periods in public library history where libraries embraced a much more outreach-focused service model. This outreach focus led to bookmobiles, home delivery, and services to institutions like prisons and hospitals. Responding to the growing populations in neighborhoods, public libraries opened branch libraries. Throughout the 20th century, opening a library building or service point and providing a collection of print materials demonstrated a library's responsiveness by promoting the dissemination of information. The development of bookmobile services followed a similar model of providing access to a smaller print collection on a regular basis to a greater number of people who could not easily access a library location. What has happened since is nothing short of a radical shift in the service model of some libraries and a disruption based on several concurrent streams in society. The resulting outreach and rapid response to community needs has allowed public libraries to more closely align with greater community needs.

The library as a responsive organization today is one that is working in concert with schools, local government, and community groups instead of as an institution set apart from the life of a community. While libraries have often been concerned with amassing collections that reflect the nature of a given user base, selecting appropriate languages, subjects, and formats, the library as a responsive organization is thoughtful in providing reference services, technology, staff, and spaces in addition to building collections. Responsive library organizations are those that listen and are present for conversations affecting the larger community. Responsive library organizations have adopted thinking similar to that found in the Manifesto for Agile Software Development (2001) that favors listening and collaborating with one's users over dictating how services should be delivered to users.

Responsive reference service in libraries depends on recognizing the evolving nature of a user population through several methods. Research findings from a Pew Internet and American Life Project study on library services indicate a clear directive that public libraries should coordinate more closely with schools (Zickuhr, Rainie, & Purcell, 2013). Libraries must no longer function as isolated entities whose sole purpose is to collect and disseminate. The expectation for what a library can do has shifted in the minds of the public—the public library now has the potential to be an agent of change. When public libraries decide to embrace this shift and seek partnership with schools, true community transformation is possible. In most communities, the public library and public schools potentially work with the same population. Initially, a public library might start from the stance that supplying books to public schools is demonstrating the coordination of schools and public libraries. What if the same public library starts by mapping the school-age library cardholders, showing where the public schools are located in a their community? This initial step allows a library to see where it already has an entry point with children who attend a local elementary school. Gathering and analyzing local school district data on achievement and performance could enable deeper understanding of the particular areas where the public library can collaborate with schools. This first analysis allows the public library to be thoughtful when approaching local schools. When the library staff are able to put their work into context, they are equipped to augment their reference service and programs. The library now has data that can inform changes to their youth services reference model and staffing based on the needs of the students. The library as a creator of and consumer of data may be a newer role, but one that is important if the library wants to respond to community needs. To that end, data literacy in library staff is crucial for any responsive model of library service to succeed. It is essential that libraries assess staff comfort with data analysis and encourage staff to build the skills necessary to find, analyze, and interpret data.

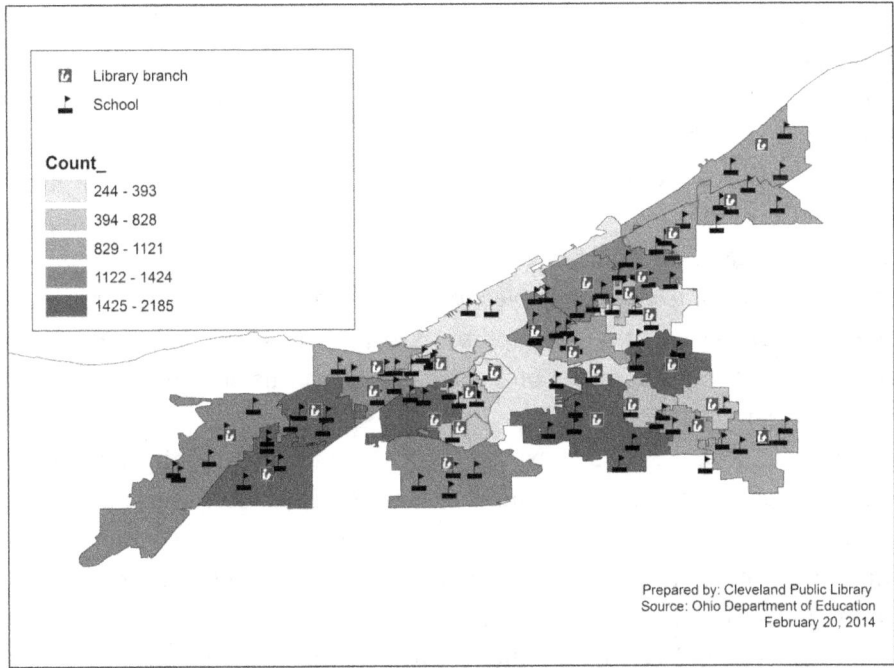

Figure 1.1. Cleveland Public Schools and Cleveland Public Library cardholders.

Identifying emerging user populations is now and has been accepted practice in all libraries across the profession. Over the years, libraries relied on staff observation, anecdotes, and self-reporting of users to inform decisions about library services and collections. Current users would inquire about a given resource, and librarians would evaluate and decide whether to provide it. The primary reason for a library to look at data was to study the habits of people currently using a library's collections and services. Data were aggregated and used to answer questions about the popularity of resources and programs that had already happened. Other research focused on marketing library services to nonusers. In both cases, the research was in line with traditional library service of delivering collections and services, and it was focused on the library's wishes rather than those of its community.

In recent years, the availability of and access to rich datasets from which to extract meaning is giving libraries the tools to identify changing community demographics and allow libraries to examine long-held ideas about the nature of library reference service. It is now possible to step away from one-size-fits-all model of library service and move toward reference services that better reflect a community's interests and aspirations. Data.gov, the home of the U.S. government's open data, has collated thousands of datasets that were previously scattered and buried in agency websites and made them readily accessible. State boards of education are publishing achievement data down to grade and school building level. Projects like GeoCommons and OpenStreetMap freely enable the general public to utilize existing maps, contribute data, and edit to add context. Finally, most of the tabular datasets from governmental open data initiatives are available in formats easily manipulated by existing spreadsheet software applications. The potential impact of the availability of this open data on library reference service is tremendous.

Once a library begins to explore data about the community, a renewed focus on responding to emerging user communities is a natural outcome. Typically, a library compiles data on current patrons' age and contact information in a user database. This database may or may not be used for marketing purposes (e.g., inviting users to a program or directing their attention to a service). Recognizing that analysis of this kind represents a small subset of data that are knowable about a user population is the first step to understanding what is possible.

The integration of data analysis into the work of a library might look like this:

> Step 1: Examination of aggregated use data leads to changes in existing library collections
>
> Step 2: Development of new outreach services to emerging user populations based on current community demographic data analysis paired with existing datasets
>
> Step 3: Design of library spaces informed by analysis of market segmentation, population projections, usage, and new data gathered by the library about community aspirations and interests

Participatory Approaches to Building Community-Centered Libraries | 27

Step 4: Library provides contributions to larger conversations about design and planning for the future of the community as an integrated community partner

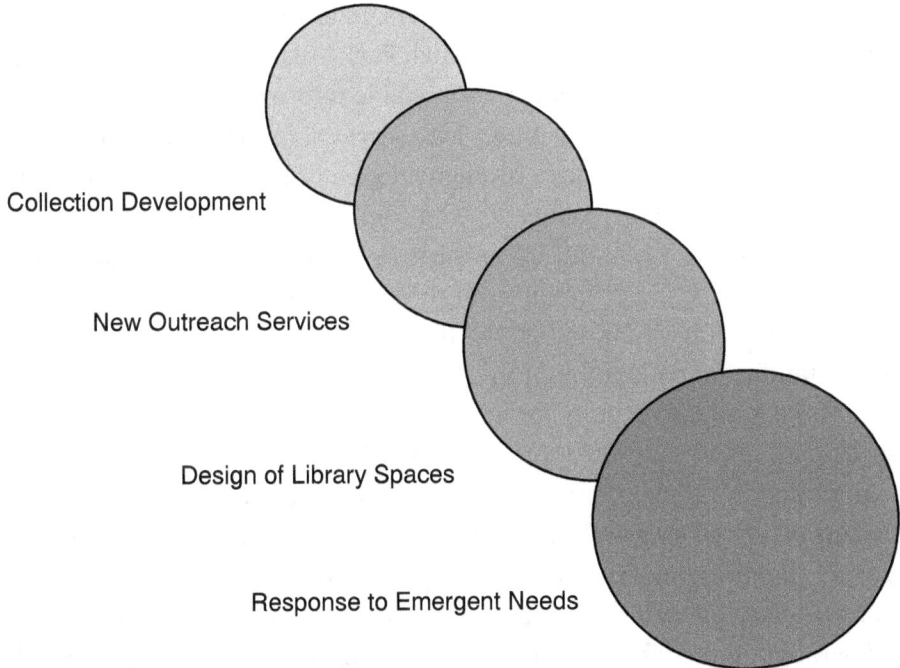

Figure 1.2. Steps for data analysis integration.

Evaluating existing aggregated use data is an accepted practice for developing a collection based on past information-seeking behavior of one's community. A library may develop collections or services based on what is popular among a particular user group and, indeed, many libraries do this. In contrast, when a library begins to look at the available demographic data while still considering the same information-seeking behavior, different outcomes are possible, even likely. Using demographic data in connection with aggregated patron use datasets are the most accessible ways a library can begin this kind of analysis. For example, the Cleveland Public Library used the most recent census data showing the number of children in each census block, coupled with existing aggregated library data about cardholders (birth through age seventeen) to reallocate programming funding for its neighborhood branches. Analyzing current data enabled the library to change existing resources and services with credibility.

Libraries that incorporate data and analysis into their everyday thinking about library service are also better able to respond quickly to catastrophic events that affect the entire community. In recent years, libraries provided shelter, Internet access, information, and the ability to connect with other services during natural disasters. In 2012, the Poudre River Public Library District responded to the High Park fire in Larimer County, Colorado, by providing Internet access, credible information on the disaster, and a place for residents to connect with services. In the aftermath of Hurricane Katrina, public libraries throughout greater New Orleans responded to community needs by connecting the community members with health and safety information, and by forming reciprocal agreements to extend library services to larger numbers of those affected (Dickerson, 2006). In this fashion, libraries strengthen ties through action that is informed by the understanding of their community.

There is an opportunity for libraries to change the nature of their own spaces and potentially affect other community spaces through design that is informed by relevant data. In this case, investigating the consumer behaviors of a given area and combining them with specific demographic data can give a more complete picture than population totals alone. In addition to these data, the community participation in co-designing library spaces brings about more vibrant and diverse experiences. In this way the branch of a public library system might share some elements of design with others in the area, but will closely reflect the local population in collections, reference services, and spaces. When libraries are engaged in this process of thoughtful design, they can participate in larger conversations taking place in the community to work collaboratively to design better neighborhoods.

LOOKING TO THE FUTURE OF PARTICIPATORY DESIGN IN LIBRARIES

Libraries that exemplify a participatory culture of learning will focus on finding strategies and mediums to:

- Be genuinely responsive to the needs of its communities and be inclusive of all communities.
- Provide multiple points of access to meaningful learning experiences that address a need or desire of the community.

- Create learning enviornments that give everyone an opportunity to participate. While not everyone has to participate, multiple points of access and mediums invite young people of different modalties and learning styles to participate. (Jenkins, 2006)

Participatory design actively involves all stakeholders in the design process in order to help ensure the project meets their needs. Participatory design involves experimenting, contextualizing, and implementing ideas to develop prototypes or models of best practice ("Participatory Design," 2011). By taking a participatory approach to design thinking, libraries can blend elements of design thinking with participatory practices. Not only might this approach help branch librarians cultivate a culture of learning that values inquiry and creative thinking, but it could ultimately help library staff at branch levels to build and sustain their capacity to organically identify and respond to challenges in their learning.

We propose that libraries incubate participatory design practices in conjunction *with* their communities, by blending the principles of participatory design thinking with Brian Mathews' (Associate Dean for Outreach and Learning at Virginia Tech's University Libraries) model of *innovation hubs* (Mathews, 2013) to help library staff and communities identify current strengths in services and programming as well as pivot points for change and growth. Teams could be interdepartmental and would include community members who would be part of the ideation and implementation processes. By using a combination of participatory design thinking principles and an innovation hub approach, libraries and their communities can function as a team and as an "incubator" site who authentically and organically organize their approach to testing ideas and strategies, identify themes and patterns that emerge from that collaborative work, and systematically document and reflect on their collaborative work.

By going beyond the traditional approach of a library advisory committee and embedding community members as part of the design team at each branch or innovation hub, libraries can truly adopt a more participatory way of meeting communities at their point of need. This continuum of design thinking is an ongoing cycle of building, learning, and assessing in which these ongoing cycles of inquiry can inform each other. As libraries and their communities work together as an incubation hub who use design thinking to identify challenges, prototype possible solutions and strategies, implement and test those working ideas, and then reflect on and learn from those efforts, innovative practices will emerge. The design thinking that anchors this approach is powerful because it is a "process for framing and solving problems and discovering new opportunities. It's a powerful protocol that can lead to truly innovative outcomes" (Silvers, 2013).

As a library moves along this "continuum of innovation" (Silvers, 2013) as a community of learners, it will be important to explore not only how these practices impact the library's community, but also to examine how participatory design impacts the library staff and the library as an organization. Mike Murawski, as director of education and public programs for the Portland Art Museum in Portland, Oregon, has been leading conversations in the world of art and museum education about the ways participatory design and practices with communities impacts the working environment of the museum organization. At the 2013 National Art Education Conference, Murawski, along with several colleagues, led conversations around these questions as part of a presentation on how museums might go deeper with a culture of participation: "How does an institution's hierarchy, leadership, and organizational structure actually enable (or disable) participatory practice? How could museum educators at various levels become more involved in fostering an institutional culture focused on visitor experience and engagement? Could these values find ways of 'trickling up' from participatory programs and smaller-scale education projects or exhibitions?" (Murawski, 2013, March 20).

As a tangible outcome, these innovation and design teams can develop a "playbook" of *best practices* and *pedagogy* that will help both staff and members of the library's learning community grow their capacity to be effective learning designers who can identify best practices for identifying learning outcomes, creative approaches to teaching and learning, and strategies for assessing learning in multiple modes. Through this participatory design approach that embraces a hybrid of design thinking and innovation hubs, libraries and their communities, as a *comprehensive* community of learners, can collaboratively compose a learning playbook that documents and shares best practices for teaching, learning, and assessment by themes emerging from the daily work rooted in the needs of the community.

By recasting libraries as innovation hubs, libraries and their communities can collectively document and compose the narratives of learning in terms of processes and products, what strategies and ideated solutions worked or did not work and why, successes, challenges, and next steps. Participatory design thinking is in a sense akin to "running plays" in football; however, these innovation hubs "run plays" for innovative learning practices and vet the best approaches through experience and reflection. The process of participatory design as innovation hubs and the end product of a "learning and participatory playbook" will enable libraries and communities to:

1. Function as a community of learners as staff at the building level, as well as collaborative communities of learning across other branches.
2. Coposition librarians as colearners with our neighborhood and/or local communities.
3. Utilize participatory design as a vehicle for branches and their communities to self-identify goals they want to target related to the larger goals of the both the library's strategic plan and community goals, while developing emerging practices for achieving those goals.

This incubator mindset that uses participatory design thinking can enable branch staff, community members, and library administration to have a "foolproof" climate for growing staff and community confidence, capacity, and skill sets, and to help all stakeholders implement what educator George Couros (2013) identifies as practices of innovation.

These practices of innovation not only support original and strategic thinking, but they are also a means of trust and relationship building between the library and the community; this approach blurs the line and se separateness paratness of institution and community by bringing them together as an entity working collaboratively. By building this playbook "from the ground up" so that our work is rooted thoughtfully in theory, action, and reflection, the innovation hub team will be able to grow a culture of participatory learning where inquiry, creating, and sharing are woven into opportunities of the library experiences that encourage people to join as well as initiate communities of learning. In this way, people will:

1. Have many chances to exercise creativity through diverse media, tools, and practices
2. Adopt an ethos of colearning, respecting each person's skills and knowledge
3. Experience heightened motivation and engagement through meaningful play

32 | Reimagining Reference in the 21st Century

4. Experience activities and experiences that feel relevant to learners' identities, interests, and needs
5. Honor rich connections between the worlds of home, school, work, community, and the world at large (Reilly, Jenkins, Vartabedian, & Felt, 2012)

PRESENT-DAY PRACTICES: PUBLIC LIBRARIES AND SCHOOL LIBRARIES, ONE COMMUNITY

How might this approach look in contemporary times in a library? In the fall of 2013, the Gwinnett County Public Library (GCPL) and Norcross High

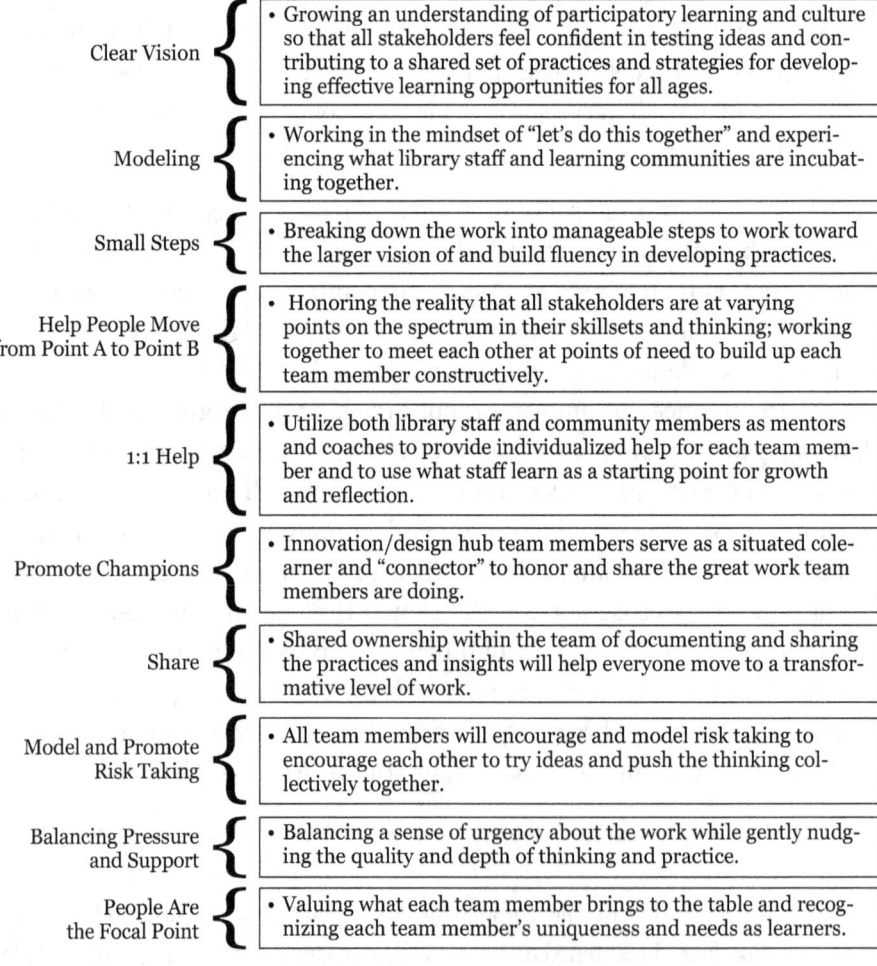

Figure 1.3. Practices of Innovation by George Couros (2013).

School (NHS) Media Center in metro Atlanta decided to apply participatory design principles as a collaborative partnership to serve Gwinnett County teens. Library staff of GCPL—Christopher Baker, Steve Thomas, Amy Billings, and Michael Casey—along with Norcross High School Media Center specialists Buffy J. Hamilton and Jennifer Lund engaged in a series of meetings to identify areas of student interest, need, and possibilities for learning experiences that would emphasize creative design and play. The team was committed to being inclusive of many kinds of learners and to developing learning activities that were connected, not separately branded events, which moved along a "continuum of innovation" (Silvers, 2013).

The result was utilizing Teen Tech Week 2014 as a starting point to provide students with opportunities to experiment with low-tech and high-tech mediums for creating content and engaging in original design. Students with diverse interests came to the Norcross High School Media Center that week to work with embroidery floss, duct tape, MaKey MaKey kits, and squishy circuits (Hamilton, 2014, March 12; Hamilton, 2014, March 16). The participating teens loved having time during the day to relax, socialize, problem solve, and create together in a foolproof setting; Hamilton and Lund were thrilled that they could offer opportunities for playful learning during the day that could either spark or nurture existing interest. The feedback from the teens was so positive that a self-facilitated and collaborative crafting area for students has been built into the Norcross High School Media Center's new learning studio redesign of its physical space and services for 2014–2015.

Figure 1.4. Students craft duct tape designs (original photograph by Buffy J. Hamilton).

The final event of Teen Tech Week 2014 was a 3-D design and printing demonstration in the Norcross High School Media Center that was cohosted by the partnership team and staff. The event included a hands-on demonstration of the Makerbot 3D printer and a presentation by GCPL staff to the students, discussing the history and future of 3-D design and the role such technology plays in numerous educational disciplines and business. Most students who participated had never seen a 3-D printer in person, and they were fascinated by the possibilities for designing and creating with such technology (Hamilton, 2014, March 19). The excitement, interest, and spirit of curiosity generated during this drop-in event over three hours left teens and library staff energized.

Figure 1.5. Students learn about 3-D printing (original photograph by Buffy J. Hamilton).

The learning experiences woven into Teen Tech Week 2014 were then followed by a series of three after school events where library staff from both libraries worked with technology education teacher Joe Floyd and his NHS Robotics Club members for two hours each week to discuss and demonstrate some of the more complex principles of computer-aided design and materials printing. The club members were able to both learn from library staff and also teach library staff various aspects of 3-D printing. These two smaller events helped prepare library and high school staff for a larger collaborative event, the GCPL-NHS Summer MakerCamp 2014.

The Summer MakerCamp of June 2014 was held near NHS at the Peachtree Corners branch of the public library. Although NHS students had priority registration, the free four-day camp was open to any teen resident of Gwinnett County. Both GCPL staff and NHS librarians were pleasantly surprised when nearly fifty teens from across the county signed up for the camp. Due to space and the desire to maintain a good student-to-mentor ratio, the partnership team accepted the first twelve students that enrolled. These twelve participants represented schools from all over Gwinnett County. Casey, Baker, Thomas, Billings, Hamilton, and Lund worked together to facilitate the Summer MakerCamp. The camp, which officially lasted two hours each afternoon over four days, utilized participatory design principles to introduce guided inquiry into using tools like Tinkercad and Thingiverse, to provide students hands-on experience in crafting an original 3-D print design.

Figure 1.6. Students designing with Tinkercad at the Summer MakerCamp (original photograph by Buffy J. Hamilton).

Figure 1.7. GCPL Training Manager Christopher Baker assists teens with their original 3-D designs (original photograph by Buffy J. Hamilton).

Students used Google Chromebooks the library purchased with a state technology grant; for most of the teens, this was their first effort at using this technology platform. While students could work individually or collaboratively, every student chose to partner with at least one other teen while also tapping into the expertise of library staff members Casey and Baker. The camp quickly gelled into a relaxed yet focused community of learners who were deeply engaged with their design work and learning the basic principles of 3-D printing with the public library's Makerbot printer. Even though some participants had great distances to travel to participate in the camp, they attended daily; many requested to stay a half hour longer to hone their designs.

The larger community was also invited to see the work of the camp through a Twitter stream using the #makercamp hashtag; several parents remarked they loved the opportunity to see photos, videos, and updates from home as their children engaged in the experimental camp (see https://storify.com/stevelibrarian/gcpl-makercamp-1). The camp culminated in a final evening celebration open to the Gwinnett County community where students' creations were displayed as part of a gallery that featured refreshments and recognition of student efforts.

The partnership team relished these different activities that provided a sustained trajectory of guided participatory learning experiences to engage with teen learners and to discover their talents and passions. This initial series of scaffolded learning experiences was well-received by the community and participants; the partnership is now using the qualitative data collected from the learning community to expand these kinds of partnership-sponsored mediums for learning and to develop new opportunities for teens in 2014–2015. As staff and students incubated these strategies and approaches, everyone came together as a larger learning community to engage the community in composing the learning and interest-driven narrative for both libraries. By sharing these experiences through public blogs, library publications, and internal communications with staff at both GCPL and NHS, the experiences and insights of this collaborative learning community can be shared with a broader audience in order to spark conversations about the ways public schools and public libraries can work together to meet the learning needs of teen patrons. The partnership team is moving into a new phase of design thinking and ideation as they explore new ways to partner with local companies, nonprofits, and individuals in the community to make the most of the emerging maker movement that resonates with teens.

The partnership of the Gwinnett County Public Library and Norcross High School Media Center embodies the principles of design thinking and Mathews' conceptualization of libraries as incubation hubs of ideas and practices that are organic and responsive to the needs of a local learning community. The partnership team, in conjunction with their teen patrons, systematically organized their approach to implementing ideas and strategies, identifying themes and patterns that emerge from their collaborative work, and documenting their processes, insights, and wonderings through reflective pieces of writing on staff members' blogs, internal reports, and library industry publications. The partnership's initial work is also nudging GCPL staff and NHS faculty to think about larger questions of inquiry-driven learning, participatory practices, and a culture of learning in which roles of expert and novice are fluid as adults and teens grow and share expertise while cultivating a greater sense of trust and deeper relationships between these learning communities.

CLOSING REFLECTIONS

By letting go and sharing the locus of control with our communities, libraries can more effectively function as organic, rich sites of participation that reflect the unique qualities and needs of their citizenry. When we reimagine "reference" beyond the traditional reference interview or perceptions of scholarly research, and instead conceptualize reference as a process of helping people discover experiences to aid them in the construction of answers to their information-seeking needs, "reference" takes on a richer, authentic, and more nuanced context to bring together a community of experts and resources for problem solving and creation of new knowledge and understandings. Whether a public, academic, or school in urban, suburban, or rural communities, libraries as participatory sites of culture, learning, and practice can be catalysts for positive change. The "playbook" is always a work in progress as libraries and their communities collaboratively compose narratives together as learners.

REFERENCES

Affinity space. (2013, March 10). *Wikipedia*. Retrieved from http://en.wikipedia.org/wiki/Affinity_space

Couros, G. (2013, May 22). 10 Ideas to move innovation forward. [Web log post]. *The Principal of Change*. Retrieved from http://georgecouros.ca/blog/archives/3890

Dickerson, L. (2006). Building from disaster: Lessons from Hurricane Katrina. *Alki, 22*(1), 16–19.

Jenkins, H. (2006, October 25). Confronting the challenges of a participatory culture [Web log post]. Retrieved from http://henryjenkins.org/2006/10/confronting_the_challenges_of.html

Hamilton, B. J. (2014, March 12). Teen tech week 2014 day 1: Crafting, experimenting, and learning by doing with embroidery floss. [Web log post]. *The Unquiet Librarian*. Retrieved from http://theunquietlibrarian.wordpress.com/2014/03/12/teen-tech-week-2014-day-1-crafting-experimenting-and-learning-by-doing-with-embroidery-floss/

Hamilton, B. J. (2014, March 16). Teen tech week DIY 2014: Duct tape, squishy circuits, and MaKey MaKey. [Web log post]. *The Unquiet Librarian*. Retrieved from http://theunquietlibrarian.wordpress.com/2014/03/16/teen-tech-week-diy-2014-duct-tape-squishy-circuits-and-makey-makey/

Hamilton, B. J. (2014, March 19). Partnering for possibilities: NHS Media Center, Gwinnett County Public Library, 3D printing, and more. [Web log post]. *The Unquiet Librarian*. Retrieved from http://theunquietlibrarian.wordpress.com/2014/03/19/partnering-for-possibilities-nhs-media-center-gwinnett-county-public-library-3d-printing-and-more/

Kennedy, R. (2013, March 23). Outside the citadel, social practice art is intended to nurture. *The New York Times*. Retrieved from http://www.nytimes.com/2013/03/24/arts/design/outside-the-citadel-social-practice-art-is-intended-to-nurture.html?pagewanted=all&_r=1&

Lankes, R. D. (2012, May 20). Participatory librarianship and change agents. [Video]. Retrieved from https://www.youtube.com/watch?v=j6ppcyBV-Wo

Manifesto for agile software development. (2001). Retrieved from http://agilemanifesto.org/

Mathews, B. (2013, April 23). Hubs and centers as a transitional strategy. [Web log post]. *The Chronicle*. Retrieved from http://chronicle.com/blognetwork/theubiquitouslibrarian/2013/04/23/hubs-and-centers-as-a-transitional-strategy/

Murawski, M. (2013, March 20). Toward an even more participatory culture in art museums. *Art Museum Teaching*. Retrieved from http://artmuseumteaching.com/2013/03/20/toward-an-even-more-participatory-culture-in-art-museums/?relatedposts_exclude=1792

Murawski, M. (2013, October 14). Possibilities for evolution: Artists experimenting in art museums. *Art Museum Teaching*. Retrieved from http://artmuseumteaching.com/2013/10/14/artists-experimenting-in-art-museums/?relatedposts_exclude=1792

Participatory design. (2011, October 23). *EduTech Wiki*. Retrieved from http://edutechwiki.unige.ch/en/Participatory_design

Reilly, E., Jenkins, H., Vartabedian, V., & Felt, L. (2012, December 12). PLAY! (Participatory learning and you!). *Slideshare*. Retrieved from http://www.slideshare.net/ebreilly1/play-participatory-learning-and-you

Silvers, D. M. (2013, May 23). Design thinking in museums: Stepping into the "continuum of innovation." *Art Museum Teaching*. Retrieved from http://artmuseumteaching.com/2013/05/23/design-thinking-in-museums-stepping-into-the-continuum-of-innovation/

Simon, N. (2010). Chapter 1: Principles of participation. *The Participatory Museum*. Retrieved from http://www.participatorymuseum.org/chapter1/

Wieland, A. (2013). *Children's work: Library reading clubs Cleveland Public Library 1903–1936*. (Internal working paper).

Zickuhr, K., Rainie, L., & Purcell, K. (2013, January 22). Library services in the Digital Age. *Pew Internet and American Life Project.* Retrieved from http://libraries.pewinternet.org/2013/01/22/library-services/

2 | Guiding Learners: Information Literacy

Alesia McManus, Howard Community College, Maryland

The concept of information literacy was coined in 1974 by Paul Zurkowski, then president of the Information Industry Association (IIA) in a proposal to the National Commission on Libraries and Information Science (NCLIS) reflecting a burgeoning growth in the amount of information available to U.S. workers: "People trained in the application of information resources to their work can be called information literates" (Zurkowski as cited in Behrens, 1994, p. 310). Since then, information literacy has been defined, standardized, and integrated into higher education and K–12 curricula, and it is still a vital literacy for the 21st century. While early efforts in libraries focused on print resources and face-to-face interaction with students, information literacy instruction, or bibliographic instruction as it was known in the early days, has since evolved along with the Internet presenting new opportunities for learner engagement. This chapter will address the pedagogy of information literacy, including the development of learning outcomes and learning experiences, technology integration, learning environments, assessment, and how the American Association of School Librarians (AASL) *Standards for the 21st-Century Learner* and the Association of College and Research Libraries (ACRL) *Information Literacy Competency Standards for Higher Education (ILCSHE)* are changing in light of current educational and technological trends.

INFORMATION LITERACY DEFINED

During the 1970s and 1980s, information literacy was discussed in the library literature, and those responsible for library user education programs considered how to incorporate the concepts of information literacy not only into bibliographic instruction, but into curricula in general. Behrens (1994) notes that the "adoption of the information literacy goal was the library profession's response to having its role essentially ignored or overlooked in the education reform process" (p. 313) that occurred in the 1980s. The AASL and the Association for Educational Communications and Technology (AECT) responded with the 1988 guidelines for school library media programs, "Information Power," which were designed to assist students and staff to be effective users of information and ideas. This was followed by the publication of the 1989 report of the American Library Association (ALA) Presidential Committee on Information Literacy, which offered an information literacy definition for the profession:

> To be information literate, a person must be able to recognize when information is needed and have the ability to locate, evaluate, and use effectively the needed information. . . . Ultimately, information literate people are those how have learned how to learn. . . . Such a learning process would actively involve students in the process of:

- knowing when they have a need for information
- identifying information needed to address a given problem or issue
- finding needed information
- evaluating information
- organizing the information
- using information effectively to address the problem or issue at hand ("Presidential Committee on Information Literacy: Final Report," 1989)

THE DEVELOPMENT OF INFORMATION LITERACY STANDARDS

Once information literacy was widely understood as an important issue in the profession, the next step was to develop and implement a curriculum for information literacy. An early contribution was Carol Kuhlthau's *Information Skills for an Information Society: A Review of Research,* which Doyle (1994) describes as having "carved out a niche for information literacy" by "including library skills and computer literacy in the definition of information literacy" and by describing library skills as "proficiency in inquiry" (p. 8). Arp (1990), in an article discussing "information literacy or bibliographic instruction," notes the assessment trend in higher education whereby "institutions are tying the requirement to assess students' progress to their general education program or core curriculum" (p. 48).

This growing emphasis on assessment led the ALA Presidential Commission on Information Literacy (1989) to include "information literacy competencies in state assessment examinations" as an objective (Arp, 1990), and one of the recommendations of the report is: "State Departments of Education, Commissions on Higher Education, and Academic Governing Boards should be responsible to ensure that a climate conducive to students becoming information literate exists in their states and on their campuses." The follow-up report, "A Progress Report on Information Literacy: An Update on the American Library Association Presidential Committee on Information Literacy: Final Report" (1998), notes, for example, that the Commission for Higher Education (CHE) of the Middle States Association of Colleges and Schools included library-related questions for evaluators, and information literacy was included in its framework for outcomes assessment. This report also mentions that the AASL was preparing to release "Information Power II."

Arp & Woodard (2002) highlight the growth of standards and guidelines for integrating information literacy in the curriculum, including the ACRL's *Information Literacy Competency Standards for Higher Education (ILCSHE)* which were approved in 2000. These standards have provided the framework for information literacy pedagogy and assessment in higher education until the present. According to the introduction to the standards, the Boyer report, "Reinventing Undergraduate Education," emphasized the importance of inquiry, problem solving, and critical thinking, requiring a more self-directed learning environment for students, and thus requiring a competency-based approach to information literacy. Therefore, the standards are a "framework for assessing the information literate individual." They were also designed to "extend AASL Task Force on Information Literacy Standards . . . so that a continuum of expectations develops for students at all levels" ("Information Literacy Competency Standards for Higher Education," 2000).

DEVELOPING LEARNING OUTCOMES

ACRL's *ILCSHE* (2000) were aimed at faculty as well as librarians. Library and information literacy instruction programs have a long history of partnering with faculty to integrate library resources, and by extension information resources, into the classroom. Similarly, the K–12 standards, "Information Power: Building Partnerships for Learning," included information literacy standards for student learning, and AASL's implementation plan "Because Student Achievement IS the Bottom Line" was "a sustained effort to advance common agendas with the school library media profession and educational decision makers" (Hofmann, 2000, p. 11). Gratch-Lindauer (as cited in Arp & Woodward, 2002) undertook a synthesis of regional accreditation standards and concludes that "probably the most direct contribution the library makes to institutional goals is its role in developing clear student learning objectives for information literacy skills" (p. 128). The *ILCSHE* encourage the design of instructional activities that promote higher levels of thinking. They are based on Bloom's Taxonomy of Educational Objectives, and the sample outcomes show both lower and higher order thinking skills. The use of the ACRL and AASL standards aid in identifying the desired results (i.e., developing information literate students) and provide a framework for assessment and collecting acceptable evidence. Learning experiences may then be planned. This model is backward design (Wiggins & McTighe, 2005). See figure 2.1.

In backward design, the first step is to identify desired results by creating learning objectives or, in current terminology, student learning outcomes (SLOs). SLOs should have a subject and an action, be active, high level, and measurable. Usually actions or verbs are drawn from Bloom's Taxonomy, which is a framework for classifying SLOs in order to facilitate assessment (Anderson & Krathwohl, 2001). The verbs in Bloom's Taxonomy represent a hierarchy of cognitive processes that are in a continuum from lower order thinking skills (LOTS) to higher order thinking skills (HOTS). The *ILCSHE* use these verbs in the outcomes for the various performance indicators. For example, outcome 2.2.2 identifies keywords, synonyms, and related terms for the information needed. "Identify" is considered a "lower order" verb since it falls within the "knowledge" domain of Bloom's Taxonomy, whereas in outcome 3.2.1, examines and compares information from various sources in order to evaluate reliability, validity, accuracy, authority, timeliness, and point of view or bias, "examine and compare" are in the "analysis" domain, which is higher along the continuum (Churches, n.d.). See figure 2.2.

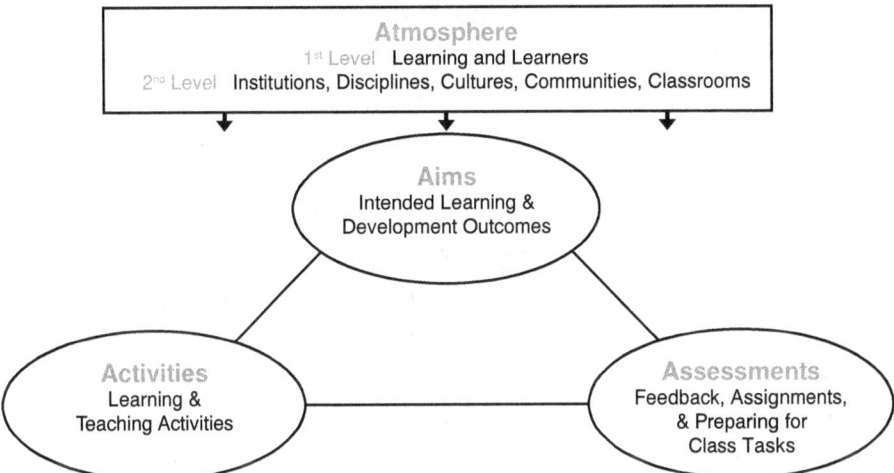

Figure 2.1. This reflects the aligned course design—backward design—principles and practices of the University of Minnesota Center for Teaching and Learning consultants generally. The diagram is built from concepts put forward by John Biggs and Catherine Tang; Grant Wiggins and Jay McTighe; James Zull; and L. Dee Fink. Courtesy of Ilene Dawn Alexander.

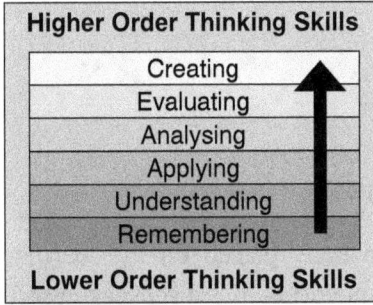

Figure 2.2. An update to Bloom's Revised Taxonomy to incorporate changes in behavior due to technology (Churches, n.d.).

For K–12 students, learning outcomes may be based on the AASL *Standards for the 21st-Century Learner* (2007) which has four main categories: 1) inquire, think critically, and gain knowledge; 2) draw conclusions, make informed decisions, apply knowledge to new situations, and create new knowledge; 3) share knowledge and participate ethically and productively as members of our democratic society; and 4) pursue personal and aesthetic growth.

DEVELOPING LEARNING EXPERIENCES

Backward design, mentioned earlier in this chapter, is an example of instructional design that is "using a systematic approach to solve an instructional problem" (Davis, 2013, p. 205). When working with faculty and teachers, backward design is a useful model for developing information literacy learning experiences and activities. Student learning outcomes define what the students will learn; assessment provides the evidence for what students have learned; and the learning activities facilitate student learning.

Farmer (2013) states that "developing and implementing literacies/learning standards require deep analysis about the knowledge, skills and dispositions that one needs in order to be what was traditionally called educated" and goes on to say that "now literacy implies that one can create knowledge communicated through emerging technologies" (p. 172). With the advent of the Internet, Google, and social media, today's learners have preferences for "digital literacy, experiential and engaged learning, interactivity and collaboration, and immediacy and connectivity in their interactions" (Williams & Chinn, 2009, p. 165). A focus on learning, rather than teaching, involves acquisition of the "products of the learning (e.g., skills, knowledge, understanding, content, and values)" and participation by learners (Alrushiedat & Olfman, 2013, p. 135). Chickering and Gamson (1987) outline good practice for engaging students in learning activities and experiences:

- Encourages contact between students and faculty.
- Develops reciprocity and cooperation among students.
- Encourages active learning.
- Gives prompt feedback.
- Emphasizes time on task.
- Communicates high expectations.
- Respects diverse talents and ways of learning.

With responsibility for learning increasingly placed on the learner, "active learning methods, such as problem-based, discovery-based, and inquiry-based learning challenge students to actively engage with information and resources to solve problems and create knowledge" (Detlor, Booker, Serenko, & Julien, 2012, p. 148). Berger (2010) cites a study that "active, rather than passive learners, are able to understand complex material and can more effectively transfer information and concepts learned in one setting to the process of solving problems encountered in another" (p. 15).

Doll (2009) points out school media librarians need instructional design skills as well. She describes the three main types of instructional design as curriculum planning, unit planning, and lesson planning. Doll's article focuses on lesson planning. The design questions that are presented are similar to what an instructor using backward design might ask:

How do students learn?
What are my students like?
What do my students need to learn?
How do I plan their instruction?
How do I deliver this instruction?
How do I assess their learning?
How do I evaluate the process? (p. 18)

The AASL *Standards for the 21st-Century Learner* (2007) outline what information literacy outcomes students should learn. The most recent AASL standards differ from the *ILCSHE* in that, in addition to skills, they also include "dispositions in action," which are the "emotions and attitudes that students display" and address "issues of student behavior" and "responsibilities" that outline expectations of students. They also include self-assessment strategies that can be used to help the student evaluate his/her own ability. The AASL standards strive to "address all aspects of the learner" (Doll, 2009, p. 19). Berger (2010) elaborates on the "nine common beliefs that support learning" in the AASL standards by highlighting the second belief, "Inquiry provides a framework for learning," and goes on to describe the Stripling Model of Inquiry, a recursive inquiry model with six phases: Connect, Wonder, Investigate, Construct, Express, and Reflect. Stripling (as cited in Berger, 2010) holds that "inquiry places students at the heart of learning by empowering them to follow their sense of wonder into new discoveries and insights about the way the world works" (p. 16).

DESIGNING LEARNING ACTIVITIES AND ASSIGNMENTS

Each assignment or activity should have an explicitly stated purpose of what knowledge, skills, or competencies the student will learn. There are many teaching and learning websites available to help teachers and instructors learn how to create assignments. For example, the Teaching Commons at DePaul University offers step-by-step guidance for course design, assignment design, and provides resources for learning activities and teaching practice. Here is a partial list of suggested assignment design strategies ("Assignment Design Strategies," n.d.):

- Clearly link each assignment to the course goals and learning objectives.
- Break large, high-stakes assignments into multiple, low-stakes assignments.

- Design assignments around real-world issues and events to engage and motivate students.
- Provide grading guidelines for the assignment in the form of rubrics and examples of acceptable and unacceptable work.
- Provide supporting structures—templates, peer review, examples, multiple drafts, guidelines for library research, etc.
- Revise assignments for next term based on student performance and feedback. Does each assignment develop student expertise in line with course learning goals?

Using the stated purpose of the assignment or activity, librarians may select or create activities to engage students in the content. One place to start is to locate websites that give examples for matching learning goals to assignment types.

Doll (2009) provides a list of methods for delivery of instruction for school media specialists (e.g., lectures, field trips, drills, demonstrations, student- or teacher-led discussions, problem-solving/brainstorming sessions, debates, group projects, dramatics, written, oral or nonprint presentations, and laboratory sessions). Berger (2010) recommends AASL's "Best Websites for Teaching and Learning" (n.d.), which "honors websites, tools, and resources of exceptional value to inquiry-based teaching and learning as embodied in the AASL *Standards for the 21st-Century Learner*."

TECHNOLOGY AND PEDAGOGY

Technology tools can be used effectively to enhance learning and should be carefully chosen based on function to support the assignment or activity learning outcomes (Sharkey & O'Connor, 2013). Referring back to Chickering and Gamson's (1987) good practices for student engagement, the appropriate technology can encourage student-teacher contact, facilitate student collaboration, offer opportunities for prompt feedback, and support diverse learning preferences. Technology can also provide flexibility for learning outside the physical classroom, since learners are able to interact with the course material when it is convenient for them. However, time management abilities may need to be reinforced, so use technology to emphasize time on task.

LEARNING ENVIRONMENTS

Active, student-centered learning occurs in physical learning environments (often referred to as face-to-face or F2F), online via learning management

Table 2.1. Examples of different types of assignments matched to various information literacy outcomes (adapted from "Matching Learning Goals to Assignment Types," n.d.).

This Kind of Assignment...	Helps Students Learn To...
Annotated bibliography	<ul><li>find and select relevant sources</li><li>summarize selected sources concisely</li><li>determine the purpose that particular sources will serve in an assignment</li><li>prepare reference lists in appropriate format</li></ul>
Peer review	<ul><li>evaluate work</li><li>reinforces students' understanding of skill and/or concepts</li><li>understand and apply assessment criteria for an assignment</li><li>be sensitive to students' feeling and perspectives</li><li>formulate constructive suggestions</li><li>work together and develop interpersonal skills</li><li>integrate, evaluate, and act on peer feedback</li><li>learn a key convention of scholarship</li></ul>
Assignment wiki or website	<ul><li>work together</li><li>synthesize existing information</li><li>prioritize and organize information</li><li>debate the quality of sources and argument</li></ul>
Journal or learning log	<ul><li>read, watch, listen carefully and critically</li><li>respond personally to selected content</li><li>differentiate between the ideas in selected content and students' own ideas about that topic</li><li>prepare to write more formally or develop a project incorporating the selected content</li><li>prepare to participate in a discussion</li></ul>
Argument or debate	<ul><li>identify an arguable issue</li><li>find and present supporting evidence</li><li>organize/prioritize information</li><li>analyze, predict, address, and adapt to audience(s)</li></ul>
Portfolios or sample work	<ul><li>assess their own work</li><li>develop metacognitive awareness</li><li>assemble materials with an outside audience in mind</li><li>showcase their best work</li></ul>

systems, tutorials, interactive modules, and simulations, or a hybrid of the two (blended learning). Blended learning is a combination of F2F and online learning that "includes the conveniences of online interaction without the loss of F2F contact" (Alrushiedat & Olfman, 2013, p. 135). The flipped classroom model, where students complete activities online before F2F contact, is an example of blending learning.

Physical learning environments are designed to facilitate learning through the use of flexible space that enables learners to work individually, collaboratively, and interactively (Sharkey & O'Connor, 2013). Libraries have sought to expand their role through use of space by employing the information or learning commons model. Weiner, Doan, & Kirkwood (2010) describe a learning commons as a "multifunctional, flexible space that deeply integrates the library into the lives of students with other campus departments and services" and as "neutral space that brings partners together to support learning initiatives" (p. 194). Individual research assistance is one of the primary services offered. Libraries have also expanded their role in the virtual learning space by embedding librarians in online courses, and integrating library content and information literacy activities into learning management systems such as Blackboard, Canvas, Moodle, and Desire2Learn.

Pulling it all together is the metaphor of "blended librarianship," where librarians are partners with teachers, collaborating with campus departments such as instructional media and e-learning to enhance learning. "Blended librarians are bedfellows with those embedded librarians who focus on being integrated into the college and university educational process" (and the primary and secondary educational process as well). "Standing at the intersection of learning and knowledge hub, online or on campus, the blended librarian is the leader, who acts as the mediator and guide, to accessing and making sense of the ever expanding universe of information in all the forms it takes" (Zabel, Shank, & Bell, 2011, p. 109). Sharkey and O'Connor (2013) note that a "key component of having a successful hybrid learning environment is to consider what technologies are available within the institution as well as freely available on the web, and then identify how their core purpose or functionality matches learning outcomes, integrates into activities or projects, and complements the types of assessment to be conducted" (p. 37).

INFORMATION LITERACY ASSESSMENT

In order to improve learning, it is important to assess information literacy programs, activities, and assignments. The ACRL and AASL standards exist to help libraries evaluate the information literacy competency of their students. Assessment is time- and resource-consuming, and Lindauer, Arp, and Woodward (2004) point out that "learning is complex and multidimensional and any serious attempt to assess learning must take a multi-methods approach" (p. 122), and that, in addition to learning outcomes, it is "equally important to measure and document personal experiences that directly contribute to the development of information literate individuals, such as specific indicators that capture the quality of the learning environment and learner self-assessment of skills and instruction/learning satisfaction ratings" (p. 123). Lindauer, Arp, and Woodward present "three arenas" of measurement for information literacy assessment, including learning environments, information literacy program components, and student learning outcomes.

Learning Environment
Curriculum
Cocurricular, independent, and service-learning opportunities
Space use
UX design

Information Literacy Program Components
Courses
Workshops
"One-shots"
Reference encounters
Individual research assistance
Online tutorials and modules

Student Learning Outcomes
Performance measurements on tests
Course-embedded assignments
Rubrics
Program portfolios
Course grades
Self-assessment
Attitude and satisfaction surveys

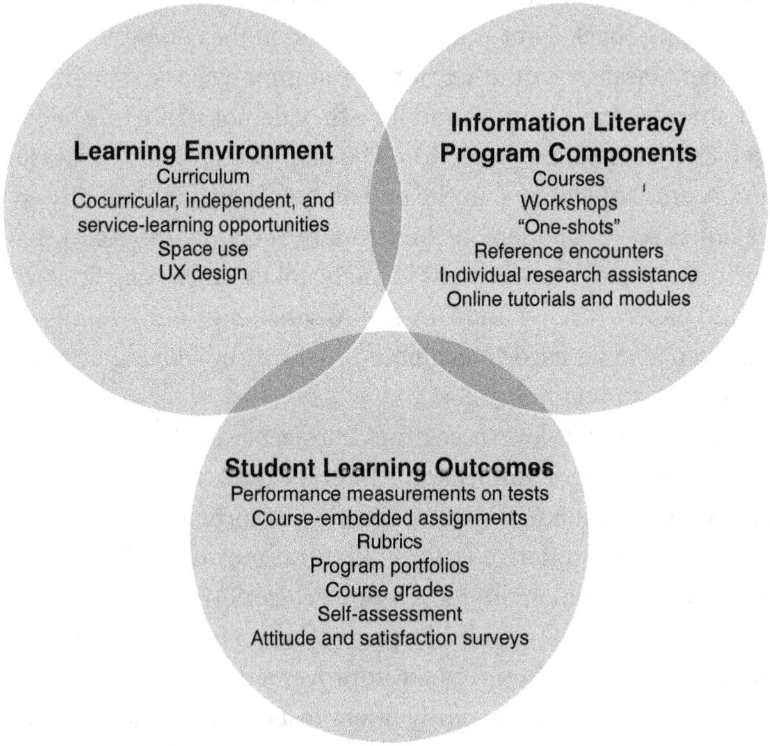

Figure 2.3. The three arenas of information literacy assessment (adapted from Lindauer, Arp, & Woodard, 2004).

There are a variety of assessment approaches depending on the goal of the assessment. Sharkey and O'Connor (2013) describe three types of assessment: "assessment for learning, assessment as learning, and assessment of learning" (p. 36). Assessment for learning helps "instructors analyze the effectiveness of various teaching and learning activities used," while assessment as learning asks students to "critically reflect and analyze how and what they learn," and educators often "merge assessment for learning and assessment as learning," which collectively describes formative assessment (p. 36). They elaborate that "the goal of formative assessment is to *monitor student learning* to provide ongoing feedback that can be used by instructors to improve their teaching and by students to improve their learning" (p. 36). It is considered to be "low stakes," which means that they have low or no point value ("Whys and Hows of Assessment," n.d.). Classroom assessment techniques (CATs) such as the "one-minute paper" or "K-W-L" can be used to evaluate classroom presentations, often referred to as "one-shots" in the literature. They can also be used in courses to obtain ongoing feedback from students enrolled in the course. The third type of assessment, assessment of learning or summative assessment, "focuses on what students have learned and how they demonstrate this knowledge" (Sharkey & O'Connor, 2013, p. 36). "The goal of summative assessment is to *evaluate student learning* at the end of an instructional unit by comparing it against some standard or benchmark" such as the ACRL or AASL standards. Summative assessment is "high stakes," including final projects, exams, and papers ("Whys and Hows of Assessment," n.d.). Summative assessment can also be used to evaluate programs by looking at sample assignments and student portfolios.

Two early national-level assessment projects were ProjectSAILS (Standardized Assessment of Information Literacy Skills) and the Educational Testing System National Higher Education Information and Communications Technology Initiative (ETS-ICT), now known as iSkills, which are standardized information literacy tests. ProjectSAILS began in 2001 at Kent State University to "enable libraries to document skill levels for groups of students and to pinpoint areas for improvement" ("Information Literacy Test," n.d.). ProjectSAILS currently offers tests for individuals as well as a cohort test for groups of students. By using the cohort test, institutions can compare their results to other similar institutions as well as to institutions who also offer the cohort test. iSkills is an "outcomes-based assessment that measures the ability to think critically in a digital environment through a range of real-world tasks" and that offers individual and group data ("The ISkills™ Assessment," n.d.).

Another tool for both formative and summative assessments is a rubric that can be used to evaluate both course-based assignments as well as programs of study through the assessment of sample materials or portfolios. A rubric is "a scoring tool that identifies the various criteria relevant to an assignment or learning outcome, and then explicitly states the possible levels of achievement along a continuum" (poor to excellent or novice to expert) ("What Are Rubrics?," n.d.). Some of the most widely used rubrics are the Association of American Colleges and Universities' (AAC&U) VALUE Rubrics, where VALUE stands for "Valid Assessment of Learning in Undergraduate Education." In 2007–2009, "teams of faculty and other educational professionals from over one hundred higher education institutions engaged . . . to develop sixteen VALUE rubrics for the Liberal Education and America's Promise (LEAP) Essential Learning Outcomes," including one for information literacy ("VALUE: Valid Assessment of Learning in Undergraduate Education," n.d.). The Rubric Assessment of Information Literacy Skills (RAILS) project is "an Institute and Museum Library Services (IMLS)-funded research project designed to investigate an analytic rubric approach to information literacy assessment in higher education" and to offer a clearinghouse to share locally adapted rubrics and the results of using those rubrics. The RAILS project uses the AAC&U VALUE information literacy rubric and the *ILCSHE* as a starting point ("RAILS Rubric Assessment of Information Literacy Skills," n.d.). School media specialists can assess student learning in similar ways using "rubrics, checklists, and portfolios," as well as CATs (Doll, 2009).

INFORMATION LITERACY FOR THE 21ST CENTURY

The AASL published the *Standards for the 21st-Century Learner* in 2007, and there are efforts to align them to the Common Core State Standards (CCSS). The CCSS initiative

> is a state-led effort that established a single set of clear educational standards for kindergarten through 12th grade in English language arts and mathematics that states voluntarily adopt.

> The standards are designed to ensure that students graduating from high school are prepared to enter credit bearing entry courses in two or four year college programs or enter the workforce. ("Implementing the Common Core State Standards," n.d.)

Forty-five states have adopted CCSS at this time. Canino-Fluit (2013) provides a case study for assessment using the statewide program, the Empire State Information Fluency Continuum, which uses the Stripling Model of Inquiry:

> These assessments, when used in CCSS-aligned lessons, can become the foundation of process portfolios by creating a paper trail of students' thinking and research processes, allowing the teacher and school librarian to monitor and evaluate each student's acquisition of the . . . Benchmark Skills needed to meet the Common Core State Standards. (Canino-Fluit, 2013, p. 47)

In 2011, the ACRL created a task force to review the *ILCSHE,* which recommended that the standards be "extensively revised" (Bell, 2013). According to Craig Gibson (as cited in Bell 2013):

> We now need an expanded set of literacies—those that take us beyond textual information, that emphasizes student participation in creating new content, that encourages students to develop metacognitive abilities and different parts of the brain, that create more and deeper opportunities for collaboration among librarians, faculty, instructional designers, technologists and students themselves. . . . This is a new learning environment where students lead curriculum projects as often as faculty.

On the website for the ACRL *ILCSHE* Task Force, "The Future of the Standards" section discusses areas that the current standards do not support effectively in light of today's learning environment. For example, the standards do not:

- Address the globalized information environment.
- Recognize students as content creators and curators as well as consumers and evaluators.
- Address ongoing challenges with student learning in a multi-faceted, multi-format, media-rich environment.

- Sufficiently address the need to position IL as a set of concepts and practices integral to student learning in all disciplines.
- Emphasize the need for metacognitive and dispositional dimensions of learning throughout ALL steps of conducting research.
- Position student learning of information concepts and practices as a cumulative, recursive, developmental endeavor (but instead suggest that information literacy is "additive" in increments).
- Address scholarly communication, publishing, or knowledge of data sources. ("The Future of The Standards," n.d.)

Farmer (2013) says that the "AASL's learning standards could be used as one springboard for thought, particularly in terms of articulating learning" (p. 171). She points out that the AASL standards "cleverly sidestepped the problematic term 'information literacy' when it used learners as its linchpin" (p. 172). Information literacy is problematic because "academicians seem more comfortable with the terms 'critical thinking' and 'research skills'" (p. 173). A possible indicator of this is that the latest draft of the Middle States Commission on Higher Education Characteristics of Excellence no longer includes the term "information literacy," but does include "technological competency" and "critical analysis and reasoning" in the general education program criteria ("Accreditation Standards Review Process Continues," n.d.). Farmer also mentions that academic librarians can work with school media specialists on college readiness and with special libraries on workplace readiness.

The interim report for the ACRL *ILCSHE* Task Force says that the goal for the draft *Framework for Information Literacy for Higher Education* is "to present information literacy as a network of understandings, core abilities, affective factors, and metacognitive components" ("Interim Report: Information Literacy Competency Standards for Higher Education Task Force," 2013). Metaliteracy and threshold concepts are two new elements. Hofer, Townsend, and Brunetti (as cited in "The Future of the Standards," n.d.) explain threshold concepts as "the core ideas and processes in any discipline that define the discipline, but that are so ingrained that they often go unspoken or unrecognized by the practitioner." They provide a description of threshold concepts based on the work of Jan Meyer and Ray Land:

- Transformative—cause the learner to experience a shift in perspective.
- Integrative—bring together separate concepts (often identified as learning objectives) into a unified whole.
- Irreversible—once grasped, cannot be un-grasped.
- Bounded—may help define the boundaries of a particular discipline, are perhaps unique to the discipline.
- Troublesome—usually difficult or counterintuitive ideas that can cause students to hit a roadblock in their learning.

Mackey and Jacobson (as cited in "The Future Of The Standards," n.d.) describe metaliteracy "as expanding the scope of traditional information skills ... to include the collaborative production and sharing of information in participatory digital environments."

The American Library Association published a press release on February 24, 2014, calling for comments on the first part of the initial draft of *Framework for Information Literacy for Higher Education*. The ALA wrote, "The new Framework seeks to address the interconnected nature of the abilities, practices and dispositions of the student moving away from the hierarchical and formulaic approach of the current standards" (American Library Association, Association of College and Research Libraries, 2014). The move from a competency model to framework is intentional. The first part includes the introduction and the first three threshold concepts for information literacy. The second part with the two additional threshold concepts was released in April 2014. After receiving feedback from interested parties, the task force released the second, revised draft in June 2014. This draft includes a newly revised definition of information literacy, suggestions for how to use the document, and an introduction for faculty and administrators. There are now six threshold concepts that are each encapsulated in six frames, which "encompass the definition of the Threshold concept as well as the accompanying Knowledge Practices and Abilities/Dispositions (Revised draft, 2014). While ACRL's goal is to release the final framework this fall, a communication from the ACRL executive director to the task force asks the task force to consider delaying the final draft if feedback warrants (Info Lit Standards Task Force—ACRL board meeting annual conference follow-up, 2014).

As evidenced in this chapter, librarians have and will continue to partner with faculty and teachers as well as instructional designers and others to integrate information literacy into the academic curriculum. Using the

AASL *Standards for the 21st-Century Learner* and the new *Framework for Information Literacy for Higher Education*, librarians as guiding facilitators will revise, develop, create, and assess a variety of new learning experiences, activities, assignments, and environments, enabling students to become "information literates" who have learned how to learn and can be successful in whatever life path they choose.

REFERENCES

Accreditation Standards Review Process Continues. (n.d.). *Middle States Commission on Higher Education.* Retrieved from https://www.msche.org/?Nav1=NEWS&Nav2=NEWSROOM&Nav3=STANDARDS&strPageName=

Alrushiedat, N., & Olfman, L. (2013). Aiding participation and engagement in a blended learning environment. *Journal of Information Systems Education, 24*(2), 133–145.

American Library Association, Association of College and Research Libraries. (2014, February 24). ACRL seeks feedback on draft *Framework for Information Literacy for Higher Education.* Retrieved from http://www.ala.org/news/press-releases/2014/02/acrl-seeks-feedback-draft-framework-information-literacy-higher-education

Anderson, L. W., & Krathwohl, D. R. (2001). *A taxonomy for learning, teaching, and assessing: A revision of Bloom's taxonomy of educational objectives.* New York: Longman.

Arp, L., & Woodard, B. S. (2002). Recent trends in information literacy and instruction. *Reference & User Services Quarterly, 42*(2), 124–132.

Arp, L. (1990). Information literacy or bibliographic instruction: Semantics or philosophy. *RQ, 30*(1), 46–49.

Assignment Design Strategies. (n.d.). *DePaul Teaching Commons.* Retrieved from http://teachingcommons.depaul.edu/Assignment_Design/general_strategies.html

Behrens, B. J. (1994). A conceptual analysis and historical overview of information literacy. *College and Research Libraries, 55*(4), 309–322. http://dx.doi.org/10.5860/crl_55_04_309

Bell, S. J. (2013, June 4). Rethinking ACRL's information literacy standards: The process begins. *ACRL Insider.* Retrieved from http://www.acrl.ala.org/acrlinsider/archives/7329

Berger, P. (2010). Student inquiry and Web 2.0. *School Library Monthly, 26*(5), 14–17.

Best Websites for Teaching and Learning. (n.d.). *American Association of School Librarians*. Retrieved from http://www.ala.org/aasl/standards-guidelines/best-websites

Canino-Fluit, A. (2013). Flying high with the information fluency continuum. *Knowledge Quest, 41*(5), 46–50.

Chickering, A. W., & Gamson, Z. F. (1987, March). Seven principles for good practice in undergraduate education. *AAHE Bulletin*. Retrieved from http://www.aahea.org/aahea/articles/sevenprinciples1987.htm

Churches, A. (n.d.). Bloom's digital taxonomy. [Web log post]. *Educational Origami*. Retrieved from http://edorigami.wikispaces.com/Bloom's Digital Taxonomy

Davis, A. L. (2013). Using instructional design principles to develop effective information literacy instruction. *College & Research Libraries News, 74*(4), 205–207.

Detlor, B., Booker, L., Serenko, A., & Julien, H. (2012). Student perceptions of information literacy instruction: The importance of active learning. *Education for Information, 29*(2), 147–161.

Doll, C. A. (2009). Teaching and learning by design. *Library Media Connection, 28*(2), 18–20.

Doyle, C. S. (1994). *Information literacy in an information society: A concept for the information age.* Syracuse, NY: ERIC Clearinghouse on Information and Technology.

Farmer, L. S. (2103). How AASL learning standards inform ACRL information literacy standards. *Communications in Information Literacy, 7*(2), 171–176.

The Future of the Standards. (n.d.). *Framework for Information Literacy for Higher Education*. Retrieved from http://acrl.ala.org/ilstandards/?page_id=19

Hofmann, S. (2000, January). The association's associations: AASL builds partnerships. *American Libraries, 31*(1), 11.

Implementing the Common Core State Standards. (n.d.). *Common Core State Standards Initiative*. Retrieved from http://www.corestandards.org/

Information Literacy Competency Standards for Higher Education. (2000). Association of College & Research Libraries. Retrieved from http://www.ala.org/acrl/standards/informationliteracycompetency

Info Lit Standards Task Force—ACRL board meeting annual conference follow-up [Letter written July 15, 2014 to C. Gibson, T. Jacobson, & T. Swanson]. (2014, July 15). Retrieved from http://connect.ala.org/node/223580

Interim Report: Information Literacy Competency Standards for Higher Education Task Force. (2013, September 25). *Framework for Information Literacy for Higher Education About the Revision Process.* Retrieved from http://connect.ala.org/files/Doc%206.1%20Interim%20Report%20for%20review.pdf

The iSkills™ Assessment. (n.d.). *ETS iSkills.* Retrieved from https://www.ets.org/iskills/about

Lindauer, B. G., Arp, L., & Woodard, B. S. (2004). The three arenas of information literacy assessment. *Reference & User Services Quarterly, 44*(2), 122–129.

Matching Learning Goals to Assignment Types. (n.d.). *DePaul Teaching Commons.* Retrieved from http://teachingcommons.depaul.edu/Assignment_Design/assignments_learning_goals.html

Presidential Committee on Information Literacy: Final Report. (1989). *Association of College & Research Libraries.* Retrieved from http://www.ala.org/acrl/publications/whitepapers/presidential

A Progress Report on Information Literacy: An Update on the American Library Association Presidential Committee on Information Literacy: Final Report. (1998). *Association of College & Research Libraries.* Retrieved from http://www.ala.org/acrl/publications/whitepapers/progressreport

Information Literacy Test. (n.d.). *ProjectSAILS.* Retrieved from https://www.projectsails.org/index.php

RAILS Rubric Assessment of Information Literacy Skills. (n.d.). *Institute of Museum and Library Services.* Retrieved from http://railsontrack.info/

Revised draft. (2014, June 17). Retrieved from http://acrl.ala.org/ilstandards/?page_id=133

Sharkey, J., & O'Connor, L. (2013). Establishing twenty-first-century information fluency. *Reference & User Services Quarterly, 53*(1), 33–39. http://dx.doi.org/10.5860/rusq.53n1.33

Standards for the 21st-Century Learner. (2007). *American Association of School Librarians.* Retrieved from http://www.ala.org/aasl/standards-guidelines/learning-standards

VALUE: Valid Assessment of Learning in Undergraduate Education. (n.d.). *Association of American Colleges and Universities.* Retrieved from http://www.aacu.org/value/

Weiner, S., Doan, T., & Kirkwood, H. (2010, January 1). The learning commons as a locus for information literacy. *College & Undergraduate Libraries, 17,* 192–212. http://dx.doi.org/10.1080/10691316.2010.484275

What Are Rubrics? (n.d.). *DePaul Teaching Commons*. Retrieved from http://teachingcommons.depaul.edu/Feedback_Grading/rubrics.html

Whys and Hows of Assessment. (n.d.). *Carnegie Mellon University*. Retrieved from https://www.cmu.edu/teaching/assessment/basics/formative-summative.html

Wiggins, G. P., & McTighe, J. (2005). Backward design. In *Understanding by design* (2nd ed., pp. 13–34). Alexandria, VA: Association for Supervision and Curriculum Development.

Williams, J., & Chinn, S. J. (2009). Using Web 2.0 to support the active learning experience. *Journal of Information Systems Education, 20*(2), 165–174.

Zabel, D., Shank, J. D., & Bell, S. (2011). Blended librarianship: [Re]envisioning the role of librarian as educator in the digital information age. *Reference & User Services Quarterly, 51*(2), 105–110. http://dx.doi.org/10.5860/rusq.51n2.105

3 | The Reference Interview Revisited

M. Kathleen Kern, University of Illinois at Urbana-Champaign

INTRODUCTION

The reference interview is, for the librarian, the start of the search for information. It is during the reference interview that the user communicates her question (information need) to the librarian, and the librarian clarifies and confirms her understanding of the user's request. Without the reference interview there is no understanding of what the user wants, but even in the reference interview communication can be difficult. As Taylor (1967) wrote, "Without doubt, the negotiation of a reference question is one of the most complex acts of human communication. In this act, one person tries to describe for another person not something he knows, but rather something he does not know" (p. 5). Communication between librarian and user requires more than just asking, "How may I help you?" It requires the librarian understand the user's information need with sufficient detail and clarity. This chapter will start with an exploration of information-seeking behaviors (how users interact with the library and the expectations that they bring), then present strategies and best practices for information conversations with users (the reimagined reference interview), and finally look at how the reference interview is affected by changes in communication technologies.

UNDERSTANDING USER INFORMATION NEEDS AND CONTEXTS

For the user, the reference interview is a waypoint in the search for information. It is likely that she has already tried to find the desired information, either unsuccessfully or with partial success. Even prior to the search for information, the user has formulated an idea of what is needed. This can be as specific as finding out if a favorite author has written a new book or as broad as "more about volcanoes."

Before covering the best practices of the reference interview, it is necessary to understand the information environment of the user, why he came to the library with questions, and his expectations. Kuhlthau (1991) noted that libraries are not the first resort when people are looking for information. This behavior has not changed over the intervening decades. People are likely to ask people they know, search the Internet, or even search the library's catalog and databases themselves before asking for help from a librarian. People value being self-sufficient, and developments in search technologies within and outside of the library support independence in research. Enabling users to find information independently is positive, but it is necessary to understanding the user's perspective that the library reference desk is often a place of last resort when faced with a need for information. Similarly, users may expect that the library will not have what they want, or they may place high hopes on the library and the librarian as the ultimate resource. Library anxiety and a lack of understanding of the role of the reference librarian also factor into reluctance to ask for help.

In many cases the user does not know what information is available, the amount of information that he might find, or where and how to find it. This makes communicating what is wanted challenging. Librarians know from experience that users often ask questions that are broader than the "real" information need or phrase their questions in ways that attempt to fit their need into what they expect to find rather than on what they really want to find. It is common for users to ask for "a book about X" when they actually do not care whether the information comes from a book, an article, or a website. Users who have previously searched and failed to find what they need naturally express a wider topic than desired in the hope of finding *something* relevant, when in fact a search for "scholarly articles about the impact of deforestation" would result in thousands of articles but the actual desired search for "impact of deforestation on gorillas in the Congo" will yield a number of research articles that is more manageable.

There also is a gap between the librarian and the user in that the librarian knows, sometimes too well, what type and amount of information might be available, but then can constrict the exploration of the user's question by trying to fit what she thinks the user needs into what she, as an expert, knows about how information is published and organized. For example, a user who is "researching gun-related deaths" might encounter a librarian who knows that there are yearly U.S. government statistics on deaths from gun violence. In this interaction, if the librarian moves forward to searching too quickly or asks leading questions, the information presented to the user may not match the actual information need of looking into the causes of gun violence.

As a librarian in Taylor's (1967) study noted, "Unless you are sure what the why is, you can never be sure what it is the person really wants. What's he going to do with the information . . . ? We can't help him unless we understand his needs as well as he does" (p. 13). Understanding the user's needs so thoroughly is lofty and often not fully attainable, but we can ask questions to understand what the user wants and how the information might be used. The Ohio Library Council (2008) has developed "The 6 Pieces of Evidence" that librarians need to know about a user's question. Paraphrasing:

1. The basic question being asked.
2. *How* and *why* will the information be useful?
3. *Who* is asking?
4. *What* type and amount of information is needed?
5. Prior knowledge the user brings.
6. Is there a deadline *when* this is needed?

Collecting this information is not a game of Twenty Questions. Understanding the user's information need is more than a checklist and requires engaging in a conversation.

CREATING A CONVERSATION: THE ART AND STRATEGY OF THE REFERENCE INTERVIEW

Decades of practicing librarians and communication researchers have developed techniques that can be learned by any public service-minded library worker. The *Guidelines for Behavioral Performance of Reference and Information Services Providers* from the Reference and User Services Association (2004; hereafter referred to as the *Behavioral Guidelines*) codify the best practices for the reference interview, with special attention to how these are manifested in both in-person and remote (online and telephone) communications.

Knowledge of these guidelines alone will not make someone proficient at conversing with users. There is an art to an effective reference interview to engage the user in a conversation to focus and clarify the information need. An art must be practiced to be refined, and every individual will have his own stylistic elements or "voice." Additionally, different types of libraries will have their own norms for communication as communities and populations will influence communication style. For example, working with lawyers requires more formality than working with teenagers. Learning standard best practices for the reference interview is the best place to start in developing the skills and art of the reference interview; after that is it up to the individual to refine skills and style through experience and reflection.

IT STARTS WITH CUSTOMER SERVICE

The *Behavioral Guidelines* start with sections on approachability and interest. These critical skills are, in essence, good customer service. They are what we hope for whenever we expect something (service) from someone else, be it a bank, the Bureau of Motor Vehicles, or a department store. If we reflect on our expectations as customers, we have a pretty clear idea of what approachability and interest look like. In the day-to-day of our work life it can be more difficult to keep in mind our demeanor and how we appear to our users. There are also people who may not be naturally inclined toward providing pleasant customer service. Having them work at a reference desk (or any other user services point in a library) is a poor choice.

Smiling, making eye contact, using a welcoming tone, and exhibiting positive body language such as nodding and keeping an open posture are all ways that we exhibit approachability and interest. Users are sometimes hesitant to approach the librarian for a variety of reasons, as discussed above. Some libraries have changed their reference desk signs to read "Ask Us" or "Ask Here" in an attempt to clarify that the purpose of the reference desk is to help and to answer questions. Nonetheless, a librarian who appears absorbed in working on her computer or in reading a book will deter users from asking questions or will hear the preface, "Sorry to interrupt you, but . . ." Users should never feel like their questions are an imposition.

Stay aware of people as they approach your desk, look up, and greet them. Stay engaged during the rest of the reference interaction through *active listening,* which involves attentive listening and responses that reflect your interest and understanding. Interest is shown through nodding, affirmative statements like, "That is an interesting topic," encouraging statements such as, "Can you tell me more about that," and rephrasing of the information need, "As I understand it, you are looking for . . ."

Approachability and interest are easier in face-to-face interactions, since telephone and online interactions lack the ability to see body language. (Note that the telephone and instant messaging also can mask negative body language as well, as long as you can maintain a pleasant verbal or written tone.) As salespeople know, if you aren't feeling it, faking it with a smile will help you to stay calm and sound pleasant when talking on the telephone. Online, it is necessary to express encouragement and interest in writing. Most libraries and librarians do not use emoticons in text or email, as they are not considered professional and may not be appropriately interpreted by all users.

BEYOND INTEREST: BUILDING RAPPORT AND REFLECTING EMPATHY

Expressing interest in a user's topic and being welcoming not only is good customer service, but it encourages users to open up and talk more freely about their topic. The balance of friendliness and professionalism will be situational and specific not only to the library, but to the librarian and the individual interaction. That is not to say that you cannot be both friendly and professional at the same time. Our demeanor should adapt to the hesitant undergraduate and to the harried businessperson, reflecting empathy or efficiency or whatever will appropriately connect with each user.

Reflecting the user's level of formality is a good way to establish the right level of rapport. A clear way to think about this is in email, where if a person addresses the email as "Dear Ms. Kern," I will respond in kind, but if the person opens the email with, "Hi," I will reply with "Hi, X" or "Hello, Y." It is probably wise to err on the side of being slightly more formal than the user to maintain his confidence in you as a trusted professional.

There are ways to create rapport without being the user's buddy and while remaining established as the person who can help. Marie L. Radford (2006) writes about the role of self-disclosure in creating a connection with users online. Users share something about their state of mind when they say things like, "This might be a stupid question," or, "The library's website is really confusing." It is easy to gloss over these statements, but they are opportunities to show you are listening and to connect through either a similar self-disclosure ("It sometimes takes me awhile to find things, too.") or through reassurance ("That's actually a really good question; we get that question a lot."). Inclusive language also will involve the user in the conversation, particularly during the process of searching for the information. "Let's see what we can find" builds more engagement than "I'll let you know what I find."

As with any customer-service interaction, people will bring with them whatever mood they are in that day, and it might be a bad mood. They may specifically be frustrated with the library or sad about something else in their lives. Even when the user's negative emotions seem directed at the library, it is best to not take the interaction personally. Keep in mind that people have days where their emotions spill over, even when encountering a person who seems to have this mood every day. Empathy is important. Try to work out with this person what will help improve the situation, at least in terms of the person's information need. If it is a regular user of the library, think about what you know about this person that might help you to have empathy and stay calm and kind. Perhaps she is an older person feeling a loss of self-sufficiency due to changes in how to use the library, or he is a parent trying to get something done before the end of story time.

Creating an environment, face-to-face or online, where the user feels welcome, listened to, and comfortable with you as a librarian who can assist is vital to the success of the rest of the reference interview, where you will learn about the user's information need.

IN THEIR OWN WORDS: OPEN-ENDED QUESTIONS

The reference interview should feel more like a conversation than an interrogation. There are a few question-asking strategies that will help you and the user to avoid feeling like you are in a television police drama.

Start the question part of the reference interview with open-ended questions that do not proscribe options but rather solicit the user to come up with his own answers. This will encourage the user to explain his information need in his own language and will engage both of you with the topic. The technique of *neutral questioning* takes open-ended questions a step further by avoiding questions that, while open, might still be directive or focus on the information rather than the information need. "What type of information do you need?" is an open-ended question but focuses on the information; "How will you use this information?" focuses on the user. Neutral questioning "provides users with control—with the freedom to unfold their stories in a human way—and while helping the librarian to avoid premature diagnosis, allows users to retain control over the description of need and directs the interaction to the most pertinent aspects of the user's experience" (Dervin & Dewdney, 1986, p. 5).

Think about open-ended and neutral questions in terms of how you might converse with a friend about a recent vacation:

Where are you going?
When are you leaving?
Why made you think of the Channel Islands? I've never heard of them.
What do you plan to do there?

In a library context, keeping in mind "The 6 Pieces of Evidence," you might ask:

What interests you most about coffee?
What do you want to know about coffee roasting?
What do you already know about the process?
How do you plan to use this information?

Sometimes we encounter users who do not seem vested in their research questions or who do not seem able to define what they need at all. When this is the case, it might be because of an *imposed query*. Imposed queries occur when 1) the user is asking the question on behalf of someone else or 2) the information need originates from outside of the user and the user has not internalized it. The former is typical of a secretary or parent acting as proxy for the person who will ultimately use the information. It is possible that the user will need to confer with the other party to clarify what is needed. The latter situation is most frequent when the information need arises from an assignment and the student has not yet really settled on a topic that is of interest or has not given much thought to the assigned topic. In this situation, the techniques of open-ended and neutral questioning can engage the student in thinking about the topic and finding angles that are of interest.

Open-ended questions also help to narrow the user's question to something that is manageable and closer to the actual information need. As mentioned, users often do not know what information might be available and think from their own frustrated searching attempts that what they need might be too specific, so they cast their net widely. Open-ended questions get the user to provide more specifics in a gentle way that does not seem like a librarian scavenger hunt.

FOCUS AS NEEDED: CLOSED-ENDED QUESTIONS

Not all open-ended questions need to be neutral, and not all questions you ask need to be open-ended. There is a place in the reference conversation for closed-ended questions. Closed-ended questions present a limited number of options, such as yes/no or multiple choices. They should be employed judiciously and after you have a solid understanding of the user's research question so that you avoid guiding the user's responses. If the librarian leads the user's responses, time will be wasted and the user might end up with information that does not really fit. Many people, when presented with a list of options, will not voice that their response is something not on that list. I have done this a few times, much to my embarrassment, and had to restart a reference interview to get back to what the user actually wanted to know.

Closed-ended questions can wrap up the questioning phase by providing precision and clarification once you know something about the user's question. "Are you interested in contemporary or historical coffee roasting?" "Will you be roasting coffee at home or in a commercial environment?" "How technical do you need this information to be?"

Confirming your understanding of the user's information need is an important part of the reference interview, even when the user's responses are on the computer screen in front of you. In the back-and-forth of any conversation, understanding can be lost or important information left out. Once you have an understanding of who the user is, what information is wanted when, and how it might be useful, paraphrase and seek confirmation. "So, you are looking for information on commercial coffee roasting techniques and equipment in the mid-20th century for a novel you are writing. You would like some diagrams or pictures as well. Is that correct?" This provides the user with the opportunity to add or correct your understanding.

The *Behavioral Guidelines* are presented as a numbered list, and that is a good way to think about how a reference interview might progress. You have to be approachable to be asked questions and to appear welcoming, and open-ended questions should typically precede closed-ended questions. However, it is not strictly a linear process; interest and active listening should be present throughout the interaction with the user, and the librarian can ask any question at any time.

SEARCHING

Once the user's information need is understood, the librarian can start to search. Librarians are trained to find, and this is where they feel most expert. There can be a tendency to shortcut the reference interview to jump to the searching. Sometimes it will be necessary to do some preliminary searching to get an understanding of the topic or to discover the breadth of information available and then use that to ask more questions of the user. More typically, searching should be held until you have confirmed with the user that you understand the information need. If you are typing while you are talking to someone face-to-face, you will appear uninterested and disengaged. If you are searching while the user is responding to questions asked over the phone or online, you might miss what the person is saying by being too focused on what you are doing.

Searching with the user is encouraged in many library environments because it: 1) teaches users how to search so that they find information independently in the future, 2) builds rapport, 3) helps the user be able to add or modify your understanding of his information need during the search process if he is present and involved, and 4) allows for more immediate evaluation of the information that is found. However, in some environments the librarian provides the service of searching while the user does something else and then presents the information that is found.

When the user is still present and searching side-by-side with the librarian, the search process is part of the reference interview and the librarian should attend to instructing the user in how to choose where to search, thinking about search strategies and terms, and evaluating the information. It is a good technique to involve the user in the search decisions, particularly when you are hoping to instruct the user, by asking for input such as, "What search terms would you use?" Another technique is to model the librarian thought process and detail why you chose a particular database or search term. For example, "adolescents" is more formal than "teenagers" and is likely the term that will be used by academic writers in journal articles.

It is easiest to search with the user when he is present in person, but the librarian can guide the user through searching over the telephone or online as well by narrating the search process as it happens and by inviting the user to follow along on his computer. Some virtual reference software allows for cobrowsing so that the user and librarian can see the same computer screen. Screen-capture software such as Jing can be used to create quick on-the-fly videos of an online search that librarians can share with a user to show a process that might be confusing, or where written or verbal instructions have already failed. If using a video or a prewritten set of instructions, be sure to not just send the user away. Make it clear that this is part of an ongoing interaction and that you want the person to return to talk to you, or that you will give the person some time to read/follow the instructions and then will check back with him. The interaction might go like this:

> Librarian: I am going to send a quick video that will show how to get into the database and the search I did for articles. Is that ok?
>
> Patron: Sure.
>
> Librarian: Please watch that and follow along. I'll check back with you in a couple of minutes to make sure that you are finding what you need.

Whether you are instructing a user and searching together or are doing the search for a user and providing the answer, the user's evaluation of the search results is what makes a reference encounter successful. Did you meet the user's information need? Librarians have noted that they do not receive as many factual "ready reference" questions as they once did. Questions today are more likely to require that the user determine what is the best information. For example, there are many books, articles, and websites on becoming an entrepreneur. Is the information found going to be useful for *this particular* user? If not, why not? Is there something more to the question? Or specific about what the user expects? Finding this out requires the librarian to ask if the information is useful and why or why not. Do not just do a search and leave the user to look at a list of books or articles. Ask if any of them seem useful. If your environment has you select information for the user, ask for confirmation that the material found is on target. This allows you to note as well that there is other information that was not included, and that your searching can be adjusted if the user wants different or additional material.

Librarians tend to love information and love searching. This is not necessarily true with users. Keep the user's time in mind and her level of prior knowledge and involvement. A person working on a PhD might want *everything* and should learn about a variety of databases and sources. The high school student or the parent helping with a science fair project will not. A user may even lose interest sooner than the librarian. Finding out the amount of information and the scope of the project will help avoid overwhelming the user. Present searching different places one by one and check in with the user about if he wants more or different information. Some people will surprise you by wanting to learn more. Others will surprise you by "satisficing" or accepting the information that is quick and easy even if it does not appear to the librarian to be an exact match with the understood question.

CONCLUDING THE CONVERSATION

Evaluation of results takes time, so the librarian might need to give the user some space and then return to ask if the information was what was needed. This is easiest in person where you can walk away and then return later to a patron if he is still there. On the telephone and online it can be more difficult, as people may not want to stay on the line while they read and evaluate the information. With an online chat, informing the user that you will give her some time to read and then will come back and ask if that is what she wanted is one strategy, but sometimes she will leave anyway. On the telephone, it is awkward to hang on the line with someone who is reading, so in these cases the best situation might be to just invite the user to give a quick look over the results and, after confirming that they seem on track, to invite him to call back if more or different information is needed.

In-person and telephone reference interviews generally have a defined end, like most conversations. The librarian asks the user if the information is what is needed, and there is a "Thank you," a "Have a nice day," and an invitation to return with more questions. In chat and instant messaging interactions, conversational etiquette is not quite as developed and clear. Librarians may find that the user leaves the conversation at unexpected junctures. Was it a technical problem with the chat software? An unhappy user? Something I said? It could be equally likely that the person went to get lunch or that she was satisfied with the help received and felt she could search on her own from that point. In my own online, text-based conversations (instant messaging, for instance), communication tends to trickle off as people are watching television, talking to others in the same room, writing emails, and so forth, and it is possible that this casual approach to conversational etiquette and cues affects how users interact with the librarian as well. It can be unsettling at first to not have a tidy end to the reference interview, but it is best not to take it personally.

Sometimes we never really know, because the patron thinks that the book or article is right for what she wants, but without having the chance for a full evaluation. This is where encouraging the user to return and having a pleasant interaction are both important. People must be willing to return and also feel that the librarian will welcome their question again, even if it is a similar question to one already asked.

REFLECTION AND CHANGE

The fundamentals of communication between users and librarians are enduring but not static; new technologies have affected how we communicate, what users expect, and what we can learn about the reference encounter. The *Behavioral Guidelines* text was first published in 1996 and revised by the Reference and User Services Association in 2004 to incorporate remote communications, such as those conducted via instant messaging. New communications technologies are slow to evolve (e.g., the telephone has been in use for over one hundred years). Even instant messaging is over twenty-five years old. Libraries continue to monitor what communication technologies our patrons use in their daily lives, and some experiment with these, such as FaceTime and video chat, to determine if these are avenues for communication with the library that patrons will want. The tenants of the reference interview—understanding the user's information need, creating a conversation, active listening, open- and closed-ended questions, and inclusion of the user in the search process—may need some adjustment to handle effectively with new communication modes. However, just as the development of guidelines for chat reference interviews were informed by in-person and telephone strategies, so will future developments be informed by the reference interviews of chat, telephone, and in-person.

In looking at the reimagining of reference services, we need an awareness of changes in communication technologies, but more revolutionary might be discovering ways to better understand and converse with users. Research into user information-seeking behavior and interpersonal communication has provided librarians with a solid basis for how to conduct an effective reference interview. Analysis of transcripts from virtual reference interactions have enriched and will continue to enrich our understanding of how both users and librarians communicate about information. New methodologies and new researchers, both within and outside of library science, explore how to have more successful conversations, how people approach their information needs, and how these can be applied within libraries and other information-seeking environments.

The improvement of the reference interview relies on three things: a desire to help the user, a curiosity to learn from others (colleagues, researchers, and users), and the thoughtfulness to reflect on your own practice as a librarian. Self-reflection on both successful and unsatisfactory reference interactions grows the ability to identify and correct mistakes in communication and to refine an individual approach and voice in the reference interview.

REFERENCES

Dervin, B., & Dewdney, P. (1986). Neutral questioning: A new approach to the reference interview. *Research Quarterly, 25*(4), 506–513.

Kuhlthau, C. C. (1991). Inside the search process: Information seeking from the user's perspective. *Journal of the American Society for Information Science, 42*(5), 361–371.

Ohio Library Council. (2008). The 6 pieces of evidence. Retrieved from http://www.olc.org/ore/2pieces.htm

Radford, M. L. (2006). Encountering virtual users: A qualitative investigation of interpersonal communication in chat reference *Journal of the American Society for Information Science and Technology, 57*(8), 1046–1059. http://dx.doi.org/10.1002/asi.20374

Reference and User Services Association. (2004). *Guidelines for behavioral performance of reference and information services providers*. Retrieved from http://www.ala.org/rusa/resources/guidelines/guidelinesbehavioral

Taylor, R. (1967). *Question-negotiation and information seeking in libraries. Studies in the man-system interface in libraries, report no. 3*. Bethlehem, PA: Center for the Information Sciences, Lehigh University. Retrieved from www.dtic.mil/dtic/tr/fulltext/u2/659468.pdf

4 | Readers' Advisory Services as Reference Services

Jessica E. Moyer, University of Wisconsin-Milwaukee

WHY ARE WE EVEN TALKING ABOUT READERS' ADVISORY?

Many of you may ask, "Why is a chapter on readers' advisory even in a book about reference services?" And that's a very good question to ask. Anyone who spends time observing a public library reference services point will see that readers' advisory (RA) questions are nearly as common as those for tech support, which means every reference librarian who is working or wants to work in a public library must be both familiar with RA services and be able to provide them as a regular part of her reference duties. In their recent overview of readers' advisory, *Library Journal* found that 100% of respondents offered some type of RA services and "Some 84% of respondents say RA is important or very important to the library's mission already" (Thornton-Verma & Schwartz, 2014). We are many years past the point where RA services are optional or something only done by specialized library staff. Readers' advisory services are a regular and everyday part of public library reference services, but this is a significant change that is yet to fully permeate the profession.

As a library science educator and RA evangelist, I teach reference and RA services courses (we talk about the reference interview in the RA class, and RA questions and sources are a part of every reference class) as well write books, make conference presentations, and speak to continuing education groups. In this chapter, I will review recent advances, the current state of practice, current and upcoming challenges for reference librarians providing RA services, and conclude with a peek into the future of RA services for the reference librarian.

Do We Even Need Readers' Advisory Services Now That We Have Amazon?

Before we can get into the main part of this chapter, we need to address the elephants in the room: Google and Amazon. How many times have we heard: "We don't need librarians anymore. We can just Google it." or "Amazon has all the books I'll ever need, and they make suggestions. Why bother with the library?" These are not only perfectly valid questions, but ones that we must have a good answer for if we hope to ever get the full support of the community. This has become an even more important consideration in recent years because of the plethora of automated advisor services. It is impossible to watch Netflix without getting suggestions of what to view next. Hulu even sends emails to its Hulu Plus customers with notifications of newly arrived shows they think you would like based on your previous viewing history.

In terms of RA, libraries have three main strengths. First, Amazon suggests books based on what others have purchased and/or similar subject areas. Neither of these may be the kind of material a patron wants, and it takes a trained librarian to understand the reader's mood and needs, and then match the person with the right story. Second, all of these systems are limited to what they are selling or have licensed. Never can they suggest from the full variety of materials that is contained within a library system. Any regular online television viewer knows that it is impossible to get HBO shows streamed without an HBO subscription, which means they are never suggested by the automated services. Yet these are some of the most popular DVDs in most public library collections. Third, you cannot have a conversation with Amazon or any of the other systems. Whether face-to-face or online, many readers yearn for a human connection in reading suggestions. It is one reason that peer-to-peer suggestions are highly valued by readers, and that human connection is something librarians are trained and ready to provide every day. It is a lot harder to tell an automated system that you are not really in the mood for your usual dark and dreary crime stories, but a well-trained librarian knows the importance of asking, "What kind of reading experience are you in the mood for today?" Finally, we need to remember that Amazon is in the business of selling books, while libraries are in the business of matching patrons and stories.

WHERE ARE READER SERVICES NOW?

Death of Reference = The Rise of Readers' Advisory

The last 30 years have seen significant changes in reference services. Indeed, many experts have proclaimed the death of reference since the rise of the World Wide Web and easy-to-use search engines. As reported in *Library Journal,* "the library [Arlington Heights] had an 85% drop in reference transactions between 1999 (259,024 interactions) and 2008 (38,077); over three years of observation, 94% of the print reference collection was never touched by a librarian" (Hadro, 2012). And yet it is not all doom and gloom, as "reference work is not dead; it's merely reinvented. Reference is now local—and encompasses programming and services" (Vnuk, 2012). The death of reference may have been exaggerated, but it has certainly changed a great deal in the last 20 years, and the increase of RA services is one significant part of the change. Readers' advisory services are becomingly increasingly integrated into regular reference services, both in person and online.

Many of the same librarians who argued about the death of reference will agree that RA has been on the rise since its rebirth in the 1980s. Evidence abounds for the increased professional acceptance and interest in RA services.

For example, the third edition of Kay Cassell's textbook, *Reference and Information Services: An Introduction,* can be found in the RA section of the publisher's website. Recent additions include horror, mystery, science fiction, and historical fiction, not to mention the more professional development-oriented titles like *The Readers' Advisory Handbook* (Moyer & Stover, 2010), the third edition of Joyce G. Saricks' classic, *Readers' Advisory Service in the Public Library* (2005), and the youth-oriented *Connecting Boys With Books: What Libraries Can Do* (Sullivan, 2009). Libraries Unlimited continues to publish the successful *Genreflecting: A Guide to Popular Reading Interests* (now in its seventh edition), the spinoff Genreflecting series, and the Read On series. Together, their 2014 catalog has more than five pages of RA services titles.

Readers' advisory services programs are some of the most popular offered at conferences, both local and national. The 2012 Public Library Association (PLA) conference featured many RA services offerings, ranging from a preconference with Nancy Pearl to programs on social media book groups, young adult crossover titles, and "Leaders as readers: What happens when directors choose reading as a core initiative" (Educational Sessions & Handouts, 2012). 2014 will be no different. A program on social media and RA services was presented both in person and as part of the virtual program; a group of RA experts discussed top trends and titles in nonfiction; and a mix of librarians and media professionals presented a session about improving RA for listeners of audiobooks.

Professional education is slowly catching up, and more MLIS programs are teaching RA services courses. Recently, both the University of Illinois and the University of Wisconsin-Milwaukee permanently added RA services courses to their library science curriculum. *Library Journal*, in their recent survey of library services, notes that nearly 60% of librarians had some RA coursework in their MLIS programs (Thornton-Verma & Schwartz, 2014).

Whether or not traditional reference is dead is still up for debate, but that is something that is well covered in other chapters of this book. However, it is clear that RA services have experienced a renaissance and become an important part of modern reference services in public libraries.

Face-to-Face or Traditional Information Services

Since the RA renaissance of the 1980s (Saricks & Brown, 1987), face-to-face RA services provided at traditional public library services desk have been the default. In the early years, some libraries split reference and RA services, and only specially trained librarians provided RA services. While this worked at the beginning, it soon became clear that patrons had trouble knowing where to go to ask their questions. Additionally, many of the RA services only provided desks located in the fiction collection. As RA services have been expanded into nonfiction (more on this later), this distinction became increasingly troublesome, and most libraries have abandoned segregated service points. Some smaller libraries have gone so far as to combine reference services, circulation, and IT help into the same service area. The San José Public Library even offers customized tours and consulting on their new service model (Tour Module, 2014). Today, nearly all public libraries offer RA services as the same physical location as their information services, a combination that may be challenging for some staff, but one that works well for library patrons.

Additionally, just as many libraries have adopted the roving model of reference service, RA services happen in stacks as well as at a physical desk. Experienced librarians know that patrons wandering the fiction collection are often in need of RA assistance. Mobile technologies and wireless Internet have made answering questions and suggesting titles as easy from any point in the library as at the physical service desk.

Readers' advisory does not take place just inside the library walls either. The 2014 *Library Journal* Mover and Shaker Erin Shea meets commuters at the railway station, first bringing business and other titles she believe they will enjoy, and later leading a book group at a nearby bar. This approach came about after Sheryl Sandberg's book, *Lean In*, had circulated more than 75 times in a month. In Salem, Oregon, Robin Beerbower creates an extensive annual "best of" brochure that she not only passes out at the reference desk, but uses as the basis for several presentations to community groups as well as a regular column in her local newspaper. Lawrence, Kansas, may have to close their library for a week to update their barcodes, but it is not stopping them from providing library services, as they put together pop-up libraries at the local park. Attendees need only bring their library card and family members to these special story times, where staff will provide a variety of books for all ages.

It's Not Just Fiction Anymore

The 2004 PLA preconference, "Crossing the Aisle: Connecting Fiction and Nonfiction," marked a turning point in RA toward a widespread acceptance of nonfiction materials as leisure reading. That same year, reading scholar Robert Burgin published *Nonfiction Readers' Advisory*, a collection of scholarly and professional essays on nonfiction reading interests. In 2006, Sarah Statz Cords published *The Real Story,* the first librarian guide to nonfiction reading interests, and Saricks' 2005 edition of *Readers' Advisory Services in the Public Library* included nonfiction as well as fiction. Definitions of RA services started to move away from adults reading fiction to embrace all ages, reading all types of materials, in all formats. In 2008, when NoveList announced that the new NoveList Plus and NoveList K–8 Plus would include nonfiction, readers' advisors rejoiced at finally being able to use their most trusted database for all kinds of reading interests (Novelist Timeline, 2014).

WHAT ARE SOME OF OUR RECENT INNOVATIONS?

Online Services

Just as RA services have merged into physical information services, they are increasingly part of online virtual reference services. Whether by chat or email, RA questions are asked and answered every day. Some libraries have moved beyond these basic offerings into innovative services that reach out to patrons. The Kansas City Public Library uses Facebook to offer weekly RA suggestions in their "Reading Refresh" program. This weekly event is used by regular and new readers from around the world, as the Kansas City Public Library doesn't limit its Facebook service to verified patrons. Kaite Stover, founder of Reading Refresh, has written about social media and RA in several forums. If you missed her virtual or in-person presentations at PLA 2014, try her article in *Reference and User Services Quarterly* (2009), "Stalking the Wild Appeal Factor: Readers' Advisory and Social Networking Sites."

An Asynchronous Alternative: Form-Based Readers' Advisory

One alternative to the desk versus virtual debate is providing reader services in an asynchronous format. Readers can submit requests either in person at the library, or more often, online at any time of day or night. Pioneered by Williamsburg Regional Library in their program "Looking for a Good Book?":

> Williamsburg Regional Library's award-winning *Looking for a Good Book?* service began in October, 2003. Since then, over 1000 readers have taken advantage of the service, using either the Library's paper or Web-based questionnaire to create a profile of their personal reading interests. Librarians have then used those profiles to develop custom reading lists, based on books and authors that the readers have already enjoyed as well as on the readers' literary likes and dislikes. (Looking for a Good Book Reader Profile Forms, n.d.)

In the last ten years, so many libraries have followed their example and so many are interested in beginning a program that ALA Editions has already one full section of a six-week e-course, "Rethinking Readers' Advisory: An Interactive Approach," and WebJunction has hosted a webinar by Seattle public librarians. Their resource page includes a valuable set of links to other libraries' forms and programs for anyone interested in starting a new service (Serving Readers: Beyond the Basics, 2013).

Readers' Advisory in Academic Libraries

Readers' advisory services are not limited to public libraries. School librarians practice RA every day as they match students with books for free reading or school assignments. Additionally, academic libraries have started to realize that RA is something they should consider offering, especially on college campuses where students do not have regular or easy access to public library collections. In 2010, Venta Silins discussed this trend and highlighted several strategies for providing academic RA (Silins, 2010). Loyola Marymount University has even created an RA LibGuide, "Reading for Fun!" (2013).

Some would even argue that the bread and butter of academic reference, suggesting which database to consult for research articles, is another form of RA. It certainly takes knowledge of all the available options, an understanding of the user, and a knack for suggesting the one that will best meet the user's needs. Sometimes it is EBSCO Academic Search Premier; sometimes it's the Gale Virtual Reference Library. The best librarians know how to go beyond subject-based needs and incorporate the unique factors of the database and the needs of the patron.

IMPROVEMENT IN SERVICES: ARE WE GETTING BETTER?

While reference services have been extensively assessed, evaluated, and critiqued, there has been significantly less for RA services due to its more recent rise and to the lack of faculty in LIS programs with research agendas focusing on RA services. In the late 1990s and early 2000s, Kenneth Shearer was one of those few, and he led several RA services evaluation studies along with Catherine Ross and Robert Burgin. A thorough review of their work can be found in *Research-Based Readers' Advisory* (Moyer, 2008), along with discussion of the much-cited *Library Journal* article by Mary K. Chelton, "Readers' Advisory 101" (2003), which listed the most common mistakes made by librarians providing RA services to students in Chelton's course on RA services. Like the earlier work by Ross, Shearer, and Burgin, RA services questions were often dismissed, ignored, or brushed off. In general, they were not treated with the same professional respect as reference questions asked at the same locations.

But that was more than ten years ago. Readers' advisory has come a long way since then, but have library experiences improved too? Since 2008, students in my reference and RA services classes have also gone out and asked RA questions at public libraries across the United States (thanks to online education, I get to teach students in many different physical locations). At the 2013 ALISE Conference, I presented the first update on the status of RA services at a poster session along with doctoral students Renee Kaspusniak and Jennifer Thiele (Moyer, Kaspusniak, & Thiele, 2013). In addition to analyzing our results, I also communicated with Chelton about any changes in the services her students were experiencing. We drew three main conclusions. First, RA services are improving. Students are getting more professional and courteous services in most libraries, and the use of RA services tools like NoveList is increasing. Second, we also concluded is that there are still major regional differences. Twin Cities libraries performed the best (possibly due to the longtime pro-reader services culture fostered at the Hennepin system), while students in Queens are still mostly receiving poor and/or unprofessional services. Third, additional research found that RA services are heavily promoted and regular training is supported for libraries in the Twin Cities metro area, especially those that are part of the Hennepin system.

CHALLENGES

What About E-Books? Don't They Change Everything?

This may be the simplest question of all; the answer is an emphatic *no*. While there is no doubt that e-books and other digital materials are providing no end of collection development challenges, from the service side they really have not changed our core business. If anything, they have broadened our service population by allowing us to reach and serve users with limited access to physical collections. In the end, the advent of e-books is really just the addition of a new format. A quick look back at library and publishing history will show that nearly the same issues and arguments came around when dime novels and mass-market paperbacks became the popular reading material of choice. It may have taken over 70 years for libraries to embrace, collect, and catalog genre fiction mass-market paperbacks; let's hope it will not take so long to fully accept e-books. Regardless of whether readers will be enjoying their books in print or on a Nook, Kindle, or iPad, it is still the same story and requires the same kind of RA services. Really, it is no different than asking if patrons prefer paperbacks over hardcovers.

I Can't Provide Readers' Advisory Services. I Don't Read!

The long-running excuse of librarians not interested in providing RA services is that they themselves don't read enough. And while an extensive personal knowledge of authors and titles was needed in the early days, it has been many years since professional library staff relied solely on personal knowledge. In fact, relying on personal knowledge is a poor excuse for professional services, which would never be tolerated in a reference transaction. Just as when providing reference services, librarians providing RA services can and should be using professional tools. Not every library may have money for a NoveList subscription, but their local consortium or state might. And there are plenty of individual resource titles published every year by Libraries Unlimited and ALA Editions, not to mention dozens of excellent websites. This sentiment seems to be changing, as a recent blog post, "Tips for the Reluctant Readers' Advisor" gives seven simple suggestions that can be tried by even the busiest librarian (Backer, 2014). Additionally, in *Library Journal*'s "The State of Readers Advisory," they note, "another respondent challenges the idea that "only voracious readers can provide effective RA service" (Thornton-Verma & Schwartz, 2014). Instead, "We stress that they don't have to have read everything, that there are tools and resources for them" (Thornton-Verma & Schwartz, 2014). Until it is professionally acceptable to say "I can't help you find out about measles because I've never had them" in a reference transaction, it is unacceptable for librarians to wimp out on RA questions with the classic, "I don't read that kind of book, so I can't help you." We have tools for providing RA services; let's make sure that we are using them.

WHAT SHOULD READERS' ADVISORY LOOK LIKE IN THE NEXT TEN TO TWENTY YEARS? WHAT DO WE NEED TO DO TO MAKE THIS HAPPEN?

Will the RA renaissance continue to flourish as we march on into the 21st century? Or like traditional reference, will it succumb to the powers of Google? Nothing is certain, but I would like to think that RA services will continue to play an important role in public libraries and be considered a core service. If we have learned anything from the recent e-book explosion, it is that e-book users read more books, and when nonreaders obtain an e-reading device, they can become readers. Despite the naysaying of the National Endowment for the Arts at the beginning of this century (Reading at Risk, 2004), it seems that we are and will remain a nation of readers, even if the format in which most of the stories are consumed has changed. As long as this is the case, then libraries must continue to provide, support, and expand their RA services and consider them an integral part of reference services for modern public libraries. And there is support for this. *Library Journal* reports "the importance of RA is not declining. In fact, more than half of respondents say RA increased in importance in the last three years, and 54% say RA will be even more important three years from now" (Thornton-Verma & Schwartz, 2014).

Part of the expansion of services will mean looking past the traditional book and into providing advisory services for all the media consumed by library patrons. As much as it may grate on more traditional librarians, the days of providing RA services for printed fiction are over. Instead, we must continue to expand, such as we have done with nonfiction. Graphic novels, audiobooks, music, and movies are all part of today's public library collection—and they deserve advisory services too. We are making progress in some areas; audiobooks not only have several RA texts as resources, but NoveList announced that they will be added to editions of NoveList Plus in 2014. We just need to keep moving forward until we are providing full advisory services for all the media collections.

Like many other areas of library services, RA services are not stagnant, but will be forever evolving to keep up with the latest in technology and society; we just need to make sure that we are ready and able to adapt and evolve. It is widely accepted that many patrons want their information needs met as fast and as simply as possible. As Vnuk (2012) writes, "While they once might have been willing to wait a few minutes for an answer to a question, today they often expect an answer instantly, if not sooner." It may have taken several years, but libraries (and vendors) have adapted well to providing digital audiobooks. I hope that we all remember this difficult lesson and do not wait too long to provide collections with a wide selection and an easy-to-use interface. The audiobook challenges of the early 2000s lost libraries a small but significant chunk of the audiobook market. The market for leisure reading materials, as we transition from print to digital, is much larger. Losing even a small part of this group could have severe and long-term consequences for libraries. Let's make sure to remember that the best library services are when patrons can make a human connection with a well-trained librarian and are provided access to a range of materials and formats that meet their needs.

REFERENCES

ALA Store. (2014). Readers' advisory. Retrieved from http://www.alastore.ala.org/SearchResult.aspx?CategoryID=197

Backer, J. (2014). Tips for the reluctant readers' advisor. [Web log post]. *BCALA Readers' Advisory Interest Group: What Are You Reading?* Retrieved from http://whatareyoureadingblog.com/2014/02/27/tips-for-the-reluctant-readers-advisor/

Chelton, M. K. (2003). Readers' advisory 101. *Library Journal, 128*(8), 38–39.

Hadro, J. (2012, March 16). Reports of the death of reference may be exaggerated. *Library Journal*. Retrieved from http://lj.libraryjournal.com/2012/03/shows-events/pla/reports-of-reference-death-may-be-exaggerated-pla-2012/#_

Erin Shea—Movers & Shakers 2014—Marketers. (2014, March 12). *Library Journal*. Retrieved from http://lj.libraryjournal.com/2014/03/people/movers-shakers-2014/erin-shea-movers-shakers-2014-marketers/

Moyer, J. E. (Ed.). (2008). *Research-based readers' advisory*. Chicago: American Library Association.

Moyer, J. E., Kaspusniak, R. B., & Thiele, J. H. (2013). Are we getting any better? Using secret shopper assignments to evaluate reader services [Poster]. Conference of the Association for Library and Information Science Education.

NoveList Timeline. (2014). *NoveList*. Retrieved from http://www.ebscohost.com/novelist/about-novelist/the-novelist-story

Educational Sessions & Handouts. (2012). *Public Library Association Conference*. Retrieved from http://2012.placonference.org/programs

Reading at Risk: A Survey of Literary Reading in America. (2004). *National Endowment for the Arts*. Retrieved from http://arts.gov/publications/reading-risk-survey-literary-reading-america-0

Reading for Fun! (2013). *Loyola Marymount University*. Retrieved from http://libguides.lmu.edu/reading

Reading Refresh, The Kansas City Public Library. (n.d.). Retrieved from https://www.facebook.com/kclibrary/posts/10151285422544412

Rethinking Readers' Advisory: An Interactive Approach. (2014). *American Library Association*. Retrieved from http://www.ala.org/news/press-releases/2013/08/rethinking-readers-advisory-interactive-approach

Tour Module. (2014). *San José Public Library*. Retrieved from http://www.sjpl.org/sjwtour

Saricks, J., & Brown, N. (1987). *Readers' advisory service in the public library*. Chicago: American Library Association.

Serving Readers: Beyond the Basics. (2013). *OCLC WebJunction*. Retrieved from http://www.webjunction.org/events/webjunction/Serving_Readers_Beyond_the_Basics.html

Silins, V. (2010, July). Readers' advisory in the academic library: Issues and ideas. *Libraries Unlimited*. Retrieved from http://www.readersadvisoronline.com/ranews/jul2010/silins.html

Stover, K. M. (2009). Stalking the wild appeal factor: Readers' advisory and social networking sites. *Reference and User Services Quarterly, 48*(3), 243–269.

Thornton-Verma, H., & Schwartz, M. (2014, February 3). The state of readers' advisory. *Library Journal*. Retrieved from http://lj.libraryjournal.com/2014/02/library-services/the-state-of-readers-advisory/

Vnuk, R. (2012, May 15). Reference reality. *Booklist Online*. Retrieved from http://www.booklistonline.com/Reference-Reality-Rebecca-Vnuk/pid=5446396

Looking for a Good Book Reader Profile Forms. (n.d.). *Williamsburg Regional Library*. Retrieved from http://www.wrl.org/books-and-reading/adults/find-good-book/looking-good-book-reader-profile-forms

Part 2
CONTENT AND INFORMATION SOURCES

5 | Reference Publishing in the 21st Century: Lead, Follow, or Get Out of the Way

Rolf Janke, Mission Bell Media

INTRODUCTION

Reference publishing is changing and in many ways it is a dramatic change—dramatic enough that some publishers have ceased publishing reference works altogether, while other publishers are seizing the opportunity to reinvent themselves in an effort to survive and grow. Just after the turn of the century, reference publishers followed the digital path that journal publishers had paved a decade earlier.

While digital reference and journals differ, they both are products that package pieces of information into a unified whole. As journals gained wide acceptance in digital formats, reference publishers forged ahead and created e-reference or e-book versions of their reference works. This was a sustainable change for the publishers, but there was a new universe of competitors, business models, and economic changes on the horizon that now threatens the existence of the traditional reference publisher.

This is not a chapter of why, when, and how reference publishers will become extinct. It is more a view of how most reference publishers have survived thus far and, more importantly, a glimpse of the key factors a reference publisher needs to keep at the forefront in order to stay in business in the future. This chapter gives on-the-ground insight, revealing what reference publishers are talking about behind the scenes. This information can also alert and educate librarians as to how this segment of the publishing business is currently being strategically redefined.

Like every book or article that discusses change and transition in a business, this chapter presents a point of view, not necessarily definitive answers. It is also important to note that there is very little public information on reference publishers' revenues, unit sales, and other key metrics that would be useful to make comparisons and even predictions on the performance of those publishers and the industry. To start the conversation, two leading reference publishers give current insight to the reference market with a brief question and answer interview. Their thoughts and observations are both insightful and encouraging.

THE SHIFT IN THE SUSTAINABLE GROWTH EQUATION

Reference publishers in many ways are resilient survivors. Yes, other publishing mediums have endured tough challenges, but if you examine the last decade, the variables in the formula for sustainable growth in reference have shifted, making room for new ones that cannot be ignored. Reference publishers were very traditional creatures and for generations stayed the course of a very simple business model of producing authoritative content packaged in book form. But in a digital era, many learned that an entrepreneurial focus was key to building a new generation of reference works. The old model for reference was built around the singular concept that print was king, and publishers enjoyed economies of scale within that infrastructure, which was built to churn out print and nothing but print on a fairly linear workflow model.

However, with the transition from print to digital, there has now been a major paradigm shift in how publishers approach creating content, how librarians purchase content, and how end users discover content. This huge shift across the entire business model has caused a decline in the use of reference products. Ultimately, it has made for an overall decline in reference publishing sales. Remember, these publishers had built a straightforward profit model that had worked for years, and this shift caused a total upheaval across all aspects of production and sales.

To survive, publishers moved from the standard infrastructure built for print to account for the new digital realm. This meant making changes at all levels and investing in new technologies and product development to support the digital environment. The workflow model became much more dynamic, with several new stages added to the publication process, along

REFERENCE PUBLISHER SPOTLIGHT:
DAMON ZUCCA, OXFORD UNIVERSITY PRESS

1. With the multitudes of changes in technology and content dissemination, is there an endpoint where the "how, when, why" reference content is more important than the actual value of the content?

Reference publishers, like all publishers, have to produce content that meets the needs of a particular audience. In this sense, the value of the content we publish is inseparable from how that material is being delivered and used. Because the fast pace of technological change is likely to continue for the foreseeable future, I think reference publishers will be actively engaging these how, when, why questions for a long time to come. The exciting side of all this is that publishers need not stand passively on the sidelines, but can have an active role in shaping new research behaviors by delivering content and services in new ways that might directly influence our audience's practices and expectations. If we are to play this part, reference publishers need to embrace change, embrace technology, and stay close to our audience. I think the toughest challenges in the current environment are how to balance the long-term planning that is essential to execute large-scale reference projects with the flexibility needed to accommodate changing demands of our audience. The only way through is for digital publishing platforms or partners to give us this flexibility.

2. Is it becoming more difficult to convince academics to author and edit reference content?

Reference publishing is at its core a highly social endeavor that depends on successfully mobilizing large numbers of scholars. Projects languish or come together unevenly if authors and editors do not believe in the vision for the project. In this period of digital transition, as traditional reference publishers have struggled to find their place within a new and evolving information ecosystem, we have also struggled with formulating compelling narratives for why busy academics should want to devote time and effort to our projects. At the same time, online publishing offers publishers the chance to tell new stories and in new ways that I find can resonate with academics. For one thing, there is great opportunity for increased use of the content we publish, and the promise of reaching a large audience is one of the most persuasive reasons we have for participating in reference projects. Online also gives publishers new ways to do the sort of community building that is so vital for developing large collaborative reference works. I think the key is connecting a virtuous circle between our authors and users. What reference services do our academic authors want to use? Once we have answered this question, publishers need to develop engaged communities of authors/users around active reference hubs involved in a continuous process of interrogating and defining fields of academic inquiry.

3. How have the economics of reference publishing changed, and are there new business models that can "happily" exist between librarians and publishers?

The biggest challenge we face now as print fades is that we are selling to a more concentrated universe of institutions that have substantial budgets for digital collection development, and this leaves out many of the smaller publics and school libraries especially that had previously been a large part of the core reference market. At these large institutional libraries, digital reference products are now competing for budget share with an ever-growing range of online products and services. In the not-so-distant past, reference librarians with their own collection budget made purchase decisions based on which reference titles were most relevant to their patrons. Now reference publishers have to work very hard to show relevance to the whole category, let alone something as specific as a title. I find, budget pressures aside, there is a lot of goodwill between librarians and reference publishers as we have felt our way through the digital transition together.

Looking ahead, I think a test of this happy relationship will come as reference publishers inevitably begin to introduce business models around their online offerings that target individuals.

REFERENCE PUBLISHER SPOTLIGHT:
VINCE BURNS, VICE PRESIDENT, ABC-CLIO

1. Is reference relevant?

Print and digital reference materials *are* relevant today. Just witness (as I have recently) a high school student and music fan disappear into a corner for hours with a copy of the *Encyclopedia of Indie Rock* (2008) or a military buff immerse himself in all 3,000 pages of the *American Civil War* (2013).

Sure, reference books aren't the only game in the information town anymore. And there are almost an infinite number of places online to find information on the Civil War or independent music. But Wikipedia doesn't have the authority of a master military historian who has spent his life researching the Civil War and the last five years assembling the experts to make sense of it in six volumes. Sure, there may be an "entry" on Second Battle of Bull Run in Wikipedia to tell you who won and who lost, but I'd rather have Professor Spencer Tucker curate his six-volume encyclopedia on the American Civil War than be left to the tender mercies of Wikipedia's anonymous contributors. Yes, reference publishing has changed dramatically in the last ten years. Publishers have come and gone. The changes have (rightfully) forced information publishers to be relevant or fold up. As a result, books that can do nothing more than tell us who, what, when, and where about something struggle to be relevant. Those that can tell us why still have a lot to say.

2. Do you think this is the end of an era for encyclopedias?

Encyclopedias are only one format for the publishing genre called "reference." And, yes, the A–Z format isn't as indispensable as it once was. But there's a place for encyclopedias. (Don't try and take the *Encyclopedia of Heavy Metal Music* away from my seventeen-year-old.) Depending on your definition of reference, there are actually many ways to organize a reference book:

> topically, thematically, chronologically, by content type, plus many other possibilities. We consider the needs of our end user and the most appropriate format for the information to be presented before we decide on an organization for a project.
>
> Example: We publish a strong list in social history (a.k.a., "daily life through history"). In this area the encyclopedia is an inefficient (at best) format. Instead, our books in social history take a thematic or geographic or chronological approach (the latter is especially appropriate if we're including primary sources). The result can be a very compelling documentary "trip" through history, one primary source at a time. The encyclopedia format would never work for projects like this.
>
> So reference isn't synonymous with the venerable A–Z. And even the encyclopedia isn't dead. We're making a mistake if we ask librarians to turn in books like the *Encyclopedia of Heavy Metal Music,* which brings together in one place a whole range of knowledge and context not available elsewhere. At least that's what my seventeen-year-old says.

with additional costs. As a direct result, new pain points were created that required smart financial decisions on what to include or not include with any reference product.

Only a handful of publishers could afford to make this change. Many of the smaller publishers simply cancelled their reference program. During this transition, print reference was still a viable format, but nowhere close to the numbers of units sold they had seen before the turn of the 21st century. Many would argue the prediction that for every lost print sale there was a digital version sold to equal the revenue balance, but that scenario never happened.

While the sales curve for print was slowly in decline, the sales curve for e-books was an even slower ascent. Possible answers as to why this happened can be explained as variables that emerged, which soon became a significant and in some cases a confrontational part of the sustainable growth equation. By confrontational, it means that as a publisher, you did not have any control over most of these factors, yet these variables were the determiners between sustainable growth or the abandonment of the reference market altogether. The short list of these new variables would certainly include:

- Technology
- Topic selection
- Usage
- Currency
- Added value
- Faculty
- Free
- Collections, bundles, and databases
- Textbooks
- Aggregators

Technology

Now, technology is sovereign in the publishing world. Technology can save you money, can cost you money, and can make you money—it all depends on how you use it. Technology can allow for new creativity, experimenting with new product ideas for content. Technology can decrease the cycle time in developing content. Technology can provide more services to your customer and all end users. Technology can introduce an innovative mindset to your editorial program. The list seems endless, and it is easy to get lost and lose focus.

This is the challenge for the publisher. Think of the publishers you know and ask their viewpoint on technology. Are they leading by building their own technologies? Do they have the funds to invest in the latest and greatest? Are they more conservative, following what others have done? Do they replicate what has been successful in the past? Are they simply not in a position to afford the costs to keep up with technology? A publisher's decision on where they stand on technology could be the ultimate determining factor in their ability not only to survive but to sustain growth. There are risks at all levels—being in the forefront, following that lead, or sticking to the paradigm of the past. There is no way of escaping the technology question.

Topic Selection

CEOs of publishing companies always ask their reference staff, "When will you run out of topics to publish?" As a publisher in the social and behavioral sciences, there is a very broad and far-reaching selection of topics for publishing reference works. Is there a saturation point in a certain discipline? Duplication in the reference business is not an economically good idea, since most libraries only have the budget to buy one reference source on a topic—if they buy that one at all. As a history publisher, is there a point of saturation when you have covered all of the major, significant historical events? Probably the disciplines that are changing the most are science and medicine, so would one ever reach saturation covering those topics? Publishers are aware that in some subject areas, there is not much room left to publish, which like these other variables presents a significant challenge.

A standard aspect of reference works is that they are not confined to just a single volume, unlike textbooks or popular novels. Multivolume works or, more specifically, encyclopedias represent the true depth of a topic or discipline. Multivolume works also represent a higher cost to produce by the publisher, and of course that means a higher price to the librarian. In the current economic climate, sales of multivolume works are on the decline, in print and in e-book format. It is an expense many publishers simply cannot afford anymore, and it is a cost that is often too expensive for the library to consider. This is a major shift in the editorial business model, and it is challenging publishers to move from "select a topic and attach a volume count" to focusing on single-volume publishing. These economies present challenges to the publisher on topic selection, as they have to adapt large topics into smaller formats.

Usage

This is a significant variable because it is one that clearly distinguishes the value between print and digital reference works. Defining how often a print work was used is very difficult. Visiting an academic library, an encyclopedia on the Cold War, which had been published almost twenty years ago, sat on a shelf. From its apparent condition, it seemed like the encyclopedia had never been used. The library bought this valuable, authoritative work on a significant event but does not really have proof on how many times it was actually used. In contrast, if that library had that same title in an e-book format, it would have access to usage statistics that the publisher and/or aggregator provide. The librarians could easily find out how many times it was used, which would then provide metrics as to its value to their collection.

What librarians may not realize is that the idea of usage statistics to a reference publisher is a scary proposition. Although many publishers research their topics with librarian advisory boards for approval, it still does not guarantee the ultimate success of a title in the long run. The cycle here is that in order to stay in business, publishers had to maintain a certain number of product offerings each year and even produce incrementally more year after year. As usage data became more and more available to the librarian, this data was also available to the publisher. How often were their works being accessed? In most cases the usage data was sobering.

Defining the metrics behind e-book usage data is not an exact science, but unlike print it does demonstrate to the library the relevancy of what they have purchased as a single title and even an entire collection. It also creates some benchmarks that go beyond sales statistics for publishers to consider as they enter the editorial meetings where decisions are made on whether to publish a certain title or not. Having new access to usage information is changing both the buying and publishing process, and it is complicating the decision-making process on all sides.

Currency

The issue of maintaining currency in a reference work takes us back to the traditional publishing infrastructure that was built for print. It was very unusual for most print reference works to be updated—not only on a regular basis, but on an infrequent one as well. Did that mean the topic did not change over time? Of course there were updates and changes, especially in medical and science works. In the print model, producing updates or new editions was a slow process, from writing to development and through the production process. There were also costs involved, and unless it was a significant update, say with more than 50% new material, it was probably frowned upon by librarians and hard to justify purchasing the revised edition. There were also instances where by the time the new edition of the reference source was ready for publication, it could already be outdated.

With the onset of the digital world, everyone believed it would be the solution for keeping reference works up-to-date. No formal statistics or data are available to show new edition/update sales of digital reference, and this may be due to the fact that there just are not that many being offered. Even with the introduction of e-reference, publishers are still a bit wary of producing revised works. Some of the same issues of old apply, which are mostly financial. A new investment is still required to update an existing work. If you cannot reach a satisfactory percentage of new material, it probably will not sell. Also, reference publishers seek out awards and positive reviews as a huge part of their marketing campaigns. New or revised editions are often not included in the review and awards process, which inhibits new sales.

Added Value

Added value is the concept of attaching something new alongside the content of a traditional reference work. As soon as reference works were digitized and offered as e-books, the shopping list of added-value components instantly began to materialize. Examples of added-value components are images, sound files, software, and video. Probably the most desirable to end users is video. Video can add tremendous value to any reference work, whether a children's, historical, or medical title. It is a brilliant way to illustrate a reference article, especially for an emerging generation that has been surrounded by video influences from birth. Librarians are very eager to see more works contain video elements.

For reference publishers, the cost for video changed the entire production and profit structure. The costs of video production add to the cost of the product, and the publisher would need to be conservative in raising the publication price just to absorb these new costs. A publisher rolled out a set of multimedia encyclopedias, which basically meant that there were links to video clips that were specifically chosen for a particular article. After the introduction of the first titles, it was interesting to learn that the most accessed entries were the ones with video clips. It was a tangible example of how added-value features could increase usage and currency. The balancing act for publishers is to use video technology strategically, since it is cost prohibitive to add this feature to all titles.

Faculty

Faculty members are considered a variable because there is an interesting dilemma related to faculty that perplexes many publishers. Since academic faculty are actually the ones publishers rely on to write and edit the content going into reference products, then why do faculty not encourage students to use those products and cite them in their research? While this is not the case for every faculty member, it is a common theme with librarians caught in the middle. Libraries on the average have hundreds of authoritative reference works containing thousands of signed articles on their shelves and/or stored in e-book collections. With this in mind, there becomes a steady and existing relationship between publisher and librarian. How can the publisher significantly increase the academic value of their products in the eyes of the faculty and make them an integral member of this relationship?

One way to increase visibility of reference products to faculty is to use faculty as a prediscoverability tool. In moderated sessions between publishers and librarians, when the discussion about discoverability arises, so does the concept of marketing reference works directly to faculty to make them aware of their existence. If faculty members are aware of newly published reference works and the authoritative value they represent, they might recommend them for purchase to the librarians and advise their students to seek them out in their research. Faculty can be allies of publishers, helping publishers to move reference works from the problematic to transformational.

Free

The public expectation that information is available for free is another one of those challenging variables that has anguished publishers. There are two components here, Wikipedia and open access. While there may be other factors, these two are true representatives and sit at opposite ends of the "get it for free" spectrum. There is not much one can say about Wikipedia that has not been said already that would introduce any new insights as to how and why Wikipedia should not be a factor in a student's research assignment. However, it is a factor, and reference publishers have for the most part moved on from recognizing Wikipedia for what it represents—that it is available for free and it is not going away. More people have used Wikipedia in the past decade than have used the *Encyclopedia Britannica* in the past two centuries. It is impressive in this landscape to see publishers who discuss creating content that has value and relevancy. Although their products might serve a very small audience, they will serve a definite purpose that is worth the publisher's investment. It is not free, but it does have incredible and credible value to the end user.

Open access journals are scholarly journals that are available for free online. These journals are either subsidized or the article authors are required to pay to have their articles made available. There are emerging discussions amongst publishers whether or not the same model can apply to reference, which is more complex. The easiest solution would be if an organization were to subsidize an open access journal. An example of this is the *Stanford Encyclopedia of Philosophy*. It is a large, dynamic, and free encyclopedia with a strong subsidy funding it. An author-funded article model would not be attractive to most academics; there is limited benefit to paying money to write a brief article that does not add any weight to their academic careers in contrast to a standard journal article.

Collections, Bundles, and Databases

For a publisher, all departments, from editorial to sales and marketing, come together to put into action a plan for collections and bundles. As e-books became increasingly popular, so did the strategy of building collections or bundles of e-books grouped in a variety of ways, such as by discipline or copyright year. The methodology behind building collections was pretty simple, and libraries took advantage of this option. Collections were often offered at a discount and provided libraries with an easy way to send hundreds of e-books into their collection at the push of a button. From a business perspective, collections are a win-win proposition. Publishers enjoy receiving big checks, and libraries enjoyed the flexibility of determining where they could get these collections from (either through aggregators or direct from the publisher), as well as their affordability.

As a key variable in a sustainable growth equation, publishers will continue to build new collection strategies, new pricing models, and new ways to add value—all of which require more of one thing: content. An editor can often feel like their job is to feed the machine, produce more content, and make the machine bigger. The danger here is that the value of a single form reference work becomes somewhat diluted in the quest for more; the identity of the individual work can get lost in these huge collection packages.

While hard to prove, one just needs to sit through a publisher's consortia sales presentation as they negotiate the price of large e-reference collections. It is rare for anyone from either the publishing or consortia side to discuss the value of any of the particular titles within the collection. The danger in all of this rapid change in the marketplace is that with publishers moving fast in a survival effort, they can at times lose their focus on what got them there in the first place.

Textbooks

Textbooks are a variable because this market on the academic landscape is changing as well. It is a multibillion dollar business that is on the edge now. Technology—including smartphones and tablets, the government, and new distance-learning models—has publishers frantically trying to figure out their own survival. There was never really any direct correlation between a textbook and a reference work, except for the fact that they both might be following a specific curriculum outline for a specific discipline.

Reference works do not really contain any pedagogical or supplemental aids like textbooks do; however, they both serve a valuable purpose in the traditional classroom environment. The ongoing paradigm shift in higher education is more transformational than traditional.

The content in a college textbook is not necessarily changing whether in print or digital format, but the departure from the traditional classroom and teacher-student landscape is changing dramatically. The popularity of the commercial universities, such as the University of Phoenix, has attracted a new generation of student seeking an online education, not just for the academic credentials, but for the convenience as well.

Where do reference works fit in or around these new educational models? Selling reference works directly to commercial online universities is not an easy task. The economic structure and decision-making process is different from the standard academic market. The content might fit a particular course or discipline from a curriculum standpoint, but due to the online infrastructure, it is hard for them to justify why your product is worth the cost. Oftentimes reference works are not even considered because many courses do not require research assignments and faculty do not see a need beyond what is available on the Internet. Yet these new educational models should be not overlooked by publishers; it would be wise to seek out ways to work with them and not against them.

Aggregators

When the larger reference publishers first moved into the new digital space, most of their content was self-hosted on their own platforms. It was a challenging transition, but it worked in their favor. Publishers who hosted their own content were in control of such things as pricing, access, and ownership of content vs. leasing. What they were not in control of was a desire by librarians to have all of their reference content on one common platform. Publishers simply became observers as they watched the emergence of e-book aggregators, companies with a one-stop shopping solution providing all their digital content on one platform. At first, publishers were wary of sending their content to each and every aggregator. Each aggregator had their own distribution and business model, which appealed to a certain segment of libraries. As a result, it seemed that e-book aggregators segmented the e-reference global market. Librarians had choices and selected the vendor that was best equipped to fit their collection development needs at a price that was affordable.

The wary reference publisher then became more aggressive and decided to license their content to all of the major e-book aggregators. The debate still remains if this was an offensive move to generate more revenue or a defensive move because everyone else was doing it. There are two strong aggregators who specialize in reference, Credo Reference and Gale Virtual Reference Library (GVRL). In this changing landscape, the reference publishers are appreciative of their initiatives and execution of delivering digital reference content.

LEAD, FOLLOW, OR GET OUT OF THE WAY

Considering these variables, one can begin to see the complexities of the reference publishing business. Sustainable growth for any publisher depends on how effectively you can manage and strategize around these variables. It is constantly changing, and there are additional variables not even discussed here. Match that dynamic with the varying sizes, needs, and pressures of reference publishers, and it is clear that strong survival skills are necessary.

It is impossible for one publisher to address all these variables equally. A wise tactic would be to take each variable and define how they want to approach it. Do they want to lead, follow, or get out of the way? By examining their strengths, mission, and brand and being honest with their weaknesses, budget constraints, and deficiencies, each publisher can decide where they can be innovators and leaders, and where they can step back and follow the lead of their competitors. Everyone wishes for that magic map that shows where this journey leads, but awareness, examination, and excitement for the future are great first steps as we charge ahead.

6 | Wikipedia, User-Generated Content, and the Future of Reference Sources

*Phoebe Ayers, Wikimedia Foundation
and University of California, Davis*

Every month, millions of reference questions—ranging from bar bets to homework queries, from television watchers curious about the next episode to doctors getting up to speed on obscure diseases—are answered by consulting Wikipedia (http://wikipedia.org), the free online encyclopedia. Just over half a billion people access Wikipedia's 31 million articles in over 200 languages every month, making it by far the most-used reference work in the world. Given this extraordinary reach, what should the relationship between librarians and Wikipedia be? What role do we have in ensuring that our patrons and students use it appropriately and well, and how can libraries and librarians help make the site better? And what lessons can we draw from evaluating Wikipedia to apply to other user-generated reference resources?

This chapter will explore the relationship between librarians and the world's largest reference work. It will give a brief overview of how Wikipedia works and how librarians can contribute. It will then examine other user-generated content sites and the benefits and challenges of such projects.

HOW WIKIPEDIA WORKS

Wikipedia is always changing. Each day, thousands of edits are made to thousands of articles, in a collective process of writing and editing by largely anonymous contributors. Some edits add whole new paragraphs, references, and ideas; some simply fix a typo, or add a category or a picture. Most edits make articles incrementally better. Some edits are not constructive; however, these can be quickly "reverted" by other editors who simply change the article back to the previous version.

All of this is possible because Wikipedia is based on a wiki, a type of website invented in 1995 by Ward Cunningham, that allows for immediate changes to be made by anyone accessing it. While Wikipedia has become the best-known wiki since it was begun in 2001, the free software that it runs on, MediaWiki (http://mediawiki.org), is available for download and use by anyone and is widely used by other sites.

Wikipedia is run by a nonprofit foundation, the Wikimedia Foundation (http://wikimediafoundation.org), which provides the infrastructure to run Wikipedia and has the overall mission of collecting and disseminating freely licensed educational content. The Wikimedia Foundation is based in San Francisco and is financed entirely by private donations, which mostly come from Wikipedia readers and average under $30. As of 2014, there are around 200 paid staff at the Wikimedia Foundation, who work with a large global community of volunteers to support the behind-the-scenes work of the project, such as keeping Wikipedia online, improving the site's code, legal support, and event organizing. Additionally, there is a network of 40 Wikimedia chapters around the world that support activities in their local geographies, as well as many informal volunteer groups.

The Wikimedia Foundation also runs ten "sister projects" in addition to Wikipedia. In particular, reference librarians should be familiar with Wikimedia Commons (http://commons.wikimedia.org), which is an enormous repository of meticulously categorized, freely licensed photos and other media; Wiktionary (http://wiktionary.org), a multilingual dictionary project; Wikisource (http://wikisource.org), a repository for public domain source texts; and Wikivoyage (http://wikivoyage.org), a global travel guide. A complete list of projects is available at http://wikimediafoundation.org/wiki/Our_projects.

Each of these projects is written by volunteer editors. Editors do many jobs on the Wikimedia projects, including writing, copyediting, and adding references to articles, welcoming newcomers, organizing WikiP-rojects, and deleting articles when needed. None of this work is centrally organized. Editors work collaboratively but independently, operating within editorial guidelines and keeping an eye on each other's edits, but without top-down oversight.

While no one group is responsible for editorial decisions, there is an extensive network of policies and guidelines that have been developed over the years by contributors. These core editorial policies include:

- Neutral point of view (or NPOV): This is the concept that Wikipedia articles should not take a particular side, or point of view, but rather should reflect what reputable published sources and scholarly consensus has to say. Articles should reflect all major points of view in disputed topics (but not overweight minority views).
- No original research: Wikipedia is a tertiary source; it is not a forum for publishing original discoveries or research. Original work should be published elsewhere first, where it can be subject to traditional peer review.
- Verifiability: Information in Wikipedia should be factual, but also verifiable via reliable outside published sources.
- Free content: Wikipedia's entries, photographs, and media are all free—in cost, but also freely licensed so that others may use and reuse them (this is described later in more depth). This means, for instance, that text copied from other places (such as organization websites) will be deleted unless it can be proved to be compatibly licensed.
- Wikipedia is an encyclopedia: This guideline helps shape what Wikipedia is and how topics are covered. It also helps define what Wikipedia is not; for example, the site is not meant as a business directory.

There are also many behavioral policies that shape how contributors interact with each other. These include the ideas of maintaining civility toward fellow contributors, not using Wikipedia to promote yourself or your organization, and being bold in making needed changes and edits. One of the most important concepts is that edits speak for themselves; regardless of whether someone is an expert in a subject, that person is expected to contribute in accordance with Wikipedia's editorial and behavioral norms. Simply claiming to be an authority on a topic is not enough; edits still need to be backed up by citations to sources that can be checked by others (though lack of access to subscription resources can sometimes hinder editors in this endeavor).

In general, editorial and other disputes are solved by contributors talking things through on article and project discussion pages. If that does not work, other editors may step in, and in extreme cases, contributors may be temporarily blocked from editing.

Wikipedia in Other Languages

Wikipedia editions exist in 287 languages, and around 220 of those have more than 1,000 articles. These Wikipedias range from the very large, with over a million articles (English, German, Spanish), to the quite small, with just a few thousand entries (Tibetan, Somali). These editions do not typically rely on translations; instead, editors working in these languages usually write articles from scratch. Multilingual contributors are always needed, as there is often a great deal to do (and a much smaller community to do it) in the smaller language editions.

If a corresponding article exists in another language in Wikipedia, a link will appear to it on the left-hand sidebar. For reference librarians, these links can also provide a quick way to find translations of terms or names. These "interlanguage links" are maintained, along with other data such as traditional authority file identifiers, in the centralized database Wikidata (http://wikidata.org), which can be updated as articles are added.

EVALUATING ARTICLES

Wikipedia differs from most traditional reference sources not just in the method of production and in its huge breadth of coverage, but also in the consistency of articles. Each article is a work in progress; articles are started at various times, worked on by different people, and are in different stages of being shaped by Wikipedia guidelines. Thus, some articles are comprehensive and accurate, with 20 or more pages; others are short, unreferenced stubs that are poorly written and are missing major areas.

Assessing the difference is a core task both for Wikipedia editors and for reference librarians guiding patrons. When evaluating Wikipedia articles, beyond looking at the article itself, you can also look at the article talk page and editing history to get a sense of how the page was produced. Specific elements to look at include:

- The text of the article: Is it well written? Are there gaps in the coverage of a subject (e.g., in a biography, is there no mention of a person's early life)?
- The references: Are facts and any potentially questionable statements in the article footnoted to outside sources? Are these references to reliable, scholarly publications when possible? Is there a bibliography of further reading?

- Warning messages: Are there any warning boxes (such as "this article needs additional citations") at the top of the page? These messages are meant to identify articles needing work for both readers and editors, and they provide a major part of how Wikipedia maintenance is done. Any editor can leave them on an article when they think there is a problem, and any editor can remove them once they fix the issue.
- The article talk page: The "talk" or discussion page is a separate wiki page that you can get to by clicking on the "talk" tab at the top of the article. Every article has an associated talk page that is meant for discussion of the article by editors, as well as providing a place for readers to leave comments. Looking at the talk page can give you a quick indication of whether there have been any major disputes associated with writing the article.
- The article history: You can get to the complete production history of any article by clicking the "view history" tab at the top of the article. This shows you, edit by edit, all of the changes that have been made to the article since it was created, who made them, and when. Clicking on the date of each edit shows you the article as it was at that time. Edit histories can be long and cumbersome, but quickly browsing through the history can give you a sense of whether lots of people have worked on the article or only a few; whether there have been any dramatic changes (such as sections being removed or vandalism); and whether the article has been updated recently. In general, the more people who have worked on the article the better it tends to be; however, lots of vandalism or disputes over the text may render the article incomplete or disjointed.

For more materials on how to evaluate articles, including handouts and presentations, see Wikimedia Outreach at http://outreach.wikimedia.org/wiki/Evaluating_articles.

CONTRIBUTING TO WIKIPEDIA

While volunteers contribute millions of hours of work to make Wikipedia what it is—a recent study by Geiger and Halfaker (2013) estimated over 100 million hours of work had gone into Wikipedia in total, and 41 million hours in the English Wikipedia—the number of active editors (around 80,000 total, and 30,000 on the English Wikipedia) is surprisingly small considering the size of the project, and more help is always needed. Wikipedia also suffers from an imbalance in contributors. As of 2013, only about 1 in 5 active editors on the English Wikipedia is female, and editors are concentrated in Europe and North America.

Many librarians edit Wikipedia as individual contributors. Whether fact-checking, building bibliographies, polishing prose, or documenting little-known corners of the world, the work of Wikipedia fits with librarians' professional skills. And there is always plenty to do—articles need to be rewritten to be clearer; [citation needed] tags need to be replaced with sources; references need to be formatted or improved; and outdated information needs to be updated.

To get started as an editor, the steps are simple: create an account, find a topic that interests you, and start by copyediting or adding sources. The help pages (linked from the left-hand sidebar on Wikipedia) give several excellent tutorials for starting out, and the Wikipedia Teahouse (https://en.wikipedia.org/wiki/WP:TEAHOUSE) provides a space for newcomers. For those who are interested in writing about libraries and library science topics, WikiProject Libraries on the English Wikipedia (https://en.wikipedia.org/wiki/Wikipedia:WikiProject_Libraries) is an effort to bring contributors together around the subject.

Asking Questions on Wikipedia

One little-known area of Wikipedia is the reference desk, where editors and readers can ask each other questions (and answer them) on any subject. "Leave a question here," the page promises, "and we'll get back to you." Dozens of questions are posted every day, sometimes with quick factual answers and sometimes leading to extended, opinionated discussion. Access the reference desk (and help add answers) at https://en.wikipedia.org/wiki/WP:RD. There are also separate help desks for people with questions about Wikipedia itself.

Contributing Institutionally

As reference professionals, there are also several ways to participate institutionally. This includes acting as educators in how Wikipedia works. For such a commonly used reference source, few people understand the nuts and bolts of Wikipedia. Libraries can also support local Wikipedia volunteers by hosting and promoting events. Finally, libraries with public domain collections can add these to Wikimedia projects.

Wikipedia Loves Libraries

Wikipedia Loves Libraries (http://en.wikipedia.org/wiki/Wikipedia:Wikipedia_Loves_Libraries) is a grassroots effort, begun by Wikimedians in New York City in 2011, to hold Wikipedia events in libraries everywhere in October and November (coinciding with Open Access Week). Depending on the type of library and institution, events might include a backstage tour for Wikipedians (for instance, if a library has special collections to show off); an editor community meetup or edit-a-thon (which just requires the library provide the community with a meeting room and Internet access); or hosting a training workshop on how to edit. A list of some different library projects and ideas is available at http://outreach.wikimedia.org/wiki/Libraries. Hundreds of libraries have participated from around the United States and the world.

Sharing Collections via Wikimedia Commons

For libraries that have special collections and archives that are freely licensed or in the public domain, making those collections available online through Wikimedia Commons is an option. There are many major collections from archives, museums, and libraries now uploaded to Wikimedia Commons, including image collections from the National Archives and Records Administration (NARA), the British Museum and British Library, the Library of Congress, the New York Public Library, and many more. These rich collections of public domain images are a treasure trove for researchers and Wikipedians alike. Adding these images to Wikimedia Commons means that it is possible for editors to use them in Wikipedia articles, and it also means that the images will get deeply categorized by volunteers. Texts and manuscripts can go on Wikisource, where they will be categorized and transcribed. This type of project supports the mission of the contributing institution as well. As David Ferriero, the archivist of the United States, said in 2012 about NARA's experiences contributing to Wikipedia: "Our work with Wikipedia is . . . great for us because it takes our goals of transparency, public participation, and collaboration to a new level" (Ferriero, 2012).

GLAM and Wikipedians-in-Residence

In 2010, a young Australian historian, Liam Wyatt, offered his services as a volunteer Wikipedian to the British Museum for a summer. He helped train museum staff in how to edit Wikipedia, assisted Wikipedians with gaining access to the museum's curatorial knowledge, and helped the museum share its treasures by adding photos of its collections to Wikimedia Commons. He also coordinated Wikipedians to improve articles about several of the museum's important artifacts and collections, such as the Hoxne Hoard and the Rosetta Stone. Wyatt coined the term GLAM, standing for "Galleries, Libraries, Archives, and Museums," a term that stuck in the Wikimedia world for projects relating to working with cultural institutions.

The project sparked interest by many other cultural institutions, and positions like this, called "Wikipedians-in-Residence," have subsequently been adopted by dozens of cultural institutions around the world. Wikipedians-in-Residence focus on increasing public exposure to and appreciation of the institution's collections, while also educating staff and volunteers, and making the Wikimedia projects more accurate and comprehensive in their coverage of cultural heritage materials. Find out more about Wikipedians-in-Residence projects at http://glamwiki.org.

Projects to contribute to Wikipedia like the ones detailed above help point the way toward a future where libraries can share their collections and institutional knowledge, and librarians can share their reference skills, with a much larger audience than has ever previously been possible. Improving Wikipedia can be seen as a way of meeting users where they are, and allows librarians to answer current and future reference questions from a global audience who might not otherwise have the opportunity to access a library of any kind.

USER-GENERATED AND OPEN CONTENT

Wikipedia is an example of "user-generated content"—work that is written by a large number of people who are also the work's users or readers, rather than being written and edited solely by a selected team of writers and editors. Wikipedia is also open content, a term that describes work that is freely licensed and thus can be freely reused and remixed. Though Wikipedia is one of the most successful and widely used examples of both user-generated content and open content, there are many other reference websites and projects that are produced by their users. "User-generated content" is a broad term, and these sites come in many types, though all share the characteristic of being written by large groups of (generally volunteer) contributors.

The following will categorize some types of user-generated content sites that are particularly useful for reference librarians, and outline some broad ways to think about analyzing current and future user-generated works.

Reference Services and Sites

User-generated content sites that are meant explicitly as reference works aim to be reliable, and sometimes scholarly, resources. This category includes several specialty dictionary and encyclopedia projects, which may review user contributions before accepting them—a process that helps ensure consistency but adds an administrative burden for the site. One example is the Encyclopedia of Life (EOL) (http://eol.org/), which collects data about all life on Earth—animals, plants, and bacteria—from many other open collections on the web (including Wikipedia and Wikimedia Commons) and aims to consolidate information about each species. While readers can contribute, they must be signed up first and contributions are reviewed.

Another example of a reference project is OpenStreetMap (OSM) (http://www.openstreetmap.org/), which aims to build a map of the world with open, freely licensed data. It is based on map data from governments and includes user contributions, including point-based edits (such as additions of historical landmarks) and GPS traces. Because the OSM data is open, other open content projects (such as LocalWiki, http://localwiki.org, which is an effort to build wikis for community information) can use it in mapping applications.

Curated Collections

User-generated collections of materials often bring to mind photo sites like the nonprofit Wikimedia Commons or commercial Flickr (http://flickr.com), but user-built collections can also include bibliographic databases and archives, such as the shared database of references built by Mendeley users (http://mendeley.com), the collection of pre- and post-prints at the physics and math arXiv (http://arxiv.org), or the lists of books that are created by Goodreads (http://goodreads.com) community participants.

These collections may be explicitly curated (where submissions are chosen or reviewed before acceptance, such as the EOL's datasets), lightly curated (like Wikimedia Commons, where volunteers review images for copyright status), or essentially uncurated (like Mendeley's database).

Encouraging broad participation and having clear inclusion standards are key for these sites—the larger the collection and the more authoritative and detailed the metadata, the more useful the collection.

Question-Answering, Education, and How-To Sites

Anyone who has ever searched online for the solution to an odd computer problem is familiar with this category of sites and their potential usefulness in answering questions. Hundreds of thousands of reference questions a day are answered online by other users, often in forums meant for conversation on a topic (childcare, cooking, a particular type of camera), sometimes in sites largely meant for publishing other content, such as blogs that have built a community in the comments section, and sometimes in dedicated question and answer (Q&A) sites, like Quora (http://www.quora.com) or Stack-Exchange, which runs 114 specialty Q&A sites on various topics (http://stackexchange.com/).

The quality and value of Q&A and review sites comes from the aggregate of individual answers, which give the information seeker a variety of perspectives to triangulate her own experience against. Amazon (http://amazon.com), which depends heavily on user-provided reviews to sell products, knows this and exploits their tremendous data resources to provide features like "most helpful favorable review" and "most helpful negative review."

Some user-generated sites exist explicitly to teach skills and share educational information. For example, the site WikiHow (http://wikihow.com) uses an open wiki community to write how-to articles. WikiHow provides a reference resource for those looking for instructions on building, making, or doing things, ranging from "How to ask someone on a date" to "How to breed goldfish."

Discussion and Sharing Sites: Social Media

What makes media "social?" The term is loosely used to encompass anything that is meant as a place for people to connect to one another through sharing (often personal) information and content. Many sites have social features, even if that is not their main purpose. It can also be a fraught term; many long-term Wikipedia contributors resist any description of Wikipedia as social media, despite its active community and discussion aspects, arguing that they are there to write an encyclopedia, not for idle chatter. Facebook, Twitter, and YouTube are the giants of this sphere, each providing platforms for publishing and sharing. Blogging sites and aggregators also provide publishing platforms, some with large communities. One example is Global Voices (http://globalvoicesonline.org/), which features citizen reporting and writing from around the world, and also serves as a community of people interested in international news and little-covered stories. Another example is the long-running MetaFilter (http://metafilter.com), whose community curates and discusses interesting stories from around the web.

For these sites, as with other types of user-generated content sites, having a vibrant community where members find enjoyment and value in participating is critical to attracting new members and long-term success.

EVALUATING USER-GENERATED CONTENT

All user-generated sites and projects can be analyzed along a few dimensions, including who contributes and why, site guidelines and mechanisms for assuring authority, and site purpose. Specific questions to ask include:

- Are submissions moderated or peer reviewed, or displayed directly as received?
- Who can sign up as a contributor, and are there standards for who can contribute? Are potential motivations for contributors clear (that is, is there a clear mission or purpose that contributors work toward)?
- How quickly is the site updated (or submissions accepted)? If the site includes quickly changing topics, are these current? If the site depends on user-provided review and curation (such as Wikipedia's editors checking new edits), does this review actually happen?
- If it is a site that depends on a variety of individual perspectives (such as a Q&A site or review site), are there a diversity of replies? Are questions answered, and is there a respectful community around discussions?
- What are the motivations of the site publisher, and are they for-profit or nonprofit? Is contributed content simply a means for the site owners to make money by getting more clicks from search results? Who is the intended audience of the site?
- If the site uses material from many sources (like the EOL), are those sources (and their licenses) clearly indicated? If the site is meant for academic or reference purposes, does it also point to other relevant resources?
- Is the content freely licensed or under copyright, and is the content's license (or copyright) clearly indicated?

Why Does Openness Matter?

Who owns the content posted on a user-generated site? Is reusing something you find on a user-generated site a copyright violation—and if so, against whom? The answers to these questions reveal what an end user can do with the site's content, but may also have implications for contributor motivations.

Wikipedia and the other Wikimedia projects are licensed with the Creative Commons Attribution-ShareAlike license (abbreviated as CC-BY-SA). There are several Creative Commons licenses offering various combinations of requiring author attribution, granting the ability to commercially reuse material, and requiring that remixed materials also be shared under a Creative Commons license. Read more about the Creative Commons licenses at http://creativecommons.org/licenses/. The fact that Wikipedia is licensed under Creative Commons means that only material that is freely licensed or in the public domain can be added to Wikipedia, and that while Wikipedia editors do retain their copyright, they also agree that their contributions will be licensed CC-BY-SA.

The license specifies that anyone can freely reuse, share, and adapt the material on Wikipedia as long as they agree to the terms of the license—that the source of material must be attributed, and if you alter or build upon it, you must license your resulting work under CC-BY-SA as well. This means that as long as you follow these terms, you can (for instance) translate a Wikipedia article into another language, adapt it for a class, or use a picture from Wikimedia Commons in a presentation without getting explicit permission first.

An open license means that contributors are explicitly making their work available for the public good. This can be an important, motivating factor for Wikipedia contributors and others who choose to freely license their work.

Understanding open licensing is a critical task for all librarians. Many other user-generated sites are also licensed under Creative Commons licenses, but certainly not all. If it is not specified, the kind of reuse that an open license makes possible is not allowed.

Open licensing also means that content that originated on one site may (quite legitimately) turn up on another. For instance, photos from Flickr that are Creative Commons licensed are routinely harvested for use in Wikimedia Commons, which aims to collect all useful open-licensed media. In another case of reuse, in recent years a few publishers have been collecting Wikipedia articles into books and selling these online. If the publisher clearly cites the source and respects the licensing terms, this is a legitimate reuse, though many of these publishers do not do this. Sometimes reuse is not obvious. As of 2014, data from Wikipedia helps fuel Google's "knowledge graph," the box that displays quick information about a search subject on the right-hand side of search results. Though there is a link to the source, it is also unclear that Wikipedia can be edited if the information is wrong.

LOOKING FORWARD: USER EXPECTATIONS AND THE FUTURE OF WIKIPEDIA, USER-GENERATED CONTENT, AND REFERENCE SOURCES

It seems clear that along with increased global Internet access, the need and desire to access Wikipedia is not ceasing anytime soon. The user-generated model that Wikipedia helped pioneer enables extraordinary resources that would be very difficult to produce with a traditional authorship model—for instance, a vast collection of photos of national monuments from around the world (from the Wiki Loves Monuments contest, http://www.wikilovesmonuments.org/) or important articles about health translated into dozens of underserved languages, as led by Wiki Project Med on Wikipedia (http://meta.wikimedia.org/wiki/Wiki_Project_Med).

But for the many millions of Wikipedia users, information is available and easy to search for, but it is not necessarily complete or polished. Does the fact that people use it anyway indicate a change in user expectations, or is it simply a reflection of the various needs of information seekers—for times an incomplete or brief answer is better than none at all? For everyone who uses Q&A sites and forums to find the answer to questions, answers do not need to necessarily come from a credentialed expert (and there might not even be an easy way to find an expert to answer some questions). And for many—perhaps the vast majority—of those readers who use Wikipedia and other user-generated sites, they may not know or consider who has produced the information they are using.

Wikipedia continues to grow in usage, but it also faces a worrying trend. For the past several years, there has been a drop-off in the numbers of active editors who are contributing to the project. This matters because without a sustained active contributor base, the project is unsustainable, as there is a large amount of ongoing work (such as triaging and reviewing

> **FURTHER READING ABOUT WIKIPEDIA AND USER-GENERATED CONTENT**
>
> Ayers, P., Matthews, C., & Yates, B. (2008). *How Wikipedia works: And how you can be a part of it.* San Francisco: No Starch Press. Retrieved from http://howwikipediaworks.net. A guide to Wikipedia's culture and how to participate as an editor.
>
> Broughton, J. (2008). *Wikipedia: The missing manual.* Sebastapol: O'Reilly. A how-to guide about how to edit Wikipedia, focusing on the nuts and bolts of working on the site.
>
> Lih, A. (2009). *The Wikipedia revolution: How a bunch of nobodies created the world's greatest encyclopedia.* New York: Hyperion. A history of the early days of Wikipedia, focusing on the people and events that created the site.
>
> Reagle, J. (2010). *Good faith collaboration: The culture of Wikipedia.* Cambridge: MIT Press. A scholarly work that analyzes Wikipedia's principles and cultural norms in a historical context.
>
> Tomaiuolo, N. (2012). *UContent: The information professional's guide to user-generated content.* Medford, NJ: Information Today. Defines user-generated content and covers a wide variety of user-generated projects and how to participate in them.
>
> Wikipedia Education Project. (n.d.). Retrieved from http://education.wikimedia.org. Resources for using Wikipedia as an educator or librarian, including handouts on how to teach with and contribute to Wikipedia.

new contributions, updating entries to match new developments, and acculturating new contributors) that has to be done simply to keep the project operational and maintain quality.

All reference works, whether traditionally published or created by a community of users, face similar concerns. Successful reference works must provide high-quality information, develop a sustainable publishing and business model, make sure the work is accessible over the long term, and gather an audience of curious readers. But user-generated sites face additional concerns, including keeping an active community of contributors satisfied, attracting new contributors, converting readers into contributors, and making sure that the site is not taken over by spam or excess bureaucracy that might hinder contribution. The unique challenge of user-generated works is that contributions are not guaranteed; simply because it is possible to review an entry, add information, or answer a question does not mean that it will happen. Thinking about contributor motivations and project sustainability is an important part of critical analysis of these reference works, as well as something that each project must tackle in order to survive. More than ever before, these reference sources do not exist in a vacuum, but rely on their community of readers and contributors.

The benefits of a user-generated and open model that encourages participation, sharing, critical thinking, and reuse, continue to be demonstrated by Wikipedia and many other projects. But the future of reference publishing is not assured by either a traditional or user-generated model. Each faces challenges.

REFERENCES

Ferriero, D. (2012, July 14). Prepared remarks of archivist of the United States David S. Ferriero at the closing plenary at Wikimania 2012, Lisner Auditorium, George Washington University, Washington, DC. Retrieved from http://www.archives.gov/about/speeches/2012/7-14-2012.html

Geiger, R. S., & Halfaker, A. (2013). Using edit sessions to measure participation in Wikipedia. *Proceedings of the 2013 ACM Conference on Computer Supported Cooperative Work* (pp. 861–870). New York: ACM. http://dx.doi.org/10.1145/2441776.2441873

Part 3

TOOLS AND TECHNOLOGIES

7 | Discovery Tools

Michael Courtney, Indiana University

WHAT IS DISCOVERY?

When S. R. Ranganathan provided the directive *save the time of the reader* (his fourth law of library science), he undoubtedly may not have predicted the significant shift in information distribution that is being fully realized in the 21st century as library collections have moved quickly to include, and in many cases replace print counterparts, a vast array of digital and electronic content (1931, p. 337). What Ranganathan fully understood, though, and why this simple phrase is still entirely relevant in spite of itself, is that it has been unwittingly responsible for library administrative reform ever since. Whereas his era was more concerned with shelf arrangement, catalog development, and the noticeable inclusion of standard bibliographies that would serve to uncover the library's resources to its users, contemporary libraries now face a new and complex dilemma—one that Lorcan Dempsey acknowledged as a shift in user focus (and need), wherein "the context of information use and creation has changed as it transitions from a world of physical distribution to one of digital distribution" (2012). Such a shift has necessitated the development of tools to aid in the discovery of resources and, to be sure, resource discovery is arguably one of the most pressing issues that concerns libraries today. Technological innovation in an increasingly online world has changed not only the availability of information resources, but also how those resources are being used and discovered. As Dempsey and others have accurately noted, changes in information format have altered access paradigms to the point that it is not often entirely necessary to visit the physical library to consult resources. Rather, the focus has shifted from the localized information repository (the physical library) to the vast network of information that surrounds us in a virtual sense.

While the library has traditionally relied on the catalog, research guides, knowledgeable staff, and other finding aids, the arrangements of which are designed to orient the user to the information's organizational structure, the modern challenge that is presented concerns leveraging networked technology with new, more appropriate tools to facilitate resource discovery. The concept of discovery is not entirely new, however much the pragmatic approach of realizing information discovery has radically changed. Historically, librarians (and libraries) have developed tools all along to aid the user in identifying relevant information amongst an enormous pool of resources. Some parallels to our modern dilemma of information access can be made as far back as the 17th century, when more economical book production methods arose, creating an increase in information (and, in turn, knowledge) accessibility, as is the case today. The development of tools to aid in accessibility, from printed catalogs to bibliographies and beyond, gradually demanded classification systems as a means of collecting and cataloging growing collections, many of which are still employed in the present day. Former concerns of serendipitous information retrieval and a collection's browsability still resonate loudly centuries later. The concept of discovery of information across a network, however, has its roots in the classical field of information retrieval, the focus of which traditionally concerned relevant document searching across static, fixed, and typically text-based collections. In this model, the user is presumed to have a finite understanding of the information need insomuch as the user is able to accurately express the need to conduct a search within the system. In this approach, more contemporary concerns of the search process (e.g., information literacy and discovery) are theoretically ignored, limiting the effectiveness overall of the information retrieval system. Conversely, *information* or *resource* discovery, according to Clifford A. Lynch, "can be used to describe a complex collection of activities that can range from simply locating a well-specified digital object on the network all the way through lengthy iterative research activities . . . often involv[ing] the searching of various types of directories, catalogs, or other descriptive databases" and typically operating on "surrogates (such as descriptions) of actual networked information resources" (1995, p. 1506). The terms information discovery and resource discovery, while having subtle, nuanced differences, are often used interchangeably in this regard.

Implicit in the concept of discovery is an effort by the user to locate (or, in effect, explore) the unknown. A user may have in mind characteristics or general knowledge of an overall information need, but here the emphasis is on locating resources that are unknown yet underscore the base need. From a library perspective, discovery tools allow users to not only discover "hidden" collections and uncover, serendipitously, new information relevant to the overall need, but also to facilitate navigation through library collections that have become increasingly complex and diverse in format. Such tools, which contemporarily have morphed from federated search capabilities (single query searching across multiple resources, or databases, the results of which are aggregated and displayed to the user, and typically referred to as metasearching) to discovery layers, web-scale discovery services, and beyond, will be the focus of the remainder of this chapter.

WEB-SCALE DISCOVERY

Web-scale discovery tools, or services, allow a user to "search seamlessly across a wide range of local and remote content and provide relevance-ranked results" and additionally to have "the ambitious goal of providing a single point of entry into a library's collections" (Breeding, 2014, p. 25). Perhaps more succinctly, Jason Vaughn suggests web-scale discovery "can be considered as deep discovery within a vast ocean of content" (2011, p. 5). The structure of a web-scale discovery tool employs a central index (or, variously, base index or unified index) of content that has been preharvested, from which a user can search across localized collections, open access resources, and subscription-based resources, all using a feature-rich discovery layer. Currently, the four major vendors of web-scale discovery tools that offer both a central index and a discovery layer are EBSCO (EBSCO Discovery Service), ProQuest (Serials Solutions' Summon), OCLC (WorldCat Local), and Ex Libris (Primo Central Index). The central index, as is in the case of the major vendors mentioned previously, is a collection of citations and full text from publishers, subscription databases, and open-source collections, as well as MARC records from library catalogs. Metadata from local collections that have been digitized, in addition to content from institutional repositories, may further enhance the central index. The discovery layer, or the user interface, allows for interactive search and display of content within a library system, such as a web-scale discovery index. Of course, discovery layers are not entirely a new concept within libraries—many discovery layer interfaces are currently deployed as end user search interfaces for online public access catalogs. Web-scale discovery services have unique and distinct qualities that make them desirable to libraries: they allow for simple, single searching across the central index; they are responsive and quick; they typically offer a variety of methods for refining search results, such as facets and sorting capabilities; they provide relevance ranked search results; and they allow the user to connect directly with full text whenever appropriate.

In addition to their robust search capabilities that empower the concept of discovery for the end user, web-scale discovery services exhibit an extremely powerful system for indexing an amazing array of content, regardless of where the service is hosted. In addition to integrated library system records, a web-scale discovery service can index a library's digital collections, content from institutional repositories, in addition to other locally created and hosted digital content. Increasingly, this allows libraries the opportunity to uncover for users "hidden" or deep content that may otherwise go undiscovered in general searching. Further, preindexed and remotely hosted content, including e-books, full-text journals, article abstracts, and open access content, the sum of which can seem astronomical to many libraries, can vastly improve resource discovery by the end user in groundbreaking ways. In short, web-scale discovery services provide a unique, seamless, and rapid method for discovery and delivery of relevance ranked content from a vast and rich index.

It should not be surprising that web-scale discovery has evolved (and continues to do so) out of a complex online networked environment where users have become accustomed to a simple, Google-like search functionality that attempts to satisfy search needs in rapid succession across an almost limitless volume of information. Libraries continue to struggle with a perceptibly impossible task—either being a tertiary outpost for users seeking information beyond web-based search engines or simply not being of perceived value to end users in an increasingly connected, online sphere. Where libraries are positioned best to utilize web-scale discovery services, perhaps, lies in the ability to employ (or even develop) a discovery tool that can significantly increase the use (and discoverability) of the content that has been acquired, licensed, or purchased at great and ongoing costs. Competing interests of end users (e.g., using any information that is most easily discovered (such as through Google) regardless of quality, reliability, and other accepted benchmarks of valuation) and a desire for seamless, rapid search results have necessitated the introduction of such discovery tools across libraries of all types.

CLOSING THE CONTENT GAP

As discovery tools have evolved over the past decade, they have greatly improved access to library collections, connecting users not just with deeper levels of library content, but also incorporating many of the features and tools that users have come to expect with open web-based resources, such as much-improved relevance ranked search results across disparate content formats as well as the look and feel of online portals that are frequently used by the general public. Increasingly, end user expectations of what such discovery tools can actually do is in direct contrast with both capability and compatibility. This, in its primacy, is a discussion of mitigating the content gap already present in all discovery tools. While the fact remains that no discovery service can quite meet the unrealistic expectations of end users (i.e., to discover anything, anytime, instantly), there is much that can be done to increase available content, across all platforms, within discovery services.

There are two significant points that comprise moving positively in this direction. One is, as Marshall Breeding suggests, "a matter of business decisions and strategies," while the other hinges upon libraries' subject expertise and inherent ability to link the user with credible, authoritative resources that exist outside of the immediate purvey of the web-scale discovery index, especially content that is openly accessible on the web but may not be properly indexed within the discovery tool itself (2012, p. 29). Regarding the former, many publishers exert strict control over content, preferring that it be made available through proprietary discovery systems where search result rankings and placement of content within such queries can be manipulated at their own discretion. It would seem obvious, then, that without cooperative efforts amongst all content providers in providing and sharing access to information, discovery tools by and large are powerless in discovering and accessing a significant volume of information. Further, not all databases and information resources play universally well with discovery tools, requiring a researcher to be aware of resources that exist outside of the discovery tool's capabilities in order to perform a more exhaustive search.

To further compound the matter, open web collections, such as the Victorian Women Writers Project, created by and hosted at Indiana University, might only be discoverable by an end user if the content were either indexed by the discovery tool or the user already possessed a general knowledge of the resource (or, counter to the implicit nature of a discovery system, the user simply employed an open web-based search tool). It is a truism that discovery tools are necessarily limited by their lack of comprehensiveness and that "it's not until discovery services truly provide access to a comprehensive representation of all the library's collection components that they can achieve their true potential" (Breeding, 2012, p. 29). Of course, this is a rather simple observation to make. Common sense would dictate that comprehensiveness within a discovery system is an enormous undertaking. The Open Discovery Initiative, a working group of the National Information Standards Organization, has been established to define best practices and standards for index-based library discovery services and to provide transparency in the ways that content is represented. Such standards and practices would prove essential to libraries in evaluating discovery systems that are best suited given the library's unique collections.

ADDING VALUE TO DISCOVERY

Significant progress has been made in recent years as more libraries have adopted discovery systems to their cache of tools aimed at increasing discoverability of resources for the end user. However, there are many improvements to be made (and looked forward to in future) that will serve to add value to the discovery process. To ensure access and discoverability of resources within the library's collections, inside its discovery system index, and across the open web, libraries must provide adequate content description through descriptive and subject cataloging, consider the organization of resources within the greater collection (via classification schema and indexing services), and make general provisions for access over time (preservation, archiving, etc.). Tangentially, the presentation of search results within a discovery system directly influences the system's overall effectiveness. An end user will naturally want the best (and most relevant) results to appear first, and it is a logical extension of thought that search relevancy methodology will need continuous improvement across all discovery systems to meet user needs (and satisfy library expectations).

As discovery systems work on such improvements, considerations for relevancy of web-based searching will likely serve to facilitate this evolution. Marshall Breeding suggests that "library search will also benefit from a more personalized approach. Information such as the user's academic department and previous search history can be great clues regarding the kinds of materials that would be considered most relevant in the user's search results" (2012, p. 30). Additional concerns of a discovery system's ability to allow for proper browsing of the library's collection, as well as e-book discoverability through such tools, remain at the forefront of continued improvements to discovery services.

INTEGRATING TRADITIONAL TOOLS WITH DISCOVERY SYSTEMS

Traditionally, libraries facilitated the process of discovery for their patrons through a variety of means previously discussed in this chapter—the catalog, personalized reference service, bibliographies, and research guides. The need and desire for such tools has not significantly waned in the age of discovery; however, the inherent value of the traditional pathfinder, even when translated for web-based environments, is not always fully realized. Discovery system vendors and developers have recognized the need to provide access, either directly or indirectly (via linking services), to such tools and resources that are not inherently indexed within the service itself. Subject-based research guides (or pathfinders), FAQs or knowledge base articles, general help pages, librarian profiles, and other information about library outreach and programmatic events would all be potentially useful content if woven into the discovery system. Adding localized content to a web-scale discovery system is, theoretically, an easier task to accomplish than adding content from competing publishers and indexes. One such endeavor in this area is the integration of Springshare's LibGuides into Serials Solutions' Summon service. Summon's application programming interface (API) allows for more thorough integration and interplay between the two systems, giving end users more options for how they discover information by and about the library. Similarly, the EBSCO Discovery Service allows for the provision of links to frequently used content sources—such as LibGuides or other relevant library information, such as operating hours or general announcements—via specialized widgets that can be added at various levels within the system. Increasingly, libraries will see the need to add this additional content to discovery services to improve discoverability by end users.

DISCOVERY TOOL USE

To be certain, dramatic shifts in technology in the digital age, as well as responsive and meaningful approaches to such changes, have radically altered how users interact with information. Search engines such as Google, social media networks like Twitter and Facebook, and an overall cultural change have directed libraries to employ tools that work in a very similar fashion to web-based search engines due to expediency, convenience, and, perhaps most of all, ease of use. Many studies have reached the conclusion that in order for libraries to exact change and remain relevant in the 21st century, users must engage with the library quite similarly to how they engage with the online world. Such familiarity appears important to users, who through rote practice and the ubiquity of online networks in their daily lives have become not only confident in their daily practice, but also wholly comfortable with how information is presented to them within a web-based environment outside of the library. The Google search interface, a simple, single box, has become the de facto standard for information gathering amongst most undergraduate college students, for example, and has created expectations, unrealistic or not, that engaging with library tools and resources should replicate that familiarity and comfort.

The reality that libraries are faced with, though, suggests the traditional library arrangement of resources, especially via the library website, as well as the inherent complexity of library catalogs, databases, and indexes, create undue anxiety for users and serve to counteract any implied value that such tools might provide in the way of help. Counter to the argument by some librarians that discovery tools serve to "dumb down students' information search skills," it has been found that a "simpler and more direct way of information retrieval would actually free up time for instruction librarians to teach about information itself and how to engage with it in a useful way, rather than teaching the 'click here, click there' procedural steps and

Boolean search strategies which students are unlikely to use again in the future" (Cmor & Li, 2012, p. 1). Considering user search behavior, then, it would be reasonable to suggest discovery tool use is typically governed by a variety of trends already inherent (and ingrained) in user habits: users typically engage with information through resources outside of the library (e.g., the open web); users have the expectation that resource discovery and immediate availability (delivery) exist in tandem with each other; and with increasing frequency, users engage with nontraditional information sources.

It is true that users do not typically view the library as a starting point for information gathering. Most end user surveys have found that an overwhelming majority of users begin a search for information using an open web search engine such as Google. However, these impediments should not discourage libraries wishing to adopt discovery systems. Rather, they should serve as reminders that a user-centered approach that is considerate of the needs of its community of users, while remaining customized to its unique collections and strengths, will serve to facilitate resource discovery with increased satisfaction and confidence in much the same way that has become customary outside of the library environment. A recognition by libraries that Google has significantly altered user search expectations (and habits) has resulted in the increased use of resource discovery tools, and as the tools themselves become more sophisticated (improved relevancy ranking, etc.), it is becoming evident that they may well provide the search solution that is the best compromise between user expectation and realistic delivery of information. As discovery systems evolve and improve, libraries must continually reassess how their catalogs and information systems keep pace with user expectation and understanding. Some catalogs and databases perform certain search and retrieval tasks implicit in the notion of discovery far better than current discovery systems. Libraries will need to ascertain how best to leverage a discovery tool within its existing structure to best enable the end user's ability to uncover and access the most appropriate resources for his or her needs.

FUTURE DIRECTIONS: OPEN-SOURCE AND COMMERCIAL AVENUES FOR DISCOVERY

A survey of current literature will reward the searcher with countless articles about choosing the right discovery tool by using a whole host of criteria, including customizability, interoperability, and price. There are seemingly numerous options for libraries of all sizes and operating budgets, with an equal weight of professional commentary both for and against almost any solution. The main players in the commercial market for discovery systems were previously discussed, and it is worth mentioning that ongoing development in this arena will produce new contenders in the market, some of which stem from the same vendors mentioned. Ex Libris's Alma, billed as a next-generation library services framework, aims to offer a "suite" of operational functions that address selection, acquisition, digitization, and management, among other things, which can be integrated with external systems. Innovative Interface's Sierra Services Platform promises a similar set of features with open development and customization. OCLC's WorldShare Management Services is self-described as the first cooperative management service for libraries. It is a cloud-based system with enhanced end user discovery with "Google-like" searching. It is likely that many libraries may transition to these types of platforms in future, moving away from legacy integrated library systems. Alternatively, Kuali OLE (Open Library Environment), which identifies itself as the "first system designed by and for academic and research libraries for managing and delivering intellectual information," is an enterprise-ready, community-source software package aimed at managing and providing access to collections and licensed and local digital content.

Such library services platforms, incorporating discovery tools with management and delivery systems, may be seen as the next evolution of the library catalog. While next-generation catalogs do not typically fit within the outline we have formed to define resource discovery tools, they certainly present the next trend in a mix-and-match approach to library automation. Importantly, there are many open-source discovery interfaces that are being deployed successfully across library systems. The Indiana University Bloomington Libraries, for example, have combined the Blacklight catalog (an open-source Ruby on Rails engine that provides a discovery interface for Apache Solr) with the EBSCO Discovery Service. Similarly, the University of Virginia has combined its own Blacklight catalog with Ex Libris's Primo Central Index. Villanova University's VuFind catalog (an open-source library resource portal developed for and by libraries) has Serials Solutions' Summon service as its incorporated discovery layer. Other examples of open-source discovery systems include: OpenBib, a search portal currently under development that is customizable and extendable; eXtensible Catalog, which comprises four software components to provide end user discovery that works well with Drupal (an open-source content management platform); SOPAC (Social Online Public Access Catalog), a module that integrates the library catalog system with the Drupal content management system while allowing users to tag, rate, and review collections holdings, which are then incorporated into the discovery index, effectively creating a "community-driven catalog system"; and, Xerxes, a mobile-ready library portal that is customizable and provides citation management and integration features.

WHITHER LIBRARIES IN THE AGE OF DISCOVERY?

Information scientist and theorist Frederick Wilfrid Lancaster, whose own work typically centered on online retrieval, envisioned, in 1978, the future as "one of a society whose formal communication will be paperless" and "as a consequence, library problems in the long term do not relate to inadequate space or even to inadequate financial resources. They all come down to one problem only: justification for existence, simple survival" (Thompson, 1982, p. 109). Lancaster asked broadly, "can libraries . . . survive in a largely electronic world?" (p. 109). For his own part, he did try to answer this question throughout his career, but he suggested (one year later in 1979) that libraries in the year 2000 "will with only very few exceptions offer 'multisource' catalogues" that include "not only entries for all the materials held by the network or networks to which a particular library belongs, but also entries for all externally accessible databases, primary and secondary, which any member library chooses to include" (p. 110). Certainly, Lancaster may have been a bit quick to presume the state of libraries in the year 2000; however, the current development and evolution of discovery tools available to libraries may very well serve to facilitate Lancaster's wishful prognostication in the not-too-distant (and collaborative) future.

REFERENCES

Breeding, M. (2014). Web-scale discovery services. *American Libraries, 45*(1/2), 25.
Breeding, M. (2012). Looking forward to the next generation of discovery services. *Computers in Libraries, 32*(2), 28–31.

Cmor, D., & Li, X. (2012). Beyond Boolean, towards thinking: Discovery systems and information literacy. *Proceedings of the IATUL Conferences*. Retrieved from http://docs.lib.purdue.edu/iatul/2012/papers/7

Dempsey, L. (2012). Thirteen ways of looking at libraries, discovery, and the catalog: Scale, workflow, attention. *Educause Review Online*. Retrieved from http://www.educause.edu/ero/article/thirteen-ways-looking-libraries-discovery-and-catalog-scale-workflow-attention

Lynch, C. A. (1995). Networked information resource discovery: An overview of current issues. *IEEE Journal on Selected Areas in Communications*, *13*(8), 1505–1522. http://dx.doi.org/10.1109/49.464719

Ranganathan, S. R. (1931). *The five laws of library science*. Madras: The Madras Library Association.

Thompson, J. (1982). *The end of libraries*. London: Clive Bingley Limited.

Vaughn, J. (2011). Web scale discovery: What and why. *Library Technology Reports*, *47*(1), 5–11.

8 | Collaborative Virtual Reference: Past, Present, and Future Trends

Kris Johnson, AskColorado/AskAcademic Virtual Reference Cooperative

This chapter discusses collaborative virtual reference as a 21st-century library service, outlining its history and origins in North America, where it stands today, and speculation on its possible future in libraries of all types. The perspective presented is from experience gained overseeing the AskColorado/AskAcademic Virtual Reference Cooperative through its eleventh year of offering continuous 24/7 service (Johnson, 2013, 2012a, 2010), library literature, as well as information and insights gained from networking and information sharing with managers of other cooperatives in the United States and Canada. If this topic is new to you, you need to know that there is a plethora of literature about the general topic of virtual reference (e.g., see Radford's online "Virtual Reference Bibliography" (2009), which contains over 900 citations) with entire books devoted to it (books by Kern (2009) and Thomsett-Scott (2013) are particularly recommended). A good deal of the literature focuses specifically on collaborative virtual reference. For the newbie, it is understandable that the sheer volume could be overwhelming, particularly if your library is thinking about starting a virtual reference service for the first time or is wondering if you should join a collaborative effort. After reading this chapter, you should have a basic understanding of what collaborative virtual reference is, why it is important, and the role it should serve in the suite of reference outlets libraries offer to their users in the future.

The origins of collaborative virtual reference stem from the late 1990s and early 2000s. Today, collaborative virtual reference is not ubiquitous in libraries, and there are still enough differing opinions about its purpose and usefulness as a core library service that one could make the argument that it has been a key factor in promoting the reimagination conversation happening throughout this book. To begin though, a basic definition of virtual reference is in order so readers will have a common understanding and framework for how it ties into collaborative virtual reference.

The concept of virtual reference is simple. It is a library reference service provided when the librarian and user do not share the same physical space. But that is too simple, because one could apply this definition to users who write letters to libraries, sending them via the U.S. postal service (historically a popular method of reference service and one some users still engage in today). And what about telephone reference? That could be considered virtual, right? To be specific, virtual reference is a reference encounter between a user and a librarian that does not occur in the same physical space, enabled by the use of a computer (or other electronic device) and some type of software interface. The American Library Association's Reference and User Services Association (RUSA) defined virtual reference in more official language in their "Guidelines for Implementing and Maintaining Virtual Reference Services" (RUSA, 2004). The guidelines also include the following extant examples of electronic channels by which virtual reference could be carried out: videoconferencing, voice-over IP, cobrowsing, email, instant messaging (IM), and chat. This chapter will focus primarily on chat (and IM to a smaller extent), mainly because in the early days and up to the present, chat has been the channel that has fleshed out as being the most commonly utilized, and is probably what most practicing virtual reference librarians would think of when discussing virtual reference.

But this chapter is not about virtual reference in general or software options for the various electronic channels by which it could be delivered—although it will be argued that software was a major factor influencing the early direction of collaborative virtual reference. This chapter is specifically about *collaborative* virtual reference. Collaborative virtual reference is when libraries join forces to provide a virtual reference service. It is that simple—and that vague. The idea behind collaborative virtual reference is the same as the idea behind interlibrary loan, or cooperative cataloging. Libraries work together to provide the service to the users, and the result saves time for the library and the user and best utilizes the resources of all of the participating libraries. RUSA defined collaborative reference in their "Guidelines for Cooperative Reference Services": "Cooperative reference service is a process through which information assistance is provided by referring the user, or the user's queries, to staff at another institution according to a system of established procedures" (RUSA, 2006). The guidelines state that cooperative reference (called collaborative reference in this chapter) could be conducted through any modes of communication, but in reality, it is virtual reference that represents the majority of cooperative reference efforts in our libraries today. In fact, the "Guidelines for Cooperative Reference Services" were only developed in the mid-1990s (the focus at that time being on asynchronous reference), and shortly after the advent of the first chat reference services in the early 2000s, the guidelines were revised to their present state to include the new synchronous options like chat. Because the origins of chat virtual reference services were predominated by collaborative efforts, it could be argued that collaborative virtual reference was the impetus for the revision process of the guidelines in 2006. Some examples of collaborative virtual reference services include: a state- or city-wide community college library system working together to answer reference questions for students (Maricopa Community Colleges in Arizona; LRC Live 24/7 for Virginia's community colleges); libraries in the Association of Jesuit Colleges and Universities fielding reference questions for one another (Ask a Librarian AJCU); or public libraries in one state working together to field questions from users, such as AskColorado, or Ask-WA (Washington state.) One of the most important early collaborations was between the Library of Congress and OCLC, called the Collaborative Digital Reference Service (CDRS), which later became OCLC's QuestionPoint cooperative that still exists today.

So how and why did these collaborative efforts begin? Virtual reference efforts date back to the late 1980s with the advent of electronic mail and the early glimmerings of the Internet. An early "digital reference" advocate, Bernie Sloan (2006), describes very early efforts to experiment with email and crazy-sounding early Internet communication tools like MUD (Multi-User Dungeon), MOO (a programming language), and IRC (Internet Relay Chat). Sloan religiously documented the virtual reference literature in his "Digital Reference Services Bibliography," which he maintained from 2000 to 2004. His bibliography eventually comprised 700+ entries and formed the basis for Radford's "Virtual Reference Bibliography."

Despite these efforts in the 1980s and 1990s, collaborative virtual reference projects did not begin in earnest until the early 2000s with the development of chat software. Library chat software stemmed from a commercial line of software used by call centers (a.k.a., contact centers), often called live help, or live chat software. What distinguished chat software from the previous technologies, and what sparked the collaborative reference bandwagon, were the myriad features included in one large software package, as well as a fairly large ticket price. Often such software included the ability to chat live in real time with users, options for having multiple providers (librarians) logged into the same "queue" simultaneously, the ability for a librarian to chat with multiple users simultaneously, queue routing so specially marked questions could be routed to librarians based on specific criteria, cobrowsing features so librarians could view webpages along with their users on the same screen, the ability to save transcripts and send them to the user, and sophisticated back-end statistical modules, to name the most significant features. Some software companies offered multiple communication channels in one package such as chat, voice, and video conferencing. Libraries have the commercial sector to thank for the addition of chat software to library vendor offerings, due to the creation of telephone "call centers" in the 1960s and their subsequent incorporation of new technologies (like chat) into their communication offerings to customers. Examples of commercial, live chat software companies from the early 2000s include Convey Systems, Inc., Human Click, eGain, and LivePerson. McGlamery and Coffman (2000) wrote about what is probably the first proof of concept project to utilize contact center software (Webline from Cisco) by a library consortium for collaborative reference purposes.

Dozens, if not hundreds, of these live chat products exist today. Human Click was acquired by LivePerson, which along with eGain are still in business. LivePerson is currently being used by several libraries and virtual reference cooperatives in the United States and Canada, such as the Austin Community College Library and the AskOntario collaborative service, to name two. Library software vendors and library cooperatives jumped on the bandwagon and started coding their own chat software. 24/7 Reference from the MCLS cooperative in the Los Angeles area, as well as the Library of Congress, OCLC, and LSSI, were early pioneers in chat reference software for libraries. 24/7 Reference and the Library of Congress eventually merged into OCLC's QuestionPoint software we know today. Interestingly, Convey Systems, Inc. (commercial software mentioned previously) was also absorbed into the QuestionPoint family (Wanerski, 2003). LSSI's chat product was purchased by Tutor.com, which still offers a virtual reference software option in addition to their online tutoring services. Details about software in the early days are briefly covered in two seminal articles: Sloan's "Twenty Years of Virtual Reference" (2006) and Weak and Luo's "Collaborative Virtual Reference Service: Lessons from the Past Decade" (2013). Neither focus exclusively on software, but they include important software moments in the chronology and history of virtual reference in a neatly organized package and via their reference lists.

There was a plethora of these software packages available to libraries in the early 2000s, the potential for use seemed unlimited, and librarians got excited about the possibilities for virtual reference very quickly. This led to the advent of collaborative virtual reference as we know it today.

Librarians quickly became aware of the benefits of using such software for reference purposes that mimicked a face-to-face interaction. Users could now contact a library using their computers, but in real-time via chat, instead of asynchronously via email. (Email was, and still is, a useful entry point for reference questions, but has its own built-in challenges due to the time delay between submitting a question and getting an answer, and the difficulty in conducting a reference interview.) Connections could occur within seconds, and links and other information could be obtained in minutes, with transcripts sent via email as a follow-up. But there was one problem—the software was expensive. It was not exorbitantly expensive, but expensive enough that individual libraries seriously questioned the value of purchasing it, weighing the pros and cons of doing so—trying new things technologically and offering innovative services to their users—or not doing so—avoiding the expense but being behind the curve on this new trend. This is where the cooperative aspects of virtual reference began.

It was at this point that existing library cooperatives started stepping up to create pilot projects that would allow groups of libraries to share and test software. The California State University (CSU) Library system piloted early collaborative efforts, organizing a "Live Reference" symposium ("Going Where the Students Are: A Symposium on Live Reference in the CSU") in early 2001 to introduce the topic to librarians and to begin testing various software on the market. Many such cooperative efforts used existing resources and infrastructures to negotiate with vendors for discounted software contracts for their pilot projects, giving early adopter libraries in the consortia free or very low cost access to the technology. Thus collaborative virtual reference was born; out of a necessity to share the costs in order to gain access to the powerful new technology, libraries left the comforts of their traditional reference desks and began collaborating with other libraries, some reluctantly, others enthusiastically.

Much of the very early days (around 2000–2003) were marked more by software experimentation and testing as opposed to the sharing of reference questions and users, though the latter was not far behind. Again, the early adopter librarians were quick to see the potential for the software to offer a library service never before offered—one that was available any time of the day or night. This was novel, but one that appealed to creative thinkers cognizant of the changing world around them. Other services available 24/7 included increased access to ATM machines, all night grocery stores and gas stations, and easier and faster access to the Internet, providing a veritable Las Vegas of information resources available to library users any time. These prescient librarians saw a potential niche libraries could fill in this new world of 24/7 availability. Why not have librarians available 24/7? How could they do this? Collaboration to the rescue.

No library could afford to staff such a service alone, and traffic likely would not warrant devoting a single librarian to every hour of the day. But would it work if multiple institutions worked together to staff such a service and answer questions for one another? A 24/7 reference service could be a reality under this scenario. Statewide cooperatives began popping up, often with partial or full funding from Library Services and Technology Act (LSTA) monies (e.g., New Jersey in 2001, Maryland and Ohio in 2002, Colorado and Oregon in 2003). Academic systems like the CSU system in California began sharing questions in 2002. The CDRS project became OCLC's QuestionPoint, which today is trademarked virtual reference software as well as a member-based cooperative, the largest virtual reference cooperative effort in the world, with member libraries throughout the United States as well as internationally. All this stemmed from the advent of the software and a necessity to cooperate based on (primarily) a financial need.

The early days (around 2000–2005) of collaborative virtual reference were exciting. Symposia and conferences devoted to the topic abounded, the

Virtual Reference Desk (VRD) Conference being the most prominent, held annually from 1998–2005. Colorado hosted several smaller-scale Collaborative Virtual Reference Symposia in 2002, 2005, and 2007. National and local conferences offered presentations and workshops on the topic, and the library literature was (and still is) saturated with articles. Where once the professional reference conversation focused on sources, there was a huge shift to discussing the delivery and evaluation of reference services. This was a hot topic with many, although not all, librarians embracing it enthusiastically.

Collaborative virtual reference was still in the early stages when the Library 2.0 movement hit in late 2005 and early 2006, and while it did not necessarily curb enthusiasm for virtual reference, it offered alternate distractions for librarians' attentions. Facebook launched in February 2004, Meebo (an IM aggregator) in 2005, and Twitter in March 2006. Library 2.0-related topics literally became all the rage in the library literature and at conferences and workshops. In the Library 2.0 spirit and philosophy, librarians began to reflect more critically on and examine the way in which services were delivered to users, as well as the tools available to them as delivery methods. In the case of Library 2.0, many new, free, web-based communication tools became available for librarians to experiment with, Meebo, Facebook, and Twitter being three very popular ones. So what happened to collaborative virtual reference during this time? The answer is nothing, and everything. Collaborative virtual reference plowed along; OCLC's QuestionPoint gained traction and grew in membership; Tutor.com and Altarama were secondary virtual reference software vendors with some popularity; and several new statewide collaboratives formed and started offering services (e.g., North Carolina in 2004; Pennsylvania in 2006). Many libraries were still excited and on board with the service, but parallel to this, libraries not familiar with collaborative virtual reference and some veteran virtual reference libraries started using the Meebo IM widget as their primary delivery method for virtual reference. (Meebo was not the only one, but it was the most popular.) Meebo was free, web-based, hosted externally, and easy to use. The downside was there was no statistical tracking, only one librarian could log in at a time, and Meebo, like all free web tools from commercial vendors, owned the rights to track and record all usage of the service, raising serious privacy concerns. Because of these issues, Meebo and its ilk could not be used in a collaborative setting.

Concurrently, the middle-days (around 2006–2011) of collaborative virtual reference were marked by an evaluation period in which the research and literature focused less on starting a service and touting the benefits of collaborating, and more on quality of service, user and librarian perceptions of the service, best practices, and lessons learned to date. Librarians were starting to speak out about features in the chat software that, while attractive on paper, were often problematic in practice. Although cobrowsing existed, and when it worked it was a great tool, in reality the feature did not always work, and was often clunky and slow, sometimes simply due to the users of the service being on computers with older, noncompatible operating systems. The software was sometimes very slow due to large system requirements (Lupien, 2006). Often, in order to use the software, librarians had to download an application and use it from a single computer, and most software was only available on PCs, not Macs. In many libraries, each time the software was upgraded, librarians had to call IT to download the latest version because many did not have administrator rights on their computers.

It is easy to see how, on the surface, the Library 2.0 tools were so attractive, especially to libraries and librarians with limited resources and time to evaluate their options in any depth. Some managers of collaborative virtual reference services used to joke amongst themselves that chat software was like Homer Simpson's dream car: "Man does it look cool, but nothing works." Chat software was not, and is not, that bad, but the comparison was made nonetheless.

Disgruntled librarians and some early adopters of the new bright and shiny Library 2.0 tools started questioning why their libraries were pouring money and time into chat software, when you could provide reference service for free using Meebo, ICQ, Yahoo IM, or any of what became a plethora of free tools available (Houghton & Schmidt, 2005). Many libraries started using these free options instead of paying for expensive chat software. One librarian/spouse duo even created their own software, Library H3lp, which combined features and benefits from both the free Meebo-type software as well as some of the commercial options, which they offered (and still do) to libraries at a very low cost. Some libraries created IM services for their library but stayed in the collaborative service they were already part of (Evans, McHale, & Sobel, 2010). Some, however, decided to go it alone and began leaving collaborative ventures altogether.

Operations managers of cooperatives were suddenly confronted with a dilemma they had not encountered previously—libraries leaving their cooperatives in order to go it alone but with more limited service hours to their constituents. By leaving the cooperative, these libraries gave up the ability to save on software costs, offer 24/7 service to their users, and benefit from centralized management of the system. For years these managers and other proponents of collaborative virtual reference were under the impression that libraries were truly collaborating because of a desire to offer 21st-century library service to 21st-century users who would expect and demand to be able to connect with a librarian 24/7. In retrospect, however, it appears the collaborative movement was perhaps precipitated primarily out of financial need based on software alone, and not a purely altruistic effort to do for reference services what catalogers and lenders had done for cooperative cataloging and interlibrary loan. Perhaps we should have seen it coming, because Joe Janes (2000) stated so clearly the reasons libraries likely collaborate to begin with: "all these examples of interconnection and interdependence [ILL, cooperative cataloging] are the result of our being poor. Let's face the truth—if libraries as a group were better funded and supported, it's quite likely that some of these examples of sharing would not exist or be far less extensive" (p. 15). Prescient words.

Caleb Tucker-Raymond, former statewide reference service coordinator for the Oregon collaborative Answerland (formerly L-Net), in a personal email to the author, describes the middle period of collaborative virtual reference like this:

> Conferences were expensive for staff at small libraries to go to, and software was expensive too, so what emerged was a movement towards "instant messaging" and an ignorance (in some cases willful) of the formal discussion. . . . I think (some of) the broader context is that setting up a collaborative service—participating in that formal conversation—is a lot of work and perhaps considered not worth the investment in time. Also, perhaps, that formal communication channels have been mistrusted. As VR has shifted from being a special hot new thing, to part of our daily operations, has the care we put into implementing VR services declined? Has quality suffered?

The exact answers to his question are unknown, but worthy of study and a place in the conversation on the future of collaborative virtual reference.

Despite its seemingly ubiquitous nature by now, it is not definitively known how many libraries offer virtual reference in their libraries, and how many participate in collaborative virtual reference. Unlike ILL, which has become a ubiquitous library service in nearly every library of every type, virtual reference—and collaborative virtual reference in particular—are not. It is interesting to note that while the practice of ILL has not existed in the library profession for as long as the practice of reference, ILL has been a dominant part of the library environment much longer than collaborative virtual reference. The ILL code dates back to 1917, and was adopted by ALA in 1919 (RUSA, 2008). Technically, ILL has also been adopted by mainstream ILS vendors. The majority of libraries have some sort of ILS, and many of those systems have an ILL component as a standard part of the ILS package.

So how do we measure where we are with virtual reference and collaborative virtual reference today? Efforts to catalog, list, and link to virtual reference services have existed in the form of wikis. The "Chat Reference Libraries" page at the LISWiki (http://liswiki.org/wiki/List_of_libraries_providing_virtual_reference_services) is one of the longest running listings, but as it is a wiki, it is not a definitive source, and despite the name, it includes libraries doing other forms of reference besides chat. A scan of the wiki using the Wayback Machine (InternetArchive) indicates that in June 2008 there were 24 state- or province-wide virtual reference cooperatives operating in North America. A scan in March 2014 showed that number had decreased by half.

Colorado's Library Research Service (LRS) has been tracking the use of web technologies in U.S. public libraries since 2008. In 2008, 2010, and 2012, they analyzed all Colorado public libraries and a sampling of U.S. public libraries for the presence of, among many things, a chat reference service. According to the Colorado LRS reports "U.S. Public Libraries and the Use of Web Technologies, 2012," in comparison to 2008 and 2010, for public libraries in the United States: "Chat reference is still offered by many public libraries but appears to be experiencing a decline since 2010, with substantial drops at the larger libraries: libraries serving 500,000 or more dropped from 71% to 57% and those serving 100,000-499,999 fell from 49% to 38%." In Colorado, chat reference services increased in public libraries from 59% to 67%, as did text reference (1% to 4%). LRS notes that the presence of a statewide virtual reference collaborative (AskColorado) contributes to these numbers. LRS also noted an increase in text (SMS) reference in public libraries in the United States, moving from 13% to 43% in libraries serving more than 500,000 people. Could it be that for some libraries, chat reference is being replaced by text/SMS? For readers wanting more in-depth information, LRS does a good job of putting the numbers into perspective based on the population served by the public library, as opposed to simply aggregating it into one general statistic. Also keep in mind that these numbers are for public libraries only, so generalities cannot be made for academic libraries based on this data. In fact, based on observational experience, the author speculates that chat reference is not decreasing in academic libraries, as noted in public libraries by the LRS.

So where do we stand today and where will we go in the future in terms of collaborative virtual reference? Although many libraries embrace it enthusiastically, we know virtual reference—as well as collaborative virtual reference—is not ubiquitous in libraries today. We know technology plays a huge role in the implementation of virtual reference, with many distractions for libraries as technologies are quickly changing (much faster rate than for interlibrary loan, for example). Librarians have a hard time keeping up with the changes, and some that had perceived "bad experiences" with early virtual reference attempts seem unwilling to get past it in order to conceive of a positive new outcome. For many, it seems the experience for the library or librarian trumps any possible benefits of offering the service for users.

The benefits of providing a virtual reference service for users in the 21st century are many, and some libraries recognize this enough to give it a second chance. Nicol and Crook (2013) describe in detail an effort at the Washington State University, Pullman, library to bring back and revitalize a virtual reference service. The title of their article highlights an awakening of sorts at their library, and an effort to really put in the proper effort to implement a virtual reference service that will be successful. The authors say that when they finally got it together and paid attention to how the service was implemented and staffed, usage went up and it became an essential service. This is the key to implementing a successful virtual reference service and ties into the success of collaborative virtual reference. Libraries and librarians need to pay attention, do the research and become knowledgeable, and take on the responsibility for making their service a success. (Once implemented, many early efforts pooh-poohed virtual reference, but when a closer look was taken, often it was determined that the library really was not committed to the endeavor from the get-go.)

Many did, and still do, observe the service as simply a "project" or "temporary experiment." Many hard-core reference librarians also carry with them the idea that "all patrons are local" and that no one but the personnel of the user's library could possibly answer their queries with any accuracy or authority. That is a vague notion in the world we live in today. People are extremely mobile, moving frequently and often using multiple libraries simultaneously. Likewise, librarians are mobile. If "all patrons are local," then shouldn't all librarians be local as well? Meaning, you could not move from one library job to another successfully. You would be able to work in only one library. This doesn't make sense. The argument that a librarian outside of the user's main library cannot answer any of their queries just does not hold water, and the success and longevity of OCLC's QuestionPoint cooperative and other cooperatives is testament to this fact. If it could not work in practice, these cooperatives would have folded in their first years of existence. The reality is that information seeking and finding is becoming a universal reference skill that can be applied just about anywhere, anytime.

Despite software oddities, complexities, and frequent changes, the success of implementing a collaborative virtual reference service has not ever rested on the technology, but on the people behind the service. People are quirky and hold many opinions about library services that often do not meet reality, are not based on evidence, or that are not user-centered. One bad experience can taint a librarian's opinion about a service forever. The only reason collaborative virtual reference has been hampered in a quest toward ubiquity has been the human aspect. So perhaps what is needed is a stronger leadership presence nationally (ALA, for example), statewide, and locally to help libraries achieve for reference what has been done for lending and cataloging. Our leaders need to make reference services a higher priority in order for it to be effective, efficient, and elegant, and collaboration should be the cornerstone of that effort. The central focus of *Collaboration in Libraries and Learning Environments* (2013) is "that collaboration is the critical issue for the ongoing transformation and success of libraries, learning environments and learning services" (p. 87). In their chapter, Roberts and Esson write about leadership development for collaboration as the key: "leadership development for collaboration, rather than leadership in general, is the single biggest issue and the single greatest lever for success in the future" (p. 87).

Perhaps this book will lead the way toward that realization envisioned by Roberts, Esson, and the other authors represented in *Collaboration in Libraries and Learning Environments*. However, this is not the first time thought leaders have mused over reference services in recent years. *Digital Reference Service in the New Millennium: Planning, Management, and Evaluation* (2000) and *Reference Reborn: Breathing New Life into Public Services Librarianship* (2011) are in a similar vein, and truthfully, we have not seen a huge shift in reference services since their publication. We need to move from "plowing along" to "surging forward." We need to move the conversation beyond "Should we be doing virtual reference?" or "Should we be doing collaborative virtual reference?" or even "What is the state of collaborative virtual reference?" to "How are we integrating all our reference contact points (F2F, email, chat, SMS) into a seamless and elegant solution for our users, are we being successful, and what can we do to be better?" Janes echoes this in a 2008 article, stating, "When the true history of 'digital' reference is written, the verdict on its success will hinge on how well it succeeded in its mission—to be incorporated not only in the institutional framework of libraries but also, and more crucially, in the mindset of its staff and the information lives of their clientele" (p. 10). In order to get there, our library leaders need to step up and make reference services a priority, devoting funding, time, and energy to the process, and collaborative virtual reference should be a key component of that effort.

REFERENCES

Evans, L., McHale, N., & Sobel, K. (2010). Apples and oranges: Creating a hybrid virtual reference service with proprietary chat reference software and free instant messaging services. In M. Radford (Ed.), *Reference renaissance: Current and future trends* (pp. 163–174). New York: Neal-Schuman Publishers.

Houghton, S., & Schmidt, A. (2005). Web-based chat vs. instant messaging. *Online, 29*(4), 26–30.

Janes, J. (2008). An informal history (and possible future) of digital reference. *Bulletin of the American Society for Information Science and Technology, 34*(2), 8–10. http://dx.doi.org/10.1002/bult.2008.1720340204

Janes, J. (2000). Why reference is about to change forever. In D. R. Lankes, J. W. Collins, & A. S. Sakowitz (Eds.), *Digital reference service in the new millennium: Planning, management, and evaluation* (pp. 13–24). New York: Neal-Schumann Publishers.

Johnson, K. (2013). AskColorado: A collaborative virtual reference service. In B. Thomsett-Scott (Ed.), *Implementing virtual reference services: A LITA guide* (pp. 115–136). Chicago: ALA TechSource.

Johnson, K. (2012a). Collaborative virtual reference really does work, but it takes a tribe. In M. Radford (Ed.), *Leading the reference renaissance: Today's ideas for tomorrow's cutting edge services* (pp. 227–240). New York: Neal-Schuman.

Johnson, K. (2012b). Mentoring MLIS students in collaborative virtual reference: The AskColorado mentorship program. In C. Smallwood & R. Tolley-Stokes (Eds.), *Mentoring in librarianship: Essays on working with adults and students to further the profession* (pp. 120–128). Jefferson, NC: McFarland.

Johnson, K. (2010). Back to the future: The AskColorado collaborative virtual reference cooperative. *Colorado Libraries, 35*(1).

Kern, K. M. (2009). *Virtual reference best practices: Tailoring services to your library.* Chicago: American Library Association.

Lankes, D. R. (2008). Virtual reference to participatory librarianship: Expanding the conversation. *Bulletin of the American Society for Information Science and Technology, 34*(2), 11–14. http://dx.doi.org/10.1002/bult.2008.1720340205

Lankes, D. R., Collins, J. W., & Sakowitz, A. S. (Eds.). *Digital reference service in the new millennium: Planning, management, and evaluation.* New York: Neal-Schumann Publishers.

Lupien, P. (2006). Virtual reference in the age of pop-up blockers, firewalls, and service pack 2. *Online, 30*(4), 14–19.

McGlamery, S., & Coffman, S. (2000). Moving reference to the web. In D. R. Lankes, J. W. Collins, & A. S. Sakowitz (Eds.), *Digital reference service in the new millennium: Planning, management, and evaluation* (pp. 181–195). New York: Neal-Schumann Publishers.

Nicol, E. C., & Crook, L. (2013). Now it's necessary: Virtual reference services at Washington State University, Pullman. *Journal of Academic Librarianship, 39*(2), 161–168. http://dx.doi.org/10.1016/j.acalib.2012.09.017

Radford, M. (2009). Virtual reference bibliography. *Rutgers.* Retrieved from http://vrbib.rutgers.edu/index.php

Reference and User Services Association (RUSA). (2008). Interlibrary Loan Code for the United States Explanatory Supplement. Retrieved from http://www.ala.org/rusa/resources/guidelines/interlibraryloancode

Reference and User Services Association (RUSA). (2006). Guidelines for cooperative reference services. Retrieved from http://www.ala.org/rusa/resources/guidelines/guidelinescooperative

Reference and User Services Association (RUSA). (2004). Guidelines for implementing and maintaining virtual reference services. Retrieved from http://www.ala.org/rusa/resources/guidelines/virtrefguidelines

Roberts, S., & Esson, R. (2013). Leadership skills for collaboration: Future needs and challenges. In M. Melling & M. Weaver (Eds.), *Collaboration in Libraries and Learning Environments* (pp. 87–102). London: Facet Publishing.

Sloan, B. (2006). Twenty years of virtual reference. *Internet Reference Services Quarterly, 11*(2), 91–95. http://dx.doi.org/10.1300/J136v11n02_06

Thomsett-Scott, B. C. (2013). *Implementing virtual reference services: A LITA guide.* Chicago: ALA TechSource.

Wanserski, J. (2003). From AskWendt Live to QuestionPoint™: A chronology of the development of a persistently virtual reference product and service. *Internet Reference Services Quarterly, 8*(1/2), 71–94. http://dx.doi.org/10.1300/J136v08n01_07

Wanucha, M., & Hofschire, L. (2013). *U.S. public libraries and the use of web technologies, 2012 (Closer Look Report).* Denver: Colorado State Library, Library Research Service. Retrieved from http://www.lrs.org/wp-content/uploads/2013/11/WebTech2012_CloserLook.pdf

Weak, E., & Luo, L. (2013). Collaborative virtual reference service: Lessons from the past decade. *Advances in Librarianship, 37,* 81–112. http://dx.doi.org/10.1108/S0065-2830(2013)0000037008

Zabel, D. (Ed.). (2011). *Reference reborn: Breathing new life into public services librarianship.* Santa Barbara: Libraries Unlimited.

9 | The Value of Reference Services: Using Assessment to Chart the Future

Amanda Clay Powers, Mississippi State University

First, what this chapter is not. It is not focused on the current ways to assess reference services as laid out in library science textbooks (Bopp & Smith, 2011; Cassell & Hiremath, 2012). Those texts contain excellent methods for assessment of information services as reference departments have done them in the past and continue to do them. Methods such as suggestion boxes, surveys, in-house assessment, questionnaires, direct observation, and focus groups are excellent and should be used as appropriate for each community. They provide examples of traditional assessment tools and methodologies for evaluating the results.

Historically, however, evaluating reference services has been problematic, most infamously in widely reported results that only roughly half of reference questions are answered accurately (Hernon & McClure, 1986; Durrance, 1989). Marie L. Radford and Lorri M. Mun (2008) contextualize these results, as well as reviewing many of the commonly used tools explicated in reference textbooks in their excellent must-read "Reference Services in Face-to-Face and Virtual Environments." Indeed, user satisfaction and willingness to return rather than accuracy have become more accepted measures of reference success; Radford and Mun conclude in their review of the research that these have become the "global outcome measure" (p. 16) for reference success. For assessment purposes this begs the question: What creates user satisfaction and a willingness to return? Frequently there is no "right" answer today. Reference librarians are instead teaching skills for information discernment and acquisition. This work is difficult to measure, and this contributes to the challenging environment for communicating the value of reference services.

Even the word "reference" seems no longer to apply to this work, as it moves away from a simpler look-up service to an instruction format. The term will be used in this chapter to represent the work of the renamed research services, roving reference, information points, integrated service points, and so forth. Indeed, the term assessment is problematic as well in the library literature. As Hufford (2013) aptly notes, "the use of the words assessment and evaluation among librarians is sometimes ambiguous, or has changed over the years" (p. 6). This chapter will focus on assessment as it is used to evaluate the library or library services, and of specific interest, how these can be used to demonstrate the value of reference service.

This chapter will lay out a path forward for librarians and administrators to look at the assessment of reference service in new ways. The literature on assessment of library instruction is extensive, and although that discipline cannot be extricated from work at reference service points, capturing student learning is much more feasible in the classroom environment. Student learning would be an excellent measure for instruction-centered reference services; however, the pretesting and posttesting are impractical in the context of a reference transaction. The demand for new models for demonstrating library value has precipitated several experiments with direct applications to reference services, which will be reviewed here.

Librarians can no longer be satisfied with the status quo in anything. It is necessary to invest time and energy on an ongoing basis to reflect on how best to represent value and how best to improve services. Everything must always be in question, but it is up to each librarian and library administrator to chart the path of their institution. Nothing is more important than the makeup of each individual library's constituency and an examination of its established values. There is no one-size-fits-all prescription for all libraries anymore. A library should be a reflection of the needs of its community.

THE STRUCTURE OF THE GOOGLE (R)EVOLUTION

The writing was on the wall for reference services as soon as Google was born. Librarians have witnessed the changes in the types of questions being asked, and most have come through this transition intact. For the profession, this shift has been happening for decades. Reference librarians have had time to adjust to the shock, and the realities they face are now apparent, and a different breed of reference librarian has emerged. Reference services have evolved out of necessity. It was certainly a possibility that reference would become redundant. Maybe all children growing up on the Web would instinctively develop research skills. The library world watched and waited. However, it is now clear that having a computer and being able to find cat videos on the Internet does not provide the training needed to do even basic research. Libraries now know it. The faculties at universities now know it. The public is slowly becoming aware of this increasingly complex information environment. Libraries are at a tentative "new normal." In academic libraries "ready reference" work has been replaced by one-on-one in-depth research instruction, responding to the need for sophisticated searching skills. Public libraries are the center for filling ever-changing technology needs. School libraries are no longer just media centers—they are the center for training the youngest patrons about how to live online as outlined in American Association of School Librarians (AASL) *Standards for the 21st-Century Learner* (2007). There is no one else trained or able to meet patrons at this point of bewildering need.

With Google, and indeed all online information retrieval, there has been a downturn in the number of questions received at some reference desks (Dubnjakovic, 2012). This change does not reflect on a lessening need for reference services, but rather a change in the nature of this work. The difficulty is that standards in reporting the value of reference services have not universally changed. New benchmarks have yet to be perfected or widely implemented. Just as reference work is now more complex, the search for means of capturing its value reflects that complexity. Libraries are still reporting out the volume of transactions, as if they continue to accurately reflect the work of reference. In order for this profession to survive, the models of assessment must change, and it is up to reference departments and library administrators to chart this new path. Google and online databases have not killed the reference desk, but the new practice of reference is not being evaluated with the sorts of longitudinal and comparative data necessary to validate assessment results. Without careful reflection and restructuring of models, like the current transaction counts being reported to the Association of Research Libraries (Kyrillidou, Morris, & Roebuck, 2011, p. 105), reference will continue to be reported as "in decline," when that could not be farther from the truth. It is up to reference librarians to determine how to communicate the value of building relationships, creating successful user experiences, providing in-depth research instruction, training students to be online citizens, and providing a technology center. In the meantime, numbers continue to be reported, and those numbers must be as accurate as possible.

With the availability of online research resources, everyone in the library is empowered to answer questions that had been the purview of the reference department. It has always been the case that anyone visible to a patron within the library was approached for help. Reference librarians do not glow as they walk around the library, signaling their specialized research skills. Reference service is no longer tied to the room that contains the print indexes and card catalog, and all of the library staff have access to the research resources in the past reserved for reference librarians. Now everyone in the library is empowered to answer complex reference questions, even though they are lacking in the training or experience necessary to do this work effectively. One can lament these facts, hope for referrals, or train for core competencies. In terms of communicating value in this current environment, however, all these information transactions need to be counted. Indeed, ALA's Reference and User Services Association (RUSA) (2008) definitions for reference describe "information contacts" by any member of the library staff, rather than defining reference transactions as being provided by reference staff: "A reference transaction is an information contact that involves the knowledge, use, recommendations, interpretation, or instruction in the use of one or more information sources by a member of the library staff."

Patrons will ask questions over Twitter; they will go to their academic departmental liaison; they will ask the person checking out their book or wearing a nametag in the stacks. Anyone patrons have access to within the library is being called on to answer reference questions. However this new reality is handled in terms of staffing or training, it is critical that this activity is captured. This is a sea change from the siloed nature of information contact counts done in the past. This relatively simple shift must be made immediately. Everyone in the library, from the dean or director's office to cataloging and technical services, must be recording information transactions. Without this revision in thinking, even the less-than-perfect counts required today will be inaccurate. There are many ways to do this, from a wider distribution of paper tick sheets to more efficient online question tracking tools like LibAnalytics, LibStats, DeskTracker, Gimlet, and so forth. However it is done, it must be done, and it needs to be done immediately. It can be difficult to train nonreference staff to record information transactions (as opposed to directional/operational) accurately. In the short term, until there are better and more broadly implemented methods for demonstrating value, it is worth taking the time and resources to do it. It goes without saying that ideally this will be done in conjunction with training on referrals and core competencies.

TOWARD A NEW VALUATION OF REFERENCE

Reference as a practice is no longer preoccupied with linear paths or simple answers. Assessment as it relates to reference services has also become a web of interdependencies and exciting possibilities. Many innovative libraries and library scholars are pointing the way forward to new valuation models of library services and even potential uses for reference data in assessment. It is no longer only about improving the reference services themselves; libraries are now using the expertise, data, and user feedback coming from reference to respond to user needs and to the priorities of their institutions. It is important to note that many of these new areas of research require significant new skill acquisitions for libraries, either through hiring or training. No one is born knowing how to do assessment.

Megan Oakleaf has done an excellent job of demonstrating the need for libraries to identify the needs and priorities within their communities as a means for demonstrating library value in her seminal report for the Association of College and Research Libraries, *The Value of Academic Libraries* (2010). Although the report focuses on academic libraries, it also includes school, public, and special libraries. This is a must-read for anyone interested in examining how to create and translate the value of libraries, as well as providing a path forward for new studies. At the local level, each institution will have different priorities, and before reference departments can contribute, these will need to be made explicit. Many universities and university libraries have created strategic plans to determine how to meet their missions, and these plans can be excellent maps in determining a forward trajectory for reference services. Without such plans, uncovering the priorities of each institution could be challenging, but it is a critical step in being able to translate the worth of these services effectively.

Oakleaf describes possible priorities for academic libraries, including "student enrollment, student retention and graduation rates, student success, student achievement, student learning, student engagement, faculty research productivity, faculty teaching, service, and overarching institutional quality" (2010, p. 12). It is obvious that reference services contribute to successful outcomes in these areas, but communicating that value is the challenge. Is it possible to determine the effect of successful reference transactions on student retention or faculty research productivity? How can reference departments translate their contributions to these institutional priorities? A careful review of the agenda Oakleaf sets out suggests several areas reference services could measure contributions (2010, p. 12–17):

- Enhance library contribution to student job success
- Review and respond to course content, readings, reserves, and assignments
- Track and increase library contributions to faculty research productivity
- Investigate library impact on faculty grant proposals and funding
- Demonstrate and improve library support of faculty teaching

The challenge, then, is to translate the work of reference for the broader institution. Does the library offer workshops on creating a professional online presence? Do reference librarians regularly review syllabi from teaching faculty to better prepare frontline reference staff to meet patron needs? Do faculty use reference services to mine databases for citation information in preparing tenure packets? Do faculty use librarians as consultants or co-PIs on grant proposals? Do faculty consult with librarians in preparing research assignments? If they do, document it. If they do not, why not? These are essential areas for institutional success, and it is critical to look for ways reference can integrate itself into this work. Accomplishing this integration will not happen without effective community building. Creating positive relationships to support institutional success is well within the reach of reference services. It is not possible, however, to stay behind the reference desk or within the walls of the library to do this work.

Reference must be part of the conversations taking place in the library and across individual communities, working together to achieve a narrative that supports community and begins to translate the work the library does into tangible outcomes that make it obvious how integral these services are in achieving the broader institution's achievements. Reference meets the patron at the point of frustration and the place researchers are pushing the edges of their understanding. Information desks are the place they bring their impossible assignments and online tasks, and the librarians staffing these desks receive the brunt of their frustration with all parts of the library experience. Reference librarians are the humans online when they are stuck in the loop of the link resolver. Reference librarians are the ones that share their user experience with the online catalog, with interlibrary loan, with confusing web interfaces, and with library jargon. Reference librarians are also the library employees who actually use the library website, online catalog, and databases on an hourly basis. These individuals are the ones who find the broken links and discover the access problems. Reference rests at the point of need, continually observing the patrons' experience. This provides reference departments with an opportunity to aggregate this unique understanding to use in translating and meeting patron needs. The librarians at work on these desks, listening online via chat, or roving through the library are able to contribute granular patron usage experiences to constituents across the library, and these are the basis for building the relationships that will allow the reference staff to contribute to the success of their constituents.

Apart from this intimate one-on-one experience of library patrons, there are tools like LibQual+ and now Ithaka S+R's Local Faculty Survey to measure the attitudes of patrons toward the library as well as user needs and expectations. ACRL has developed a toolkit to accompany *The Value of Academic Libraries* for librarians to use, and they are working toward providing training in the skills needed for libraries to develop their own assessment programs. For reference difficulty, the READ Scale is another widely used tool (Gerlich, n.d.) for augmenting the "volume count" currently being reported from the desks, as it delineates the difficulty level of information transactions. New ethnographic and anthropological studies are providing a wealth of data on patron experiences (Booth, 2009; Foster & Gibbons, 2007; Bryant, Matthews, & Walton, 2009). Nackerud, Fransen, Peterson, and Mastel (2013) have implemented a new comprehensive model of tracking demographics for library usage by matching patron activity to individual university accounts. The new challenges this data present call for ongoing training in translating this data into value. This is where data must fit into the priorities of each institution.

The value of LibQual+ and Ithaka's newly implemented Local Faculty Survey (there are also surveys for graduate and undergraduates) is that they allow the critical comparison needed with peer institutions. Longevity is an advantage in an assessment tool, in that it provides a large dataset and longitudinal data needed for the iterative assessment process. A critical component in these surveys must be the user experience, however. For LibQual+, for example, the full assessment and complexity in the responses required result in problematic completion rates and responder complaints (the full survey must be completed to be accepted). The structure of the survey asks responders to rank their library on a 1 to 9 point scale for perceived, minimum, and desired levels of satisfaction. There are 22 core questions with options to add questions from a 100+ question pool. A LibQual+ Lite has been developed in response to these issues, and some libraries have had increased completion rates by offering incentives upon submission of the completed survey (Thompson, Kyrillidou, & Cook, 2009). These general library surveys can also contribute to qualitative assessment through features like the LibQual+ comments section. These can be invaluable for addressing service issues or uncovering areas of success.

Additionally, reference departments have been recognized as a source of relevant data for the library as a whole, particularly in the area of the library's web presence. This is due in part to virtual reference services, which provide transcripts that can be analyzed for user experience and practice. Those creating our online libraries need to know the kinds of language patrons use. The reference department is the one place that patrons actually share their language, their search strategies, and their points of research failure. Virtual reference transcripts record all of this data, and some libraries are even recording details of in-person transactions. In the past, these volumes of usage experience data have been siloed behind the walls of the reference services departments. It is imperative to analyze and translate this data to demonstrate value in moving the entire library toward its strategic goals.

The Auburn University Libraries used feedback from reference transactions to evaluate web-based discovery systems (Ellero, 2013). The Mississippi State University Libraries used virtual reference transaction data to mine point-of-need user experiences for a new library web design (Powers, Shedd, & Hill, 2011). These experiments offer ways to share collective knowledge gained in reference transactions about the needs of the various constituencies with those creating the overall web presence. Indeed, they can provide an analysis of the types of language patrons use when approaching the library with an information need. Breaking this down by status and department, a qualitative picture of the patron emerges. Those designing the library's services, both in-person and via the Web, are able to create experiences that appeal to all types of library patrons. Understanding demonstrated need, language usage, and the places online that cause difficulty for certain types of patrons creates a deeper understanding of where work must be done.

A culture of assessment is crucial to survival, however challenging allocating time and resources to creating it can be. Librarians often fall into the trap of thinking they know what people need, thinking they know the words they use, and thinking they can train them to use resources the way librarians do. Gathering empirical data and investing in relationships with the patron community frees libraries of these misapprehensions. Staying ahead of patrons while simultaneously working to meet them where they are takes a tremendous amount of time. It is a struggle to keep up with the micro-changes occurring on a day-to-day basis while creating a stable research and service environment. To step back and look at the big picture, then implement change, measure it, reevaluate, and then begin again takes time. This iterative assessment is no longer a choice. It is the only way libraries will be able to stay relevant. However, deliberate change is critical. There cannot be a response to each breath of newness. There is value in institutionalizing deliberate, responsive, and selective changes. Libraries are essential, and assessment is the strategy that provides understanding in each library's constituents, the decision makers, and purse string holders. A broadly disseminated annual report delineating progress is essential, and many libraries are providing relevant data, including methods for patrons to respond to that data, on their websites for public consumption. This transparency is being recognized as essential in demonstrating responsiveness to the needs of the constituencies, and consequently creating value. Creative and innovative assessment is no longer optional; it must become a core strength.

For any assessment to be effective in transforming services and meeting ongoing changes in the evolving information age, it must be continually uncovering problems or questions through tools like those mentioned above. It must then address the issues, implement sensible change, review the success (or lack thereof) of the responses, and then begin again. Although it is challenging to find the time or even skills to create the tools needed to find, create, and demonstrate value, it is no longer optional. The only way for individual constituencies to see the value of library services is if it is patently obvious. Libraries and reference services are not what they were, and for some in our communities that means that libraries are no longer a foregone conclusion. Progress made and goals achieved in the process of aligning libraries more closely to the goals of each institution or community must be communicated to the wider community in order to be able to survive and thrive in this evolving information world.

REFERENCES

Bopp, R. E., & Smith, L. C. (2011). *Reference and information services: An introduction*. Santa Barbara, CA: ABC-CLIO.

Booth, C. (2009). *Information innovation: Tracking student interest in emerging library technologies at Ohio University*. Chicago: Association of College and Research Libraries.

Bryant, J., Matthews, G. & Walton, G. (2009). Academic libraries and social and learning space: A case study of Loughborough University Library, UK. *Government Information Quarterly, 25*(1), 7–18.

Cassell, K., & Hiremath, U. (2012). *Reference and information services: An introduction*. Chicago, IL: ALA Neal-Schuman Publishers.

Dubnjakovic, A. (2012). Electronic resource expenditure and the decline in reference transaction statistics in academic libraries. *Journal Of Academic Librarianship, 38*(2), 94–100. http://dx.doi.org/10.1016/j.acalib.2012.01.001

Durrance, J. C. (1989). Reference success: Does the 55 percent rule tell the whole story? *Library Journal, 114*(7), 31–36.

Ellero, N. (2013). An unexpected discovery: One library's experience with web-scale discovery service (WSDS) evaluation and assessment. *Journal of Library Administration, 53*(5/6), 323–343. http://dx.doi.org/10.1080/01930826.2013.876824

Foster, N., & Gibbons, S. (2007). *Studying students: The undergraduate research report at the University of Rochester*. Chicago: Association of Research Libraries.

Gerlich, B. K. (n.d.). *The READ Scale*. Retrieved from http://readscale.org/

Hernon, P., & McClure, C. R. (1986). Unobtrusive reference testing: The 55 percent rule. *Library Journal, 111*(7), 37–41.

Hufford, J. R. (2013). A review of the literature on assessment in academic and research libraries, 2005 to August 2011. *portal: Libraries and the Academy, 13*(1), 5–35. http://dx.doi.org/10.1353/pla.2013.0005

Ithaka S+R Local Surveys. (2014). *Ithaka S + R*. Retrieved from http://sr.ithaka.org/content/ithaka-sr-local-surveys

Kyrillidou, M., Morris, S., & Roebuck, G. (2011). ARL Statistics 2009–2010. *Association of Research Libraries*. Retrieved from http://publications.arl.org/ARL-Statistics-2009-2010

Nackerud, S., Fransen, J., Peterson, K., & Mastel, K. (2013). Analyzing demographics: Assessing library use across the institution. *portal: Libraries and the Academy, 13*(2), 131–145. http://dx.doi.org/10.1353/pla.2013.0017

Oakleaf, M. (2010). *The value of academic libraries*. Chicago: Association of Research Libraries.

Powers, A. C., Shedd, J., & Hill, C. (2011). The role of virtual reference in library web site design: A qualitative source for usage data. *Journal of Web Librarianship, 5*(2), 96–113. http://dx.doi.org/10.1080/19322909.2011.573279

Radford, M. L., & Mon, L. M. (2008). Reference services in face-to-face and virtual environments. In M. L. Radford & P. Snelson (Eds.), *Academic library research: Perspectives and current trends* (pp. 1–47). Chicago: American Library Association.

Reference and User Services Association (RUSA). (2008). Definitions of reference. Retrieved from http://www.ala.org/rusa/resources/guidelines/definitionsreference

Standards for the 21st-Century Learner. (2007). *American Association of School Librarians*. Retrieved from http://www.ala.org/aasl/standards-guidelines/learning-standards

Thompson, B., Kyrillidou, M., & Cook, C. (2009). Item sampling in service quality assessment surveys to improve response rates and reduce respondent burden: The "LibQUAL+ ® Lite" example. *Performance Measurement and Metrics, 10*(1), 6–16. http://dx.doi.org/10.1108/14678040910949657

Value of academic libraries toolkit. (2010). *Association of College and Research Libraries*. Retrieved from http://www.ala.org/acrl/issues/value/valueofacademiclibrariestoolkit

Innovation in Action
STUDIES AND EXAMPLES

Alienation, Acceptance, or Ambiguity?: A Qualitative Study of Librarian and Staff Perceptions of Reference Service Change

Mara H. Sansolo, Pasco-Hernando State College, Florida, and Kaya van Beynen, University of South Florida St. Petersburg

This study focuses on the perspectives of library staff at a medium-sized academic library who directly participated in the restructuring of reference and information services from a "just-in-case" reference model (defined as librarians sitting at a traditional reference desk waiting for questions) to a "just-in-time" model (librarians only called upon to answer in-depth research questions on an as-needed basis), with the additional creation of an IT help desk. Solicited through a qualitative assessment one year after the implementation of the new service structure, library staff reaction could only be described as ambivalent and evolving. Some participants reported being emotionally supportive of the change, but were very critical of how the change was implemented; other respondents expressed ideological opposition to the restructuring, but emerged as the most vocal proponents of the new day-to-day operation. A lack of consistent and open communication furthered cross-departmental disputes and heightened perceptions of inequity. Yet at the time of the assessment, ironically, all respondents reported general satisfaction with the new service model. As academic libraries continue to experiment with new service models, they must acknowledge that employees will be ambiguous about the change and that opinions will evolve over time. This is crucial for easing employee fear, facilitating acceptance, and ultimately ensuring a continued high quality of library service delivery.

MANAGING CHANGE

As change can be difficult for some people to accept, the change management process is designed to 1) prepare employees for the change, 2) manage the process, and 3) assess, correct, and reinforce a service or the restructuring of departments or job responsibilities. Ideally during a process of organizational change, managers will try to understand their employees' mindset and build trust among all the participants. Facilitating trust during periods of organizational change can be enacted through a variety of methods, such as incorporating all people in the planning process, supporting employee training and professional development, and a combination of formal and informal discussions between supervisors and their employees.

But an individual's reaction to change can be complex, contradictory, and shift over time, and individuals can experience conflicting emotional and cognitive reactions. An emotional reaction pertains to how the individual feels about the change (anger, fear, resentment, etc.). A cognitive response relates to how the individual understands the purpose and process of the change. Piderit (2000) advanced the theory of change management by signifying the importance of employee ambivalence representing a conflict between cognitive and emotional responses to change. Employee reactions are not simply black and white; what is often labeled as resistance may only be reluctance, concern over the process, or a reflection of an individual's cautious temperament.

METHODOLOGY

After the new reference structure was implemented, it quickly became apparent that not everyone was equally happy and that cross-departmental tension was high. Conscious that it was time to reassess the situation, the heads of access and public services acknowledged that the librarians and library staff needed a safe forum to express their opinions and vent their feelings. An anonymous, qualitative assessment with open-ended questions was created to ascertain employee experiences and emotional reactions regarding the reference restructuring, to identify areas of concern, success, and to solicit ideas for improvement.

All library employees who directly worked with the new tiered reference service were asked to participate in the study: public services (reference librarians), IT/systems (systems administrators and IT desk workers), and access services (circulation/interlibrary loan staff and student workers). There was a 68% response rate; 4 librarians from public services, 7 library staff from access services (AS), and 4 staff from information technology. The purpose of the information gathered was to achieve an in-depth understanding of the key respondents' perceptions and experiences of the service transition, not a numerical or statistical representation. Thus, the small number of respondents was not detrimental to the study.

RESULTS

Interdepartmental Miscommunication

Difficulties with creating and implementing the best procedures for interdepartmental communication regarding reference services emerged as a common theme with all survey respondents. Among the AS staff, uncertainty over which librarian was "on call" and whether he or she was really available was a frequent comment. For example, "schedule becomes confusing because we are depending on a schedule that has different reference folks on it. Sometimes they forget they are scheduled, sometimes they have conflicting schedules . . . someone may have called in sick or sometimes people switch around their times and these changes aren't always communicated promptly with circ staff." Specifically, the print schedule at the circulation desk, situated for quick and easy reference, was not always kept up-to-date regarding last-minute changes. Even the reference librarians acknowledged their own lack of communication regarding issues caused by their reliance on the electronic reference calendar. Meanwhile, the students that work at the IT support desk did not maintain or communicate either a print or an electronic schedule. In this case, AS staff could only visually check whether an IT worker was sitting at the desk and available to answer IT questions.

The mode of communication between members of the various departments when they are on call for reference and information services was also an issue. At the beginning of this new service, librarians were given a walkie-talkie to carry with them when they were on call, ideally allowing them to be located anywhere in the building, but still always easily accessible if the need arose. In practice, several librarians found this mode of communication to be antiquated: "Who uses walkie talkies? That really makes the librarians look tech savvy! . . . Replace the walkie talkies with a cell phone people!" The walkie-talkies were not always reliable—the librarian would be out of range on the third floor of the library, the device might not work, or the channel frequency could be intercepted by other devices. Additionally, librarians were only scheduled to be on call during the library's busiest hours from 11 a.m. to 7 p.m.: "Although prior to 11 is definitely not a peak time, there are patrons that require in-depth reference assistance. Seeking assistance turns into a phone roulette." Finally, the IT service desk does not have a phone or walkie-talkies connecting it to the circulation desk, thus, "It's difficult to get the attention of the student IT guys since there is a column and machinery blocking out views. You also don't want to have to scream across the library to get them to notice that their assistance is needed."

Line Ups, Transfers, and Service Quality

The ideal result of this new three-tiered reference and information service model was that AS provided frontline triage, answered general questions, and referred IT and research questions either to the IT service desk or to the librarian on call. For the successful implementation of this model, a smooth transfer of students and faculty from one service point to another was essential. This transfer process emerged as a theme among the IT and librarian respondents. One IT staff member stated that, "I have found that oftentimes other departments do not properly communicate and refer to the IT department when patrons are having IT-related problems." Similarly, a librarian wondered, "If the lack of a librarian presence [sitting at the reference desk] limits the research help we may be able to provide students and faculty." A discordant relationship between the departments was perceived as the cause for this lack of transfer: "Access service staff are too prideful to ask for help and sometimes try to handle it all at once." The notion of equating transferring patrons as a "bother" was also repeatedly stated: "[Access services staff] may feel they are 'bothering' the librarians if they ask for help with non-research-related questions."

The transfer of patrons identified an associated issue: patron reaction to their transfer across the three department service points. The AS staff are very sensitive to customer service and perceived reductions to the quality of service. Thus, their concerns focus on customer complaints, for example, "[They] get annoyed as they want the first person they talk to assist them. This is especially true for those that wait in line at Circulation, only to be directed to another person for assistance." In contrast, the librarians highlight their perception that the students and faculty either have not noticed the service change, or continue to be satisfied that their questions are being answered: "I think the students and faculty are getting the same high level of service they are used to receiving. I think they care more about getting an answer than they do about who provides them with the help they need. The last assessment indicates they [the students] are happy with the level of service."

An example of the transfer between tiers of service was outlined by one AS employee. A student first went to the IT support desk (the old reference desk) for reference help. The IT workers then referred them to the circulation desk. After a quick interaction between the AS employee and the student, it was determined that the inquiry needed to be handled by a reference librarian, who then had to be summoned from her office. The employee states that "by time the reference librarian came out the patron was flustered and didn't know who could help him. . . . This can be stressful for both staff and patron alike."

A Question of Equity?

As the circulation desk is located in the immediate line of sight when entering the library, it serves as the first and most frequent point of contact for patrons. With no reference librarians at a reference desk obviously waiting for a question, many AS staff feel as though they have been handed an increased workload. As one AS worker put it, "The workload has increased significantly during peak hours. Not only do we have to handle the normal flow of patrons for quick tasks, we also now need to weed out the technologically challenged patrons to refer to the IT [desk], and the ones that need in-depth reference assistance." Compounding this issue is that although certain inquiries can be handled by an AS staff member, that does not necessarily result in a quick transaction. Some requests can take well over five minutes, causing a line to form during peak hours. One staff member wrote, "There are moments throughout the day when circulation tasks aren't quick. For instance: processing a new patron, discussion about fines, lost materials, and policies and privileges." Additionally, AS staff can feel overwhelmed and unsupported at times, which places unwanted stress on the AS staff to provide the best service possible: "In the simplest terms it feels as if we are expected to be at two or three places at once helping people."

This feeling of inequity between the costs and benefits of the service transition was further inflamed by the shorter schedule (10 a.m. to 7 p.m.) of the IT workers and the reference librarians. While these are the busiest times of the day for the library, early morning and late evening patron questions can only be answered by AS staff. Compounding this issue is the staffing of the circulation desk, as "busy times are so unpredictable I can't think of a way to double-staff at those times." There are no consistent peak times; instead, students and faculty come in brief and unpredictable waves.

Adaption to Change

Library faculty, staff, and student workers expressed a range of reactions to the change in reference service, including acknowledgment that the change was necessary, questions over fairness and equity across departments, appreciation with incremental steps, and concern over the implementation of the new service model. There was general agreement that the newly created technical support desk was a wonderful addition to the library. The comments ranged from how the new IT desk has helped the library faculty and staff with their own job, "The tech desk has been a great help"; that it provides improved service, "When it comes to technology help students have been receiving better customer service because they have people who are knowledgeable there more often to help with issues"; and finally, to observations on the students' reactions, "[The students] like having the IT support right there and have even come in on weekends looking for it."

The librarians were appreciative of change, as the previous reference service with the librarian sitting at the reference desk "limited what I could work on during my reference shift, as I needed to be sitting at the desk." Instead, the new the triage structure "allow[ed them] to work on other projects while still being 'on call' for reference," and has "definitely freed us up for other work." However, the lack of a physical reference desk made two librarians feel rootless, that the lack "essentially [made] the librarians wandering refugees."

In contrast, the AS staff complained about many of the changes. While there was acknowledgment that the change was necessary, "I understand that libraries are changing and that also means that employee responsibilities and jobs are changing," their perception of its impact on their jobs was not favorable, and that they now had more pressure "to handle things

[that] in the past they did not." Additionally, several AS staff members said that they did not have a voice in the transition and the final structure: "The changes are sometimes difficult when the party it involves does not have a say before changes are decided. Not a say to prevent these changes but a say in how to best accommodate these changes." However, the AS staff were happy with the incremental changes. They specifically appreciated the mid-step period of transition "during the transition to the one desk model while reference librarians were still scheduled this was probably the most helpful." The temporary reference specialist (an employee of the Public Services Department with a desk located in the Access Services Department) said, "The best decision in my opinion that was made to accommodate our changing jobs was to hire an additional [temporary] employee who is always on call and willing to help with all questions not just in-depth reference."

The subject of how well the faculty and staff were adapting to this transition received contradictory comments from the survey respondents. One librarian argued that "there will always be resistance from certain people no matter what the situation is," while an AS staff member stated, "Some staff are more adaptable to change than others. I do feel that as a whole they have taken on the change well and really stepped up to the plate." Another AS staff member put forward that the structure, communication, and collaboration of new tiered reference service "should probably be revisited at least once a year. Sometimes things change."

DISCUSSION

Most of the AS staff and reference librarians expressed ambiguous feelings with regards to the change in reference service, none being completely positive or hostile toward the transition. The AS staff tended to acknowledge the need to change and adapt, liking the idea of reference librarians providing flexible backup support at the circulation desk. However, they had great cognitive discontent about the specific implementation of change, were critical of the lack of consistent backup support by the reference librarians, and questioned whether their opinion on the outcome of the new service would be heard. In contrast, some of the reference librarians were emotionally concerned about not having a physical reference desk and the potential ramifications to their job of providing research assistance if they were not immediately visible to students. However, in terms of the actual process of change, the reference librarians, while acknowledging the AS staff members' concerns, were unanimously happy with the reduction of their frontline reference responsibilities.

The AS staff report feeling stressed and worried about a decline in their customer service under the new just-in-time service model, in which library management made the strategic decision that students and faculty would not be unduly burdened by waiting in line. However, the AS staff equated the wait in line as poor customer service. Particularly, AS is unable to efficiently predict and adjust the staffing levels around the variable the ebb and flow of crowds. While the new service structure outlines a clear division of responsibility in terms of question type, some patron questions overlap these divides. Territorial concern over one department "inappropriately" answering questions that belong to another department illustrates an attachment to the old service model (first place of contact answers the question) and to the belief that the old model was the only means of providing quality customer service.

IMPLICATIONS AND CONCLUSION

The use of qualitative research that examines employee perception and reaction can guide the change management of libraries considering similar transformations in their reference services. We argue that if library administrators do not try to learn and acknowledge how their employees respond to the multitude of changes at academic libraries, then they are ill-equipped to address how these responses can impede the transition and the effective management of change in our institutions.

Academic libraries, when undergoing similar transitions in reference services (or even more generally dealing with changes to their service structure), should consider the differences between emotional and cognitive support and resistance to ascertain whether they may be dealing with ambiguous reactions that might require different modes of response. Managers should utilize different communication strategies depending upon whether their employees demonstrate emotional or cognitive resistance. If the resistance is emotional, change management research suggests that informal communication may be more effective in creating an atmosphere for employees to express their negative emotional responses; while in the case of cognitive resistance, change agents may find listening for suggestions on how best to recalibrate the new service is an effective means of communication.

All participants in this study expressed a strong desire to provide a high level of customer service; it was only the means of achieving this customer service that was emotionally and cognitively dissonant. Finally, the mantra that libraries will continue to change should be emphasized; thus, any service change, no matter how radical it may seem to the participants, will in reality continue to be incremental and need recalibration with the subsequent semesters and years.

REFERENCES

Piderit, S. K. (2000). Rethinking resistance and recognizing ambivalence: A multidimensional view of attitudes toward an organizational change. *Academy of Management Review, 25*(4), 783–794.

B | Meet Your Personal Librarian

Martha Adkins, University of San Diego

One of the most important aspects of the reference interview is establishing a relationship between the patron and the librarian. This can be a difficult thing to accomplish with the barriers that often prevent patrons from approaching the reference desk in the first place: anxiety over asking for help, not knowing how or that they can ask for help, and, informed by these and perhaps the strongest barrier of all, resistance to entering the library building.

In order to confront this multifaceted obstacle in the development of the relationship between librarian and student, Copley Library at the University of San Diego (USD) instituted a Personal Librarian program in the fall 2013 semester. Each incoming student was assigned to a librarian, that student's Personal Librarian.

OVERVIEW AND VISION

Program design included reaching out to students before they arrived on campus, then periodically throughout the academic year, allowing students control over how and when they made contact with the library. Short-term goals for the program are numerous: provide one more way to welcome new students to campus; make students feel confident using the library building and services; help students feel comfortable asking for help when they need it; encourage students to explore the library and services on their own terms. The long-term goal of the program is to cultivate a meaningful relationship between students and the library not directly tied to specific assignments or courses, which will result in overall academic success.

The Personal Librarian program at USD was envisioned as a complement to the traditional subject liaison librarian and staffed reference desk models currently employed. The administration of these service models invariably is tied to physical service points, which do not foster an ongoing relationship of help-seeking: desk and virtual reference services are tied to drop-in traffic, usually at a reference desk; individual consultations are tied to the office, where librarians are often asked to meet urgent research help needs; and instruction is tied to the classroom, inside and outside the library, which anchors the information imparted to a specific assignment or class. These models are fixed in nature, and therefore make certain assumptions about student behavior. Classroom instruction assumes that information reaches the student at precisely the right moment in the research process, and that the skills related in the session will be integrated beyond this setting into future research endeavors. Another assumption is that students know when and where to ask for help and that they are confident enough to do so. These models do not take into account the wide disparity in research confidence incoming students possess, nor do they make any concessions toward anxiety or unwillingness to approach the library building or the people who work there (Martin & Park, 2010; Mellon, 1986).

The Personal Librarian program, then, was envisioned as a way to address some of the potential shortcomings in currently employed service models. Direct communication from a librarian to a student might reinforce classroom instruction or, the converse, classroom instruction might reinforce an idea introduced previously in a message from a librarian. On a more fundamental level, students would be made aware early on in their academic careers, and would be reminded regularly, that the library is a welcoming place where they might seek assistance. The personal nature of the communication between librarian and student would help build a comfort level with the library that might have taken much longer to develop, if it developed at all.

Essentially, we hoped that reaching out to students on a personal level would foster a service relationship, an added layer to the series of interactions at service points each student is also likely to experience. The importance and quality of the interactions at those service points do not diminish, but are augmented by this relationship. It bears repeating that the Personal Librarian model as envisioned and employed at USD is not meant to supersede other models or modes of outreach to students, but to be complementary. It is meant to add value to students' experiences with the library in the long run.

RESEARCH

The Personal Librarian program at Copley Library was inspired by and modeled on the Personal Librarian program for undergraduates at Yale University, which was modeled on the program at Yale's Cushing/Whitney Medical Library (E. Horning, personal communication, November 9, 2012). Research for our own Personal Librarian program included a broad survey of similar programs at academic institutions nationwide, as well as an interview with the facilitator of the program for undergraduates at Yale. Common practices observed in this research included the importance of personalized communication, the careful consideration of the content and timing of the communication, and an emphasis on not adding burden to librarians' workloads (Spak & Glover, 2007; Vine, Yang, & Appleby, 2014; E. Horning, personal communication, November 9, 2012).

Research into other institutions offering this type of programming revealed an incredible variety in the sizes of the institutions and the number of students served. In the limited sample, school sizes varied from less than 2,000 students to well over 50,000. Most libraries offer the program to first-year or freshmen students only, either as a whole or in limited groups, such as students in an honors program or international students. Other variants encountered in this research include Personal Librarian programs for faculty only; the "Personal Librarian" label attached to the traditional subject liaison model; and the label attached to librarians embedded in the classroom or involved in outreach in a digital learning environment. The research referred to here did not include the innumerable possible variants on titles of programs of this nature.

Despite the variants in Personal Librarians encountered in benchmarking scan, the scalability of this type of programming was immediately apparent. That Personal Librarian programs have been scaled up and down to meet the needs of these different student population sizes encouraged librarians at Copley Library to move forward with the implementation of the program on our campus.

PLANNING

In our first academic year implementing the Personal Librarian program, we chose to reach out to all of the approximately 1,500 new students. This number includes incoming freshmen as well as new transfer students. Each of the 15 full-time librarians participated in the program, including librarians from all departments of the library, not only reference librarians. In our initial estimation, this would give each librarian a group of approximately 100 students.

Librarians at Copley Library were able to fit the Personal Librarian program into the existing first-year experience programming on campus, namely the Preceptorial program and the Living Learning Communities (LLC) residential program. Initiated in 1973, the Preceptorial program combines the idea of a freshman seminar course with academic advising (i.e., Preceptorial instructors act as students' advisors until they declare their majors). Preceptorial courses are offered to both incoming freshmen and new transfer students. The LLC program is a more recent initiative, begun in the 2011–2012 academic year, with the goal of accommodating all first-year students by 2014. In this residential program, students who share common academic interests live and study together. The nine LLCs each have a theme and associated Preceptorial classes. In its current iteration, this program only includes incoming freshmen; transfer students, while they are assigned to Preceptorial courses, are not assigned to LLCs.

We were able to overlay our Personal Librarian program onto this existing division of incoming freshmen into nine groups of 120–180 each, with the addition of approximately 350 transfer students. The transfer student group was divided into three, and in the final allotment, we ended up with 15 groups of 75–150 students.

IMPLEMENTATION

Before the semester began, we mailed a personalized letter to each student, introducing the Personal Librarian program and the student's Personal Librarian. Letters were printed on library letterhead and signed by the coordinator of the program. We hoped that the personal touch would make an impression on students as well as their parents. In addition to briefly describing the program and introducing the librarians, the letters also invited students to the library's "New Student Bash: Carnival at the Library," a party held on the lawn outside the library at the end of the first week of classes. We also sent students a formal invitation to this event through campus mail. Library staff and faculty volunteered at the event to offer students cupcakes, lemonade, homemade carnival games, and a game-based tour of the library and library resources. Over a two-hour period, the party saw approximately 150 attendees.

Over the course of the academic year, the coordinator of the program provided the Personal Librarians with email distribution lists and email templates to share with their groups of students. This periodic communication generally promoted upcoming events or workshops in the library. We wanted to remind students of Personal Librarian contact information and availability, as well as any important deadlines. We tried to emphasize all the ways to get in touch with the library, including virtual reference services, social media, and self-guided tours.

RESULTS TO DATE

After one semester, Personal Librarians reported a range of student response numbers, from 0 to 10. The majority of Personal Librarians reported response numbers in the 3 to 6 range. The content of student-initiated communication included inquiries about jobs in the library, workshop offerings, library hours, printing services, introductions and questions about the program, and a handful of research questions, which were answered preliminarily and then forwarded to subject specialist librarians for follow-up, if necessary.

The response numbers are certainly lower than those reported by other institutions, which tend to be in the 10–30% range (Spak & Glover, 2007; Vine, Yang, & Appleby, 2014; E. Horning, personal communication, November 9, 2012). Other possible measures of the success of the program, such as gate count or reference transaction numbers, are not telling. These numbers remained mostly static in a comparison to the fall 2012 and fall 2013 semesters. One measure that may indicate the success of both the Personal Librarian program and Copley Library's growing student workshop program, and the mutual benefit of simultaneous and complementary programming, is the increase in both preregistration and attendance for workshops. Attendance numbers were up 125% in the fall 2013 semester relative to the fall 2012 semester. Preregistration numbers received an astonishing increase from 44 in the fall 2012 semester to over 222 in the fall 2013 semester. Marketing efforts for the workshop program were identical each semester; the only discernable difference was the Personal Librarian program. Most of the registrants were freshmen who would have received regular email communication from Personal Librarians.

GOING FORWARD

At the time of this writing, we are preparing for the second year of the Personal Librarian program. Participating librarians met late in the second semester of the first year to share ideas about how to proceed in this next academic year. This type of anecdotal assessment has been ongoing since implementation, and our notes will inform the next iteration of the program. Formal assessment will be implemented in this second year, integrated into assessment administered to all first-year students in November and in February. Using this existing infrastructure for the assessment component of the program further links the Personal Librarian program to the overall first-year experience for students at USD.

Looking forward, we will develop more definitive metrics for success. The initial vision for the Personal Librarian program came from an effort to increase the efficacy of reference services and thereby impact student academic success. In planning and implementing the program, we realized that the impact would be more far-reaching, and that our efforts might contribute to student retention and an overall feeling of satisfaction with the USD experience.

A final analysis of the strengths, weaknesses, opportunities, and threats of the program reveals more strengths and opportunities than weaknesses or threats. Because this is an innovative program, we see a weak spot in the lack of formal, independent assessment, and a lack of concrete metrics for success. Our goal in this regard will be to determine those metrics over the next several years. We may see threats in a lack of awareness of the program by the discipline faculty of the university, which may lead to a lack of support, albeit inadvertent, by the faculty. Another threat, though this is also an opportunity, is a gap in campus-wide programming for transfer students. The programming available for transfer students is not on par with that for incoming freshmen, in terms of offerings and level of organization, which makes this group more difficult to reach. The Personal Librarian program is in a unique position to assist in correcting this gap.

Another opportunity for the Personal Librarian program lies in broader residential life programming at USD. The associated offices will likely play a great role in helping us promote the Personal Librarian program, especially as we are able to cultivate relationships with student groups. Additionally, the implementation of an on-campus housing requirement for first- and second-year students will strengthen the reach of the Personal Librarian program to students beyond the freshman year.

The strengths of the Personal Librarian are what inspired the program in the first place and what encourage us to take on another academic year. In addition to the positive outcomes we foresee for the students, providing a venue for consistent and personalized outreach to students about the library and its services, we see this program as presenting wonderful opportunity for growth for the participating librarians. If we argue that it is wholly beneficial for students to interact with librarians within and outside the library walls, then we can also argue the converse, that it is beneficial for librarians to interact with students outside of traditional channels. In addition, we have discovered that the Personal Librarian program presents multiple opportunities for librarians to collaborate with faculty and staff from areas of campus they might not otherwise have a chance to encounter.

CONCLUSION

The first semester of the Personal Librarian program has revealed a great number of possibilities for the librarians of Copley Library. Librarians outside the reference department have been given an opportunity to interact with students in a way not normally afforded to them. All librarians are able to cultivate relationships with students, faculty, and staff beyond the confines of the library. We now have a three-pronged service model: information literacy instruction in the classroom or library as arranged between discipline faculty and liaison librarians, point-of-need instruction and assistance at the reference desk, and contact between students and librarians outside of the library, outside of the classroom. The three complement one another, with connections outside the library fostering and strengthening connections inside the library.

On a deeper level, we have learned that taking risks in outreach and reference services can benefit the whole institution. We have embraced the unknown, embarked on a program without a clear plan for assessment, recognizing that only in the long term will we be able to fully measure our success. The overwhelming support from administration and our colleagues encourages us to take on another academic year, keeping our ultimate goal of student success in mind.

REFERENCES

Martin, P. N., & Park, L. (2010). Reference desk consultation: An exploratory study of students' perceptions of reference service. *Reference & User Services Quarterly, 49*(4), 333–340. http://dx.doi.org/10.5860/rusq.49n4.333

Mellon, C. A. (1986). Library anxiety: A grounded theory and its development. *College and Research Libraries, 47*, 160–165. http://dx.doi.org/10.5860/crl_47_02_160

Spak, J. M., & Glover, J. G. (2007). The Personal Librarian Program: An evaluation of a Cushing/Whitney Medical Library outreach initiative. *Medical Reference Services Quarterly, 26*(4), 15–25. http://dx.doi.org/10.1300/J115v26n04_02

Vine, R., Yang, K. Z. J., & Appleby, J. W. (2014). Keeping it personal: Supporting collaboration, assessment & efficiency in a large Personal Librarian pilot. [2014 Ontario Library Association Super Conference Presentation.] Retrieved from https://personal.library.utoronto.ca/uploads/PersonalLibrarian-OLA-2014.pdf

Roving Reference

*Madeline Cohen and Kevin Saw, Lehman College,
City University of New York*

Over the past decade, academic libraries have experimented with new forms of providing reference services that augment and enhance services at reference desks. Roving reference is one such variation. As the name implies, the intention is to extend reference beyond a fixed place in the library to meet students at their point of need. In addition, by moving around the library building, or to locations outside it, the library itself becomes more than a place. It becomes a connection to learning, which is available where students are working and socializing.

This study will describe the rationale, implementation, and assessment of a new roving reference service inaugurated under a fall 2013 Innovative Internship awarded to Lehman College Leonard Lief Library and Kevin Saw by Metropolitan New York Library Council (METRO). The conclusions drawn from this project on the value of roving reference at Lehman College will offer recommendations that can be applied to academic libraries with comparable challenges in reinvigorating and enhancing their reference service.

BACKGROUND

The Leonard Lief Library serves Lehman College, a senior college in the City University of New York (CUNY) system. Located in the Bronx, one of the most economically challenged counties in New York State, Lehman College offers an exceptionally diverse student body, including a large Hispanic and African American population. Many Lehman students are first-generation college students, and many are nonnative English speakers.

With a mix of undergraduate and graduate programs available at Lehman College, the Leonard Lief Library serves over 10,000 undergraduate students, graduate students, and faculty and staff. The library building contains four floors, with the reference desk located on the first floor. The reference philosophy guiding all interactions is that reference is most valuable as a teaching opportunity. All reference queries, including the so-called simple questions, such as looking up books in the library catalog, are handled with instruction rather than delivering answers alone.

Given the growth of Lehman's student body, and the need for instruction in more complex information technology and information resources, it was resolved that reference assistance was needed beyond the reference desk. Chat reference was started at the library in 2011 and has been popular. The reference desk interacts with over 100 students per day, according to recent usage statistics. However, on a typical day, over 3,000 students enter the library to use resources, study spaces, and equipment.

In order to reach out to many students who use the library but are not in contact with the reference desk, the roving reference program was launched in the fall 2013 semester. Its goal was to gather quantitative and qualitative data on the often unspoken needs of the library's student population, and to assess student receptivity to offers of reference help from a roving librarian.

LITERATURE REVIEW

Most of the articles reviewed on roving reference view it in a positive light, with many articles noting benefits of having such a program. Cassell (2010) informs readers that a number of library users do not avail themselves of the reference desk because "not all users are comfortable approaching the reference desk" (p. 6). Penner (2011) adds that a roving program would benefit students who might be reluctant to leave library seating or computers to travel to the reference desk, particularly if it is located on another floor of the library. Gadsby and Qian (2012) view roving reference as an outstanding outreach and marketing tool, which helps raise awareness of available library services. Nunn and Ruane (2012) contend that personalized reference services, such as roving reference, can "have a positive impact on the library image with the user community, and will help users associate a particular trustworthy person—and a successful reference interaction—with the library, transforming it from an intimidating building with a constantly rotating desk staff to a welcoming environment" (p. 578).

METHODOLOGY

There is more than one approach to providing this service. Between different roving reference programs, there can be variations in the type of equipment used by roving librarians, marketing, staffing models, service locations, and number of hours per week. Of course, logistical decisions must be based on local needs and resources. At Lehman, roving librarians were equipped with iPads. The iPad was chosen for its portability, ample screen size, and the fact that it can be used to answer more complex research questions such as database searching. Roving librarians were also equipped with two cloth armbands to make them more easily identifiable to patrons. These armbands made clear that the individual wearing them was a librarian and available to help. One armband had "Ask Me" embroidered on it. The other said "Librarian."

The service was promoted through social media on the library's Facebook and Twitter pages. It was also marketed by posters placed throughout the library building. A large, prominent poster was placed near the circulation desk, located near the entrance. In addition to posters, small advertisement cards were made available for users to take with them. A text-a-librarian service was established, giving students the option to summon a roving librarian to their location during hours of the roving service. For the text service, a Google Voice app was installed on the iPad, alerting the roving librarian whenever a student sent a text. The number was advertised on the posters, and advertisement cards were handed out after each interaction.

DATA COLLECTION

Data was collected throughout the fall 2013 semester in order to assess the service. Two separate surveys were created using Google Docs: a librarian survey form and patron survey form. The librarian survey form was uploaded as a webpage, so it could easily be accessed and filled out using the iPad after each interaction. Patron surveys were distributed as print forms, and users were given the choice to fill it out.

The librarian survey was used to collect usage data. Information collected by the librarian survey included: total number of transactions; how the roving interaction was initiated (by librarian, patron, or by patron using the option to text a librarian); type of question with which the librarian assisted. Type of question had three categories: reference questions; technical questions; directional, policy, and other questions. Duration of the interaction was measured by indicating whether it was longer than ten minutes.

There were also subcategories for reference questions, allowing librarians to record types of questions more precisely. At the end of the survey, an open comment box was available for inputting qualitative data, such as comments on the degree of success in showing patrons how to use various resources in the library, particularly electronic databases.

The primary purpose of the patron survey was to obtain qualitative data to gauge patron opinion on roving reference service as a new service, and to determine whether individuals were satisfied with the quality of service they received. Students were asked their opinion of having a librarian available on the floor where they were working. Second, they were asked what they learned from the librarian that day. Included in this survey were two open-ended questions: What did you like about having the librarian help you today? What did you dislike about working with the librarian today? Filling out the forms was voluntary and students' names were optional. The roving librarian encouraged students to register their opinions, so the library could develop this service in a way that would benefit students most.

FINDINGS

During the fall 2013 semester, there were a total of 257 roving reference interactions. There were an average of approximately 11.7 transactions per day; an average of 4.7 interactions for every hour spent roving. Nearly 60% of these interactions were librarian-initiated, underscoring the importance of roving librarians proactively seeking patrons who may need help and offering it.

Table 1. How was the interaction initiated?

How was the interaction initiated?	Percentage
Librarian initiated	58%
Patron initiated	41.2%
Text message	.8%

Very few patrons took advantage of the text-a-librarian service. One possible reason for this might have been that texting was available only during hours when the librarian was roving, which made it difficult to advertise. The more likely reason for minimal use of texting is that it would require the student to take the initiative to call a librarian for help. Students may believe they are supposed to figure out how to use library resources by themselves and are reluctant to have attention focused on what they do not know.

Reference transactions accounted for about 37.3% of total transactions. Technical help transactions also accounted for 39%. Directional, policy, and general questions comprised the remaining 23.7%.

Table 2. Type of interaction.

Type of interaction	Percentage
Reference	37.3%
Technical	39%
Directional, policy, or other questions	23.7%

Most technical interactions (59%) were help with printing, copying, or scanning issues. The majority of reference interactions were either "Help with finding books" (41.7%) or "Research help" (40.6%).

Table 3. Type of reference interaction.

Type of reference interaction	Percentage
Find book(s) in catalog or shelf	41.7%
Research: Library, website, databases, e-books, e-journals, etc.	40.6%
Web research	1%
Citation format	11.5%
Other reference questions	5.2%

Most of the "Help with finding books" interactions were not straightforward, and they involved much more than simply assisting patrons retrieve books from the shelf. A number of patrons were looking for reserve or reference materials in the stacks. These students were shown where the reserve and reference collections are located, and how to identify these in the catalog. Students also were looking for items that were already checked out.

Of course, some patrons were not entirely certain how to read Library of Congress call numbers. In accordance with our reference philosophy, these transactions were handled with instruction rather than delivering answers.

Roving librarians had a great opportunity to provide research support once they connected with students. Most research interactions were lengthy, usually lasting anywhere from 20 minutes to one hour. Such encounters allowed roving librarians to provide personalized information literacy and research consultations to guide students through searching subject databases, retrieving articles from e-journals, citation formats, and downloading and printing articles. The roving librarian familiarized students with new library resources and brought them to a point where they could continue productively on their own.

The student survey forms had a low return rate (mainly due to limited time), but all patrons who did return the survey indicated they liked the roving reference program and were satisfied with the help they received. Comments included praise for the roving librarian's patience and willingness to teach searching and citation skills. One student wrote that because of roving reference he would be coming to the library much more often. Another student was amazed and pleased that the roving librarian walked with him from the first floor to the third floor to locate a book. Sample comments on the roving librarian's service were: "awesome," "tremendously helpful," "made a significant effort," "went step by step," "very helpful." Among the tasks and concepts students listed as having learned: narrowing searches, using databases they did not know before, citation format, and different ways of locating books and articles. One of the most insightful and gratifying comments revealed that the librarian demonstrated that finding academic journal articles was not as difficult as the student previously thought.

ASSESSMENT

Roving reference brought innovation to our reference services and proved to be a great tool for library outreach. This program enabled the library to raise awareness of many resources and services. For example, roving librarians were able to promote the reference desk, research guides, 24/7 chat service, mobile website, consultation services, and more. Opportunities to promote e-books, interlibrary loan, iPad and e-reader loans, and the mobile library catalog arose as librarians helped students find books.

Having a roving reference program also allowed the library to extend reference services to all four floors of the building. For libraries with multiple floors, roving reference is an effective means of reaching students on floors without established reference desks. Rather than maintaining multiple reference desks, mobile technology and scheduled roving provide a more flexible option that could furnish the same or better results as setting up satellite reference desks.

Roving reference was especially useful on crowded days. Many patrons are reluctant to leave their desks or computer stations to ask for help for fear of losing their spot, especially if they have to go to another floor for assistance. When a roving librarian is available, patrons in a busy library are no longer forced to choose between losing their spot or foregoing help.

Finally, having a roving reference program allowed librarians at Lehman to better connect to library patrons. When patrons receive personalized service, the librarian who helped them is no longer just a nameless figure behind the reference desk. Roving librarians will have time to introduce themselves and share some of their experiences teaching students to use databases or other library resources. Above all, if the encounter is friendly and nonthreatening, students will remember the individual librarian and be more likely to seek out that person another time. Hopefully, a positive experience with one librarian will lead to forming a good impression of all librarians being friendly, approachable, and knowing how to help students succeed in their research.

RECOMMENDATIONS

There is more to providing roving reference services than having librarians walk around the library with their choice of equipment. There are subtleties that make this service work well. When developing a roving reference program, try to adopt these procedures from the outset: 1) roving librarians should be easily identifiable to patrons; 2) roving librarians should actively seek out patrons that need help and not simply wait to be called over; and 3) roving librarians should take the opportunity to offer further assistance beyond the initial question.

It is crucial that roving librarians wear or equip themselves with something that identifies they are available to help. If a patron is unaware of the roving reference service, they will not use it. Clothing or armbands with embroidered or printed text are a good way to make roving librarians more easily identifiable. If using a cart, it can be decorated to brand its function.

Take the initiative to try to engage with patrons. Do not simply wait for patrons to call you over. One primary goals of roving reference is to engage patrons intimidated by, or who are too introverted, to approach the reference desk. The roving librarian must demonstrate a welcoming, open spirit that encourages interaction.

Above all, roving librarians should operate under the notion that users usually need more help than initially perceived. Analyze the situation and determine whether you can go further. A patron looking for books might be seeking information for a research paper or project, and would most likely appreciate an offer for research help.

CONCLUSIONS

At Lehman, the traditional reference desk will remain a visible and constant access point. Due to positive results of the first semester of roving reference, this service will be extended and refined. The value of this service to individual students makes it important to offer it, even for a limited number of hours. At the Lehman Library, only a few librarians have time to rove. Therefore, the service will be staffed on two busy days for approximately five hours per week. More promotion will be accomplished by more eye-catching posters and through social media. Maintaining the service on a regular basis is your best calling card. Satisfied students spread the word about the roving librarian to their friends.

Roving reference presents an opportunity to extend reference to all corners of the library and enhance reference as a more personal and interactive service. The very fact a librarian will walk around seeking out patrons speaks volumes about the outreach service. Roving reference is a vital part of a paradigm shift in academic libraries as learning centers, where learning takes place through connections with individual librarians, as well as with resources and technology. The future of reference is in becoming more personal and interactive. Roving reference takes libraries farther along this path.

REFERENCES

Cassell, K. A. (2010, May 10). From the reference desk to Twitter: Meeting our users on their Terms. [Meeting Presentation.] Retrieved from http://sla-princeton-trenton .pbworks.com/f/Meeting_Users'_Needs_Through_New_Reference_Service.ppt

Gadsby, J., & Qian, S. (2012). Using an iPad to redefine roving reference service in an academic library. *Library Hi Tech News, 29*(4), 1–5. http://dx.doi.org/10.1108/07419051211249446

Nunn, B., & Ruane, E. (2012). Marketing gets personal: Promoting reference staff to reach users. *Journal of Library Administration, 52*(6/7), 571–580. http://dx.doi.org/10.1080/01930826.2012.707955

Penner, K. (2011). Mobile technologies and roving reference. *Public Services Quarterly, 7*(1–2), 27–33. http://dx.doi.org/10.1080/15228959.2011.572775

D | On-Call Reference

Krista Schmidt, Western Carolina University

The way that physical reference service points have been staffed has been changing for libraries of all sizes and missions for many years. These changes —motivated by trends, budgets, and new efficiencies—include hours staffed, who staffs the desk, location of the desk, and so forth. This case study describes how a midsized academic library successfully implemented a technological solution to solve a physical staffing problem without sacrificing the fundamental mission of the department: providing timely assistance by professional librarians.

BACKGROUND AND HISTORY

Hunter Library is the sole library at Western Carolina University (WCU), located in Cullowhee, North Carolina. WCU is one of the 17 institutions of the University of North Carolina system. It is a regional comprehensive university that has increased 40% in size over the past 10 years. To meet the needs of a growing university population, the library has evolved in those 10 years, making changes and additions to resources, services, and public spaces. One major change began in the early 2000s, when the library began employing the liaison model for all new hires in the reference department. Liaisons would be responsible for broad disciplinary areas including the sciences, fine and performing arts, and education. Though reference librarians had subject responsibilities for many years, the shift to focus more on subject specificity was in part to foster stronger ties with departments and programs across campus. As more librarian-liaisons were hired, liaison responsibilities outside of staffing general reference service points and collection development increased. Librarian-liaisons were also providing more subject-specific information literacy sessions as their relationships with departments developed. These growing commitments began to put pressure on librarians' schedules. Though the reference department grew after the liaison model was implemented, peaking at nine librarians in the fall of 2007, by 2011, the department had lost one position permanently and was relying heavily on help from faculty and staff in other departments to run reference service points.

In response to these pressures, the reference (now Research and Instruction Services) department convened a Shared Reference Schedule Task Force in the spring of 2011. The task force was charged with reexamining the current staffing model of all reference services. While staffing of all service points was under discussion, the most visible service point—the reference desk—came under particular scrutiny. Desk hours occupied a very large part of all Research and Instruction Services (RIS) librarians' committed time.

Historically, Hunter Library reference librarians spent a lot of time at the reference desk, even with the assistance of nonreference librarians, staff, and temporary employees. The department had always been committed to providing excellent customer service; to accomplish that, two librarians staffed the reference desk during the busiest hours. Data presented to the task force detailed how much time was committed to double coverage over the past 20 years. Double coverage began in 1990 with just 12 hours total Monday through Thursday, not including evenings, which were also double staffed from 6 p.m. to 10 p.m. By 2011, double coverage in the evenings had ended but daytime double coverage expanded to 30 hours a week Monday through Friday. After examining these trends, discussing the department's workload, and committing to maintaining responsive reference services, the task force made several recommendations for scheduling and staffing changes.

TEMPORARY FIXES AND MAJOR CHANGES

The first changes the task force made were to the schedule. In addition to Monday through Friday reference service responsibilities, RIS librarians also worked Saturdays and Sundays, averaging four weekend days per semester. Weekend work created scheduling difficulties on Fridays when librarians who had worked a preceding weekend day were out of the office, leaving the department short two librarians every Friday. The task force studied past service point statistics and then proposed reducing hours during the least busy times of nights and weekends, as well as for breaks. This was approved and put into place for the fall of 2011.

The double coverage versus single staffing conundrum remained. The department had already tried using "shadowing" as a replacement for double coverage in the summer and early fall of 2010. Shadowing required only one person to be at the desk, while the second person, or "shadow," would work in an office behind the desk and come out to the desk when a queue formed. After a few short months, it became apparent that this was not working since shadowing still required committed time from two librarians. Shadowing was abandoned completely when the department was able to hire a fixed-term, full-time librarian. Double coverage was reinstated but at a lower level, only seven hours per week. The task force continued to search for solutions; one member polled listserv members for ideas. Her question was, "Our reference department is exploring ways to provide backup at the reference desk when the desk is single staffed. At our library the offices are scattered, and it is not possible to see when the person at the desk needs help. We are curious: how does your library provide backup for librarians at the reference desk?" The answers ranged from using wireless doorbells to instant messaging (IM) to using tiered/triage reference.

The task force debated the feasibility of these ideas. Members thought that the long-term potential for these solutions meshing well with our customer service philosophy was unsatisfactory. Some would not work well given the distance of some offices from the desk; others, such as tiered reference, were incompatible with our reference philosophy. The task force and department ultimately agreed that we would use both phone and IM for requesting backup help during single coverage, a continuation of previous practice. This was still not optimal, as an on-duty librarian might still be forced to leave a queue waiting for help should no one be available via phone or IM. Also, those librarians with offices right behind the reference desk shouldered more requests for assistance simply due to their proximity, prompting some complaints about equitability of responsibility.

FROM IDEA TO SOLUTION

As the fall semester progressed, the task force discussed finding a better alternative to the blind-phoning of offices or sending a broadcast call using IM for help. No workable hardware solution seemed to present itself, and the software solutions that the task force had already considered were unsatisfactory. The task force, however, had not considered the growing world of tablet applications (apps) to solve the backup problem.

Work productivity apps designed for individuals have been popular for years and provide a breadth of solutions, so it made sense to investigate existing productivity apps for a solution for a group. Based on both task force and departmental discussions, the successful app would need to be technologically simple, easy for patrons and busy librarians to use, and send clear notifications to both those needing help and those responding to help. After several fruitless attempts to locate such an app, it was decided to approach the library's systems unit to see if they would help develop an application in-house. After several brainstorming sessions, requirements were refined and the technology was agreed upon. The development process was quite iterative, as several initial ideas did not function as desired or could not be made to work. But by the following spring, the final product was ready for pilot testing at the desk.

The "Call Button," an Android-based app, runs on a tablet that is mounted in a locked kiosk at the reference desk. The app's appearance is that of a large, white round button on a black background, with the words "Press for Assistance" centered in large lettering on the button. Once pushed, the app sends a message to a specially designated queue of the existing virtual reference platform. When the call is received in the queue, all logged-in users are notified that help is needed at the reference desk. The librarian who responds simply types in her name and the app sends the patron an automatic message (e.g., "Krista is on her way") that displays on the tablet screen. At the same time the patron message is generated, all logged-in librarians are notified that the call for help has been answered and by whom.

THE PILOT PROJECT AND FULL INTEGRATION

In mid-spring of 2012, the Call Button testing began. The pilot project called for the tablet—with the app running on the desktop—to be kept behind the desk for "call-a-colleague" use, for example, when the on-duty librarian needed backup help. During that time, the app was debugged, the look and feel were refined, and several workflow procedures were clarified. For the pilot phase, RIS department members agreed that the Call Button would be used from 8 a.m. to 5 p.m.; there were no evening hours since physical backup was unavailable after standard business hours. Existing departmental policy already requested that all available librarians monitor virtual reference, which meant that since the app was seamlessly integrated into that platform, any logged-in librarian was also automatically monitoring the Call Button queue. During the pilot, the Call Button was used sparingly, with only 15 uses recorded, and some of those were for testing or troubleshooting. It was possible that this low number was due to physical location—it was not yet mounted in the kiosk, so it sat either in a drawer or on a shelf behind the desk—and/or the low need for reference services at the very end of the semester.

After this five-week pilot, the locking kiosk was mounted and the Call Button was ready for "just-in-time" testing. Just-in-time reference—providing service at the desk when a need arises—was in contrast to traditional "just-in-case" reference during WCU's May minimester (a 12-day short semester where classes meet for eight hours a day and the library is typically deserted). Just-in-case reference required a reference member to be at the desk and staff all three service points (desk, phone, virtual reference) for several hours regardless of patron activity. Just-in-time reference service still required librarians to be assigned to desk shifts; however, staffing it was done by forwarding the phone to the on-duty librarian's office and using the virtual reference platform to respond to online questions and any in-person patrons who used the Call Button. At a shift change, the oncoming librarian came to the desk and performed a visual scan of the area and library activity. If there were no immediate needs, she forwarded the phone to her office where she monitored all three service points.

During this pilot phase, RIS members were not required to switch to just-in-time staffing as some still felt uncomfortable with the app serving as the "face" of the desk. However, many did try just-in-time reference. For those who still preferred to sit at the service point, the app was used for call-a-colleague backup or to call for assistance when they were away from the desk assisting a patron. Statistics indicate that the app had very high use during the minimester, with 28 calls recorded in just four weeks.

At the beginning of summer semester in June 2012, the department put the Call Button app into place permanently. We agreed that during the fall, spring, and summer semesters, we would single staff the desk and use the Call Button from 8 a.m. to 5 p.m. for requesting backup help. During breaks and the minimester, the desk would be single staffed from 8 a.m. to 5 p.m., and librarians had the option of using just-in-time reference, thus could staff the desk from their offices. Procedures for daily setup and takedown of the tablet were also established. The librarian at the reference desk for the first morning shift would get the tablet, start up the app, and secure the device in the kiosk. The librarian working the 5–6 p.m. hour would take the tablet out of the kiosk, lock it up, and set it to charge.

Though the app was fully integrated before the fall semester, there was no external advertising or marketing. The department thought it would be best to wait until after using it for a standard academic semester. This delay necessitated more patron education than intended; some patrons were uncertain if they should push the button or not and would leave without help. There were also a few patrons who, as they made eye contact with a waiting librarian, pressed the button while asking, "What's this?"

MEASURING SUCCESS AND LOOKING FORWARD

From summer 2012 through December 2013, the statistics captured by the virtual reference provider indicated robust use of the Call Button. There were a total of 89 uses of the Call Button from summer 2012 through the fall semester. In 2013, a total of 224 uses of the Call Button were recorded, with usage increasing drastically for the summer of 2013 compared with the summer of 2012 (13 calls in 2012, 54 in 2013). While these numbers are encouraging, there are some flaws in the statistics, including calls never answered, calls canceled, and calls made as part of the troubleshooting process. Troubleshooting calls have decreased since 2012, but it is unlikely statistics for calls never answered or calls canceled will be parsed from the main data. It is also too soon to identify any long-term trends because there is not enough data yet for meaningful interpretation.

The Call Button app has been successful, but that does not mean that all staffing issues are resolved. When using technology to solve this type of problem, human frailties must also be considered. Everyone in the department must remain sensitive to ongoing staffing issues; backup is not backup if no one is around to provide it. Other human-based issues include simple mistakes, like typing more than a name when answering the Call Button queue (which garbles the reply message) to librarians forgetting that the button is for call-a-colleague as well as for just-in-time or backup use. The latter is related to some changes to the physical setup of the kiosk that affects the app's usability. The kiosk is in a fixed position so the tablet faces patrons. When the desk gets busy, it is easy to forget about the app and revert to old habits like running around looking for help or continually asking only front office librarians for help. The next step is to upgrade the kiosk so it will be multidirectional. This will enable both a librarian view when someone is physically at the desk as well as patron view when it is necessary to leave the desk to assist someone or for just-in-time reference service.

The Call Button app has become an indispensable tool, despite some of the flaws of the current physical design. As RIS looks forward to continuing changes to services, this app will also evolve. It is doubtful that the RIS department will ever reinstate double coverage, despite some excellent benefits to both patrons and librarians. Luckily, the Call Button allows RIS to provide the timely, professional reference service that patrons want and for which the department is known across campus.

E | Peer Reference Tutoring

Michelle Twait, Gustavus Adolphus College, Minnesota

BACKGROUND

Located about an hour south of Minneapolis-St. Paul, Gustavus Adolphus College is a private, coeducational, residential liberal arts college. The college enrolls approximately 2,500 FTE students and offers only bachelor's degrees. The library, situated near the heart of campus, serves as both a social center and a popular study space. The library employs six professional librarians, ten support staff, and over 80 student employees, making it the second largest student employer on campus.

INTRODUCTION

Student learning is the compass that directs all of our library's services, and our interactions with students at the reference desk are no exception. Our philosophy of reference is learner-centered. When we discuss questions with students, our goal is to help those individuals build upon their existing strengths and grow as researchers. Instead of providing answers, we seize that opportunity as a teachable moment.

Our approach to staffing reference services has been fairly traditional. Professional librarians are at the reference desk six days a week. In addition to face-to-face consultations at the reference desk and through individual appointments, we offer a chat reference service (monitored by professional librarians). Individual librarians may choose to spend part of their shift providing "roving reference," but it has not been consistently offered in any formal way. Support staff and student employees often assist students with directional questions, but usually refer patrons to the reference desk for research assistance.

Many alternative models for staffing the reference desk focus on graduate students or support staff. The former is not an option for us, as we are an undergraduate institution and the nearest graduate program for library science is an hour away. The latter option is also problematic, since our support staff is small and they have many other responsibilities. In staffing models involving undergraduate students, some libraries have staffed the reference desk with students who are also writing center tutors (Fensom, McCarthy, Rundquist, Sherman, & White, 2006) or asked students to assist students in particular courses (Dawkins & Jackson, 1986). In some cases, peer tutors have provided research assistance through a consultation model (Auer, Seamans, & Pelletier, 2001). Other libraries have employed undergraduate reference assistants when faced with budget cuts, severe time or staffing limitations (Connell & Mileham, 2006; Judd, McLane, & Osborne, 1994), or increasing demand for library services.

Though there are a host of reasons for exploring alternative staffing models for reference service, our library's approach might have remained the same had we not welcomed our first intern. In 2009, we worked with the campus Career Center to establish an internship program for students interested in librarianship. Our goal was (and is) to provide students with a well-rounded introduction to the many areas of specialization within librarianship, to educate them on professional values, and to offer them opportunities to complete projects in their areas of interest. Initially, for the reference component of their internship, our interns merely spent time shadowing at the reference desk. In 2011, we expanded the scope of their involvement and began training our first "peer reference tutors."

What changed? First, while we knew our reference desk was being utilized by students and that they recognized it as a place to receive assistance, we realized that students turned to professors and peers more frequently than librarians when seeking help (Gratz & Gilbert, 2011). In addition, at least part of students' hesitation to approach librarians may be related to familiarity—they do not know us. In implementing the peer reference tutor program, we hoped that our primary users, the students, would appreciate having a fellow undergraduate available for research help. Furthermore, we wanted to provide the peer tutors with an experience that would allow them to gain a better understanding of reference work. In sum, we were motivated by a desire to mentor students and enhance our existing reference services.

SELECTION PROCESS

The first peer reference tutors were chosen from our pool of library interns. We later expanded the opportunity to students who were interested in librarianship, but who did not have time to complete an internship. Depending on whether they were an intern or simply an interested student, the hiring process differed. Interns were selected based on their application, cover letter, and grade point average. Previous library experience was preferred, but not a requirement. Students interested in peer reference, but not interning with the library, had an interview with a librarian prior to the hiring decision. Peer reference tutors are juniors or seniors, and they represent a wide range of majors. Our internships are unpaid, but students can choose to receive academic credit for the experience.

TRAINING

The librarians recognize that we cannot condense our graduate education and years of experience into a few weeks of training. Fortunately, in any given semester, we may only have one to three peer reference tutors. This simplifies the training process and allows us to get to know the students' strengths. One librarian serves as the coordinator of the peer reference program and handles most of the training. However, as all of the librarians interact with the tutors during observation time at the reference desk, the workload is more balanced. In addition, the program coordinator created a shared folder so all of the librarians have access to training materials and peer tutor schedules.

Since students may encounter reference questions that require an understanding of patron or item records, training often begins with some basic instruction on the circulation module of our integrated library system. Next, we ask them to work through practice reference questions. While some libraries utilize worksheets or quizzes (Connell & Mileham, 2006; Neuhaus, 2001), most of our training questions are derived from assignments given in reference courses at various library science graduate programs. We also compile a list of questions received at our reference desk, including questions related to research assignments that we regularly encounter. In addition, tutors spend a few hours each week observing at the reference desk. We feel it is important for tutors to shadow each of the librarians, as we have different approaches to our work and unique research strengths. For example, one librarian may be adept at finding even the most elusive statistics, while another may have keen sense for primary sources. In their observations at the reference desk, tutors are exposed to a variety of tools and strategies while also getting a glimpse into the types of questions we handle.

Peer tutors often focus on their ability to answer research questions, whereas librarians realize that reference work is much more than that. We offer training on the reference interview, proper etiquette at the reference desk, and our teaching in conjunction with the nuts-and-bolts training related to databases and search strategies. We recognize that the tutors' training needs to include discussions of our philosophy of reference and the interpersonal dimensions of reference service. For example, tutors need to be aware that their peers may be reluctant to seek help at the reference desk or may have a low sense of self-efficacy in regard to their research abilities. We tell our peer reference tutors that many students approach the reference desk with a mixture of fear, hope, and anxiety. Students may fear appearing ignorant, hope that they will receive the help they need, and feel overwhelmed by the assignment. We talk with our tutors about what it means to create a welcoming climate at the reference desk by being approachable, putting students at ease, being sensitive to a student's emotional state, and using reflective listening skills. An online guide for tutors contains practice questions, tips related to reference interview techniques, etiquette reminders, and the opening and closing procedures.

SCHEDULING

Peer reference tutors spend the first several weeks of the semester in training. Around midterm, they begin working without a librarian present. The timing is intentional, as it ensures that tutors are well-prepared and also coincides with an increase in reference traffic. Tutors are on duty primarily at night, after the librarian's shift ends (10 p.m. to midnight). This time period was chosen in recognition that students' study schedules often fall outside of our regular reference hours. We also occasionally ask tutors to cover the reference desk during staff meetings. In other words, the schedule for peer reference tutors is intended to extend our normal hours of reference service, during times when we might not otherwise be available.

DURING THE SHIFT

The librarians encourage, but do not require, peer tutors to complete practice questions, explore unfamiliar databases, and watch online tutorials during their shifts. Although some peer tutor programs ask students to work on projects for the library or other tasks in their time at the reference desk, we do not feel this is fair to our unpaid assistants. As librarians often bring their work to the reference desk, we feel it is reasonable to allow the peer reference tutors to work on their homework during their shift.

PEER TUTORS' PERSPECTIVES

At the end of each semester, peer tutors complete a short evaluation of their experience. When asked what they enjoyed most about being a peer reference tutor, students often referred to the times when they felt that they had made a difference. For example, one tutor said, "I greatly enjoyed working directly with patrons and feeling like I was actually able to help them." Another tutor found much satisfaction in being able to assist her peers: "The thing I enjoyed most about being a peer reference tutor was actually being able to answer people's questions! Every time I worked there always seemed to be at least one really flustered person who had saved something for the very last minute, and I liked being able to send them in the right direction." Yet another tutor liked the novelty and variety that reference work provides: "I really enjoyed getting the chance to see what types of assignments other students were getting, as well as the opportunity to familiarize myself with databases and questions that I wouldn't normally encounter."

Reflecting on their training, most tutors were satisfied with their preparation for the program. For instance, one tutor observed, "I especially think it was helpful to shadow the librarians at the desk." A different tutor appreciated the collaboration with staff members: "I definitely felt support from the library staff. They were all incredibly nice and I never felt awkward or uncomfortable asking for help or asking to sit and get experience at the reference desk." One tutor found the deeper conversations beneficial: "It was also helpful to get more of the theoretical aspect of how to address problems—as with the idea of the reference interview." Even the less formal aspects of the training were appreciated: "I felt it was good to simply spend time walking through the reference stacks and getting used to them and where things are and where subjects are located." One peer tutor acknowledged that there was room for additional training: "I think I would have liked to learn a little bit more about online databases and where to point students in regards to those." It is interesting to note that each peer tutor highlighted different aspects of the training process. This underscores the importance of getting to know the individual tutors and tailoring the training to suit their needs.

When asked how we might improve the program, most tutors had no suggestions. However, one peer tutor commented on promoting the program: "I think it would be great to market/promote the additional reference hours to students. It was often a bit slow at the desk between 10 p.m. and 12 a.m. If the service was marketed, it is possible that we would get more questions."

In summary, it is clear to us that peer reference tutors enjoyed their experience and appreciated the opportunity to explore this aspect of librarianship. One tutor explained, "As someone who wants to be a librarian, this was an excellent experience for me. I got to experience how it would be to do an everyday part of a reference librarian's job. It helped me to develop skills that will be very useful in my future at graduate school and as a librarian."

LIBRARIANS' PERSPECTIVES

Our experience with the program has been overwhelmingly positive, a feeling shared by staff at other libraries (Stanfield & Palmer, 2011). As librarians, we know that reference work is one of the most challenging and rewarding parts of our jobs. Yet we rarely take the time to talk about what we do and, more importantly, why we do it. Both librarians and students can benefit from highlighting and discussing our professional values. A peer reference tutor program is a wonderful opportunity to share our enthusiasm for our work with students interested in the profession.

As other authors have pointed out, having these students around creates a "mini-focus group on a daily basis" (Faix et. al., 2010, p. 101). We can ask for feedback on initiatives and get a student's perspective on our services. Even better, in serving as a peer reference tutor, students' opinions are informed by their experience, which gives them a unique insider/outsider view of our work.

Our interactions with the peer tutors were very affirming. All of the students involved in the project were enthusiastic and highly motivated. Each had a strong public service orientation and sincere desire to perform well. There was only one instance where a tutor's interpersonal skills needed improvement. In that case, the librarians approached that situation as a teaching opportunity. We offered more shadowing at the reference desk and met with the student on several occasions to discuss how best to handle certain situations and reference questions.

Other issues encountered had very little to do with the tutors themselves. For example, librarians expressed some concern that patrons would see a peer reference tutor with a librarian at the reference desk and assume that we were busy. We did our best to ensure that both persons were seated behind the desk (rather than to the side), and a sign near the tutor indicated that s/he was a peer assistant. Additionally, as one of our peer tutors pointed out, we need to improve our marketing of reference services, since students may be reluctant to approach the reference desk or unsure as to how librarians can help them. However, this is true for our reference services in general, not just an issue for our peer reference tutoring program.

Our library plans to continue the peer reference tutor program, and we expect that it will evolve over time. In addition to promoting the service more, the librarians hope to incorporate role-playing into students' training, especially during those semesters when we have more than one peer tutor (see Sheets, 1998, for more on this subject). Also, we would like to invite tutors to join the librarians in a monthly journal club where we could discuss articles related to reference services.

CONCLUSION

While there has been debate among librarians regarding the value of non-professionals in reference services, this was not our primary concern. Instead, we asked how we could create a mutually beneficial learning experience in an environment that would foster mentoring. In giving undergraduate students a chance to interact with patrons at a reference desk, we are not only providing them with a better understanding of reference work, but also of the profession as a whole.

REFERENCES

Auer, N. J., Seamans, N. H., & Pelletier, L. (2001). Peer advising in the research process: A year of student success. In J. Nims & E. Owens (Eds.), *Managing library instruction programs in academic libraries: Papers and session materials presented at the twenty-ninth National LOEX Library Instruction Conference* (pp. 25–30). Ann Arbor, MI: Pierian Press.

Connell, R. S., & Mileham, P. J. (2006). Student assistant training in a small academic library. *Public Services Quarterly, 2*(2/3), 69–84. http://dx.doi.org/10.1300/J295v02n02_06

Dawkins, W. M., & Jackson, J. (1986). Enhancing reference services: Students as assistants. *Technicalities, 6,* 4–7.

Faix, A., Bates, M., Hartman, L., Hughes, J., Schacher, C., Elliot, B., & Woods, A. (2010). Peer reference redefined: New uses for undergraduate students. *Reference Services Review, 38*(1), 90–107.

Fensom, G., McCarthy, R., Rundquist, K., Sherman, D., & White, C. B. (2006). Navigating research waters: The research mentor program at the University of New Hampshire at Manchester. *College & Undergraduate Libraries, 13*(2), 49–74. http://dx.doi.org/10.1300/J106v13n02_05

Gratz, A., & Gilbert, J. (2011). Meeting student needs at the reference desk. *Reference Services Review, 39*(3), 423–438. http://dx.doi.org/10.1108/00907321111161412

Judd, B. E., McLane, M. J., & Osborne, N. S. (1994). Valuing diversity: Students helping students. *Reference Librarian, 21*(45/46), 93–110. http://dx.doi.org/10.1300/J120v21n45_11

Neuhaus, C. (2001). Flexibility and feedback: A new approach to ongoing training for reference student assistants. *Reference Services Review, 29*(1), 53–64. http://dx.doi.org/10.1108/00907320110366813

Sheets, J. (1998). Role-playing as a training tool for reference student assistants. *Reference Services Review, 26*(1), 37–42. http://dx.doi.org/10.1108/00907329810307425

Stanfield, A., & Palmer, R. (2011). Peer-ing into the information commons: Making the most of student assistants in new library spaces. *Reference Services Review, 38*(4), 634–646. http://dx.doi.org/10.1108/00907321011090773

F | A Single Service Point

Diane Hunter and Mary E. Anderson,
University of Missouri-Kansas City

INTRODUCTION

After decades of staffing separate service desks for reference and circulation services, a renovation of the Miller Nichols Library at the University of Missouri-Kansas City in February 2011 provided the opportunity to combine multiple facets of patron assistance at a single service point. Careful design of the physical desk and cross-training of staff led to improved service to library users and more efficient use of library personnel.

HISTORY

The Miller Nichols Library always had separate service desks for reference assistance and for circulation services. The circulation desk, staffed mainly by student assistants with staff available for backup, handled directional questions, traditional circulation, interlibrary loan, and reserve functions. Circulation staff were trained to direct all reference questions to the reference desk some 30 yards away in an adjacent room. Although dedicated to providing high-quality service, staff in both departments frequently found themselves making incorrect referrals to the other desk. Reasons for incorrect referrals included misunderstanding the patron's need, questions that morphed into new questions, or patrons who needed both circulation and reference assistance. Understandably, patrons often did not know where to ask their questions. Circulation and reference had separate phone lines, and patrons were sometimes transferred back and forth when the reference interview was inadequate or the patron had multiple service needs.

For many years librarians and student assistants staffed the reference desk, answering reference and directional questions and performing other duties, such as maintaining and refilling printers, restocking office supplies, logging visitors onto computers, assisting patrons with basic technology and software questions, and acting as an intermediary between the patron and the library's technology office. The reference desk was located in the midst of the computers and printers, so referring patrons to the circulation desk for these services would have been inconvenient for the patron and caused a delay in service. Because of the physical arrangement of that reference desk, patrons could not distinguish a librarian from a student assistant, and often a librarian would be refilling printer paper while a student assistant was answering a reference question. The reference desk was staffed the same hours as the circulation desk (i.e., during all the weekday hours the library was open 7:30 a.m.–11 p.m.).

The first step in addressing these concerns came with an opportunity to upgrade the Circulation Services evening/weekend supervisor position duties to include providing reference assistance after 9:00 p.m. Reference librarians gave the individual hired for this position the same training as everyone who staffed the reference desk. Given the limited number of questions asked during that time period, this solution worked very well. Based on examination of reference question statistics, the hand-off to circulation services was eventually moved back to 8:00 p.m.

As members of the planning committee for a major renovation of the library, the head of Circulation Services and the head of Reference Services had a unique opportunity to consider further changes. Through discussions with the committee, which included library administration, and conversations with circulation and reference staff, the concept of a single service desk evolved as the best approach for students, faculty, and library staff. Much of the discussion from within the two affected departments centered on the concern that patrons continue to receive excellent service. The turning point in agreeing to implement a combined service desk came with the clarification that no decision is permanent. Openness to flexibility is vital. All agreed that if the new desk did not meet the needs of library users, the two departments would seek an alternative solution.

THE SINGLE POINT-OF-SERVICE DESK

The new desk was designed to provide two separate services, often staffed by two different groups of people, at one service point. The design took into account observations that walk-up service is best for patrons checking out books, while patrons seeking a reference consultation find being seated with a librarian more conducive to a successful interaction. The new desk is counter-height for walk-up circulation services and desk-height with patron chairs for reference assistance. To conform to the architects' aesthetics for the space, lower desks were placed at both ends of the counter, even though the plan was to provide reference service only at one end. That design feature has proven not only more pleasing to the eye, but also beneficial for times when either circulation or reference staff need an extra station to meet immediate patron demand. The second desk-height station also provides convenient ADA access to circulation services. Staff office space for Circulation Services and Interlibrary Loan are located immediately behind the service desk, partially visible to patrons, and staff in those areas are readily available to provide additional assistance at the desk.

In order for the new service desk to address building changes that progressed in stages, it had to be visible from both the stairs and the elevators east of the desk, initially the only entrances to the floor, and also from a new entrance to the west of the desk that would open with the completion of a classroom addition two and a half years later in the fall of 2013. Visibility of the desk to patrons from all entrances, as well as the ability of circulation staff to monitor the security gates at the new entrance, was rightly anticipated to be crucial. After a semester with reference service at the east end of the desk further away from the new entrance, this service moved to the west end, where reference assistance is more visible to the greatly increased number of patrons coming in the new entrance. The new arrangement places reference service closer to the circulation staff, whose assistance can be more easily called upon at busy times. The reference librarians are also more visible to circulation staff, a particular advantage when making phone referrals. The designed flexibility of the desk reinforces and supports the library staff commitment to providing excellent service. Patrons receive individualized assistance the moment they first approach the desk. Transferring a patron in person or via the phone to the appropriate staff member is nearly seamless to the patron. The single service desk provides a learning opportunity for everyone who staffs either part of the desk. Working in close proximity, librarians and staff overhear each other's communications with patrons without being intrusive. Circulation staff pick up new ways or better words to answer basic reference questions, while reference librarians learn more facts about the borrowing process. When a colleague provides erroneous or misleading information, the staff or librarian can jump in with assistance. At first, training was necessary on polite and helpful ways to insert information and to make referrals to the person at the next part of the desk. Now such behavior is the norm, and even new student assistants quickly learn the expected behaviors.

DIVISION OF LABOR/CROSS-TRAINING

With reference librarians and circulation staff working at the same service point, tasks and activities were reassigned based on position and knowledge rather than on physical proximity to the particular service. The Circulation Services Department continued to perform the primary circulation duties at the service desk. The location and staffing of the combined desk allows circulation staff and student assistants to take responsibility for tasks formerly performed by reference desk librarians and staff, such as restocking printer paper, logging guest users on the computers, troubleshooting technology and software issues, and keeping patron office supplies stocked. Instead of two separate phone extensions, all calls to the library are answered via the main circulation phone line. Circulation staff members were given a thorough training in answering basic reference questions that were received by phone, chat, text, or in person. Higher-level or more subject-specific questions are still referred to reference librarians. As a result of these changes, reference librarians staffing the desk mainly focus on answering reference questions or questions that are transferred after being vetted by circulation staff. The reference librarians also have training in basic circulation functions, allowing them to step in and pull a book from the reserve reading shelf, check out a monograph to a patron, or log on a guest when the circulation staff are attending to other patrons. With this level of cross-training, all staff can step in and assist each other as needed based upon desk activity.

IMPACT ON SERVICE

As mentioned earlier, the primary concern of librarians and staff in moving to the single service point was that patrons continue to receive excellent service. Based upon available feedback since the changes to the desk and services, in some ways patrons now receive even better service than before combining desks. Patrons now know where to ask any question and are more quickly able to get their needs met. Reference questions are easily handed on to librarians, and circulation staff and student assistants readily volunteer to step in to help with printer problems or to log a guest onto a computer. Several aspects of the single service desk contribute to improved service. Roles are clearly defined. Although librarians and staff are crossed-trained, all staff understand and are comfortable with the duties of their positions and are trained to be ready to refer questions appropriately. The effectiveness of this training is visible with new circulation student assistants who are not yet fully trained. Their initial reluctance to refer questions highlights how well everyone else makes referrals. Incorrect referrals occur much less frequently and are less obtrusive. To the patron it appears more like getting help from multiple people than being passed back and forth.

Similarly, phone service has been simplified by having one published incoming line. Circulation staff receive incoming calls at their own desks, answering the questions they can and referring reference questions to a librarian. To ensure that calls are vetted by circulation staff, the phone at the reference desk does not have a published number and can only receive calls from campus lines. The single service desk serves well here also. If the phone call leads to a question that the circulation staff can better answer, they are close at hand to provide the information without transferring the patron back again. Overall, patron phone calls are transferred much less frequently, and multiple transfers are now nearly nonexistent.

IMPACT ON STAFFING

The single service point has greatly increased staffing flexibility by providing the opportunity to explore and test out a variety of staffing models, with little investment of time and generally little or no expense. Because at least one person from the Circulation Services Department is always staffing the desk, staffing for reference assistance is based on whether the volume and nature of the questions typical in a given hour could be handled by the circulation staff. Changes in the staffing model for reference service are based on analysis of service statistics for reference assistance, both on and off the desk, and for circulation and directional questions. Statistics are analyzed to determine the most efficient and effective staffing at various times of the day, week, and semester. As most academic libraries have experienced, the number and nature of reference questions has changed over the last decade. To provide more efficient service, the staffing model had changed from double staffing to having one person at the desk and one person as a backup from his/her office. The librarians saw the opening of the new single service point as an opportunity to experiment with different staffing models. Based on previous experience with students staffing the reference desk, the first model scheduled one person, generally a graduate student assistant, at the desk with instructions to answer only questions anticipated to take less than 10 minutes and one on-call librarian for longer questions and reference questions. When needed, circulation staff did triage and contacted the on-call librarian. The plan for circulation staff to answer all incoming calls was implemented at this time. Due in part to the exceptional skills of the graduate assistants, the 10-minute rule did not last long, and most in-person questions were answered by the person at the service desk. A chat reference service was added a few months later in the summer of 2011. Because of librarian concerns about juggling in-person and chat questions, monitoring chat was assigned to the on-call person who received relatively few other questions.

When not answering questions, librarians found they could accomplish more on their own projects at the on-call desk than at the service desk. Because so few patrons ask questions during the intersessions, circulation staffed the service desk alone with one librarian on call from his/her office for in-person, chat, and phone questions. This model proved to be very efficient while still being effective for periods between semesters and continues to be the model anytime classes are not in session.

During the 2012–2013 academic year, the on-call service was moved from the librarians' individual offices to a desk in the staff area behind the service desk. The goal was to make the on-call person more readily available to help with in-person and phone questions while in an environment less distracting than the service desk. Even though the total number of questions during most hours was not enough to justify scheduling two librarians, many librarians were still concerned that one individual handling both in-person and chat questions might diminish service excellence.

After consulting service desk usage data, the head of Circulation Services and the head of Reference Services decided that single staffing for reference service could improve the efficiency of service delivery without sacrificing quality. Beginning in fall 2013 after the initial rush of where's-my-classroom and how-do-I-get-my-textbook questions, one person staffed the reference desk, answering all questions, including chat. Circulation staff continued to answer basic reference questions when needed, and librarians provided backup from their offices on a voluntary basis. This model worked well and continued the following semester.

Having a single service point has also enabled reductions in the number of hours reference librarians staff the desk. After years of staffing the reference desk all hours the library was open, the single service point has enabled reference librarians now to staff the desk only 40 of the 88.5 hours the library is open, with no perceived reduction in meeting patron needs.

CONCLUSION

The combined single service point has proven to be an effective model for providing excellent, timely service to library users, while making the best possible use of librarian and staff time. The library will conduct a formal survey of user satisfaction in another year. In the meantime, the feedback so far indicates that patron needs are addressed more easily and with greater success under the new service model. In concert with the principles that no decision is permanent and that openness to flexibility is vital, regular review of the effectiveness of the staffing model will continue, based on accurate and detailed records of reference questions. Having both circulation and reference staff at one service point has created greater cooperation and opportunities for jointly meeting patron needs. Taking the risk to combine the two desks has proven to be successful.

Community Outreach Through LibGuides

Mandi Goodsett, Georgia Southwestern State University, and Kirstin Dougan, University of Illinois at Urbana-Champaign

INTRODUCTION

Online library guides have become a central part of academic library services and serve a wide variety of purposes—from supplementing one-shot classroom information literacy sessions to training student workers, to providing library news and updates to faculty. In some ways, library or research guides have become as commonplace as books in libraries (Gaphery & White, 2012). However, one use of online library guides that has not yet been thoroughly explored has the potential to be an especially valuable method of improving library outreach and marketing. LibGuides utilized as outreach tools enable libraries to both promote their own resources and collections and strengthen their connection with those in the broader university and local communities.

This study draws on the experience of two institutions that use LibGuides as a community outreach tool. The LibGuide platform is a content management system provided by SpringShare and used by thousands of libraries to curate and present information on any topic or subject. Outreach methods described here using LibGuides could conceivably be translated for use with other software or tools. Both libraries in this case study allow community users to take advantage of library services and collections, which is an important premise behind the use of LibGuides for outreach—without the ability to share collections with and offer services to the community, outreach in most forms would be difficult to justify.

The University of Illinois at Urbana-Champaign's Music and Performing Arts Library (UIUC MPAL) built their outreach library guides in collaboration with the Krannert Center for the Performing Arts (KCPA), which is also a part of the university. Librarians at MPAL create a guide for each month of KCPA's season (September–May). Individual tabs highlight materials from the library's collections that can supplement both preparation for and further research about a specific performance and its performers and repertoire.

Georgia Southwestern State University has also created partnerships with local performing arts organizations in conjunction with the use of LibGuides for outreach. The library guides highlight performances from outside musicians presented by the university's music department, showcase events and services of the community art center, and promote events at the Rylander Theatre, a local theatre that often hosts the performances of community groups.

REACHING OUT TO COMMUNITY PARTNERS

Neither of these endeavors could be successful without strong collaboration between the library and its partners. One of the first steps to creating an effective outreach library guide is identifying the right community partner(s). Finding willing partners should not be difficult because the library is essentially offering the organization free publicity with minimal work. However, what is more challenging is locating a partner whose activities lend themselves well to an outreach guide and whose patrons would benefit from use of the library collections. In many cases, this will be an arts organization that has regular performances or events, although experimentation with collaborations with other kinds of organizations may result in valuable connections. For example, MPAL is in the process of creating a collaborative guide with the Spurlock Museum, the local cultural history museum.

In the case of MPAL's partner, KCPA, the organization was already closely tied to the university's music department. The Krannert Center for the Performing Arts is an educational and performing arts complex that frequently hosts the performances of the University of Illinois at Urbana-Champaign orchestras, bands, choirs, theater, and dance department groups. The center's season calendar also includes internationally renowned artists and performers, which provides students and community members with opportunities to enjoy fantastic performances without travelling far. KCPA's physical proximity to MPAL (they are on opposite sides of the street) makes it convenient for community members and others to visit both on the same day. Given that MPAL's resources provide excellent resources to enhance concertgoers' experiences at the KCPA, the partnership was a natural choice.

While not every library has the benefit of having a partner like KCPA in its community, any library can find a collaborative community partner, no matter how limited the library's surroundings. Georgia Southwestern State University is located in small, rural Americus, Georgia, and the library chose its community partners from among the few arts-focused organizations in town. The benefit of outreach in a small community is that communication with these partners is simple and straightforward; there is little red tape to work through, and the leaders of these groups are often acquaintances or even friends.

Reaching out to a community partner, if a connection is not already in place, can be as simple as sending a friendly email to explain the premise of the outreach LibGuides and asking for a meeting to talk further. Collaborators outside the library will probably be unfamiliar with LibGuides, so sharing an example, especially one that is already used for outreach, will help them visualize what is possible. It is important to get input from the nonlibrary partner(s) about content and scheduling. They may have needs related to grant fulfillment and education programs that can be served by the LibGuides. Relay up front that the primary contribution of the collaborating organization will be assistance with marketing, and the majority of the work creating and maintaining the guide will be handled by the librarian. Keep in mind that some organizations will be very particular about how their image is displayed in any medium or capacity, so they may want to monitor and/or proofread the outreach library guides created for their organization carefully. Setting up a process for the collaborator to be involved in the maintenance of the guides from the beginning will ensure the organization is satisfied with their representation in the guide.

CREATING AN EFFECTIVE OUTREACH LIBRARY GUIDE

Regardless of the kind of organization with which the library collaborates, there are several elements of the LibGuide that will make it a more effective outreach tool for all involved. First of all, the LibGuide should be easy to find. While the URL for library guides might not matter when there are direct links to them on a library website, to effectively market these guides to off-campus users, a URL that is simple and memorable will be extremely helpful. For example, the MPAL KCPA LibGuides all begin uiuc.libguides.com/KCPA and end with the month and year for that guide, making it easy to remember the URL if necessary. It is possible to quickly and easily change the URL of a LibGuides under guide settings.

It also is helpful to include links to the collaborator's relevant web content, such as event logistics, as much as possible. Because the guide is not meant to serve as a replacement for the content on the collaborator's website in any way, it can be helpful to provide users with an easy way to access additional information as needed. However, it is also important to keep in mind that including too much detail from the partner organization's website could distract users from the real purpose of the guide—to connect potential patrons with library material.

To highlight library material, librarians can include links to books, audio and visual recordings, scores, and other specific items in the library catalog, as well as links to carefully constructed searches in the library catalog (see Figure 1). Information about services and programs offered by the community partner, including a detailed calendar for regularly scheduled activities, will be helpful in creating a relevant, comprehensive guide. Including a YouTube video or other visual content from outside sources that relates to the event, performance, or service will allow users to get a better sense of the topic. Because the focus of

Figure 1. Outreach library guides can include links to books, audio and visual recordings, scores, and other specific items in the library catalog.

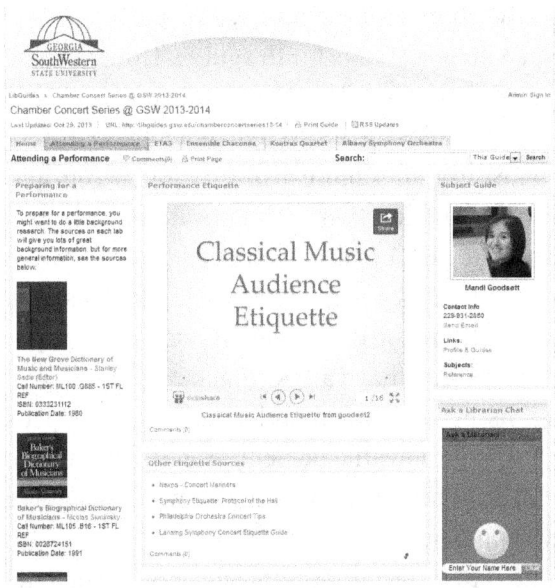

Figure 2. LibGuides can promote performance etiquette with a tab about attending performances.

the guide is promoting library services, the presence of a library chat service, if available, and contact information for the relevant reference librarian(s) can help users easily reach the library with questions. Depending on the focus of the guide, creating a tab about attending performances can provide the library with an opportunity to promote performance etiquette as well.

General best practices for any LibGuide creation also apply here. Avoid library jargon where possible, reuse material for easy guide creation, use visuals often, and be practical and restrained in the use of tabs (Gause, 2013). The strategic practices that make it easier for students to navigate library guides related to classes and research also will prove beneficial to community members accessing and exploring the library's outreach guides.

MARKETING

One of the most challenging aspects of creating an outreach library guide is marketing the guide to potential users, who are likely not regular library users and may only visit campus for performing arts events. Or, they may be regular patrons at another library on campus (e.g., science professors). Because the intended audience of the LibGuides extends beyond the institution's population (the library's typical users) to include community members, creative marketing is necessary to reach all intended users. Marketing is the aspect of outreach LibGuides that requires the most collaborative effort with the partner organization.

MPAL recognized the challenge of effective marketing after tracking the usage statistics of KCPA guides over time. At the beginning of the month, a new KCPA guide's link would be shared on the library's blog and Twitter feed, which would result in a spike in page views for the guide. However, the views would dip after this initial marketing push and would not rise again beyond the occasional spike when the guides were tweeted about again during the month. In an attempt to make the guides more visible, MPAL wrote and received an internal library grant to market them. The librarians at MPAL worked with the graphic designers at KCPA to design posters promoting the guides, and copies were hung in the KCPA and Music Building lobbies. The same design was used as an advertisement in the faculty/staff newspaper twice each semester. The ads and posters have a QR (quick response) code that links to the library webpage listing all of the monthly KCPA guides. This stable link directs users to KCPA guides for the current month without the library needing to change the QR code monthly. Statistics showed that guide usage increased after each newspaper ad placement.

Although MPAL was not able to afford to put links or advertisements in the KCPA performance programs, this would be another good form of marketing. The benefit of marketing this way is the ease with which concertgoers could access the link to the LibGuides after a performance, in addition to the specific reminder directly to the intended audience about the guides that marketing in a program can provide. Space in a performance program may be limited, however, and the use of space to advertise a LibGuide, while useful for the partner organization, may still cost the library a fee. The size of the organization may play a role here—if the organization is large, there may be less flexibility to allow a link to the LibGuide to be included in performance programs free of charge.

Another natural location for marketing would be a link for the guide on the organization's website. This could be a single, prominently placed link or, as the KCPA website does, a link to the appropriate LibGuides tab in the online calendar entry for each event. Yet another opportunity for marketing is through local newspapers, newsletters, listservs, or regular emails sent by either the library or partner organization. MPAL found marketing to be more effective when KCPA started including links to the LibGuides in their weekly highlights emails to subscribers, and the Georgia Southwestern State University Library observed a similar improvement when the Americus Art Center began including a link to their respective LibGuides in its email newsletter.

One surprisingly effective form of marketing came when the librarians at MPAL applied to and were invited to participate in a public engagement symposium at the University of Illinois at Urbana-Champaign. They created and displayed a poster, which illustrated to the UIUC community the valuable, strong collaboration between the two campus partners. A by-product of that event was that many attendants were informed about the presence of the LibGuides and encouraged to use them. While a university-wide symposium might not be a possibility for marketing at a smaller institution, any kind of professional development event to which faculty and, especially, community members are invited can be a valuable opportunity to increase word-of-mouth marketing of outreach library guides. For example, the Georgia Southwestern State University Library's guides were featured in an article for the campus-wide faculty and staff newsletter, which provided valuable exposure for the project to the university community and beyond.

If none of these forms of marketing are possible, or if additional marketing is desired, there are many other options for marketing available with varying amounts of effort required. Having an event that highlights the collaboration between the library and its partner organization would be a great opportunity to get the word out about the guides. The presence of a librarian at several performances or events to hand out flyers with links to the guides could also be helpful, although potentially time-consuming and costly. Any other kind of typical community outreach tool—online boards, local radio and TV stations, and so forth—could provide additional venues for marketing. A discussion with the cooperating partner about marketing could result in more ideas, as well as potentially more help from them in marketing the guide(s) as much as possible. Having a well-organized, thorough library guide is a great start, but it is of no help to anyone if no one knows it exists.

CONCLUSION

As reference services adapt to the changing needs of patrons, it will become increasingly necessary to emphasize the relevance and importance of libraries through connections within and between communities. LibGuides can serve as a valuable tool for the future of a reimagined reference environment that encourages these community connections. There is much additional experimentation and research that could be performed in this area. The use of LibGuides as outreach to community organizations in the arts, as described here, is only one avenue for using LibGuides in outreach among many that could be explored by libraries. Libraries of different types may find partnership through LibGuides a natural fit with certain kinds of organizations, depending on the focus of their collections. Regardless of the kind of collaboration the LibGuide highlights, one thing is clear: with strong marketing and a good partner relationship, collaborative outreach library guides can be a robust tool for marketing library collections and making community connections.

REFERENCES

Gaphery, J., & White, E. (2012). Library use of web-based research guides. *Information Technology and Libraries, 31*(1), 21–31.

Gause, R. (2013, August 26). LibGuide tips & tricks for librarians. *University of Central Florida Libraries*. Retrieved from http://guides.ucf.edu/libguides-tips

24/7 Global Virtual Reference Cooperation: The Case of QuestionPoint

Susan McGlamery, OCLC QuestionPoint

For as long as we have libraries, and people who use (or are entitled to use) those libraries, there will be a need for qualified information professionals ("librarians") to provide impartial, knowledgeable advice, tailored to specific information needs. Whether called "reference" or something else, this is a unique service provided by libraries and as such should be nurtured and promoted. Discovery tools, FAQs/guides, and search engines, while increasingly comprehensive and intuitive, still (at present) do not contain everything, nor do they intuit what the user is trying to find; this is where the librarian steps in to help. The premise of a cooperative reference service is that it should not matter too much if the librarian stepping in to help is not actually an employee of the user's home library.

Similar to cooperative cataloguing, the idea behind cooperative virtual reference is to leverage the cost of providing reference services by removing excess capacity in the system and thus achieve greater efficiencies. As applied to virtual reference, the excess capacity might be stated as follows: if 100 librarians in 100 different libraries are staffing their own chat service during a given hour and cumulatively receiving 50 chats during that hour, could those same 50 chats be handled effectively by 10 reference librarians during that same hour—and if so, what is the best way of achieving this? Cloud-based and web-scale solutions propose that going to the cloud can remove redundant local provision and create improved system-wide capacity, as well as providing other benefits unique to a web-scale service. This case study will look at the effectiveness of one cooperative virtual reference service: QuestionPoint's 24/7 Reference Service. However, the experiences related to this service and my conclusions may equally apply to other cooperative reference services.

Over 15 years ago, I started with this proposition: If content is available 24/7 through the library's website, then the librarians should be available 24/7 as well, to help the user at his point of need. Inspired by Anne Lipow ("in your face reference") and Hilary Clinton ("it takes a village"), I convened a group of reference librarians in Los Angeles to determine the feasibility of providing a 24/7 live chat service staffed by librarians. Two options were considered: 1) a central call center staffed with trained librarians, such that chats are routed to this center when the subscribing libraries are offline, or 2) a cooperative of willing libraries that agree to staff each other's chat queues, according to an agreed-upon schedule, thus extending the hours of service for all participants. Not surprisingly, given my role as the reference coordinator of a library consortium in Los Angeles, I chose the latter.

While the call center would have been easier in terms of monitoring quality, the cooperative approach provided several benefits. Sharing staffing costs among participating libraries should cost less overall, and thus be less expensive for members, and consequently more sustainable. In addition, it is more scalable. As membership in the chat cooperative increases, so do the pool of librarians who are staffing the chat queues. Another appealing aspect of the cooperative approach was political. Staffing by member libraries is more akin to a peer-to-peer network and was more politically desirable (at the time) than outsourcing to a call center. The cooperative approach also provided the opportunity for library staff development. An hour spent staffing the chat service often provided more interesting reference questions than a similar hour spent at the reference desk. Additionally, during cooperative staffing, the participating librarians were exposed to the resources, guides, and programs available at the participating libraries, thus increasing awareness of reference best practices. Finally, the cooperative approach was a natural extension of other collaborative projects undertaken by this group. Thus the 24/7 cooperative chat reference service ("the 24/7 Coop") was launched in Los Angeles on July 1, 2000, with three intrepid libraries (Santa Monica, Los Angeles Public Library, and Buena Park Library District), through a grant provided by the California State Library.

However, to ensure true 24/7 coverage, we added paid backup librarians before a year had elapsed (June 2001) to fill in the hours not covered by the member libraries. In effect this meant we ended up with a blended approach: a cooperative backed up with paid staff. Once true 24/7 service was a reality, other libraries (both within and outside California) joined. From late 2001 membership increased rapidly, and in 2004 the 24/7 Coop was acquired by OCLC and merged with the QuestionPoint service.

The 24/7 Coop today consists of about 1,000 libraries in the United States and United Kingdom, most of which agree to staff the cooperative chat queues (libraries can opt out of this, for a fee, and some have). The service has been staffed every hour of every day (24/7/365, including holidays) since June 2001 (with the exception of brief software maintenance periods). Since the launch on July 1, 2000, the service has picked up over 6 million chat requests from users across the United States and (since 2004) the United Kingdom. The average number of chats handled by the 24/7 Coop each year for the past several years averages to about 500,000 chats per year. We have achieved the vision of providing around-the-clock reference service provided by trained information professionals. Now, almost 15 years later, it is useful to see what worked, what needs improvement, and what might be interesting to explore next.

Is 24/7 reference service essential? One way to answer this question is to look at current usage statistics, to determine when the service is used most heavily during the hours the service is available. For the 24/7 Coop as a whole, close to 40% of all chat questions are asked "after-hours" (defined, for simplicity, as 10 a.m. to 6 p.m. Monday–Sunday, adjusted by time zone). This varies by library, since libraries' open hours vary. For example, New York Public Library found that 36% of their chats came in after-hours (based on when the NYPL librarians were offline). Similarly, the U.K. public library group, Enquire, found that 38% of their chats come in when Enquire librarians are offline. In 2012 we produced a webinar on this topic called "Best Practices in Virtual Reference: Keeping the Virtual Lights On" (2012) featuring speakers from NYPL and the University of California.

However, usage statistics do not tell the whole story. One appeal of a 24/7 service for many of the early participants was the promotion value of saying, "We're always here when you need us," and the belief that if users have to figure out when the service is open, they will be less inclined to use it. Fifteen years ago, many libraries were reluctant to provide a link to virtual reference because they were afraid they would be overwhelmed with traffic from eager users. This fear appears to be still present, given the non-intuitive placement/messaging around some library virtual reference services (although, to be fair, those keen to promote the service at their library may not have control over their library's website). Generally, the service is used more when it is effectively promoted, and sometimes just placing (and naming) the link in an obvious way is enough to increase usage. For example, the University of Birmingham (United Kingdom) replaced their chat form (requiring students to fill in information before submitting the question) with a chat widget, then placed the widget on the front of the student portal page. Usage increased almost immediately by over 200%, and has remained there since. Several years ago we produced a guide to "Increase Awareness for Virtual Reference Services: Best Practices for Link Placement" (2010) and since that time there have been many studies linking placement to usage. For more tips on this important topic, our webinar "Best Practices in Virtual Reference: Finding Your Virtual Reference Users Online" (2012), presented by Bill Pardue of Arlington Heights Memorial Library and Joanne John of Enquire, contains many valuable tips.

If 24/7 service is desirable, then is cooperative reference the best way to accomplish this? Some libraries are open 24/7, although not necessarily with trained reference staff available at all hours. Libraries with campuses across the world can take advantage of time zones such that most or all hours of the day can be staffed with librarians from the same institution (some schools with campuses in the United States, Middle East, and China/Australia are doing this). However, for libraries without overseas or other staffing options, cooperative reference offers a reasonable way to provide a service that might not otherwise be a possibility.

In addition to the 24/7 Coop, other groups have successfully used a "follow-the-sun" approach to take advantage of time zone differences as a way to extend chat coverage. For example, the Chasing the Sun service offers collaborative chat for medical (hospital and clinical) libraries in Australia and the United Kingdom, and the Ubib French academic chat cooperative has member libraries in France, the French West Indies, and French Polynesia (for more information, see http://www.ubib.fr/). In the public library sector, a francophone network has been discussed by libraries in France, Belgium, and Quebec.

Apart from the value of offering a chat service that is always available, there are other advantages of cooperative reference. Depending on how the service is set up, cooperative reference can provide extra help even when the local library is online. While the motivating principle behind the establishment of the 24/7 Coop was to extend the library's open hours through chat, 24/7 Coop members highly value having backup from other librarians during busy times. Percentages vary by library (for the 24/7 Coop as a whole, one-third of all 24/7 Coop chats are answered by the local library, just over 40% are picked up by other 24/7 Coop librarians, and the remainder are picked up by our paid backup staff, on average), but when backup is available during the day (including backup from the 24/7 Coop librarians as well as the backup staff), then libraries do avail themselves of this additional cover. This allows libraries to provide their users not only with extended hours of service, but also with extra business hours of chatting during busy times, when their users need it. Cooperative virtual reference allows the library to call in extra staff from its fellow 24/7 Coop librarians, on demand. This flexibility would not be possible without the cooperative staffing network.

Along with the many benefits, only some of which are outlined above, there have been challenges as well. The biggest challenges for the 24/7 Coop relate to staffing. To continue to provide the service at an affordable cost, individual 24/7 Coop members are encouraged (through subscription incentives) to take on an appropriate share of staffing the chat queues (based on size of the library's service population/FTE). However, agreeing to staff a certain number of hours per week does not automatically equate to picking up a certain number of chat sessions. The QuestionPoint software used by the 24/7 Coop has two attributes that impact staffing: it requires the librarian to pick up a chat (it is pull not push; there is no automatic assignment of the new chat to an available librarian), and it provides a question preview, which allows librarians to leave difficult questions to others. This is undesirable because it increases patron wait times and potentially increases demands on the backup staff. To solve this, we instituted a staffing guideline called the "Answering Percentage," which provides a benchmark for the number of chats each 24/7 Coop library/group is expected to pick up, based on traffic from their users. This has proven to be fairly effective, although occasional spot monitoring is still scheduled when needed.

In addition to making sure cooperative members pick up their fair share of chat traffic, it is important that the librarians provide good quality service to the chat patrons they do pick up. From its inception, quality has been a high priority for the 24/7 Coop. More than one early participant confided that "I don't mind picking up chat sessions from other libraries' patrons, but I'm not sure I want librarians from other libraries picking up chats from *my* patrons!" For the cooperative to work, the quality issue had to be addressed.

To ensure good quality service, the 24/7 Coop currently uses four related tools: common procedures, policy pages, quality review, and continuing education. The procedures are designed to set a common understanding of the level of service to be provided during chat sessions. To the extent possible, patrons should receive roughly the same type of service regardless of which librarian happens to pick them up. Naturally, the local librarian can provide definitive answers to a greater range of local questions than a 24/7 Coop librarian, but among these librarians the level of service should be roughly the same. Our "24/7 Policies" document, supplemented by the "24/7 Best Practices," is continually revised in consultation with the "24/7 Reference Advisory Board." The policies provide guidelines on service levels, how to handle various types of patrons (rude, persistent, homework help, etc.), when follow-up should be used, and so forth.

Ideally, 24/7 Coop librarians should be able to step into the shoes of the patron's own librarian and provide as much assistance as possible during the chat session. To accomplish this, the 24/7 Coop librarians need quick access to the policies and resources of each cooperative library. This is provided by the 24/7 Coop policy pages (basically, a standard template for each 24/7 Coop library member, maintained by each library) and accessible from the chat monitor whenever a librarian is in session with that library's user. Without the policy pages, the 24/7 Coop librarians would be much less effective in providing assistance to users at diverse libraries.

In addition to the 24/7 Coop policies and the policy pages, we provide training events such as webinars and quality tips posted in the QuestionPoint blog and listserv (which also provides a discussion forum). But if a 24/7 Coop librarian fails to provide good service, then that session may be referred to our quality review service. 24/7 Coop librarians can send any session to the quality team, who review the session and provide constructive comments to the chatting librarian. Less than 1% of 24/7 Coop sessions were sent to quality in 2013, and some of those were not complaints, but rather compliments to the chatting librarians. The quality process provides another piece of the staff development benefits of cooperative reference.

What's next for cooperative virtual reference? The 24/7 Coop fosters a thriving community of reference librarians spanning the United States, the United Kingdom, and beyond (recently, we welcomed the American University in Cairo to our group). The 24/7 Coop libraries came together primarily to extend the hours of chat service they could provide to their users, but additional cooperative opportunities are possible. We have made attempts at subject referral among members but more could be done, such as establishing communities of interest by subject. These referral networks have been limited to libraries using QuestionPoint software. Is there a way to open referral up to libraries using other software tools, thus creating more synergies with the widest possible participation? In addition, could we bring our users into this community in a meaningful way? Currently, we engage with the users to answer their direct enquiries, one-to-one. Consumer-facing answer services (Yahoo!Answers, for example) take a different approach. Could we blend the expertise of librarians to build communities with our users, to the mutual benefit of both? Whatever the answers, cooperative virtual reference has provided one way for librarians to reach beyond their doors and work with colleagues around the world, many of whom they will never meet. The potential inherent in this has yet to be fully realized, and it continues to be an exciting area to explore.

REFERENCES

Best practices in virtual reference: Finding your virtual reference users online. (2012, May 17). *OCLC*. Retrieved from http://www.oclc.org/events/2012/Best_Practices_in_VirtualRef3-May17.en.html

Best practices in virtual reference: Keeping the virtual lights on. (2012, March 6). *OCLC*. Retrieved from http://www.oclc.org/events/2012/Best_Practices_in_VirtualRef1-March6.en.html

Increase awareness for virtual reference services: Best practices for link placement. (2010). *OCLC*. Retrieved from http://www.oclc.org/content/dam/oclc/services/brochures/214348usb_QuestionPoint_Link_Placement.pdf

I | Serving the "Somewhere Out There" Patron: The View From the Digital Cooperative Reference Desk

Nicolette Warisse Sosulski, Portage District Library, Michigan

Having worked with chat reference patrons for 10 years in public and academic settings, I have, I calculate, passed the 10,000-hour mark—explored by neurologist Daniel Levitin and made famous by Malcolm Gladwell (2000)—required for mastery of a subject. While "mastering" an ever-changing discipline such as reference may be a bold claim, over this length of time I have identified some of the challenges of working with what I have dubbed the "Somewhere Out There Patron" (SOTP). Although there is some truth to the statement "It's all reference," which is attributed variously to David Lankes, Joe Janes, Steve Coffman, Anne Lipow, and other luminaries, this is oversimplification. Librarians going into chat reference, especially in cooperative settings, have some explicit and marked differences that they should anticipate from reference in a face-to-face, phone, or even another virtual setting, such as email. The aspects of anonymity, free access by clicking in via a link from a web search from anywhere in the world, synchronous library contact, and 24/7 access can make chat ref, and especially cooperative chat ref, a whole different ballgame.

What does my chat experience look like? While some of it was gained as a graduate library assistant at the University of Washington, one decade of it was as a backup chat librarian for the 24/7 reference cooperative started by Susan McGlamery and Carol Bonnefil in California, which then joined with QuestionPoint chat reference service for OCLC. I covered 8–22 hours a week of chat shifts for the public, academic, military, and Spanish queues for a cooperative of libraries from Washington State to New York, London,

Edinburgh, and Mexico. Except for Mexico, all of these locales, and some in between, had both public and academic libraries as members, hundreds of libraries in total, none of which was my "home" library as the librarian. I would log in for a shift, and, as questions came into the queues, I would grab them to answer—in real time. Because I also have a daytime, full-time job, many of my shifts were either in the early hours of the morning before my 9–5 (more or less) job, or on evenings or weekends, most notably and challengingly, Sunday evenings and nights. Sunday nights produce the most hair-raising shifts of the week, as homework assignments successfully ignored during the rest of the weekend loom, with due dates of midnight Sunday local time or class on Monday, inducing panic in multitudes of students who have not worked (or have not worked productively) up to that time.

As a result of a substantial part of my experience working in these types of shifts, I may be more conscious of the differences between chat reference, especially cooperative chat, and other reference, as well as the particular challenges of the SOTP. My experiences are representative of those delivering services in cooperative chat reference, but my opinions or conclusions are my own, rather than those of any current or previous employer. In addressing these differences, I will organize my thoughts with the classic reporter questions: who, what, where, when, why, and how.

WHO

"Who *is* this person?"

Always foremost in the librarian's mind in many a chat reference interaction, this is one question that is often never answered in the course of the transaction—and yet, to do our jobs best, we need to tailor a response to the patron and his or her age, intelligence, education level, native language, technical familiarity, and mental state. In a face-to-face environment, we can get a lot of context clues from appearance, voice, and accent. On the phone, we at least have the last two (more with caller ID). Email is challenging, but sometimes the email address can be mapped to a patron record, giving more information—and we have time to check these things out. In chat, we may get what seems to be a grossly misspelled query full of text jargon and no syntax. However, addressing meaning to those misspellings takes a lot of time and context, which one may not have. Misspellings can be the result of:

1. Youth (is this a third grader?)
2. Lack of education or spelling training
3. Innate inability to spell, despite extensive education
4. Poor typing skills
5. English being the second language
6. Technical issues, such as a key that sticks, a lag in transmission of responses, or a program refreshing
7. The use of a version of text speak with which the librarian is not familiar
8. The patron's suffering from deadline-induced panic and possibly abundant caffeine intake

Depending on why the query is so garbled, the appropriate resources sent for the query "so i nede 2 no abt the presdnt" could vary drastically: grade school President's Day assignment, community college introductory creative writing class, college analysis of president impact for political history, person preparing for citizenship exam, or adult layman trying to make sense of something seen on CNN or Fox. The librarian might have just one chance to send a response that the patron will then use to evaluate the utility of the service and librarians in general. Balancing this with speed expected in the chat medium and the increased necessity of clarity only to be obtained through a reference interview (and one that has to replace the context clues about the patron) adds an onus on the librarian that does not exist to the same extent in other modalities, but is critical. Ask the questions. You do not have time, but you do not have the luxury to omit doing so. If you send something that the patron thinks is way off base, you may never have another chance. When she hangs up, that is it (lots of patrons do not log in with any way of contacting them by email afterward).

"I mean, who *are* these people?"

In cooperative chat, the possibility of having to juggle two or more patrons is increased. Due to the accelerated sense of time passing that seems to affect the chat patron, if people are waiting in line, you usually do not have the luxury of waiting until you are done with the previous patron interaction. You pick up the next person in queue and click back and forth. Unless the patron is told otherwise, he often assumes that he is the only person the librarian is assisting.

WHAT

"WTH does this patron need? (What source are we using?)"
"What is the subject of her information need?"

Since the patron cannot see what you are doing and where you are getting information, sending the source of your answer becomes even more important than in face-to-face interaction, just as the reference interview becomes more necessary—at a time when, start to finish, we might be aiming at a 20-minute or shorter interaction (guidelines may vary depending on library or cooperative policies). Does the patron need a website or an academic article (to which, depending on the resources of the queue the patron logged in on, we may not have access)? The patron may not think she needs the source right now, but she did not have the benefit of watching the librarian go into that red, white, and blue book behind her chair or seeing her navigate to that site about med something plus. Later, tracing back where the information came from might be more challenging, especially if this patron logged in anonymously (and may log in on a regular basis through any number of libraries), which makes it more difficult to trace a transcript and find what she was given.

The other "what" is the subject about which the patron is asking. Given the opportunity to be anonymous, the patron may ask about things or situations that he would not be comfortable asking in real life. In my and my colleagues' experience, the cooperative chat librarian gets more questions on sex, tattoos gone bad, violence in relationships, and firsthand symptoms of depression or illness than many reference desks—because they cannot be traced back. It then behooves us to have ready access to reputable and relevant sources on these topics, and to be twice as diligent about checking out links to see if they still work. Sometimes at night, I have had a person who needs to be talking to a hotline. This is a high-stakes interaction that should not be a reference query, but requires a far better than adequate referral. Sometimes the agencies serving people with health needs have closed down, but their sites live on forever on the Internet. Click every link you refer to a patron, to make sure that they are still viable. It is always important in any reference transaction to verify accessibility of sources, but sending a person in crisis to an out-of-service crisis hotline is to be avoided at all costs.

WHERE

"Where" did that come from? Where does he live, go to school, or work?

Although we have touched on the permeability of patron access through the web in the "who" section, the "where" may seem to approach this again. Where refers to the libraries or queue through which the patron reached you, the libraries or queue with which the patron may or may not have an affiliation, and which of those might own the question or be better for answering the query than the one through which the patron reached you. After a decade of work on the Sunday night shift, there are times I assume that every student out there, online or in place, blew off the library orientation session that was so strongly recommended by the academic program.

1. A patron with a card from a public library in Pennsylvania logs in through a public library in California but is actually at a university in California.
2. A patron with a card from a public library in New Jersey who attends a college in New Jersey.
3. A patron with no library card at all who is eligible for one in Pennsylvania and is doing a high school assignment.
4. A patron from Nigeria logs into a university library in California because he knows that the university is strong in the discipline the patron is studying.
5. A patron from Chile logs into New York Public because it is the biggest library she can think of.
6. A patron from Australia logs in because we are open.

Patron 1 or 2 may belong to a library that subscribes to the service, go to a college that may or may not subscribe to the service, and could be logging in to a library that subscribes but to which he or she has no affiliation.

A number of questions have to be answered in rapid-fire succession.

- What does the service owe the member?
- What does the member library owe the member?
- Who "owns" the question, or at least, the resources to best answer that question?
- What library should the patron be navigated to in order to best answer that question?

If the patron is examining the contribution of natural disasters to the incidence of post-traumatic stress disorder in a given geographic population, and is investigating this at an upper baccalaureate, master's, or PhD level, the public library is not going to be the place, in all likelihood, where resources reside to best answer that question. Anecdotally, from 10 years of desk experience in physical libraries and possessing the same number of years of cooperative chat reference experience, I can emphatically state that chat librarians get this sort of query/institution mismatch at a frequency which exceeds that of brick-and-mortar libraries, even accounting for the rise of online degree programs. Several assumptions usually hold true.

1. The patron does not want to go anywhere else if they do not have to.
2. The patron with a card feels that the possession of that card entitles them to service.
3. The patron, if not told about the riches of her academic library, may never use it and may well continue to use the less-optimal library for future similar interactions.
4. The librarian will want to help the patron navigate to the best set of resources for which he is eligible.
5. Time-strapped patrons may not comprehend how much better the optimum library is for the query, and if this is not made explicit, may accuse the librarian of not wanting to help or trying to pass the buck. That reflects badly on the library and service through which the patron logged in.

The librarian needs an elevator speech or script that explains quickly and clearly the difference between the types of resources available at each institution. When questions of authentication come up, as they will and should (sending a patron to a place where their authentication does not work is a fine way to lose patrons), explain that you are not asking about library card or student registration status to look for an excuse not to help the patron, but because the good stuff requires a login/membership/subscription, just like cable TV or a prime Internet music service. Since the patron may or may not be listening (that paper is now due in 3 hours 46 minutes), you need to reiterate that you are asking her about the library card/registration *not to send them to another library in person in the morning,* but to see what good stuff the patron is eligible to get into, and to get into the good stuff *right now.*

Another subject to be raised is the value the patron may gain, time permitting, from the use of a subject specialist liaison. My own way of describing this is to use an analogy taken from the medical field. Chat is urgent care; walking into the library may be like making an appointment with your own physician; meeting the subject specialist liaison is like consulting a medical specialist. If you have cancer, you want the oncologist; if this is a high-stakes or in-depth assignment, the subject specialist liaison is the very best option.

WHEN/WHY

"You are all that is open at 3:00 a.m."
"It's due in four hours."
"It's Christmas."
"It's Friday night on a four-day weekend and I am bored."
"I cannot drive, and anyway, mom does not know my homework is not done."

Not all chat reference is 24/7, 365 days a year; however, the cooperative chat reference model is one aimed at expanding hours beyond those that an independent library could offer, and the one I worked at, the largest service of its kind, was originally named 24/7 for that very reason. This leads to some patrons—many—reaching them during times when services elsewhere are reduced or absent. Queries may be encountered not because a patron feels that this is a library question, but because, since we are open and nobody else is, he might as well give it a try, and if the librarian indicates this is not a service that can be rendered at this time, perhaps the patron can push the matter in case there is wiggle room. Many of these are queries that the vast majority of the patrons would never dream of asking at a physical desk. Matters like this, which usually are not ideally suited to cooperative chat reference include (and please remember that I covered a combination of public and academic queues, yielding a wider variety of queries than might ordinarily be experienced by some other situations):

- Monetary or registration issues with the patron's account
- Interviews the patron was supposed to do with a teacher or librarian during school hours
- Tech support on something that the patron has purchased—a phone, vacuum cleaner, television, computer, watch, video game, personal pedometer, washing machine, or car—this list only includes items I personally was asked to troubleshoot but belongs to a universe of tech support that is far more extensive

- Physics, chemistry, or mathematics tutoring
- Manuscript editing and proofreading
- Résumé editing and compilation
- Summarizing a book that the patron has not read for which there are no summaries of the length or degree of complexity required extant
- Transcription of several pages of a physical book in the collection, which may not be anywhere near the location the librarian is working from
- Medical diagnosis or advice, especially dealing with a call as to whether the ER is necessary
- Legal diagnosis or advice
- Psychological help
- Tax help at 11 p.m. on April 15 (or any time)
- Christmas eve/day assembly/attempt to use a gift, or a Thanksgiving turkey crisis
- Holiday weekend crank calls by tweens in an attempt to shock a librarian

The librarian looks at how she can balance and work around constraints of privacy (account information), expertise (tutoring, professional services, some consumer products), and geography (we actually are not sitting at laptops in the stacks, truly we are not) to deliver some assistance to a patron who may be in a situation he considers desperate for whom there are no other free professionals readily available. In this situation, referrals to services or explanatory pages, along with David Tyckoson's first "R" of reference—reassurance—are the best that the profession can provide (2013). Explanations that the account cannot be accessed due to measures protecting the patron's privacy or the interview cannot happen due to other patrons waiting may not be heard, but should be offered.

HOW

"It's the computer . . ."

Everything gets kicked up a notch by synchronous service via computers and the Internet. Since there are often lines waiting on chat queues, the librarian is frequently serving multiple patrons, each of whom may be totally unaware of the others. Each thinks that she is the only one, and the instantaneous replies to some questions not requiring research somehow seem to feed expectations that each query can be answered as rapidly. I think of patrons as experiencing "patron time," which seems to be much slower than "librarian time"—the amount of time it takes to find a difficult-to-find date or citation seems to fly by, while the same unit of time spent in front of a chat screen when the answer has not come seems to drag endlessly. There can be assumptions on both sides that lack of action means that the connection has been lost, and a premature ending of the session may ensue.

This cutting of the connection is frustrating and should be avoided if at all possible, as session endings in chat have a finality to them that no other mode of reference has. When patrons disconnect, they are gone—extremely gone if they did not log in with any kind of name or email address. This comes through for the librarian just as a patron misunderstands a post to the chat session and disconnects, not knowing that the source he needs is just about to be sent. In person, one can occasionally catch up with a departing patron or hunt the person down in the library ("Mrs. Robinson, I finally found the answer!"). In email reference, one can reply multiple times. In many libraries, when call ID is present, one can call a disconnected patron back to convey additional information. In chat, one can sometimes only sigh and notate a "lost call."

How to avoid that disconnect? Sending multiple items for the patron to review and choose from while the librarian searches for others is one way of buying time. Remembering to address the patron and confirm links were received and can be opened is critical, particularly if no response is received from the patron. The patron should see something new on the screen every 30 seconds or less, which is especially challenging if the librarian is working with three or more patrons simultaneously. Even if preliminary signals, such as a color indicator, tell the librarian that the patron is no longer there, the librarian should continue sending messages until the system indicates unequivocally that the patron has disconnected —the "Lazarus" patron phenomenon, in which a session connection wanes and then recovers, is all too common.

Cooperative chat reference is a useful, highly valued mode of reference. I have had numerous patrons thank me, and the library providing the service, for this just-in-time, anytime, anywhere assistance. Its users are ubiquitous and varied. Providing that service is a mind-sharpening roller coaster ride that is exhilarating to the librarian who brings her A game.

After a decade, my personal conclusions as to optimizing services for this type of patron are as follows:

1. A critical level of experience in this modality drastically improves service. On the OCLC cooperative, service by backup librarians was traditionally rendered by people with at least 5 and up to 30 hours per week of chat shifts (now at least 15). I personally noticed that a drop in hours resulted in a blunting of skills—typing speed, reactive ability, source finding—each summer, when there were fewer needed and hours per librarian dropped. Each fall, there was a readjustment period. Although in fairness a library might want to have everybody staff chat shifts, service might be optimized by consolidating those shifts among fewer librarians. This would seem to be supported by research done by Christine Tobias (2011) at Michigan State University (MSU). Chat sessions answered by QuestionPoint backup librarians showed up as highest in patron satisfaction and answer quality, even for patrons of MSU. This, I posit, has nothing to do with any shortfalls of Michigan State's librarians, many of whom I know and professionally revere, but with the constant practice in the chat environment that the QuestionPoint librarians had.
2. Some kind of cooperative backdoor environment for the chat librarian should be fostered, by which people engaged in providing this service are connected. In addition to training, probationary periods, and knowledge bases, which are all very useful, a back channel chat for cooperative librarians is in place for the service. If you, as a librarian, get stuck, you have synchronous professional backup and can learn from other librarians in real time. That backup was critical to my development as a chat reference professional. Twitter crowdsourcing, as explored by Courtney Young's recent column in *The Reference Librarian,* might be another means of achieving this goal (2014).

Although some highly regarded authorities state that "all reference is local," there are times that expertise in the reference medium may provide a better user experience than local knowledge (Tobias, 2011). As we continue to provide 24/7, 365-day reference services as cooperatives, this type of training and backup, tailored to the expectations of the medium and patron base needs to be ongoing and in the forefront of the minds of those offering the service, and from where we sit, we see the value of being there whenever the information need strikes.

Where could this type of service be going in the future? I find it difficult, if not dangerous, to speculate on means of service delivery, as technology advances make what was unimaginable yesterday practical today and obsolete tomorrow. I will state that I can only see the need and appetite for remotely practiced synchronous reference increasing. Remote provision of education cuts across time zones and area codes, and reference should keep pace. In June 2014, the National Center for Education Statistics released data showing the number and percentage of students enrolled at Title IV institutions by distance education enrollment status. Of 21,147,055 students enrolled in fall 2012, 12.5%, were enrolled exclusively in distance education courses, with 13.3% enrolled in some distance course. The remaining 74.2% did not participate in distance education (Institute of Education Sciences, 2012). Among workers, the American Community Survey reported that the rate of those who telecommute rose by 29% for some teleworking and 17.7% for those teleworking exclusively between 2005 and 2010 (Mateyka, Rapino, & Landivar, 2012). As librarians and libraries reach out to these remote users, and as these patrons look to us for point-of-need information, our only real choice, in terms of coverage, efficiency, and affordability, is to band together to meet their needs where they are. Just like your phone or your computer, but a world better.

REFERENCES

Gladwell, M. (2000). *The tipping point: How little things can make a big difference*. Boston; London: Little, Brown.

Institute of Education Sciences. (2012). Enrollment in distance education courses, by state: Fall 2012. National Center for Education Statistics. Retrieved from http://nces.ed.gov/pubs2014/2014023.pdf

Mateyka, P. J., Rapino, M. A., & Landivar, L. C. (2012). Home-based workers in the United States: 2010. U.S. Department of Commerce, Economics and Statistics Administration, U.S. Census Bureau. Retrieved from http://www.census.gov/prod/2012pubs/p70-132.pdf

Tobias, C. (2011). Cooperative virtual reference assessment: Service process, service quality, and user perception. Poster presented at Michigan Library Association Annual Conference, October 26.

Tyckoson, D. A. (2013). 4 R's of the reference interview. *Reference Interview 101* [Online Course]. Retrieved from http://www.classes.ala.org/mod/resource/view.php?id=20180

Young, C. L. (2014). Crowdsourcing the virtual reference interview with Twitter. *The Reference Librarian, 55*(2), 172–174. http://dx.doi.org/10.1080/02763877.2014.879030

J | Integration of Library Resources Into the Course Management System

Janet Pinkley, California State University, Channel Islands, and Margaret Driscoll, University of California, Santa Barbara

BACKGROUND

Channel Islands (CI) is one of 23 campuses within the California State University (CSU) system. CI is 11 years old and is the only four-year public institution of higher education in Ventura County, California. Since the University's inception, the John Spoor Broome Library has aimed to provide services to support student learning and this has taken the library "where the students are": the campus-wide course management system, Blackboard. As a young university we were afforded opportunities to build services and collaborate with information technology (IT) in ways that might be more challenging for more established institutions.

The library began with one library service integrated into Blackboard in fall 2006. Over time the library has been able to increase the number of services being integrated into Blackboard. Currently, the library is able to provide students access to necessary materials to complete course requirements through the library's electronic reserves (e-reserves), print reserves, and streaming A/V, as well as support research-based assignments through embedded course guides. The integration of library resources into Blackboard directly supports the library mission of "enhancing the CI mission of interdisciplinary, international, multicultural, and service learning through active collaboration with students, faculty, and staff to plan, implement, promote, and access the use of collections and services and support student learning via its robust information literacy program" (CSU Channel Islands, 2013).

EARLY IMPLEMENTATION

In the months leading up to fall semester 2006, a strategic decision was made to discontinue using a third-party service for hosting e-reserves in favor of integrating this library service directly into Blackboard. This move was prompted by a number of important principles identified by the library:

- The desire to place the library and its services "where the students are" to best serve their academic needs by providing easy access to authoritative and academic materials (and offset the growing ubiquitous use of general Internet searching for research)
- The library could participate in the campus-wide effort to reduce student authentication to access various university services from many to one log-in/password combination
- An early understanding of the exorbitant costs students bear for textbooks and learning materials and the role the library could play in providing affordable materials

Where the Students Are

Every course offered at CI is provided with, and encouraged to use, a digital course site in Blackboard. In fact, the CSU Accessible Technology Initiative (ATI) states a goal to have every campus "implement policies and procedures to promote the posting of all required curricular and instructional resources (including print-based and multimedia materials) in a central, accessible electronic location" (Smith, 2013). Due to this imperative, the vast majority of faculty utilize Blackboard as their course informational warehouse where they post the syllabus, announcements, assignments, and so forth, even when all class sessions meet in a weekly face-to-face environment. Blackboard, then, is the default location for students to visit on a regular basis for important class information and activities.

The Broome Library is self-identified as a digital teaching library, and while still being a vital physical place on campus, is less focused on physical collections than more established university libraries. Combined with an already-established e-reserves service of scanned documents for course readings, integrating this service into Blackboard was a natural fit. Additionally, as will be outlined a bit later, linking directly to journal articles in the library's subscription databases provides immediate access to, and familiarity with, recommended research platforms for academic work. This acts as a subtle library- and faculty-endorsed recommendation to bypass general Internet searching for academic research.

Student Authentication

Prior to Blackboard integration, access to e-reserves required the library to provide a separate login and password for each class. This login/password combination was in addition to several required to access other university services. At one time students and faculty needed to regularly visit more than five individually secured, web-hosted university sites, each requiring unique authentication. The CI campus began working diligently on a portal scheme to provide single-entry authentication to the various campus resources. A link to the library's homepage is included in the entry portal; however, the library took this opportunity to embed e-reserves directly into Blackboard and eliminate the added authentication. Providing access through Blackboard still maintained registered-student-only admission to the copyrighted materials contained within e-reserves to retain our claim to abiding by academic fair use.

Textbook Costs

Library staff members were well aware of the rising costs of college textbooks and the burden this placed upon our students. Additionally, through librarians working closely with faculty members, it became clear that readings from a variety of sources could either effectively supplement the textbook for greater learning outcomes or, in some cases, replace the textbook altogether. Readings gathered from a variety of sources had the ability to greatly enhance various viewpoints on the course topic in ways that textbooks sometimes did not. Additionally, assigning academic journal articles provided advanced opportunities for students to become familiar with reading scholarly works and one day (perhaps) joining the "conversation" by publishing their own research.

In the years following the integration of e-reserves into Blackboard at CI, the entire CSU system undertook an Affordable Learning Solutions initiative that included promotion of free and low-cost learning objects as well as academic readings (California State University, 2012). The library, because of our already-established stance on providing the e-reserves service, became the CI campus leader for this initiative with both a website for faculty (Driscoll, 2013) and a CSU system-wide webinar presentation on September 2012 entitled "Campus ALS Efforts and Outcomes @ CSU Channel Islands" that can be found on the California State University Affordable Solutions webpage (California State University, 2012).

Menu Options in Blackboard

A link directly to the library homepage is located on the campus-wide authentication portal rather than in each Blackboard course. At the course level, it was decided to maintain separate menu choices for the various library services. Some were handled as macro-additions (included in every course during initial course population each semester), while others were added to the menu choices by library staff on a micro level (only in those courses utilizing the service). Individual instructors have the ability to hide menu choices from the student view if they are not desired. The e-reserves menu choice was selected as a macro-addition along with external links, which is used for streaming A/V. Print reserves and course guide menu choices are micro-additions.

E-RESERVES

Academic libraries across the country provide reserves services, both electronic and print, so there is significant understanding of best practices for providing these services. Each campus library deals with the educational demands for their materials in much the same way; however, integrating these library resources into Blackboard at CI heightened the need for developing systems and workflows to maximize the ability of library staff to meet the growing needs. Even prior to contributing to the Affordable Learning Solutions initiative on campus, the library's e-reserves service took into account three substantial legal imperatives:

   1. Accessibility (ADA Section 508 compliant)

The State of California is a strong proponent for the rights of the disabled, and in response the CSU Board of Trustees articulated their commitment in Executive Order 926 (EO 926) (Reed, 2004) relating to the policy on disability support and accommodations. Additionally, the Office of the Chancellor issued Coded Memorandum AA-2013-03, which states that "technology access for individuals with disabilities must provide comparable functionality, affordability, and timeliness and should be delivered in as seamless a manner as possible" (Smith, 2013). Broome Library responded to these directives by placing a high importance on producing ADA Section 508-compliant documents for all scanned e-reserves materials. This has not necessarily proven to be easy in all circumstances. The library researched and selected ABBYY FineReader scanning and optical character recognition (OCR) software to use in conjunction with Adobe Acrobat Pro to create accessible PDF documents. Because we add a copyright coversheet to each PDF, whenever either of these software packages were upgraded, difficulties with the final merged document occurred. Software settings and merging processes had to be reestablished every year or so in order to continue producing accessible PDF files.

2. Fair Use

The library course reserves coordinator (coauthor of this case study) was responsible for understanding, abiding by, and educating faculty on the aspects of copyright law applicable to nonprofit educational institutions and libraries. The coordinator developed a systematic process for determining copyright/fair use status and acceptable quantities, as well as prior electronic availability, for all materials prior to scanning for e-reserves use.

3. Subscription database licensing agreements

Most subscription database licenses with major vendors stipulate that users be directed to a journal volume or article via a durable link to the database rather than extracting an article in PDF and redistributing the digital file. Most faculty members are, of course, unaware of these license stipulations. Therefore, the library endeavors to increase awareness and educate faculty in order to ensure the proper distribution of subscription database materials.

All three of the above required diligence and continued conversation to assure that the library e-reserves service provided academic materials identified by faculty in a legally acceptable manner. On occasion the course reserves coordinator, while conducting other work within a faculty member's Blackboard site, would run across materials posted that were not in compliance with accessibility, copyright/fair use, or licensing agreements. It was important that all materials housed within the e-reserves tab of each course site, and thus associated with the library, be in compliance with all three legal imperatives. Therefore, the coordinator communicated and organized efforts with faculty on a regular basis throughout the academic year.

PRINT RESERVES

The Broome Library utilizes Ex Libris' Voyager integrated library system (ILS). The Circulation Module includes a print reserves functionality that marries catalog records with course information and circulation parameters specifically identified for print reserves materials. The Online Public Access Catalog (OPAC) is customizable to include a print reserves search tab that allows discoverability by academic department, professor name, and course number. The results list indicates specific materials placed on print reserve as well as material availability. While searchable from the OPAC, it again seemed important to place this capability "where the students are," and an embedded link to print reserves became the second generation of instructor-selected library materials in Blackboard.

The first iteration of the link displayed the results of a search for specific course materials. This required print reserves staff to generate and maintain course-specific URL links, which proved to be unsustainable over time. The decision was made to provide a generic link to the print reserves search tab in the OPAC rather than to the individual course results so that we could maintain awareness that print reserves were available for the course with less micro-effort. Not only did this provide Blackboard access to library print reserve materials, but it also engendered an awareness of the library OPAC as a whole within Blackboard.

STREAMING VIDEO

In 2008, the library began offering a streaming A/V service to enhance student learning by increasing availability of instructor-selected library-owned content. Through this service selected DVD or VHS materials owned by the library are converted into Flash video files. The files are linked within Blackboard to a specific course, making them available only to students enrolled in that course.

Classroom Implications

Streaming A/V is one way the library can help support the flipped classroom model of instruction. This allows for students to view library-owned videos and content from home, reserving classroom time for discussion and instruction. This also greatly increases student access to the video, avoiding being unable to view a single copy of the physical video placed on reserve because someone else was watching it.

Accessibility

As mentioned previously, the CSU system promotes accessibility of resources and technology for all students. It is a challenge, both budgetary and time-wise, to make all streaming videos accessible. As such, we ask faculty to indicate to our streaming video coordinator if they have any students that require accommodation for the viewing of streaming A/V without identifying the individual student. This allows the library to send out specific videos for closed captioning, making that streaming video accessible to students with disabilities.

Authentication and Student Access

Students access course-related video content through their course within Blackboard. This allows only students enrolled in a course to view content streamed. There has been some question about streaming video and copyright compliance. The 2011 federal court case, *Association for Information Media and Equipment, et al, vs. The Regents of the University of California, et al.*, affirms that academic institutions, in this case UCLA, are not in violation of copyright by digitizing and streaming library-owned videos and making them available to students on their password-protected Intranet (Ass'n for Info. Media & Equip. v. Regents of the Univ. of Cal., 2012)

COURSE GUIDES

Another service offered by the Broome Library is the integration of either general subject- or course-specific guides in Blackboard. In 2010, the library migrated from HTML-based subject guides on the library's website that were comprised of a list of links, much like print pathfinders, to using Library á la Carte. Library á la Carte is open-source software, similar to LibGuides, that enables librarians to create webpages and subject guides without special programming languages or knowledge of web design. The initial motivation for Library á la Carte was to update outdated and visually unappealing subject guides. However, during the implementation phase of Library á la Carte, we quickly realized the potential for using subject guides within Blackboard and to again get the library "where the students are."

General Subject Guides

Some courses, due to the nature of the coursework, the curriculum, or student projects, do not need course-specific subject guides. Faculty will often request that the general subject guide be posted in their course for students to access library resources for their discipline. This allows students access to library resources at their point of need and directs them to the most relevant resources for a particular discipline.

Course-Specific Guides

In contrast to the general courses mentioned above, there are some courses that have such detailed content that it is necessary to tailor a guide specifically for the curriculum of the course. Interest in these course-specific guides primarily stems from librarians promoting the service to faculty during library instruction. The librarian utilizes the syllabus for the course to make the most relevant guide of library resources for students in that particular course. The reference/instruction librarian and circulation supervisor who serves as the Library á la Carte administrator (coauthor of this case study) then creates a menu choice on the course control panel labeled "Library Resources," which links to the course guide.

CHALLENGES

Permissions to Blackboard

The road to embedding Broome Library materials into Blackboard was paved with gold from the beginning. In the early days of CI, the Blackboard administrator position fell within the organizational structure of the library. Therefore, it was not difficult to obtain access rights or to influence macro-level menu choices for library services. Within the academic IT world, there are grave concerns regarding security and privacy. Giving individuals other than faculty and students access to Blackboard is not taken lightly; in fact, there are a variety of access profiles built into Blackboard that allow fine-tuning of what functions and modules to which individual logins are granted access. As time went by, the Blackboard administrator position was blended into the campus-wide IT organizational structure. Selected services within the library were, however, grandfathered in, with sysadmin access, which allowed the addition of appropriate menu choices, uploading of course content (documents and web links), managing content and access to streaming server content, and copying content from course to course and semester to semester. Without a doubt, the library takes this access very seriously and treats it with great respect. Several times over the years other access profiles were applied to library staff with varied success, with an end goal of allowing library staff to add and manage content without having access to student information.

Communication

As within any organization, communication, both internal and external, is a reoccurring challenge. In relation to our Blackboard-integrated library services, one of the communication challenges is advertising and promoting the services. As a small institution there is a false sense of security that the library does not need to advertise its services because the faculty are already aware of them. However, for an institution that is growing each year, hiring on new tenure-track faculty, and with a large number of courses taught by adjunct faculty, a large portion of teaching faculty are unaware of how the library can support their instruction material needs.

Communicating the processing time required for the various services and scheduling use of the services each semester also proves to be a challenge. Although we aim to process all items as quickly as possible, the work is still detail-oriented and time-consuming. Ensuring that faculty have a clear understanding of the amount of time required from submission to availability continues to require ongoing dialog.

Reoccurring use of services has its communication challenges as well. Some faculty are adept at transferring course materials within Blackboard from one semester to another or one course to another, while others are less comfortable with the technology and require assistance from the library. Additionally, streaming A/V materials require an extra step on the server side to make them available for a new set of students. Faculty, of course, are not always aware that course content does not transfer automatically, so remembering to request assistance in a timely manner can be problematic.

Coordination

Internal coordination of these services also comes with a unique set of considerations. Although there are established workflows for each of the service areas, there is only one permanent staff member assigned to each area. Since no individual can be present all of the time, the result is that the specific service coordinators need to rely on colleagues to facilitate communication that includes intake of materials, requests for services, and so forth. Therefore, all library staff members need at least a basic understanding of the behind-the-scenes processes, average processing time and workflow, and how students access these services.

CONCLUSION

Eight years after the decision to integrate our first service, e-reserves, into Blackboard, it is easy to see that this was the right decision. The integration of library services into Blackboard has been well received by faculty and students, the services are appreciated, and they continue to grow. Therefore, the continued investment of staff time and energy is warranted, even with the knowledge that we will need to continue to adjust workflows, identify creative staffing, and even seek funding for additional staffing to accommodate and sustain increased usage. By continuing to provide integrated library services, the library is playing a direct role in student success, even for those students who may never step foot in the library. Hopefully, case studies such as this will serve as a discussion point for other libraries as they work toward gaining access to their own campus CMS for embedding library resources and services "where the students are."

REFERENCES

Ass'n for Info. Media & Equip. v. Regents of the Univ. of Cal., Case No. 2:10-cv-09378-CBM (MANx), C.D. Cal, 2012 U.S. Dist., (2012). Retrieved from http://law.justia.com/cases/federal/district-courts/california/cacdce/2:2010 cv09378/489296/16/

California State University. (2012). Affordable learning solutions. Retrieved from http://als.csuprojects.org/

CSU Channel Islands. (2013). About: John Spoor Broome Library mission. Retrieved from http://library.csuci.edu/about/

Driscoll, M. A. (2013). Affordable learning at Channel Islands—Textbooks & beyond. Retrieved from http://alacarte.library.csuci.edu/subject-guide/69

Reed, C. B. (2004, December 20). Memorandum: The California State University Board of Trustees policy on disability support and accommodations—Executive order number 926. Retrieved from http://www.calstate.edu/eo/EO-926.html

Smith, E. P. (2013, January 29). Memorandum: Accessible technology initiative. Retrieved from http://www.calstate.edu/AcadAff/codedmemos/AA-2013-03.html

K | Negotiating Space for the Library: Embedding Library Resources and Services Into a University Learning Management System

Jolanda-Pieta van Arnhem and James Williams,
College of Charleston

INTRODUCTION

The College of Charleston Libraries is an academic research library located in Charleston, South Carolina, and is comprised of Addlestone Library, the Communications Museum, Grice Marine Resources Library, the Avery Research Center for African American History and Culture, and the Lowcountry Graduate Center. Addlestone Library is the flagship institution and the central library for campus faculty and students. The library serves approximately 10,506 undergraduate students and 1,217 graduate students (Quick facts: 2012–2013, 2013). The library's charge is not only to support the present academic and research requirements of the undergraduate and faculty population, but also to expand its collections as needed in order to provide resources and services congruent with future instructional and research requirements at the institution. The library's long-term goals and objectives are tied to the projected growth of the student body and the evolving needs of both students and faculty in the digital age (Addlestone Library mission, goals, and vision statement, n.d.).

In 2010 the campus Information Technology (IT) Department announced that it would retire the existing content management system, WebCT, and implement the Desire to Learn (D2L) learning management system platform (LMS) in May of 2011 (WebCT is being decommissioned, 2011). The library took this opportunity to collaborate with the campus IT department to embed library resources and services into the new learning management system in an effort to meet the changing needs of patrons and the university. In the existing WebCT platform, library resources and services were disconnected and viewed as two separate systems. Students and faculty did not have direct access to library services or resources (e.g., the library website, catalog, databases, electronic reserves, subject guides, or the recently implemented virtual chat with a librarian service) from within the LMS. At best, faculty could include links to these resources and services on the libraries' portion of the college website from within their courses. To add to users' frustration, access to most library resources required separate usernames and passwords for each system.

The campus adoption of D2L, branded "OAKS," provided the first opportunity for the library to advocate for a permanent, embedded presence in the college's learning management system. As we learned through the process, this presence had to be continuously renegotiated, with the needs of the library and its patrons not always apparent to IT and other stakeholders on campus, or even within the library itself.

CONNECTING LIBRARY RESOURCES AND SERVICES TO THE CAMPUS LMS

Determining Needs and Creating the Plan

The task of defining and embedding library services and resources into the campus LMS requires constant collaboration between faculty both in and outside the libraries, as well as with various departments in the library and IT. Since this project began in 2010, the library has continued to actively negotiate with all the stakeholders involved in order to identify, update, and retain key resources and services to be embedded into the campus LMS. Numerous topics have had to be considered. Initially, it was vital that library staff receive training on the new system, since many were not familiar with D2L or had even used its predecessor, WebCT. It was also important to decide what services and resources were the most important to include in the initial rollout of the new campus LMS, and to make sure that services worked as expected and provided a seamless user experience.

Initial requests from the library to IT during the 2010–2011 academic year included LMS development server test accounts, staff training, and individual development courses in order to identify key services, resources, and points of failure that needed to be resolved or included in the new LMS.

After reviewing the features available in D2L, it was determined that access to the library website as well as links to key student library services would be beneficial. Single sign-on to library resources was also requested, in order to allow on-campus users to automatically authenticate by IP, and off-campus users to authenticate against Active Directory. The library was also interested in creating a single sign-on from within the LMS for interlibrary loan and My Library Accounts, where patrons could view current checkouts, fines, renew books, and update personal information in order to simplify access to library services for the user.

Investigating New Embedded Librarianship Opportunities

The adoption of a new campus LMS also provided opportunities for the library to explore different models of embedded librarianship. The LMS afforded librarians new methods of delivering content to the classroom and to the user, regardless of location, and provided a single container to deliver individualized services to faculty and students. Considering the LMS as a new point of service provided the opportunity to rethink existing delivery models and broaden existing definitions of embedded librarianship. It provided a key building block to aid in the anticipated need to deliver more and more library instruction virtually (College of Charleston Libraries annual plan 2011–12, 2011). With these ideas in mind, the library developed a system for requesting an embedded course librarian within the LMS. There was some initial concern from all involved about defining roles for an embedded librarian, as well as how to manage requests. After much consideration, the "librarian" role was defined and a procedure for managing requests developed. Faculty can request an embedded librarian in their course using the "Request a Librarian" form available on the D2L homepage. This form was created and is maintained by the library. Requests to assign a librarian to a particular course section are submitted to the head of reference and the instruction coordinator. After a librarian is assigned, the faculty member can add her to their course using the "Add Users" option from the "Classlist."

Librarians embedded in the campus LMS can create widgets, customize the navigation bar, and create and edit homepages in order to facilitate adding course-specific research guides and customized LibGuide widgets within the LMS. The librarian can also participate in "Discussions" in the course and is included on the course "Classlist" to facilitate email contact with the students and faculty. The librarian cannot see any student work or the gradebook, or create or modify course content; however she is able to view course content (OAKS FAQ, n.d.).

Preparing for Roll-Out: Tutorials and Training for Faculty and Students

The library collaborated with the campus IT department to create student-focused video tutorials that were available on the library YouTube channel available for faculty to embed in their D2L courses. Tutorial topics included logging in and general course navigation, using the discussions tool, and how to take a quiz and submit assignments.

Joint training sessions by the library and the IT department were held on campus in order to inform faculty about embedding library resources and services into their D2L courses. Information was also provided during the new faculty orientation activities in fall and spring. Additionally, information was added to the library's "Faculty Services" guide in an effort to provide documentation for library staff and faculty on integrating library services in our campus LMS.

Launching D2L with a Library Presence

The new campus learning management system went live in May 2011. For the initial launch, the library website as well as key links to library services were included in the default navigation of all course templates, thus providing seamless integration to library resources and services for students with minimal effort on part of the instructor.

The team was also able to provide a standard "Student Library Services" D2L system widget as part of the default course homepage. The widget included a live interactive chat feature, initially powered by Meebo, which provided students with instant access to a librarian during reference desk hours from within D2L. The "Student Library Services" widget also provided users with links to key services and resources such as their My Library Account, interlibrary loan services, electronic reserves, research consultation requests, off-campus access to library materials, and the library's hours.

CONNECTING LIBRARY RESOURCES AND SERVICES TO THE CAMPUS LMS REDUX

A number of Library requests could not be implemented during the initial launch of the campus LMS in May 2011. One of the requests that could not be fulfilled was the ability to provide subject- or discipline-specific library resources at the course level. This would require significant programming time and expertise from our IT department and librarians and was not a project priority at the time. Over the course of this project, the library and campus IT department have continued to collaborate in order to provide seamless integration to key library services. A significant improvement for the users has been the implementation of single sign-on to library resources, simplifying access to library services and resources both on and off campus. There have also been a number of changes in services and resources offered by the library, as well as two major updates to the D2L platform since this project began.

Migrating Electronic Reserves (e-Reserves) to the LMS

In an effort to collapse duplicative systems and provide access to library electronic reserves from a single point of access for the user, the library decided to migrate our existing electronic reserves (e-reserves) system to the campus LMS. The migration not only eliminated the need for students to maintain additional passwords and to go outside of the LMS to view electronic materials from their instructors, but it also reduced annual spending from the library budget by allowing us to discontinue paying the annual fees associated with the existing e-reserves system.

In order to migrate existing e-reserves courses and move users to the LMS, new procedures and roles had to be developed. Similar to the embedded librarian presence, the library created and maintains a "Request Course Reserves in OAKS" form for faculty to request the service. A role was created for the circulation department that allows library staff to access the "Content" area of a faculty member's course and add electronic reserves material. After the content has been added, a screenshot of the content area is taken and emailed to the faculty member as confirmation that the electronic reserves have been established.

Changes at the Reference Desk

In fall 2011, the library implemented a peer staffing program and combined two service points in the library into a single "Information" desk in an effort to provide library patrons with consistent, in-person and virtual assistance, research, and information support, as well as IT support for students. The project required collaborative efforts between the library and the campus IT department, and it utilized full-time and temporary staff from the reference department and the student computing support department (part of campus IT). This included many student workers that would join with reference librarians and IT staff on desk shifts. As a result of merging the service points, students could now access library and IT resources and services from a single location, whether in person or virtually via the LMS. Also in preparation for this change, and to provide additional reference support for online learning, the library licensed and began configuring LibAnswers Knowledge Base. Using this system, students can find answers to frequently asked questions. If the question is asked over instant message, the staff member who responds to the query can add new questions not covered in the system to Knowledge Base at the time of the transaction. Knowledge Base provides a place all staff can consult in order to give consistent responses to queries in all formats. Knowledge Base even has a query spy feature to see questions that were typed but not submitted.

The Day Meebo Died

On July 11, 2012, Google shut down Meebo, a very popular free IM chat client in libraries (Tay, 2012). Our library was an active user, and like many other libraries, Meebo powered our "IM a Librarian" service. The chat widget was also an integral part to our presence in the campus LMS, and was featured in the "Student Library Services" widget on every course using the default course homepage. We were seeing an increased use of the virtual chat widget from previous years and expected this trend to continue when we implemented peer staffing and a single "Information" desk at the library. Virtual chat was also an integral service for the future, as more courses were offered online at our institution. Fortunately, Springshare was due to release LibChat, an IM service that could be integrated into LibGuides and LibAnswers (Meebo going away, 2012). Our library was already using LibGuides and negotiating to acquire LibAnswers, and decided to smooth the transition from Meebo by making the impromptu decision to pay for an IM service and adopt the new LibChat platform. The transition to LibChat was relatively seamless, with minor issues related to browsers and mobile devices. New widget code was created; however, the library experienced multiple delays from our campus IT department in changing the code to the "Student Library Services" widget in the LMS, and the chat feature was down for a short period of time. This experience showed us that some services may be worth paying for earlier rather than later and that the library needed more control over the library content that was offered in the LMS.

LMS Upgrades (Or When Stuff Breaks)

A month after Meebo died, our campus IT department informed us that they would be rolling out a major upgrade to D2L (version 10) in 2013. Based on our previous experiences, we requested to have librarian beta testers and accounts on the development server in order to identify any points of failure or new services that needed to be included in LMS upgrade rollout. The LMS upgrade broke many of the widget features we had added that called an application programming interface (API): for example, a dropdown list of all of our Springshare LibGuides. After lengthy testing, and based on our previous experiences, we elected to create a "false" widget that was actually just an image promoting library services that linked out to an external page managed by the library.

Reconfiguring the LMS widget provided the library with more control and direct access to change, add, or update information included in the LMS. The change also provided the library with the opportunity to provide additional access to library resources and services, such as our newly adopted "Ask Us" Knowledge Base.

The LMS upgrade created an entirely different look and feel for the campus LMS, and it provided a great opportunity for the library to rebrand the library services widget to reflect the changes in the organization and staffing of the information desk. The upgrade also required new student-focused tutorials to help aid

Figure 1. Desire2Learn (D2L) linked image "Library Services" system widget.

in the transition. In an effort to increase campus awareness about using library services within the LMS, the revised tutorials were made available on the Library YouTube channel, IT OAKS Support blog, "How Do I" library Knowledge Base, and the IT Student Computing Support blog as well. Tutorial topics included logging in and course navigation, course content, communication tools, grade tools, and management tools.

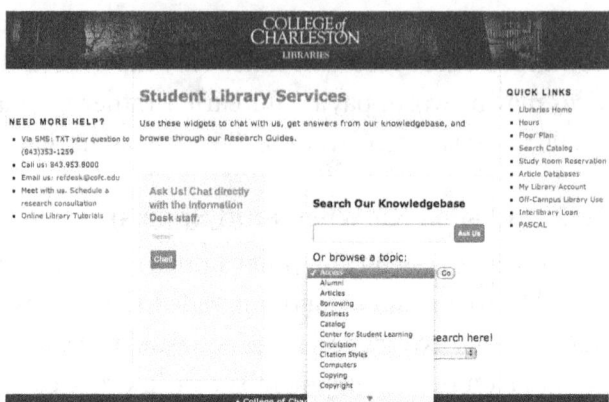

Figure 2. Desire2Learn (D2L) "Library Services" system widget external page, managed by the library.

In May 2014, the IT department rolled out a second major upgrade to D2L, version 10.3. The library and IT continued to collaborate on joint efforts to embed library resources and services in the campus LMS. Student tutorials were revised by the library, captioned with YouTube's automatic timing feature, and published as a playlist on the library YouTube channel. The playlist was shared on the previously mentioned distribution points. The creation of a single playlist for all the new LMS tutorials is a new marketing strategy and provides added convenience for users. Faculty who want to embed the tutorials in their LMS courses can do so with a single embed code, and viewers can review multiple related topics in a single location. New tutorials can easily be added to the playlist as they are created, and embedded playlists are automatically updated without any further action required.

The upgrade coincides with the library's website redesign project. In order to provide uninterrupted service and maintain existing links in the LMS for the Student Library Services widget, redirects will need to be coordinated and maintained by the library for all the pages hosted on the library website.

CONCLUSION

Embedding library services and resources into our campus LMS has been a vehicle for change at our library. It has allowed us to collaborate with partners outside the library, provide outreach and training to the campus, and work toward our anticipated growing need to deliver library instruction and research services virtually on a 24/7 schedule. The project has also helped us prepare to fully participate in online learning at our institution and evaluate our needs. For example, as online and hybrid course offerings continue to expand at our institution, it is imperative that the library continues and collaborate with our campus IT department on: implementing web conferencing capabilities into our LMS, expanding access to our newly adopted discovery service, and creating and delivering resources, training, and instruction at the point of need in order to provide a fuller embedded librarian experience for our patrons.

The project has helped to support the library's strategic goals to improve technological infrastructure and enable smooth transitions to new technologies (College of Charleston Libraries annual plan 2011–12, 2011). For example, in fall 2013 the campus IT department integrated GoogleApps into the campus LMS, prompting the need for instruction for students and additional tutorials that can be embedded in faculty courses to help increase adoption (Study skills workshops 201, n.d.). The D2L 10.3 upgrade in May 2014 included additional integrated features in the LMS, including the adoption of the campus-hosted video sharing platform Kaltura, and a campus license for VoiceThread. The library plans to continue collaborating with IT to produce student tutorials and provide instruction in the use of these newly integrated D2L services.

Embedding library services and resources into the campus LMS has proven to demand continual reassessment of current and emerging technologies required to serve library patrons. For example, as streaming video services increase and access to VHS resources are removed from campus, the library is collaborating with IT to provide education, tutorials, and training for faculty on how to seamlessly use library streaming collections in their LMS courses. These services and resources help to ensure the delivery of content to the classroom and to the user, regardless of location. As a whole, our opinion is that embedding library resources and services into the campus LMS is both beneficial and useful; however, we have found that a clear plan of assessment of our efforts is a missing piece of the puzzle, making it difficult to evaluate fully.

Moving forward, we have added Google Analytics to the external "Library Services" widget page in order to determine how many individuals are

> **ADDITIONAL RESOURCES**
>
> College of Charleston Libraries YouTube channel. (n.d.). Retrieved from http://www.youtube.com/playlist?list=PLPMd8f8re-v51C0jQ4Nd9wgErUsW79mQp
>
> Faculty services [LibGuide]. (n.d.). College of Charleston. Retrieved from http://libguides.library.cofc.edu/content.php?pid=121337&sid=1170780
>
> Request course reserves in OAKS [Web form]. (n.d.). College of Charleston. Retrieved from http://cofc.edu/library/faculty/eres/course/index.php
>
> Request a librarian [Web form]. (n.d.). College of Charleston. Retrieved from http://cofc.edu/library/libraries/request-a-librarian/index.php
>
> Student library services. (n.d.). College of Charleston. Retrieved from http://media.library.cofc.edu/widgets.html

using it. We hope to determine the number of unique logins that occur over the course of each term to gauge usage by faculty and students more exactly if this data can be retrieved from the D2L system by our campus IT department. We would like to compare this to other usage statistics, such as the number of clicks on the Library Services widget. We also plan to collect our own data on the number of faculty using D2L for course reserves and the number of e-reserves courses migrated. It would be beneficial to determine how much of our IM traffic, LibGuide usage, and Ask Us Knowledge Base queries are generated from the Library Services widget in the LMS. Thanks to the analytics provided in YouTube, we do know how many views our online tutorials have received. The total overall number of views for each D2L version of tutorials has increased since 2011; however, we do not know how many of our students are watching them or how many faculty are actively embedding the tutorials in their courses.

Increased marketing of embedded library resources and services in the LMS, as well as a survey of student and faculty usage, is certainly warranted to better understand the needs of our patrons. Much of this data could be used to further develop a tailored embedded librarian program that emphasizes student-centered learning in order to ensure that students at the university receive thoughtful instruction in information literacy and digital fluency.

What we have learned from the experience is that embedded librarianship has to be more than just resources and services. It must be predicated on relationships built with the community of users across campus, especially the faculty. The library is well aware of the value of creating and maintaining those relationships. It takes a community development approach to interweave the right services and resources at the correct point of need in order to avoid the trap of developing time- and resource-intensive "one shots" of limited value. This kind of development, based on listening to the community and recognizing their knowledge about their own needs, can drive us to new opportunities afforded by coproduction with the community. Faculty can tell us not only about their subject areas, but their experience with students as a diverse body of learners who often need tailored approaches to create an entryway to lead them to better resources, and the ability to select better resources on their own. This approach to embedded librarianship requires constant, iterative effort and continuous evaluation and assessment in order to meet the needs of the users most effectively.

REFERENCES

Addlestone Library mission, goals, and vision statement. (n.d.). College of Charleston. Retrieved from http://www.cofc.edu/library/libraries/mission.php

College of Charleston Libraries annual plan 2011–12. (2011, June 29). College of Charleston. Retrieved from http://www.cofc.edu/library/docs/goals_objectives

Meebo going away, LibChat coming your way . . . see it at ALA! (2012, June 12). Retrieved from http://blog.springshare.com/2012/06/12/meebo-going-away-libchat-coming-your-way-see-it-at-ala/

OAKS FAQ: Answers to frequently asked questions regarding OAKS. (n.d.). College of Charleston. Retrieved from http://it.cofc.edu/education/webctoaks/oaks/oaks-faq.php

Quick facts: 2012–2013. (2013, January). College of Charleston. Retrieved from http://irp.cofc.edu/docs/quick-facts/2012-2013%20Quick%20Facts.pdf

Study skills workshops 201: Google Apps. (n.d.). College of Charleston. Retrieved from http://libguides.library.cofc.edu/googleoaks

Tay, A. (2012, June 10). Meebo Messenger, Meebo Me discontinued July 11, 2012. Retrieved from http://lisnews.org/meebo_messenger_meebo_me_discontinued_july_11_2012

WebCT is being decommissioned on May 14. (2011, May 12). College of Charleston. Retrieved from http://blogs.cofc.edu/it/tag/webct/

L | **Boosting User Engagement With Online Social Tools**

Georgina Parsons, Brunel University London, United Kingdom

INTRODUCTION AND BACKGROUND

In the past, online library services have been centered around the catalog and basic account functions, with additional noninteractive content, such as library information and news, book lists (for example, prize winners), and events calendars.

The advent of social media and rich variety of new online tools have led users, especially from the younger generations, to have higher expectations of all online experiences. Their website usage should be seamless, interactive, and personalized—as simple as Google, as social as Facebook, and as immediate as Twitter.

This has triggered a growing need for libraries to look into simple and fast ways to enhance their online presence to meet, and take advantage of, these new expectations and ideas. Rising to these challenges is beneficial to libraries in increasing satisfaction and usage, and ensuring a new generation of users continues to see libraries as a core part of their lives.

This article looks at the principles of integrating social tools into online library services, and the benefits of doing so, with examples looking in particular at the integration of ChiliFresh's Connections platform.

DEVELOPMENT OF ONLINE SOCIAL TOOLS FOR THE LIBRARY

The ChiliFresh platform began as a ratings and reviews engine, taking advantage of the possibilities of online crowdsourcing in order to offer user-generated content through the library catalog. In this way, users who were not directly engaged with the library were targeted more, with the offering of a "real-life" service that can be seen as more relevant to them, due to reviews coming from peers rather than librarians. This builds on the solid foundations of libraries always having offered valuable content above basic metadata, in library recommendations and publisher enrichment, by adding to this mix the human side of patron interaction and response.

Using a global platform offers the possibility to use international content rather than just reviews from a library's own patrons, in order to allow for a rapid install and visibility even if the library's users do not engage quickly. The flexibility in moderation procedures means staff involvement does not need to be too demanding, but the option remains to ensure full moderation before user content becomes visible, allaying concerns often raised over the appropriateness of user-generated content. An often-stated attraction of new technologies and tools is their flexibility for the end user, but the customization for the administrator is equally key.

In addition to reviews and ratings within the catalog itself, the availability of simple widgets allows for pushing the library out to other sites, for example, embedding content within the county website or local schools' sites, to display lists of the top-rated content or most recent reviews. Along with the promotional aspect, this can encourage engagement with the community where users want to see their reviews highlighted online on official sites; this almost competitive aspect can be appealing to some user groups.

The expansion of the reviews and ratings engine into the broader Connections product reflects the rapid development of social tools online and other companies' social plugins, to bring the end user the fuller social experience but within the context of the library. With Connections, users can share book lists, create a profile and wish lists, recommend items to each other very simply (as they would on Facebook), but all the while remaining within the library's online environment. This adds the elements of interactivity and personalization to the traditional library interface.

New functions such as online book clubs and discussion groups allow for greater patron interaction; users can manage their involvement in particular areas, or library staff can maintain a presence within the platform and moderate or spark interaction. As well as deciding how much practical input the library should have in these features, the level of customization is also a library choice; each feature in the platform has an administrative area allowing the library full control over the wording, style, and settings, in order for the appropriate level of local branding and oversight to be achieved.

Another key aspect in the modern online experience is the personalization of services, where users expect, or desire, relevant information only. The Connections recommendations function aims to achieve this with personalized recommendations based not only on the user's interests and past or present reads, but also on her networks of friends and groups within the system. Again, this retains a focus on the content being a peer-based system rather than a recommendations engine based on library, publisher, or machine-driven data, with the anticipated result of being seen as a more valuable service and more "in touch" with the users.

Additional add-ons allow users the choice of interacting in their preferred method, and choice is one more modern expectation. As well as the personalization of the Connections interface (so users do not have to see areas of content they are not personally interested in), there are additional add-ons in the product suite. For example, does the library have a lot of younger users who spend significant time on Facebook? Perhaps they can be reached with the ChiliFresh Facebook application, which is undergoing rapid development and is in use, amongst others, at Dallas Public Library (2014). Is there a large group of users who prefer their mobile device to a PC (or perhaps don't have a PC)? They can be offered the mobile application (Cromaine Library, 2014; Jessamine County Public Library, 2014), which allows mobile-friendly catalog access enhanced with reviews and other user content; again, this is offered as a simple install without additional work required from the library system vendor.

The features mentioned so far cover additional, enhanced content aiming to improve the feel and utility of library services, but we must remember that the core library functions remain as important as ever. New social tools do not neglect these. Account management becomes easier as users who see their library on Facebook, for example, are reminded of their loans and can simply use the Facebook app to renew items without needing to exit the site and log in to the library catalog. Similarly, resource discovery is improved. It is no longer just about having an online catalog, as there are so many other sites competing for users' attention and offering additional, perhaps more attractive, content and experiences. Enhancing the online catalog with modern tools and pushing it further (both in itself and out to other sites so it becomes more visible) becomes a necessity, as discovery is a core feature underpinning any strong library service.

BENEFITS AND OUTCOMES OF USING SOCIAL TOOLS

Many of the following points around the benefits of using social tools are again general and should be considered in developing a library's online presence in any way. Useful in evaluating the potential impact of online developments, the practical comparisons here continue to use the ChiliFresh platform as an example.

A fundamental benefit, and probably the underlying reason for adopting any new online tool, is that of creating a better user experience. Users love to share, and adapting the online library experience so that it becomes more personal will engage users more. They can share what they like (as much or as little) in whichever method they prefer, whether just reviews, discussion groups, or book clubs, either as a participant or running their own, whether for fun or for student projects. Making the experience enjoyable should increase retention of users.

As well as being enjoyable, there is an element of simplicity and security in such an online platform. The ease with which users can contribute in, for example, book clubs, whilst remaining relatively anonymous and safe online, encourages the shyer library users to engage in discussions and offers them the ability to dip in and out with no pressure. This can then perhaps develop into further physical engagement at the library.

User choice is another benefit. Offering options to users, such as managing their account in the catalog or in Facebook, is important in increasing library exposure and making patrons' lives easier. A wider online presence also builds on the relationship with patrons between their physical visits.

Implementing anything new inevitably takes staff time, but many new tools have low maintenance requirements, which is often a key consideration in choosing add-on products. The provision of ChiliFresh promotional tools, such as graphics, bookmarks, and widgets for both online and physical promotions, is a useful time-saver, but there is still work required in obtaining and implementing these. Similarly, clear interfaces ensure users do not need assistance being led through them, and simple installs and customizable maintenance settings, for example, regarding moderation, allow library staff to spend as much, or as little, time as is available with the new platform.

However, whilst a simple and rapid product implementation is possible, one cannot underestimate the benefits of staff engagement, with its twofold advantages. Staff time spent promoting the new features, leading book clubs, triggering discussion areas, and so on can engender more activity from the users. Additionally, staff usage of the tools can result in improved physical library interactions, as they can share their personal experiences of the platform and thus market the new tools more efficiently. This blending of physical and online interactions is a critical aspect where the crossover should be seamless.

Improving users' library experience is key, but benefits to the library itself must not be forgotten. A wider range of tools can lead to an increase in the visibility of library stock. There is additional serendipity on social sites, as users go from friend to club to recommendation, and so on, which highlights stock more broadly and increases discovery, thus also potentially increasing usage of materials. Promotion of stock online in lists, clubs, discussion areas, and using widgets to highlight user reviews (which can reach different or more people than simple library recommendations) all help to boost library usage. Visual widgets, such as the book carousel on the Pierce County Public Library System catalog (2014), add the visual element that is becoming more crucial, to ensure library catalogs appear as modern as other search engines, and to draw users in to items in an attractive manner. Libraries often see an increase in loans and reservations of highlighted items as a result of such prominent visual advertising.

One other key focus with ChiliFresh products is their integration; library enthusiasm for trying new sites and engagement tools can risk resulting in a disparate selection of sites and content without seamlessness. While it is key to be present where users are, or want the library to be (e.g., having a Facebook page), there must also be seamless integration between additional tools and the main library content or site, so that users do not feel lost or have to accustom themselves to multiple interfaces. ChiliFresh's complete integration within the catalog, such as that at Salt Lake County (2014) or the Libraries of South Australia (2014), uses lightboxes for additional interaction, such as ratings, reviews, adding items to bookshelves, and leading users smoothly into ChiliFresh features. The user does not have to navigate a cluttered interface, but has easy links to open interactive content, which still does not remove him from the core library site.

This focus of Connections in creating one library "hub," where users can access the library's own content as well as peer content and can make new connections, ensures that the user is not drawn away from the library. In times when there are many sources of information, especially in the online world, this aspect of building on the library as the core, essential point of reference, on which other experiences are built, provides the benefit of ensuring that the library remains the central focus.

CONCLUSION

The traditional online library catalog remains a core service with important functions. However, the increasing expectations for online experiences must be built in to ensure that the library remains relevant online, and the examples discussed demonstrate how some simple work with new products can boost user engagement and improve user interaction with libraries in the online environment. Social media and many new technologies are built around communication and interaction, so library interaction through such tools can reposition their online presence from static sites that provide news and stock information, to lively places for conversation and exchange.

Integrating social tools such as the ChiliFresh platform into the catalog means that, while the library catalog remains the central point of reference, the addition of user-generated content, personalization, choice, and interaction shifts the online experience so that it becomes about the user, not the library. And after all, enhancing the life of the user is a core purpose of libraries.

REFERENCES

Cromaine Library Mobile app. (2014). Retrieved from https://itunes.apple.com /us/app/cromaine-library-mobile/id642385074?mt=8

Dallas Public Library. (2014). *Facebook*. Retrieved from http://facebook.com /dallaslibrary

Jessamine County Public Library app. (2014). Retrieved from https://play.google .com/store/apps/details?id=com.chilifresh.jcpl&hl=en

Libraries of South Australia. (2014). Retrieved from http://sapln.ent.sirsidynix.net.au/

Pierce County Public Library System catalog. (2014). Retrieved from http:// polariscatalog.piercecountylibrary.org/polaris/

Salt Lake County Library catalog. (2014). Retrieved from http://catalog.slcolibrary .org/polaris/

You Have a Question, So Tweet Me Maybe: A Study in Using Twitter for Reference

Amanda L. Folk, University of Pittsburgh at Greensburg

The Millstein Library at the University of Pittsburgh at Greensburg (UPG), an undergraduate-serving, regional campus of the University of Pittsburgh, launched a pilot of its @MillsteinLib Twitter account in late August 2013. Prior to this launch, the library's existing references services required our students to come to us, whether it was coming to the physical library building or to the library's website. The rationale behind the launch of @MillsteinLib was to experiment with a new reference medium that existed in a space that many of the students already used. The implementation of a Twitter account was also an opportunity to extend the existing "A" Team brand, created to promote reference and instruction, into the realm of social media. In addition to @MillsteinLib, students were encouraged to use #asktheateam to hashtag their questions. Prior to implementing @MillsteinLib, no literature about Twitter as a reference medium was located, so it seemed that the Millstein Library might have something to contribute to the field by piloting such a service.

TWITTER AS A REFERENCE MEDIUM

After the librarians at the Millstein Library received permission from the University Library System (ULS) administration at the University of Pittsburgh, we drafted a Twitter policy working document describing how we would interact with students who tweeted us questions and how this service would be staffed. In general, the @MillsteinLib account would be staffed from 8:30 a.m. to 6:00 p.m. Monday through Thursday, and 8:30 a.m. to

5:00 p.m. on Friday. We used the existing on-call schedule for the reference desk to set up the coverage of the account by the three librarians, Pat Duck, Amanda Folk, and Anna Mary Williford. Although the existing on-call schedule was used to determine coverage, a librarian might be responsible for fielding reference questions on Twitter even if she was not at the physical reference desk. The on-call librarian was responsible for checking the @MillsteinLib account and #asktheateam approximately every 30 minutes during her shift. The following guidelines were given for responding to questions:

- Type in the user's "handle" proceeded by the "@" sign. (e.g., @MillsteinLib). This will alert the user that the librarian is responding to his/her question.
- Answer the question as completely as possible while being mindful of the character limit. If necessary, you can spill over into a second tweet, but be sure to include the user's handle in the second tweet as well as the first. If a question would be better handled over email, send the user a direct message, which is a private message between two users, asking for his/her email address. Also, provide the user with your email address at this time.
- Include your initials at the end of your response, so the user knows which librarian helped him/her.
- Record the question in your individual DeskTracker account, selecting the off desk option, using the instant message/chat option as the venue, and adding "Millstein Twitter" in the notes field. The question type, patron group, and subject of question will vary.

Despite our intention to use Twitter as a reference medium, we did realize that it was not the best vehicle for more in-depth questions. We hoped that students would be interested in asking basic questions, such as "What hours are you open today?" or "Do you have color printing?" For students who are already regular Twitter users, we believed it would be an easy way to ask these basic questions, as easy as sending a text message. We decided that if students did ask questions that would require a more lengthy exchange, we would send them a direct message asking if we could contact them via email.

On November 19, we received our first question on the @MillsteinLib account through Twitter's direct message feature. The student asked if we have a scanner or fax machine in the library, which is a question we receive frequently. Like a regular tweet, the direct message feature only allows one to enter 140 characters at a time. However, since it is a private message between two people, sending two messages does not look as sloppy as it would if it were tweeted publicly.

Figure 1. First question received on the @MillsteinLib account.

On December 11, a student sent a tweet directly to @MillsteinLib asking if we carry a particular book about cell biology. Unfortunately, this tweet was sent after 6 p.m., so a response from the library was not immediate.

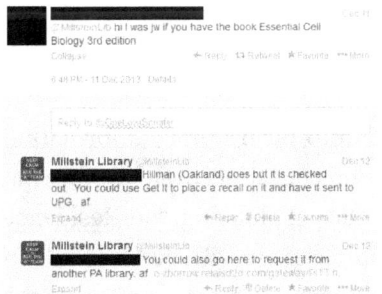

Figure 2. Second question received on the @MillsteinLib account.

In addition to receiving one other question on the Twitter account, we received questions from students on various Facebook accounts. On December 3, a student sent a private message to the Friends of the Millstein Library Facebook page to ask if there would be extended hours during finals. This is interesting, because this Facebook page has not been promoted to students. Also, one of the librarians fielded a reference question from a student on her personal Facebook account just a few days later.

In October, before we had received any questions, one of the librarians was invited to meet with the "Advertising: Strategy and Practice" course, in which the students had just learned about using Twitter and other social media sites for promotional purposes. The course instructors thought this would be a great way for the students to apply what they had learned, for the library to get valuable feedback from our target audience, and to promote the @MillsteinLib account. It is impossible to say if the changes we made to @MillsteinLib based on the feedback from these students led to the reference questions being asked. Despite this, we did receive some perspective about how undergraduate students on our campus are willing or are not willing to interact with a campus department on social media.

DESIGN

The original profile picture for the @MillsteinLib account was of our iconic stained glass window with Bruiser the Bobcat, the campus mascot. We received feedback that the picture of the building seemed too impersonal, so we changed our profile picture to reflect the "A" Team brand created to promote reference and instruction. We used the previous profile picture as our background image.

The descriptive information in our profile box originally said "Need some help? Have a question? The librarians are here to help! Send us a tweet, direct message, or use #asktheateam." Based on student feedback, we changed the third sentence to include the three librarians' names, so our account had a more personal feel.

CONTENT

Initially, the Twitter account was not intended to push library information to our users. However, after meeting with our colleague Brian Root, who had implemented a Twitter account for the Office of Housing and Residence Life, we decided that we did need to interact and engage with our students in some way. Although all three librarians were responsible for monitoring the @MillsteinLib account and answering questions, I took the lead in generating content for the account. I started by posting some "fun" photos of the library as we prepared for the upcoming school year, as well as some library humor. Toward the end of the semester, when stress levels were running high, I posted some funny cat pictures, which some of the students retweeted. I hoped that the lighthearted posts would make the students feel more comfortable approaching the librarians to ask questions, either online or in person. I also started to post older pictures from the UPG Visual History site—pictures that I thought students might find interesting or funny. For example, the women's basketball team implemented a Twitter account about the same time as the library, so I posted a picture of the first women's basketball team and mentioned them in the tweet. I tried to tweet or retweet almost every weekday in order to keep the level of activity up. Whenever character limits allowed, I used the #PittGreensburg hashtag so that students, faculty, or staff who searched for this hashtag on Twitter would see the @MillsteinLib tweets.

Root also suggested that we use contests to engage the students, since his department had some success with this. The first few contests that I

CONTEST TIME! We've hidden a delicious prize in the Library. Find the books about the drink that helps you make it through the day after a long night of studying, and you'll win something that will help you to buy some of it on campus. If you find it, make sure you tweet a picture of it to @MillsteinLib, post a picture of it on this Facebook page, or email a picture of it to Amanda (alfolk@pitt.edu). HAVE A BLAST!

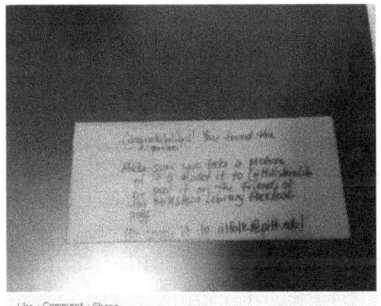

Figure 3. Using Facebook for longer posts, including contest instructions.

tweeted were related to pictures from the UPG Visual History site, and the prizes were 2 GB library flash drives. Participation in these early contests was hit-or-miss. Some contests did not have any participants, while others had a couple. I learned that while our students like anything that is free, they are most interested in free food and drink. With the help of the Friends of the Millstein Library, I purchased "bucks" for campus dining services. For the next contest, I wrapped up $10 worth of "bucks" and hid them in books about coffee in the library's main stacks. I gave hints about where students might be able to find the prize. The initial contest announcement was posted on the Friends of the Millstein Library Facebook page, which updates to our Twitter feed, so I could exceed the 140 character limit.

After the Office of Housing and Residence Life retweeted the contest, two students worked together to find the "bucks" and sent a picture of them holding the prize as proof. I also tried a contest in which students were asked to submit pictures of studying for finals in the library for a chance to win "bucks" for coffee. This contest did not have any participants. This last contest was not retweeted by other departments, which means we might have to ask other campus social media users to help promote our contests. I regularly retweet other campus departments on the @MillsteinLib account, so this promotion would not be one-sided.

PROMOTION

Prior to implementing the @MillsteinLib account, the library routinely used bookmarks and postcards to promote our services, including LibGuides, the SAILS test, and the "A" Team. I worked with the library's administrative assistant, Diane Hughes, to create Twitter-specific postcards in Microsoft Publisher. In addition to being available at the reference desk, we handed them out in library instruction sessions and placed them in tabletop displays around the library. Hughes also created images of these postcards that could be posted on the campus digital signage system and included in the campus's weekly news electronic bulletin, the *Intercom*. The flyer advertising our fall hours also featured the new Twitter service, and the existing LibGuide boxes promoting the "A" Team were updated to reflect the new service.

The majority of our followers came from the Freshman Seminar courses that were offered in the fall. In addition to giving the students the postcards, we told them that we would give them more free University Library System (ULS) swag, such as coin purses or sticky note books, if they showed us that they were following the @MillsteinLib account.

Students mentioned that they were hesitant to follow campus departments on Twitter because they did not want faculty and staff to read their tweets, especially if they have not made their accounts private. Some students thought that being up front in a funny way about this tension on promotional material might make them more likely to follow @MillsteinLib. One possibility would be to put #wedontcreep #noreally on some of our promotional material. I intend to work with Hughes to create new promotional material that reflects these suggestions.

CONCLUSION

The implementation of Twitter as a reference medium was intentionally launched as a pilot; we really did not have any idea of what to expect but thought it was worth trying. The maintenance of the account took about 15–30 minutes a day, including posting content and monitoring the account for questions. Some days monitoring the account or thinking of new content was difficult to manage, but most days @MillsteinLib was not an inconvenience or a burden on my workload. The development and monitoring of contests was the most labor-intensive aspect of this pilot, and this work usually had little reward since participation was low. Having said that, finding material to post was often a fun task, and the implementation of @MillsteinLib provided the opportunity to interact with other campus departments that were also trying to create a social media presence to engage our students.

Two of the three questions that we received in the first semester of the @MillsteinLib pilot came in after the librarians had left for the day. For the spring semester, the night supervisor, Jim Vikartosky, will also be monitoring the account and answering any questions that are posted. This means that, for the most part, the @MillsteinLib account will be monitored during the library's normal Monday–Friday operating hours. We have already started to advertise these extended hours on signage in the physical library, as well as in the @MillsteinLib Twitter profile.

I will be assessing @MillsteinLib and making recommendations for the future of the account as a part of a ULS leadership development program. While the account has not received many reference questions at this time, it might be worth keeping the account if it allows the library to connect with students in a different way or with other campus departments, such as admissions or athletics. However, if there is not a substantial increase in questions, followers, or retweets, it might be worth discontinuing the @MillsteinLib account and exploring a different social media vehicle to facilitate these types of interactions. The Pitt-Greensburg campus uses MAP-Works to aid with retention efforts and distributes surveys to students throughout the academic year. In the past the library has had the opportunity to add questions to the survey, and it might be worth including a question about how (or if) the students want to connect with library or ask the librarians questions through social media.

ADVICE

Listed below is some advice for libraries that are thinking about trying Twitter as a reference medium.

- If your library has student employees, talk to them about how they think their peers might like to interact with the library using social media. This is something I did not do but should have.
- Conduct a focus group with targeted users, even if it is informal.
- Before committing to the new service, even in the form of a pilot, be honest about how much staff time you will have to dedicate to daily maintenance and monitoring.
- Create and agree upon a policy document, so everyone knows what is expected in terms of coverage and responding to patrons.
- Team up with other colleagues or departments who have used or tried to use social media to engage students. Find out what has worked for them and what has not.

- Show some personality while maintaining a level of professionalism.
- Make sure students know there is an actual person communicating with them on Twitter, not just "The Library."
- Make sure the service is staffed in the evening and at night.
- Be prepared to post information almost daily, even if you are simply retweeting information from another person, department, or organization.
- Create an account for a URL shortening service, like Goo.gl or Bitly. Not only will this save you some precious characters when posting links, but it will also tell you how many people clicked on the link. This can help you determine what kind of content appeals to your users.
- Pictures, pictures, pictures. Students seemed to favorite and retweet tweets that included pictures more often than ones with no pictures.
- Create lists to group the accounts that you follow, especially for accounts related to your campus. This will make it easier to monitor what is happening around campus and to retweet information that might be useful or interesting to your followers.
- Do not be afraid to discontinue the service if it there is no return on investment.

Embedding LibraryThing for Libraries in the Online Library Catalog

Amanda Viana, Norton Public Library, Massachusetts

BACKGROUND

The Norton Public Library is located in the town of Norton, Massachusetts, serving a population of 19,000 residents, approximately half of whom are library card holders. The Norton Public Library is a member of the Southeastern Automated Information Library System (SAILS) network, serving libraries in southeastern Massachusetts. SAILS is responsible for running and supporting the network's online catalog.

The SAILS network is a multitype consortium that includes public, academic, and K–12 libraries. SAILS has the largest number of full-time member libraries in the state, serving over 70 libraries in more than 40 communities, with a total of 474,452 patrons. The network is dedicated to serving the diverse needs of the member libraries and patrons. The mission of SAILS includes "[working] cooperatively with its members to promote the collection and sharing of library resources" and "[encouraging] the joint use of technology—24/7 online collections & services; managed by the network" (SAILS, Inc., 2013, p. 1). Consistently evaluating the effectiveness of the online catalog and resources as well as suggesting and implementing improvements to the online catalog are part of fulfilling these objectives.

In fiscal year 2012, SAILS was running the SirsiDynix e-Library OPAC; however, the network membership was exploring options for a new discovery platform. The network membership wanted a discovery solution that would generally enhance the catalog beyond what the standard Syndetics package could provide. The ideal product would allow patrons to view titles in a series, link back to those titles within the catalog, and provide links to similar titles. While evaluating options the membership wished to provide enhanced discovery tools for patrons to extend the life of e-Library. The objective for enhancing the existing OPAC was to provide more user-friendly discovery tools. The network membership began to explore LibraryThing for Libraries as a temporary solution to sustain the current catalog.

EXPLORING OPTIONS FOR A NEW DISCOVERY PLATFORM

At the time the only options for enhancing the catalog open to SAILS were Encore by Innovative Interfaces, Inc. (III), EBSCO's EDS (EBSCO Discovery Service) package, or the SirsiDynix Enterprise catalog enhanced with Bowker's LibraryThing for Libraries content. Though the membership was impressed with EBSCO's and III's discovery tools, ultimately they felt it was cost prohibitive for a network of SAILS's size. In May of 2011, SAILS began exploring a transition to Enterprise.

Bowker's catalog enrichment product, LibraryThing for Libraries (LTFL), offered simple implementation at an affordable price. This product also offered additional discovery tools that could be integrated at a later date, such as book display widgets, the "BookPsychic" recommendation tool, and "Stack Map," which provides a link to a map guiding patrons to items within the facility. The SAILS membership decided to add LibraryThing for Libraries to enhance e-Library while the transition was made to the new discovery platform.

LIBRARYTHING FOR LIBRARIES

LibraryThing was created in 2005 as a personal and social book cataloging website. LibraryThing allows users to catalog their personal libraries, track what they are reading, create collections, and contribute to the database with tags, ratings, reviews, and other information about books and authors. Bowker partnered with LibraryThing to create a library product, LTFL, based on the LibraryThing model. This product takes the syndetic and social structure of LibraryThing and combines it with the readers' advisory knowledge of librarians. Content such as tags and reviews are contributed by LibraryThing users and vetted by librarians.

IMPLEMENTATION

Initially, the SAILS network invested in two LTFL products: the Catalog Enhancement Package and the Reviews Enhancement Package. The Catalog Enhancement Package allowed SAILS to embed book recommendations, keyword tags, read-alikes, series information, links to other editions, and awards. The Reviews Enhancement Package allowed patrons to rate and review titles, and to share their reviews via social media. The LTFL product supported the network's mission to provide discovery platforms with easily accessed, valuable, and user-driven content.

The SAILS network membership ultimately voted on the SirsiDynix Enterprise discovery platform. Though Enterprise provided a user interface and discovery tools that were radically different from e-Library, the implementation of the LTFL-embedded content was so successful in meeting the objectives for the online catalog that SAILS libraries decided to continue the subscription to the Catalog Enhancement Product. The Review Enhancement Product was not widely used in e-Library and was dropped.

Embedding the LTFL content in the Enterprise catalog was relatively simple. First, SirsiDynix delivered a widget that automatically added the star ratings to the results list (also known as the hit list). Next, customized code was designed via Cascading Style Sheets to build a box on each title's record, or item details page, to contain the LTFL content. Finally, another widget was designed to direct the item details page to display LTFL content. Both the item details pages and LibraryThing records use ISBNs; when an ISBN in a catalog record matches an ISBN from LibraryThing, the content automatically loads on the item details page.

The SAILS Network was very satisfied with the customer support that was provided. LTFL representatives worked closely with the network staff to ensure that the product was customized and working to their satisfaction. LTFL even temporarily created two accounts for SAILS while e-Library and Enterprise were running concurrently.

STAFF AND PATRON REACTION

Prior to the LTFL catalog enhancements, quite a few patrons at the Norton Public Library approached the OPAC with trepidation, if at all. The LTFL enhancements are similar to many online merchant user interfaces, which give the catalog a familiar look and feel that provides a level of comfort for users. Seeing familiar features such as tag clouds, star ratings, and book recommendations increased patrons' willingness to use the OPAC.

In terms of the goals of the library's reference services, the LTFL catalog enhancements give the library staff a streamlined set of tools to use for catalog instruction. The keyword tags provide a simple way for patrons to access additional materials on a particular subject or author's titles much more simply than formal subject headings. The tag cloud and read-alike suggestions provide a simple way for all staff to provide readers' advisory. The series browser lets patrons quickly and easily access the titles in a series, and one click takes them to the title's catalog record. The enhanced catalog features bolster the underlying catalog structure, and provide cohesiveness and simplicity that patrons do not seem to find in MARC records.

SAILS network libraries found the embedded readers' advisory content to be extremely effective. Not only could savvier users utilize the tools themselves, library staff members were able to provide quick answers to readers' advisory questions without leaving the online catalog. Even the best readers' advisors have gaps in their knowledge; with LTFL embedded in the catalog, library staff members can quickly utilize the user-generated and librarian-mediated content to assist patrons quickly and effectively. This streamlined approach to readers' advisory improved staff ability to guide patrons.

Many SAILS libraries still subscribe to other readers' advisory services, such as EBSCO's NoveList or "What Do I Read Next?" from Gale Cengage; however, LTFL's embedded content goes further. Users are able to connect to similar books by subject, access series lists and search the catalog for titles within the series with one click, access other editions of the title, and even view award lists. The ability to access this content without leaving the catalog or having to teach patrons to use a new interface makes LTFL an invaluable resource and readers' advisory tool.

ASSESSMENT

Statistics validate the anecdotal evidence that SAILS network library staff members have reported. SAILS began heavy promotion of Enterprise in February 2013, but continued to run e-Library concurrently until June of that year. Since LTFL was added to the Enterprise catalog in November 2012, 11,992 tags have been clicked, making tag clouds the most popular feature with patrons by far. In February 2013, there were 140 tags clicked; in January 2014, there were 1,364—an increase of 874%. The series browser has been opened 6,104 times, followed distantly by review links at 1,833 and awards browser at 1,629.

There have been some obstacles to using LTFL. As previously mentioned, the Reviews Enhancement Package was never widely used. SAILS network staff members were unsurprised by this, suspecting that users were more interested in getting content from the catalog than producing it. Since the initial launch of the Enterprise catalog, changes have been made to enhance discovery features and patrons' ability to quickly and effectively use the catalog tools. Such changes include the ability to see holdings and place holds from the results list rather than having to access the item details page. Since the LTFL content only displays on item details pages, it seems likely that fewer patrons are seeing the content. SAILS and its member libraries are currently considering ways to draw patrons' attention back to this value-rich content.

Despite these small setbacks the SAILS network has been satisfied with the valuable, user-driven content provided by LTFL. Though the changes to Enterprise may make it less likely for patrons to stumble upon the LTFL content, previous experience has shown that patrons value the information provided and are interested in utilizing the content.

BOOK DISPLAY WIDGET

The Norton Public Library was so impressed with the catalog enhancements that the library took advantage of the opportunity to subscribe to the Book Display Widget product. This tool allows the library to embed book display widgets on the library's website. Although the OPAC is a shared resource, each library does have its own interface. The library maintains its own website, however, which can feel disconnected from the library's catalog because it has a very different design. Before embedding the Book Display Widget, the only thing connecting the Norton Public Library website to the Enterprise catalog was a "search the catalog" link. The widgets display book covers on the library's website, linking directly back to the catalog. The book widgets are customizable, allowing the library to create widgets based on read-alikes, new books, themes, bestsellers, award winners, and more—and multiple widgets can be embedded simultaneously. It provides yet another level of readers' advisory that can be used virtually or with the assistance of library staff. In the year since the Book Display Widget was added in February 2013, there have been 795 clicks that take patrons from the library's website directly to a catalog record.

Like the LTFL content, the Book Display Widget was affordable and relatively simple to embed and maintain. LTFL worked with the SAILS network to index the Norton Public Library's holdings. In addition, library staff members have the option of manually entering ISBNs or using RSS feeds to populate the widget. Staff members simply log in to the LTFL site and access the Book Display Widget tools to design widgets. First, one selects a data source (catalog, ISBNs, RSS, etc.) and selects from multiple design features to customize the widget. The widget automatically matches ISBNs to the library catalog, eliminating invalid entries, and populates the widgets with cover images that link directly back to the library catalog. An HTML code is generated that must be added to the library's website. Once the code is embedded, staff members can update the widget within LTFL's website, and the changes are automatically made to the embedded widget. Aside from the initial addition of code to the library's website, no in-depth knowledge of coding is required.

CONCLUSION

Ultimately, LTFL allowed the SAILS network to bolster their discovery platform and underlying cataloging structure with enhanced content. The Norton Public Library has been able to harness the power of that content to support the library's reference service goals and improve readers' advisory services inside and outside the library. The LTFL features enhance the syndetic structure and allow library staff to perform catalog instruction as they provide readers' advisory services. It also allows patrons the ability to use readers' advisory tools remotely, empowering them to take full advantage of the catalog. LTFL-embedded content allows the library to improve traditional readers' advisory services and provide passive readers' advisory tools for patron discovery.

REFERENCES

LibraryThing for Libraries. (2014). Retrieved from http://www.bowker.com/en-US/products/servlib_ltfl.shtml

SAILS, Inc. (2013). FY 2013 annual report of SAILS, Inc. Retrieved from http://www.sailsinc.org/annualreport2013.pdf

O | CrowdAsk: Crowdsourcing Reference and Library Help

Ilana Stonebraker and Tao Zhang, Purdue University

INTRODUCTION

Help information regarding library resources and tools is a critical part of library services, but is often fragmented and undermaintained. There have been some efforts to create searchable help content, but adding new questions and answers, as well as validating and updating answers that may be out of date, inevitably takes up librarians' valuable time. More importantly, the traditional model of librarians passively waiting for users to seek help—while most users find help outside libraries—has not changed. Users, especially students, tend to seek reference help from faculty advisors and their peers. This kind of knowledge sharing does not have a well-structured platform within the library environment, and expert knowledge is not well utilized.

To address these needs, we developed a crowdsourcing web-based help system (CrowdAsk) for academic libraries. By definition, crowdsourcing is the practice of obtaining needed services, ideas, or content by soliciting contributions from a large group of people and especially from the online community rather than from traditional employees or suppliers. CrowdAsk allows users (particularly undergraduate students) to ask and answer open questions related to library resources. In both the public and library contexts, crowdsourcing has emerged as a distributed problem-solving and content production model. Existing crowdsourcing platforms, such as Stack Exchange, incentivize the user base to become involved in the project through a variety of means including gamification. Common implementation of gamification involves the use of scoring elements of games (e.g., scores, points, levels, and badges) in a work or educational context.

CROWDASK

The library help system we developed is a new paradigm to shift the traditional reference help model that has been focused on the needs of users familiar with the libraries. This project took an explicitly user-experience-centric and reference-centric standpoint on crowdsourcing. CrowdAsk provides librarians and users with an online, community-driven, and persistent help information source. It follows the emerging trend of crowdsourcing with the ultimate goal of building a shared knowledge base as well as a thriving user community, where the previous fragmented help information can be curated and better utilized. Users receive research help from not only librarians, but also a community of researchers with expertise and shared interests. Therefore, this help system could improve user understanding and utilization of library resources and user engagement of libraries and librarians. Librarians are able to spend more time on other mission-critical tasks (e.g., information literacy and data management services), and users may find additional collaboration and learning opportunities from the community.

Similar questions and answers systems exist for the general public. For example, Stack Exchange (http://stackexchange.com/) is a network of sites on diverse topics in which users can freely ask and answer questions. Although Stack Exchange is open for the public to propose new sites within its network, building a new and open-source library help system allows more flexibility of functionalities and customization of user experience. By making CrowdAsk open source, other libraries could potentially adapt our system and integrate it with their web presence, thus creating a broader impact for enhancing existing library reference services. CrowdAsk was developed with funds from a 2013 Institute of Museum and Library Services (IMLS) Sparks! Ignition Grant awarded to Purdue University Libraries.

FEATURES OF CROWDASK

A screenshot of the CrowdAsk main interface is shown in Figure 1. CrowdAsk can be accessed at http://crowdask.lib.purdue.edu. The interface lists questions that have been asked by users, the number of answers, answers, and votes received for a question.

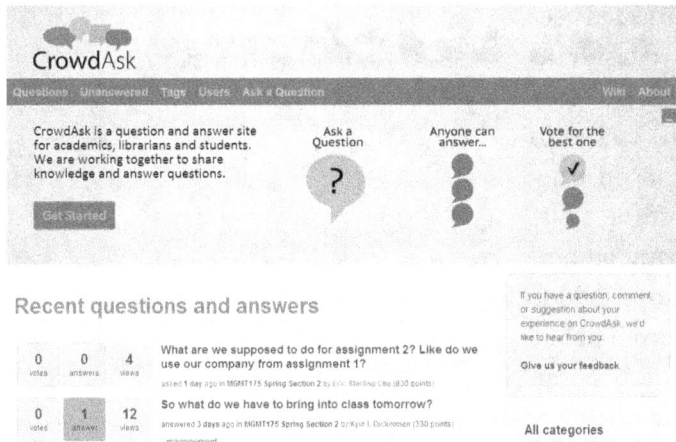

Figure 1. Main interface of CrowdAsk.

User Roles and Points

Each user role is associated with a set of privileges. An anonymous user can only browse and view questions, answers, and comments. By default, all registered users have the following privileges: 1) ask new questions; 2) answer existing questions; 3) post comments to questions and answers for clarifications; 4) mark an answer to his/her own question as accepted; 5) vote up and down answers; 6) create tags and select categories; 7) set bounties for questions to encourage answers.

Whenever a user asks a question, answers a question, or votes on a question or answer, he receives points. He also receives points for his answer being selected as best. The point values can be adjusted on the administrative interface of CrowdAsk. The system will automatically assign additional privileges to a user based on the user's points, "leveling up" that user to a new user role. Additional privileges include closing votes of the user's question, reopening votes of a question, and locking any question so the question will not accept new answers. A moderator (designated by the administrator of CrowdAsk) has the ability to close and reopen votes of a question or answer. Note that if the vote for a question is closed, the votes of the question's answers are also closed.

Questions and Answers

A question can have multiple answers, but only one answer can be marked as accepted (best answer). An example of a question page is shown in Figure 2.

An authenticated user can mark a question as her favorite. A question can be locked to prevent unconstructive and off-topic discussions. An administrator can also hide questions from public view. A question can be protected so that the question will not accept votes. The list of answers is ordered by up votes by default and also can be ordered by time the answers were posted or edited, number of views, and number of answers.

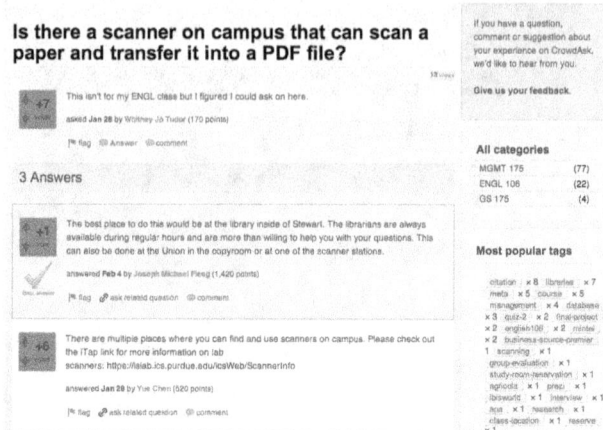

Figure 2. Example question page of CrowdAsk.

Tags and Categories

An authenticated user can assign existing tags to the question she asks or create her own tags organically. Categories support a hierarchical structure for questions and user roles. Usually tags are subjects. Categories reflect communities or groups of users, such as a class or department. An authenticated user can assign or modify an existing category to the question the user created. A question has none or only one category. A category is associated with a list of questions in the category. Users can use categories to browse related questions. The moderator role can be associated with one or more categories.

Badges

In order to encourage positive behavior, badges also are included in CrowdAsk. In the administrative interface, administrators can create an unlimited number of badges. We have implemented 23 badges in our system. Some example badges we have implemented include "Knowledgeable" (having at least one answer selected as best answer); "Commentator" (left at least 10 comments); "Good Answer" (answer with more than 25 up votes); and "Outstanding Contributor" (left 25 or more comments, and answered 20 questions or more).

Bounties

A user can assign a bounty to a question when the user first creates the question. A user must have at least 120 points to assign a bounty. Bounty points for a question can be set from 20 to 100. Once the user has set a bounty, the system deducts the point from the user and stores the point in a secured table. All bounties are paid for upfront and are nonrefundable under any circumstances to prevent students from revoking their bounties after getting the answer they wanted, and thus gaming the system. Once the user selects a best answer for the bounty question, the answerer gets the bounty points.

INITIAL TEST RESULTS

In the spring 2014 semester, we implemented CrowdAsk with three undergraduate courses at Purdue, including English 106 (First-Year Composition), Management 175 (Information Strategies for Management), and General Studies 175 (Information Strategies for Hospitality and Tourism Management). English 106 is a required course for all incoming students, and it is aimed at providing students essential skills for researching a topic and presenting the topic in various written formats. Management 175 and General Studies 175 are required courses designed to develop students' information-gathering, evaluation, and presentation skills in the two disciplines. In total these three courses included 12 class sessions and over 370 students. We introduced CrowdAsk to the students at the beginning of semester and frequently encouraged students to use CrowdAsk in the classes when they needed help researching a topic. We added the link to CrowdAsk in the course management system as part of the course resources. We also coordinated with librarians at Purdue University Libraries to provide necessary reference help on CrowdAsk. The overall usage data of CrowdAsk between January 5, 2014, and April 2, 2014, is provided in Table 1.

Data from Google Analytics showed that from January 5, 2014, to April 2, 2014, CrowdAsk had 1,150 visits from 474 unique visitors. The total number of page views was 14,715, with average 12.8 pages per visit. The average visit duration was 6 minutes and 7 seconds. This shows that CrowdAsk attracted a good amount of traffic from the classes. The students were engaged with CrowdAsk as they stayed and viewed some amount of pages for an average visit.

Table 1. Usage data of CrowdAsk, January 5, 2014, to April 2, 2014.

Item	Amount
Registered users	211
Users who posted (questions or answers)	99
Users who voted	106
Questions	122
Answers	232
Question owners	59
Question answerers	72
Comments	14
Most votes	35
Most answers	8
Most views	92
Unanswered	5
Highest user score (registered users start from 100)	2,080
Highest number of badges	11

Preliminary analysis of the question titles and answer texts showed that users asked the following categories of questions on CrowdAsk, ordered by their frequency:

Course-related: Questions that ask for information about particular courses, for example, "Do you know how to retake the quiz on blackboard (for Management 175)?" and "How much will my writing improve throughout the semester?"

CrowdAsk-related: Questions that are about the point system, badges, and type of questions on CrowdAsk. Example questions include "How do you earn points on CrowdAsk?," "May I know the full list of badges and how to achieve them?," and "Are we only allowed to ask academic-related questions here?"

Library services or resources: Questions that are about where to find certain information and how to access physical and electronic resources, for example, "Is there a way to search the libraries catalog just for movies?," "How do I reserve a study room at library?," and "How do you get the actual article to come up on Business Source Premier instead of just the abstract?"

How-to: Questions that ask for instructions, for example, "What is a good website to use to do a voiceover on Prezi?" and "How to analyze the financial tables of a company?"

Conceptual: Questions that are conceptual, abstract, and do not involve specific contexts, for example, "What is the best citation management software?" and "Could someone tell me what is the meaning of APA citation?"

Most questions on CrowdAsk fit into one of these categories, but some questions could be assigned to more than one category, for example, "How do I find the DOI for an IBISWorld article?" This question was asked by a student in the Management 175 class, but the answer could be useful for other library users.

We recruited four student participants for the user test of CrowdAsk. Three participants were from the current users and received high points in the system; the other participant did not use CrowdAsk before the test. The test tasks included: 1) registration and login; 2) ask a question and assign tags to the question; 3) propose an answer to an existing question; 4) select the best answer to the question asked earlier; 5) view user profile and understand user privileges; and 6) explore other features of CrowdAsk, including tags, categories, and site search. Participants explored CrowdAsk before they performed the six test tasks. During the test tasks, they were encouraged to talk aloud about their expectations, difficulties, and general comments about using CrowdAsk. After the tasks, participants responded to open questions about their experience using CrowdAsk.

Overall, participants' task performance showed that basic tasks—such as browsing existing questions, asking and answering a question, selecting the best answer, and voting for questions and answers—were easy and without major obstacles. Participants completed the test tasks within reasonable time duration (averaging approximately two minutes) and did not require assistance. We observed that participants tended to not assign tags to their questions. The major reason was that they did not use tags in general and did not find tags particularly useful for them. This suggests that proper intervention (e.g., adding/editing tags) may be necessary during the initial launch of CrowdAsk. Participants commented that the meaning of badges and user levels were not clear to them. Badges are shown on user profile pages, but the user needs to move the mouse cursor over each badge in order to see its corresponding rule. Similarly, user level and privilege information is shown on the user profile page, but not on the list of questions page. Two experienced users of CrowdAsk did not know that they have additional privileges (e.g., editing questions and answers) due to their high points in the system. Consequently, we noticed that only a few users used their editorial privileges on CrowdAsk. User participation in the content management will be critical if CrowdAsk continues to grow as a user community. Therefore, we have proposed new interface designs to address these issues and promote awareness of features such as points, badges, and privileges among CrowdAsk users.

We also collected user feedback on CrowdAsk through course evaluations. In general, students liked the idea of asking questions and helping each other on CrowdAsk, without emailing teachers all the time. A few students thought they did not have questions to ask, and some questions and answers on CrowdAsk were vague, which reinforces the importance of user guidance and editorial intervention (i.e., clarifying questions and answers through editing and comments, as well as building useful content).

The above preliminary findings indicate that CrowdAsk is effective in terms of meeting users' information needs beyond traditional library reference help. Users have asked various types of questions and reached high levels of scores and badges in a relatively short time period. We will continue to assess CrowdAsk through content analysis and user testing. Our future research based on additional data from CrowdAsk will cover important issues such as subject expert participation, user motivation, and the development of the crowdsourcing community.

A NEW LIBRARY HELP SERVICE PARADIGM

Rather than replacing or improving existing digital reference models, CrowdAsk is focused on reimagining reference in the 21st century. Users are becoming more comfortable in Web 2.0 systems like Wikipedia, Facebook, and YouTube, where user-generated content is the norm. Our current systems disenfranchise our expert students, allowing them only to act as passive information gatherers and not authoritative sources in their lives. In addition, the new Association of College and Research Libraries (ACRL) *Framework for Information Literacy for Higher Education* call for more attention on the "vital role of collaboration," including wikis and digital communities and their "potential for increasing student understanding of the processes of knowledge creation and scholarship" (Association of College and Research Libraries, 2014). CrowdAsk encourages users to participate in knowledge creation with other members of their academic community. It has the potential of not only providing additional useful information for students, but also assisting in fulfilling our mission as librarians to educate and encourage an information-literate and informed populace.

Acknowledgments

This work is supported by IMLS grant LG-46-13-0239-13. The views and opinions expressed are those of the authors and do not necessarily reflect the views of the IMLS.

REFERENCES

Association of College and Research Libraries. (2014). Draft for comment: Framework for information literacy for higher education. Retrieved from http://acrl.ala.org/ilstandards/wp-content/uploads/2014/02/Framework-for-IL-for-HE-Draft-1-Part-1.pdf

P | The *Guide to Reference*: A Solution for Teaching Reference Sources

Denise Beaubien Bennett, University of Florida

CHALLENGES OF TEACHING SOURCES IN LIS PROGRAMS

When and how should future reference librarians and reference service staff learn reference sources? Recent research studies (Adkins & Erdelez, 2006; Agotsto, Rozaklis, MacDonald, & Abels, 2010; Bossaller & Adkins, 2011; O'Connor, 2011) and observations and local practices (Hogan, 2009; Kern, 2009; Kieft, 2011; Robbins, 2012; Thomsett-Scott, 2012) point toward an acknowledgment by library and information science (LIS) educators and by practicing librarians that learning specific sources, with the exception of a few truly universal sources (O'Connor, 2011; Rabina, 2013), is a task best suited as a component of on-the-job training for several reasons.

From the perspective of LIS instructors, reducing the time and energy spent on teaching sources offers several benefits. Instructors could instead focus more on the conceptual skills, such as conducting the reference interview, techniques for evaluating sources, strategies for matching a patron with an audience-appropriate source or response, the ethics and responsibilities of reference services, and managing and evaluating reference services. Sources and formats that a future professional will "need to know" are widely divergent and dependent on the specific library where the person is employed, and the difference at present is highly dependent on library type. Distance students or those in online programs may not have ready access to sources in either print or electronic format, resulting in an uneven learning experience and frustration for all concerned. In LIS coursework, the student typically is not working with "real" questions and may not have the opportunity to practice the reference interview and match sources with "real" patrons. Each of these factors provides a strong argument for de-emphasizing the teaching of sources in the basic reference course, and instead using a well-designed tool that provides a base for instructors and students to select and examine a customized set of sources that are appropriate for individual needs.

AUDIENCE FOR AN ON-THE-JOB TRAINING TOOL

To provide quality service, reference staffers will need at some point to learn and to keep up to date on reference sources. A single tool that supports a range of "just-in-case" to "just-in-time" functions, from a systematic approach to learning several sources to an ability to select locally held and used sources to serving as a quick look-up function at the point of need, can be used by all reference service providers at any stage of their careers.

An on-the-job training tool can serve a much greater audience than beginning professionals. Reference assistants and student workers who provide any level of reference service must be trained in relevant sources for assisting their patrons, since most of them only learn about reference sources on the job, if at all. Reference collections have expanded beyond a few shelves in easy reach of the desk, to include both online sources and volumes sent to the circulating stacks. Reference providers may not be sitting at a service desk near the reference stacks when responding to queries. Librarians who are specialists, whether in a subject discipline or in an area of librarianship, may find themselves staffing a chat service and suddenly realizing that they are not well-suited to answering a question that is beyond their comfort levels. For anyone working under a policy that chat questions are to be answered and not just referred, the right tool can serve as a ubiquitous colleague when knowledgeable humans are not available for rapid consultation.

When reference providers assume or verify that their patrons have already "checked the Internet" before seeking assistance, knowing some quality sources where the patron may not have looked is helpful, especially when those sources have been vetted for quality and accuracy in a tool that also indicates which sources are efficient to use. In addition to helping answer specific reference questions, a reference source tool can assist with reference collection management decisions, such as developing a reference collection in a new topic or discipline, choosing to purchase a source in print or online format, updating (or not) with a new edition after assessing its added value, and weeding items to the circulating stacks or to be withdrawn. A source tool can also assist with instruction planning, aiding the instructor in identifying tools appropriate to the audience and to the discipline.

Finally, online catalogs and broad discovery tools are not always helpful for limiting the retrieved items to reference sources with quick look-up functionality. An online tool that can provide vetted and organized training and is specialized for reference sources is useful in all of the circumstances outlined above. The online *Guide to Reference* (http://guidetoreference.org) is that one-stop tool to support both teaching and training functions as well as just-in-time reference.

THE *GUIDE TO REFERENCE* TODAY

The *Guide to Reference Books* served librarians throughout the 20th century as a learning tool and finding aid to reference sources. Published in 11 print editions from 1902 through 1996, the *Guide* began as a product of Columbia University's general reference department, but along the way, contributing editors from other large research libraries were welcomed. For a fuller history on the *Guide*, please consult an essay written by Robert Kieft, the general editor and pilot of the *Guide to Reference,* from initial conversations about the online edition until its launch in 2009 (Kieft, 2011).

The *Guide to Reference* includes trusted go-to sources that have stood at least some test of time and utility; it is not a review medium of new sources. It is format-agnostic, including both print and online sources, and it includes sources that are free but authoritative, or sources that require purchase or licensing but are held at enough libraries to be reasonably available to readers of the *Guide*. The selection and annotation activities are performed by subject and genre specialists. The primary audience of the *Guide* has been English-speaking academic and large public libraries in North America, but the scope is gradually expanding to serve a wider range of library types and locations around the world.

As the definition of a "reference source" blurs, sources in the *Guide* include websites, web pages, blogs, search engines, and full-text databases as well as the traditional array of encyclopedias, handbooks, and indexes.

A source only appears in one format; its annotation may identify the format options and describe the relationships (if any) between online and print versions. New reference works or editions are not automatically included in the *Guide*, but when an edition is updated, its older counterpart is eliminated. Libraries are encouraged to retain the older print editions of the *Guide to Reference Books* for consultation when older sources seem appropriate.

The LIS section within the *Guide to Reference* includes much more than reference sources; it serves as a broad sampling of books, websites, key periodicals, and blogs, and it describes career resources and other basic tools useful in professional practice. The section is capable of guiding the basic needs of LIS students, library assistants, and beginning professionals.

Whether used in LIS instruction or in on-the-job training, the *Guide to Reference* supports several options for learning sources. Beyond the function of identifying the best resources for answering specific questions, learners can study the taxonomy of one or more disciplines, evaluate different resources based on their annotations, and create lists of resources for class projects. Editors' guides assist the user by providing an introduction to the discipline and to the types of reference sources used to support information and research needs. They discuss characteristics of the literature outside the scope of annotations, and they address how those sources can be applied in reference service and in supporting patrons' work.

The reader is encouraged to peruse the annotations of entries in the same subcategory as known items. An annotation may contain extensive cross-references to related sources that are not described separately as well as comparisons to related sources, indications of appropriate audiences for the source, and other details that provide significant added value. Annotations may provide a comparison across sources or a discussion of the cost-benefit to acquiring a newer edition of a work, supporting librarians with collection decisions appropriate for their user groups. The annotations help novices and experts alike to learn "which source to use when" by indicating audience and depth of coverage.

An advantage to an online version of the *Guide to Reference* is the support of hyperlinking. Record annotations may include links to related records within the *Guide* and links to further information on publishers' sites. Online sources include either a direct hyperlink or, in the case of some licensed sources, a link to its description and licensing details. Any ISBNs and ISSNs in the records can link to local holdings via WorldCat or, when using the Firefox web browser, via the LibX tool.

Personalization and social tools add value to the *Guide to Reference*. Users can mark and create lists of selected or locally held sources. Creating a personal or course-wide account enables the addition of user notes, which can be set as personal to the account holder or as global to be visible to all users of the *Guide*. These interactive features for lists and notes afford possibilities for LIS course exercises and for reference department activities, such as reference desk training and collection weeding. The ability to export records makes the compilation of local instructional materials and subject portals easier. Librarians and trainees can use the notes feature to advise each other and the editorial team about the qualities and usefulness of sources, the relationships among sources, sources that should be considered as candidates for entry, revisions to the browsing taxonomy, and topics that should be covered or dropped.

Keeping the content of the *Guide to Reference* up-to-date is a never-ending task. One disturbing trend is noting that high-quality and well-established websites that were freely available for more than a decade, such as BUBL LINK and Intute, no longer exist. Users begged for these tools to be sustained, but developers began to discontinue updating these sites and eventually removed the outdated sites completely. When grant funding runs out or the volunteer force evaporates, sites can no longer be maintained and eventually must be retired. To track these and other developments, and to keep the *Guide* as accurate as possible, the editors of the *Guide* invite LIS students to critique the source selection and annotation content, to recommend enhancements where appropriate, and to take on assignments to develop and maintain the *Guide* in a manner that is helpful to them at present and in the future.

THE FUTURE OF THE *GUIDE TO REFERENCE* AND ITS POTENTIAL

The *Guide to Reference* is available in an online format as an annual subscription, with portability, updatability, linking and sharing functions, and convenient access at the top of the feature list. However, several potential customers have requested non-online options. The most frequent concern is an inability to accommodate another addition to their continuations/subscription budget. Less frequently expressed are problematic online access and the advantages of the print format for quick consultation. To address these concerns, the *Guide* is producing snapshot segments of topics that have been identified by subscribers as most useful. These segments will be offered as e-books or in a print on demand format. Scheduled for production in 2014 are segments on: medicine and health, essential general reference and library science sources, business and economics, and genealogy and biography. Additional topics or regular updates of any of these topics will be generated if the segments are assessed as useful and successful.

The *Guide to Reference* can retain its current format to provide relatively brief annotated records, editors' guides, and functionality to mark, note, and share records, and create lists.

But with support, the *Guide* can expand its current features to include:

- Expanded scope to include more sources of interest to public libraries and to those beyond North America.
- Additional in-depth guides to subject disciplines, perhaps affiliated with ALCTS/CMDS Sudden Selector's Series published by a division of the American Library Association.
- Expanded annotations to include a deeper evaluation and comparison across sources, and increased situational advice regarding use.
- Links to review sites and to "best reference source" lists.
- Additional segments on reference interview tactics, to provide one-stop access to assist reference service providers in better understanding a patron's query on the journey to identifying some efficient and appropriate sources for specific audiences and disciplines.
- Regular updates of the print/e-book segments to facilitate purchase by libraries that are unable to sustain a continued subscription or unable to successfully access the online *Guide*.
- Comparative analysis content in the form of bullet points, flow charts, tables, and other visualization formats that are easily digestible by busy or stressed users, acknowledging how much (or how little) reference staff will search or read background information about reference sources at the point of need.
- Repository of real-life reference questions, optionally augmented with the reference interview or with the strategy for choosing the consulted sources.

The online *Guide to Reference* has dipped into the era of social networking by incorporating features to encourage feedback from users at all levels of experience while still funneling suggestions through its contributing editors. The balance between displaying all input while continuing to assure the authority behind the *Guide* will be determined by its users and by their expressed preferences. Future plans, when funding permits, include moving the *Guide* to a contemporary and more flexible platform that can clearly credit all contributions and suggestions.

ROLE OF THE LIBRARY COMMUNITY

The library community can assist in developing and maintaining the *Guide to Reference* to the desired level of usefulness through several channels. Volunteer assignments for contributing editors become available on a frequent and irregular basis. Subject specialists and reference librarians who work with or near large reference collections are valued participants because they are in a position to assess a wide range of sources. Librarians who are looking for publication outlets and for opportunities to assist their fellow professionals are invited to add an "edited work" credit to their résumés. Teams of new and veteran reference service providers can bring a well-rounded perspective to the intrinsic and audience-specific value of sources. LIS students are invited through their coursework to accept the challenge of choosing a more useful set of sources or providing more comparative annotations than the subject "experts" have done.

As with many tools, the long-term health of the *Guide to Reference* is dependent on two major factors: the continuing interest of contributing editors and the support of subscribers/licensors to cover the production costs. The editors of the *Guide* encourage participation at any of the levels described above. While the *Guide's* form, function, and features will depend on the engaged participation of its users, it can remain a viable tool for learning and finding reference sources for librarians, library assistants, and LIS students for as long as reference service is provided.

REFERENCES

Adkins, D., & Erdelez, S. (2006). An exploratory survey of reference source instruction in LIS courses. *Reference & User Services Quarterly, 46*(2), 50–60. http://dx.doi.org/10.5860/rusq.46n2.50

Agosto, D. E., Rozaklis, L., MacDonald, C., & Abels, E. G. (2010). Barriers and challenges to teaching reference in today's electronic information environment. *Journal of Education for Library & Information Science, 51*(3), 177–186.

Bossaller, J. S., & Adkins, D. (2011). Envisioning the future of reference instruction: LIS students' and practitioners' opinions on print and online sources. *Reference & User Services Quarterly, 51*(2), 153–162. http://dx.doi.org/10.5860/rusq.51n2.153

Kern, M. K. (2009). Teaching reference: Ten questions from a first attempt. *Reference & User Services Quarterly, 48*(4), 330–333. http://dx.doi.org/10.5860/rusq.48n4.330

Kieft, R. H. (2011). The *Guide to Reference* and learning reference librarianship. In D. Zabel (Ed.), *Reference reborn: Breathing new life into public services librarianship* (339–354). Santa Barbara: Libraries Unlimited.

O'Connor, L. G. (2011). The education of reference librarians: A detailed survey and analysis. In D. Zabel (Ed.), *Reference reborn: Breathing new life into public services librarianship* (317–338). Santa Barbara: Libraries Unlimited.

Rabina, D. (2013). Reference materials in LIS instruction: A Delphi study. *Journal of Education for Library & Information Science, 54*(1), 108–123.

Robbins, S. (2012). Moving a general reference course online: Issues and considerations. *Reference Librarian, 53*(1), 12–23. http://dx.doi.org/10.1080/02763877.2011.591689

Thomsett-Scott, B. (2012). Creating a formal program to train LIS students for reference services. *Reference Librarian, 53*(1), 41–59. http://dx.doi.org/10.1080/02763877.2011.591666

Reference to Patrons With Disabilities

Michael Saar, Lamar University, Texas

INTRODUCTION

Starting college can be a stressful time for anyone. Far from the safety of home and the structure of the K–12 education system, students can quickly feel overwhelmed and intimidated by the accountability expected of them in higher education. This stress may be amplified for individuals entering college with a disability, leading to frustration, especially in environments that are not welcoming or accommodating to individuals with disabilities. The Mary and John Gray Library at Lamar University has recently initiated a multiphased, concentrated effort to provide greater outreach and accessibility to its patrons with disabilities. The initiative is comprised of five phases. This study will examine the first two phases that have been completed and discuss the future phases of the project.

In addition to the legal requirements held through laws such as the Americans with Disabilities Act, the library as a profession has historically emphasized the ethical obligation to provide equal access to all users. The American Library Association clearly highlights the importance of this issue in the first clause of the organization's code of ethics (2006). Despite this importance, the amount of research conducted in the library literature on the provision of library services to patrons with disabilities has been disappointing. Several studies provide suggestions on physical alterations to library spaces to accommodate users with disabilities (Wade, 2003, Copeland, 2011), while other articles stress the need for adequate training for library staff in working with people with disabilities (Charles, 2005,

Tinerella & Dick, 2005, Black, Burks, Taylor, & Walker, 2006). Dequin, Schilling, and Huang's 1988 study on the attitudes of academic librarians toward persons with disabilities is illuminating, stating that only 50% of librarians expressed comfort in working with users with disabilities. A common thread in the above cited literature is the importance of creating a welcoming environment for users with disabilities. While some of these works discuss the importance of the physical atmosphere, of interest to this author in particular were examinations on the atmosphere created by library policy and personnel. Several articles mention the necessity of creating this welcoming environment beginning with Needham's 1977 article, which discusses the attitudinal barriers that prevent users with disabilities from feeling welcome in the library. The importance of creating a welcoming environment for users with disabilities in academia is emphasized outside of the library literature as well. In Graham-Smith and Lafayette's 2004 study of classroom accommodations for users with disabilities, the respondents overwhelmingly stated that a caring staff and safe environment would be the most beneficial to their academic success.

Without adequate support from faculty and staff, the challenges faced by students with disabilities in postsecondary education may become overwhelming and impede progress toward educational goals. Retention rates for students with disabilities are lower than those who do not have disabilities (National Center for Education Statistics National Center for Education Statistics 2011a; 2011b). Although there are many factors that contribute to a student's academic success, the university library certainly has an important role to play, which includes providing adequate resources and staff support for student research to simply offering a welcoming environment for students to work and study in. In addition to evaluating the overall environment, the current study also explores evidence of students' abilities to be efficient and effective users of information. While there are many ways to define these capabilities, the author has chosen to use the Association of College and Research Libraries' (ACRL) Information Literacy Competency Standards for Higher Education (2006), which lists five basic competencies of effective information users: defining and articulating the information needs, accessing information effectively and efficiently, evaluating information critically, using information effectively, and using information ethically and legally. Due to the prevalence and importance of the topics of a welcoming environment and effective research skills in the literature, the current study examined both of these areas closely.

BACKGROUND

The germ of this project began in the fall of 2011, when library faculty members decided to utilize the university's larger-than-average population of students who are deaf or hard of hearing to investigate their needs and expectations for library use. Located in Beaumont, Texas, about 80 miles east of Houston, Lamar University is one of only two institutions in the country to offer a doctoral degree in deaf studies and deaf education. Because of this program, the population of students who are deaf or hard of hearing at Lamar University is higher than those at other public four-year colleges and universities. A team of library faculty surveyed the students who are deaf or hard of hearing at the University to determine ways they could better serve them. The study demonstrated that while the library does a satisfactory job of providing a welcoming environment for these students, there was definite room for improvement, particularly in the area of communication (Saar & Arthur-Okor, 2013). With this information, the library decided to reevaluate its service to both its users who are deaf or hard of hearing and patrons with disabilities as a whole.

While many of the steps undertaken to improve library services can be accomplished on a departmental or even individual level, it was quickly decided that one of strongest ways to demonstrate institutional commitment to excellent service for patrons with disabilities was to have the support of the entire library behind it. This was confirmed with the unanimous decision to make accessibility one of the goals of the library's current strategic plan. This decision led to the formation of a library accessibility committee through which the plan outlined in this study was initiated and enacted. The committee set up a multiphase plan to revise library service to users with disabilities: evaluation of users' attitudes toward the library, communication of library services to patrons with disabilities, assessment of library facilities and resources, training of library staff, and outreach to other faculty and staff working with students with disabilities.

EVALUATION

Although some evaluation was completed with the original study, it was decided more in-depth analysis could provide insight into needs or areas that had not been addressed previously. This was achieved through a closer examination of the focus group session conducted in late 2011. The focus group, consisting of 11 doctoral students in the deaf studies and deaf education department, was an open-ended discussion of various issues related to the students' library service guided by the author. As the surveys collected prior to this discussion had indicated, communication was a problem in the library. Emphasis was given to this topic but the participants were not limited to any one topic. To better understand the information gleaned from the focus group session, the author analyzed the discussion for references to the qualities of communication, information literacy, and library environment. The latter two areas were chosen based on their importance in the literature, as noted in the introduction, while the topic of communication was selected based on its prominence in the 2011 survey. The analysis was done using the Coding Analysis Toolkit (http://cat.ucsur.pitt.edu/) an open-source software program hosted by the University of Pittsburgh.

The analysis was achieved by examining the transcribed responses given in the focus group for references to communication, information literacy, and the library environment. As statements often built upon one another, transcriptions were evaluated on a paragraph level rather than sentence by sentence. This allowed for a more accurate representation of the speaker's response. For the purpose of this analysis, a paragraph was defined as an uninterrupted response to either the interviewer's question or another participant's response. Once another person began speaking, a new respondent's paragraph began. Since all responses were interpreted through a single American Sign Language (ASL) interpreter, it was easy to determine when one response began and another ended. When a respondent referenced multiple elements in a paragraph, all applicable responses were coded. For each of the three areas analyzed (communication, information literacy, and environment), the author noted if the speaker's response indicated a positive, negative, or neutral association with the topic. A total of 111 paragraphs were analyzed.

References pertaining to communication dealt with the explicit act of communicating information from the library to the user, including both the communication act and any resources involved. Respondent experiences of a positive communication with library staff or technologies were noted as a positive reference, while negative instances were noted as such.

Comments that dealt with communication without reference to actual library experiences were listed as general/neutral responses. The majority of these comments referred to preferences regarding communication methods and technologies.

References pertaining to information literacy deal with any of the five competencies detailed in the ACRL information literacy standards cited above. Any instance that demonstrated a poor grasp of these skills and concepts was noted as a negative reference to information literacy, whereas a positive demonstration was noted as such. One response demonstrated both positive and negative aspects and was recorded as exhibiting both. Where the concept was discussed generally or no determination could be made, the response was listed as a general reference to information literacy.

Paragraphs regarding the library environment include references to librarian attitudes to patrons, ability of patrons to be self-sufficient, willingness of library staff to assist patrons, flexibility of library staff, and concern for the patron's overall library experience. Specific library experiences shared by the respondents were recorded as positive or negative based on the nature of the experience. Mentions of experiences outside of Lamar University's library or preferences in terms of environment were recorded as general comments.

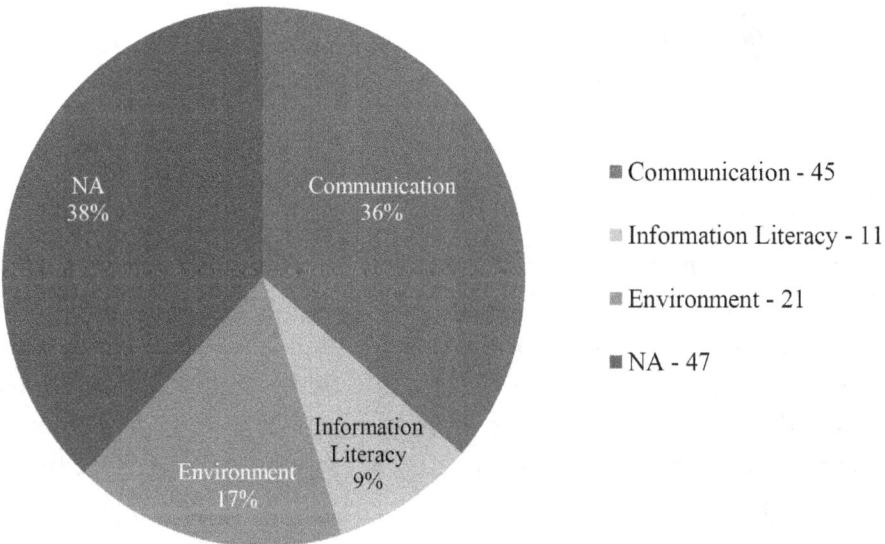

Figure 1. Paragraph references by code.

A total of 124 instances were coded among the 111 paragraphs (see Figure 1). This accounts for 13 instances of paragraphs being assigned multiple codes. A substantial portion, 47 or 37.9% of the paragraphs were coded as not applicable to any of the three categories. Out of the remaining paragraphs, the majority dealt with communication (36.9% of responses), with environmental and information literacy issues representing 16.94% and 8.87% of the responses, respectively. With over one-third of the responses related to communication, it is clear that this issue is important to the students interviewed in the focus group.

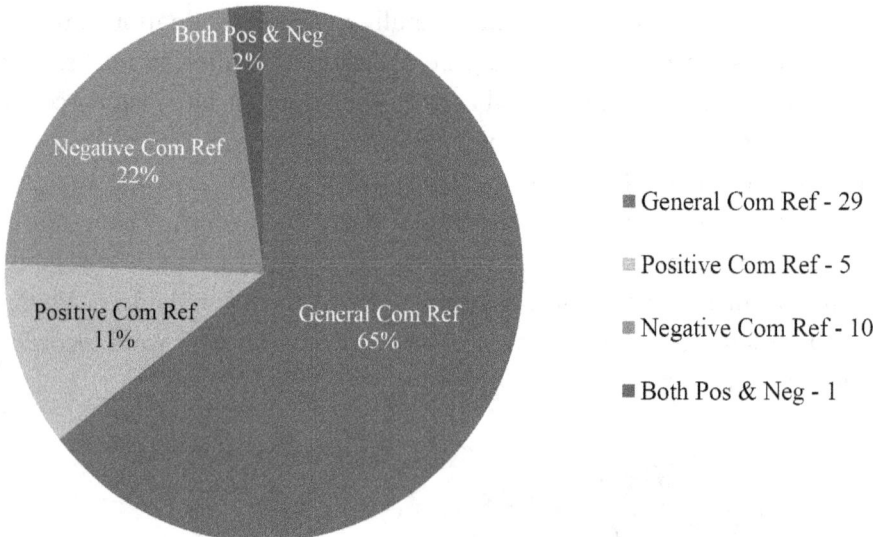

Figure 2. Communication references.

While this information is not surprising given the emphasis of the focus group, upon examining the breakdown of communication-coded responses, the author was surprised to discover twice as many negative communication experiences with the library as positive ones (see Figure 2). Many of these arose from a failure of the communication process between library staff and a student. One notable example of this is through the library's communication of the hours for the ASL interpreters the library employs. The student's frustration in recounting this experience is palpable:

> We went in the summertime, and it was always the wrong time. Like, for example, my class was in the morning and I had

a break, and I ran over to the library and it's like, they're available tomorrow, in the morning. Ok, fine. So then I went over there, "Oh, they're not here, they'll be here in the afternoon." It's like, what? And so it was always the wrong time. (Personal communication, November 5, 2011)

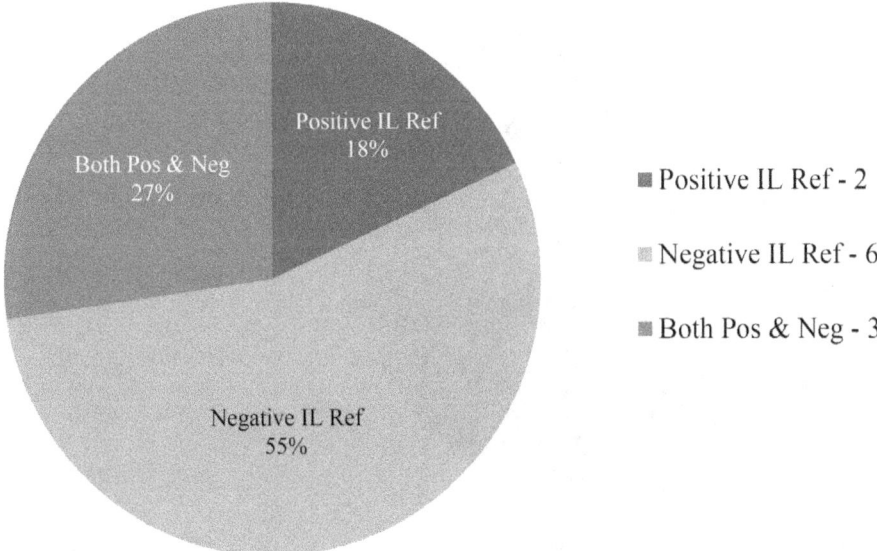

Figure 3. Information literacy references.

Similarly, upon examining the references coded for information literacy skills, the author discovered double the amount of negative indicators as positive ones (see Figure 3). These negative indicators ranged from the minor (misnaming databases) to more glaring errors, such as refusal to explore nonelectronic sources or the inability to properly formulate and execute search strategies. In one instance the respondent claimed the library did not have any resources on deaf studies before 1998, when in fact the library subscribes to several journals covering this topic during the time period mentioned. Despite these statements revealing their underdeveloped information literacy skills, the students almost universally demonstrated confidence in their research abilities, especially compared to other students. As one respondent notes, "As doctoral students, we already know what we need. A lot of times undergrad students come into college and they are just clueless; they don't know what kinds of services are available" (Personal communication). While information literacy abilities were not an emphasis of this focus group session, the information gleaned from it indicates the library needs to be more aggressive in passing on these skills to students with disabilities at all levels of their college education.

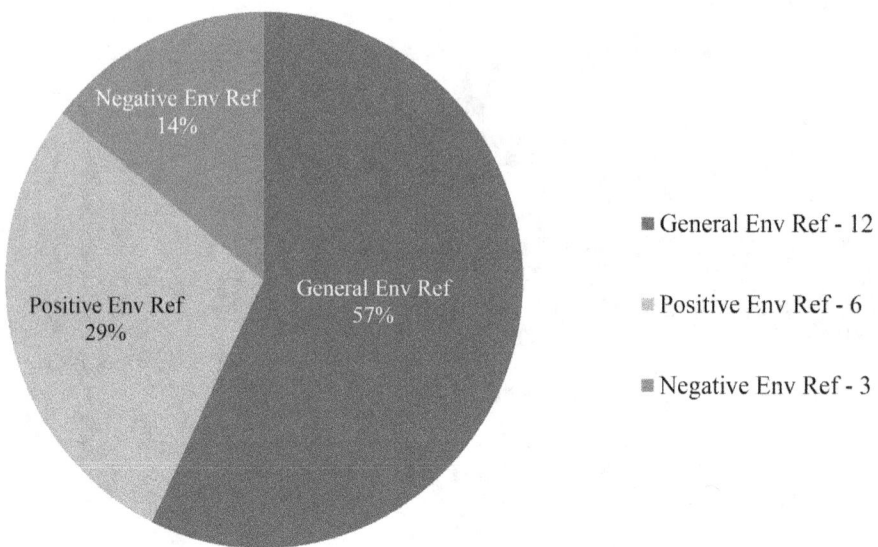

Figure 4. Environment references.

The environmental references were more favorable, with twice as many positive experiences listed as negative ones (see Figure 4). Many of these responses spoke generally about qualities that allow for self-sufficiency in student research (providing accessible equipment, captioning for videos, etc.) and did not reference the university library specifically. Other responses referred to interactions with library staff. While these comments also spoke of libraries in the general sense, they allude to the necessity of the library staff having greater sensitivity and adaptability to these users' needs. One student provides an example of the type of interactions she hopes to avoid:

> And sometimes it may be that people are like, "Ah! Oh! I have to look at a . . . I have to talk to deaf person" . . . and they freak out! There's no need to freak out. . . . "Oh my gosh! Oh-oh! Oh here they are! Oh my gosh! Oh! What do I do?!" No! There's no need for that. (Personal communication)

These results reaffirmed the need to dramatically improve communication, and the demonstrated information literacy ability indicated these efforts should be focused on communicating research skills. The responses regarding environmental preferences provide both direction in assessing the library's current resources and services, and in the way library staff should, or more to the point should *not*, communicate with students with disabilities.

COMMUNICATION

Based on this information, the accessibility committee prioritized improving the library's communication with patrons with disabilities. The first step was the creation of a page (http://vmlibweb.lamar.edu/service/deaf.htm) on the library website listing the weekly hours for the ASL interpreters. This immediately addressed a specific concern of the focus group regarding poor communication of interpreter hours. Additionally a LibGuide for students with disabilities (http://libguides.lamar.edu/access) was created allowing an easily updatable, centralized location of information that would be of interest to students. Included in this guide are hours of specialized services and locations and descriptions of accessible resources. Announcements of both the ASL interpreter hours and the separate LibGuide were distributed to students with disabilities via the office of Services for Students with Disabilities (SFSWD) email list.

This first step addressed the immediate communication concerns, but in order to take a more proactive approach to establishing a relationship with its patrons with disabilities, the library created the position of liaison to students with disabilities. Days after the official announcement of the liaison position, several students who are blind requested a meeting with the liaison and the head of the SFSWD office to discuss a recent library incident involving a student worker. Operating off of misinformation, services were delayed to one of these students, and the emotionally charged and politically incorrect term "handicap" was used to refer to one of the library computers reserved for users with disabilities. While the circumstances that led to the meeting were quite unfortunate, the meeting itself was an excellent opportunity for the library to more demonstrably show its sincerity in improving services to users with disabilities. The liaison met with three students and listened to their concerns surrounding the incident and with library services in general. Afterward, the liaison addressed several ways the problems will be rectified, including sending a reminder to all staff on the accessible computers policy and person-first language for addressing people with disabilities. Based on this initial encounter, it appeared the decision to create a liaison specifically for users with disabilities was an excellent one. The students at the meeting expressed their appreciation that someone was available to hear their concerns and offer solutions to both the immediate and future issues. All three students in attendance also indicated that having an opportunity to share the challenges they experienced in accessing library resources with a sympathetic ear was valuable. This event began a working relationship with the students that has grown quite strong in the relatively short time since the liaison position was created. As a testament to the strengthening relationship between the library and this patron population, the library liaison was recently asked to be the faculty advisor to the newly reinstated on-campus group for students with disabilities. It is the hope of the library that this relationship will continue to grow and provide a way to both keep users abreast of library developments and keep the library aware of the needs and concerns of this patron group.

ASSESSMENT

While establishing strong communication is crucial, without action it is meaningless. The third phase of the library's plan to improve services entails assessing and updating the facility and its resources for optimum accessibility. Because any alterations to the physical building may necessitate the allocation of money beyond the library's standard operating budget, the accessibility committee decided to recommend using an outside consultant to assess the physical building's ADA compliance. At the time of writing, that assessment has not yet occurred. The majority of the completed work on this phase has occurred through assessing the library's electronic resources. The library relied heavily on the assistive technology checklists from the University of Washington's DO-IT Center (http://www.washington.edu/doit/) to evaluate the accessibility of both electronic hardware and software. Table 1 shows the initial assessment and status of accessible resources in the Mary and John Gray Library broken down by type of disability and includes some examples of products when available. Product listings do not indicate an endorsement or preference for a particular item. Certain areas that are underrepresented (resources for users with a physical disability and some items for users who are blind) are being considered by the library for purchase. Areas

Table 1. Accessible equipment checklist.

Equipment	Vendor	Status
Low Vision		
23" monitors	Various	HAVE
Screen enlargement software	MAGic/Built In	HAVE
Large type keyboards	MAGic Large Print	HAVE
Blindness		
Braille embosser (printer)	Romeo Attache Pro	Considering
Optical character recognition software	Open Book/Kurzweil 1000/AB-BYY Fine Reader Professional/ Text Cloner Pro	Considering
Designated scanner	Various	Considering
Screen reading software	JAWS/Built In	HAVE
Mobility Impairments		
Speech recognition software	Dragon Naturally Speaking/Windows Speech Recognition	Alternative
Alternative entry options	Mouth Stick	Considering
	Sip and Puff Switch	Considering
Alternative pointers	Joystick/Trackball	Considering
Head pointing systems	Headmouse Extreme	Considering
Keyboard adaptations	IntelliKeys /Switch Click USB	Alternative
Onscreen keyboard	ScreenDoors2000/WiVik/Windows	Alternative
Learning Disabilities		
Optical character recognition software	WYNN/Kurzweil 3000	Considering
Skills enhancement software	CO:Writer/Word processing features	Alternative
Writing/brainstorming/organizing software	Inspiration	Alternative
Speech output	Write Out Loud/Read&Write Gold	Alternative
Deaf/Hard of Hearing		
Visual alternatives	Deepfreeze/Windows Alerts	HAVE
Video relay service	Sorenson	HAVE

labeled "alternative" indicate resources that the library possesses as a low or no-cost alternative. In many instances, these items are found in the "ease of access" slate of options included with the Windows 7 operating system used in library computers.

FUTURE PHASES

With the first phase completed and significant progress in the second and third phases, the library is optimistic about transforming into a more welcoming environment. In addition to these steps, two future phases remain: training and outreach. Instituting a regular training program for library employees in working with users with disabilities will help ensure a positive future for the library's communication efforts. Although excellent service to all patrons is always the goal, users with disabilities may require additional sensitivity that not all employees are aware of, and training will help stress the need for flexibility and care. While the library's communication efforts aim at reaching students with disabilities, outreach to the wider university is crucial to improving awareness of services. The accessibility committee hopes to reach out to faculty who regularly work with students with disabilities, such as the Deaf Studies and Deaf Education Department. The prevalence of negative information literacy references in the focus group indicates, and the literature confirms, that students with disabilities often struggle academically. The library hopes to encourage faculty to bring students in for information literacy sessions or use the library's online information literacy tools to increase their abilities in that area.

Having discovered that communication was perceived as a negative factor in the library's interactions with students with disabilities, the library decided to focus its efforts on improving these relationships through a five phase process. Evaluating responses from a library focus group comprised of students who are deaf or hard of hearing provided illuminating context for the accessibility committee to direct its efforts. The committee has worked to improve communication by providing easily updatable electronic information as well as creating a library liaison position for students with disabilities. In addition, the library is in the process of evaluating the accessibility of its physical environment and resources. With training and outreach as the final steps of the process, the library hopes to position itself as a desirable and welcoming location for users with disabilities on campus.

REFERENCES

American Library Association. (2006). Code of ethics of the American Library Association. Retrieved from http://www.ala.org/advocacy/proethics/codeofethics/codeethics

Association of College and Research Libraries. (2006). Information literacy competency standards for higher education. Retrieved from http://www.ala.org/acrl/standards/informationliteracycompetency

Black, W., Burks, A., Taylor, M., & Walker, J. E. (2006). Special needs: Envisioning a spectrum of library services. *Tennessee Libraries, 56*(1), 26–40.

Charles, S. (2005). Person first, disability second: Disability awareness training in libraries. *Library Review, 54*(8), 453–458. http://dx.doi.org/10.1108/00242530510619147

Copeland, C. A. (2011). Library and information center accessibility: The differently-able patron's perspective. *Technical Services Quarterly, 28*(2), 223–241. http://dx.doi.org/10.1080/07317131.2011.546281

Dequin, H. C., Schilling, I., & Huang, S. (1988). The attitudes of academic librarians toward disabled persons. *Journal of Academic Librarianship, 14*(1), 28–31.

DO-IT. (2014). University of Washington. Retrieved from http://www.washington.edu/doit/

Graham-Smith, S., & Lafayette, S. (2004). Quality disability support for promoting belonging and academic success within the college community. *College Student Journal, 38*(1), 90–99.

National Center for Education Statistics. (2011a). Table 345. *Digest of Education Statistics 2011*. Retrieved from http://nces.ed.gov/programs/digest/d11/tables/dt11_345.asp

National Center for Education Statistics. (2011b). Table 402. *Digest of Education Statistics 2011*. Retrieved from http://nces.ed.gov/programs/digest/d11/tables/dt11_402.asp

Needham, W. L. (1977). Academic library service to handicapped students. *Journal of Academic Librarianship, 3*(5), 273–279.

Saar, M., & Arthur-Okor, H. (2013). Reference services for the deaf and hard of hearing. *Reference Services Review, 41*(3) 434–452. http://dx.doi.org/10.1108/RSR-12-2012-0083

Tinerella, V. P., & Dick, M. A. (2005). Academic reference service for the visually impaired. *College & Research Libraries News, 66*(1), 29–32.

Wade, G. L. (2003). Serving the visually impaired user. *Portal: Libraries & the Academy, 3* (2), 307–313. http://dx.doi.org/10.1353/pla.2003.0048

R | Discovery Service: Goals, Evaluation, and Implementation of OhioLINK Academic Consortium

Ron Burns, EBSCO, and Theda Schwing, OhioLINK

The implementation of a discovery service at any institution can be a complex undertaking. Implementing discovery at a multi-institution consortium has its own challenges as well as benefits, which can provide valuable information for a wide range of libraries that will be undergoing the process.

BACKGROUND

The Ohio Library and Information Network (OhioLINK) is a consortium of 90 academic libraries and the State Library of Ohio. Together, the libraries work together to provide Ohio's 600,000 students and faculty with the information they need to fulfill their research objectives. OhioLINK and its member libraries provide access to nearly 50 million books, 17 million electronic journal articles, more than 81,000 e-books, 45,000 electronic theses and dissertations, more than 100 electronic databases, and thousands of images and videos.

Since large amounts of digital content in different silos became available, OhioLINK's goal has been making access to these resources as seamless as possible for its members. The federated search product that libraries had been using was less than ideal, and OhioLINK began to envision a product that could be both simple to use while providing high-quality results in a single search. They began to imagine discovery for all OhioLINK content—articles, books, and data.

In October 2008, OhioLINK issued an invitation to negotiate with any vendors able to build a state-of-the-art, unified search interface for all

OhioLINK content and that of its members. The development of the tool faced delays for various reasons. Meanwhile, vendors had created their own discovery tools and began to make them available, and some OhioLINK member institutions believed that by waiting for the OhioLINK resources, users were being deprived of a tool that would help them find and choose relevant solutions from an ever-increasing number of potential options. Several institutions purchased commercial discovery tools independently.

In 2012, OhioLINK made the decision to investigate purchasing a single discovery tool that could be used across the consortium, and it created a discovery task force to develop the criteria that would be used to evaluate the commercial discovery products. OhioLINK needed a tool that had the ability to meet the needs of the wide range of member libraries; it had to provide what the libraries at the top research universities required while also offering a support structure that could assist the smaller institutions with implementation and maintenance. Another requirement was that the discovery layer index would have to cover at least 80% of all OhioLINK content, and searches would need to return the most relevant results, regardless of the content provider.

Using these criteria as its guide, OhioLINK selected EBSCO Discovery Service (EDS) in December 2012, which included LinkSource and the EBSCO A-to-Z product (which will soon be replaced by the next level holdings and link management tools from EBSCO called Full Text Finder). EBSCO exceeded the minimum coverage criteria and was able to bring more into the mix that reflected the resources many OhioLINK institutions subscribed to at the time. Through evaluation, it was clear that quality search/relevancy ranking was a critical component of, and a major differentiator among, the commercial services. Content also played a direct role in the case of EDS, which was able to utilize content that is not available through other discovery services (such as the subject indexes that are part of databases like PsycINFO, Inspec, and CINAHL). This approach to discovery leveraged detailed indexing to optimize search relevancy, which in turn had a major impact on relevancy and ultimate value for end users.

OhioLINK and EBSCO agreed to limit the implementation of EDS to 15 institutions each quarter at the most, in order to optimize and customize the implementation for each university. The goal was to ensure that each university could maximize the OhioLINK initiative by making their instance of

EDS seamless with their own local resources (e.g., catalog, special widgets, and special collections). At the time of this article's writing, EDS continues to be implemented at OhioLINK libraries, with a current total of 65 member libraries using EDS, and while each library still has the option to use other discovery services, an increase in EDS participation is anticipated.

IMPLEMENTATION

Several factors have contributed to the success of the EDS implementation for OhioLINK members.

1. OhioLINK hired a project manager named Eliza Sproat to lead its side of the project, which helped the implementation proceed efficiently. The project manager gave EBSCO one point of contact who could then set priorities and disseminate information to the libraries based on OhioLINK's overall needs. In particular, Sproat was able to provide information from OhioLINK's consortial Integrated Library System (ILS) vendor, Innovative, more quickly than if the team from EBSCO had had to obtain it on their own across multiple libraries.

    Sproat also organized a weekly task list that included an aggregation of questions she received during the week from OhioLINK members. This task list was one of the items discussed on a weekly call with EBSCO. The project manager was able to keep these calls productive by tabling issues that needed further discussion and bringing those issues back to the front when a decision had been made by consortium members so that executable tasks had priority at any given time.

2. For EBSCO, there were four designated people assigned to work on the project. They were specialists in various areas of discovery tool integration, including catalog integration, knowledge base/link resolver, and the discovery layer itself.

3. Monthly training sessions were held in a central location—the State Library of Ohio in Columbus. Additional training sessions were held in Cincinnati, Cleveland, Akron, Bowling Green, and Youngstown to reach the northern and southern parts of the state.

    OhioLINK coordinated the sessions and handled the registration. The focus was on providing everything the libraries needed to know to implement EDS. Training included a brief overview of EDS; customization options for EDS, knowledge base, and link resolver management; and the opportunity to complete questionnaires identifying how the project was proceeding from the members' point of view. These overview sessions transitioned to more hands-on training sessions, putting more focus on EBSCOadmin and knowledge base administration.

The training sessions allowed for greater collaboration between the libraries. A few libraries had implemented EDS before OhioLINK selected it as a consortial offering and were able to provide helpful feedback and advice to those going through the process. This allowed for useful discussions on integrating EDS in library instruction in addition to implementation topics such as default settings and options.

4. The OhioLINK Central Catalog Coordinator Anita Cook created an export guideline with screenshots and instructions so that all libraries would know how to export their data from the Innovative Interfaces ILS. This enabled librarians to send their catalog data to EBSCO in a timely and consistent manner so the EBSCO team could begin to work on the EDS Custom Catalog databases more quickly.

5. OhioLINK created its own EDS listserv for its member libraries where questions could be posted, ideas exchanged, and feedback given. EBSCO is not on the listserv, but the project manager forwarded questions or key topics of interest.

CHALLENGES AND CUSTOMIZATION

There were some unique challenges to working on multisite implementations, such as how the various sites would authenticate into EDS given the different proxies (e.g., on vs. off campus, guest access, etc.). Some of the other challenges related to the enormous number of resources that can be accessed through OhioLINK.

OhioLINK has incorporated seven proprietary institutional repository databases into EDS, including a central union catalog, and members can choose which of these collections to include in their individual implementations. Institutions are also able to retain the individuality of their library's information and services by branding EDS with unique names, their own logos and colors, and adding widgets, customized search boxes and toolbars, and guest access entry points.

There were challenges related to how OhioLINK content (including the Electronic Journal Center, which is a locally loaded e-journal platform with journals from major publishers) displayed in individual members' instances of EDS. One such issue was that the search results from the central catalog overwhelmed the other results. To overcome this, EBSCO created a version of the central catalog that had a differently weighted relevancy, which allowed Ohio-LINK members to better customize how they wanted their discovery service to work with their local content. In this way, EDS can act as a collective view of the library community within OhioLINK, enabling visibility into unique materials across a network of libraries, while still providing access to local resources.

EBSCO also addressed how interlibrary loan (ILL) links would display. For times when an ILL is necessary, libraries have the ability to enable a link to an ILL form right from the result list. By modifying custom links in EDS, items available through the central catalog by direct peer-to-peer requests were routed through OhioLINK's INN-Reach system and not referred to a library's ILL request form. This is an example of partnerships that EBSCO has forged with other vendors, allowing for a neutral, customized solution for each library—across EBSCO and non-EBSCO resources. Libraries also have choices about how full text links display in results. EDS offers direct linking to full text to complement the link resolver. Individual libraries can choose their preferred approach (any or all).

Some desired customizations are still being created. For example, EBSCO is working on improving the display of the central catalog's holdings in EDS, including the display of additional fields from the catalog, directly available patron hold and checkout functionality, and additional cohesiveness between catalog records and other records in the discovery service, which will heighten search functionality and eliminate duplication. The list of institutions that hold a particular item can be long, and as it is currently displayed, it is not always immediately clear if an item is available at a user's home library. Ideally, OhioLINK would like to have real-time availability of items to list the member libraries' own holdings first, followed by other OhioLINK library holdings in alphabetical order.

PRELIMINARY RESULTS AND FEEDBACK

Usage statistics show a trend of increasing sessions and custom links across all libraries, but because of the staggered implementation schedule and the number of institutions that have not implemented or just recently implemented EDS, it is difficult to ascertain much from these stats (see Figures 1 and 2).

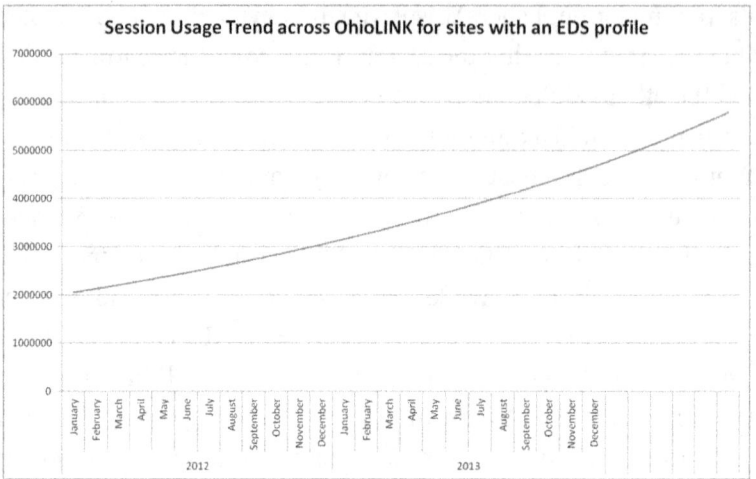

Figure 1. Shows the usage trend across OhioLINK sites that have an EDS profile with six month anticipation.

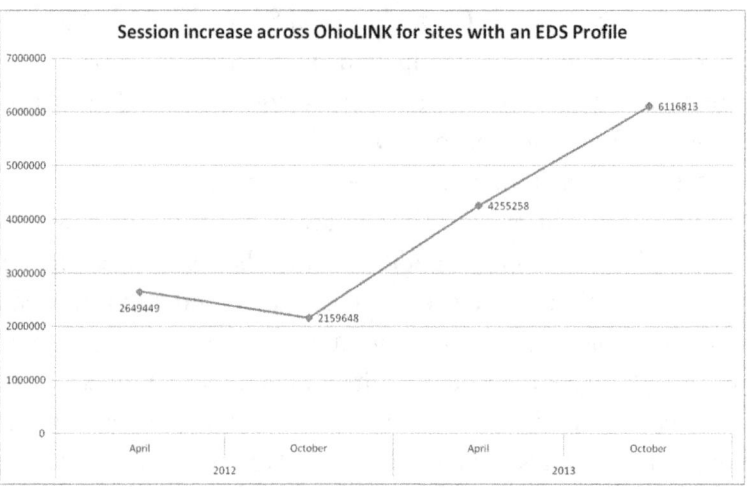

Figure 2. Session increase across OhioLINK for sites with an EDS profile. To account for natural decreases in usage during summer months and school breaks, the statistics for usage in April and October were considered.

Individual institutions that have fully implemented EDS are seeing benefits. At Shawnee State University, there has been a sizable increase in sessions since they started using EDS (see Figure 3). Suzanne Johnson-Varney, technical services librarian, attributes the success to a number of factors.

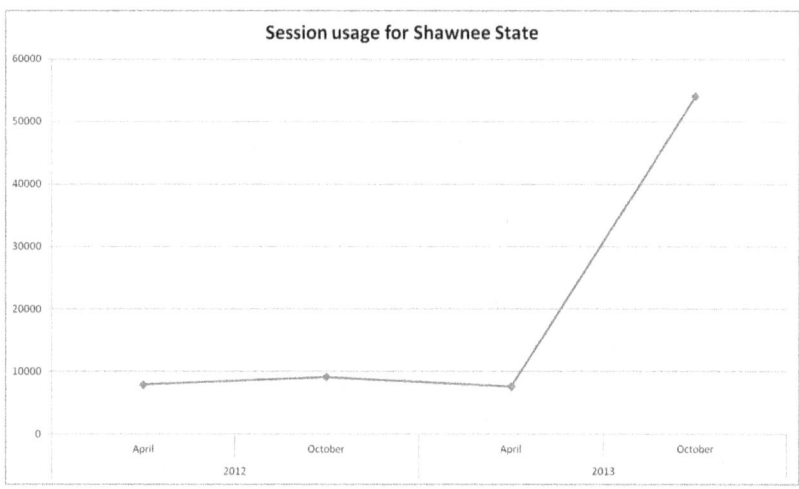

Figure 3. Session usage for Shawnee State University, which began to include EBSCO Discovery Service in the library's Information Literacy Instruction class in the fall of 2013.

When Johnson-Varney started at Shawnee State University, the searching solution with federation was not ideal (personal communication, February 12, 2014). She stated, "It was difficult to teach students how to search, and the tool required too much manual work." She sees the ease of use of EDS as a main reason why there has been an increase in off-campus usage—a major accomplishment for a school with a majority of non-traditional students. "A reason it is successful is that it isn't too library-oriented," said Johnson-Varney. "Our students don't understand Google versus library resources that they would have to pay for. It has made a huge difference in working with the students because they are getting tangible results." Another reason for the increase in adoption is that EDS is included in the library's Information Literacy Instruction class. "We need to teach kids how to use resources without being overwhelmed," says Johnson-Varney.

Johnson-Varney and her fellow librarians have been able to use the flexibility of EDS to their advantage. They have the OhioLINK catalog as a separate field because they want students to search their own holdings first. They embedded the discovery search box in LibGuides to create a one-stop shop. They tried different settings to see how they affected search results. In one case, many of the librarians thought limiting to a full-text setting as a default setting would narrow results too much, but since all of Shawnee State University's holdings are included in EDS, limiting searching in this way displays all the library's accessible online full text (subscription and open access) even if it is hosted on a remote publisher site. As a result of what they have seen, the setting has become permanent. Further, Shawnee has elected to display "SmartLinks" to PDF articles, so users have one-click access directly in the result list, something that has been shown to impact usage of the collection and perceptions of the library by end users. These links essentially bypass the link resolver, improving the accuracy of links, and eliminating confusion and dead ends that often arise for students through confusing link resolver menus.

EDS also benefits institutions that have more experienced researchers. As one of the five members of the Association of Research Libraries in OhioLINK, Ohio University has also seen an increase in sessions since implementing EDS (see Figure 4). This is largely because EDS takes a true academic approach to discovery, including not only an emphasis on peer-reviewed and other scholarly materials (not on newspaper records, for example, that can dominate results in many discovery services), but also on results from graduate and postgraduate-level resources. Researchers can dive into the special limiters associated with individual databases, allowing users to move from the larger discovery service, identify where search results came from, and organically move into the native resource to conduct more sophisticated research.

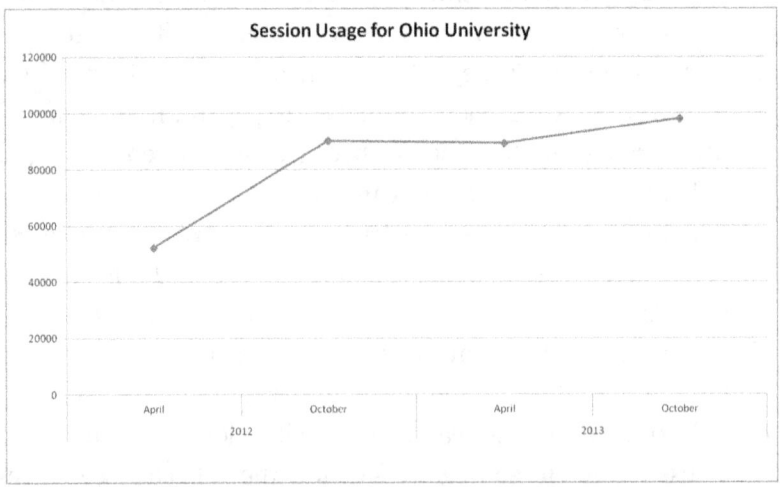

Figure 4. Session usage for Ohio University, which implemented EBSCO Discovery Service in June 2011, before OhioLINK selected it.

There are many features and enhancements to come that will continue to make this one-stop shop for research a greater resource. For example, EBSCO is undertaking a major initiative to merge thesauri from the most respected sources in the academic industry (e.g., MEDLINE, PsycINFO, Inspec) and map to a controlled vocabulary that will let users search with simple terms, yet be presented with highly relevant results that take advantage of "behind-the-scenes" mappings that will display articles using subject terms related to their search queries. In the end, EDS is a simple experience for users, with a sophisticated approach to providing the best possible results.

S | OCLC and Discovery

John McCullough, OCLC

HISTORY

OCLC is a global membership-based library cooperative representing more than 26,000 institutional members. OCLC provides a variety of services to the membership, including applications such as library management, reference, and discovery. One of OCLC's central services is the creation and maintenance of WorldCat, a publicly accessible database of the holdings of the world's libraries.

OCLC entered the web-based search space with the FirstSearch reference application in 2000, upgrading from the existing text-based interface at the same time as the initial web-based Online Public Access Catalog (OPAC) offerings were appearing from Integrated Library System (ILS) vendors. FirstSearch represented a public search interface of WorldCat titles and holdings as well as a range of databases OCLC had made available, such as ERIC and MEDLINE, and quickly became a standard database offering at many libraries. At the start of 2014, over 18,000 libraries had access to First-Search, which requires a paid subscription from the library and a log-on by the user. Like many search interfaces of the era, FirstSearch exposed a broad array of sophisticated search functions, including some specialized functions intended for use by library staff—extremely powerful for the knowledgeable user, but somewhat daunting for the more casual searcher.

In 2005, OCLC announced the Open WorldCat Initiative, which recognized that the web was trending in the direction of consolidating traffic under known brands, and believing that OCLC had the scale to establish a library brand on the web. The Open WorldCat Initiative would apply the direct-to-consumer philosophy of websites like Amazon.com to libraries and offer web-based public searching of WorldCat and other OCLC databases to all, free of charge and with no user log-on requirement. Libraries with holdings in WorldCat would not only be able to make them available through the FirstSearch interface, but also see those holdings exposed via the new, open service. This service was launched under the address of WorldCat.org.

WorldCat.org represented a significant upgrade to the user experience compared to FirstSearch. In line with the more user-friendly design ethos of the time period, in which the complexity and verbosity of early library search interfaces was dramatically reduced in the interests of usability by the average library patron, WorldCat.org offered a single search box, faceted browsing, and a general streamlining of the interface.

The Open WorldCat Initiative also included the launch of the syndication program, in which OCLC worked with partners out on the open web, starting with Yahoo and rapidly expanding to include Google, Wikipedia, and many more, to include links from title-level book displays back to Worldcat.org, and from there to local libraries. As users have expanded their starting points for searches from the library's native interfaces to the search engines, the syndication programs leverage the scale of OCLC to put a path back to libraries out where users are. More recently, OCLC has worked with partners like Blackboard to include access back to the library search from within apps like Mosaic.

The user experience of Worldcat.org was so successful that when OCLC made the decision to move into the local library discovery space in 2006, it built that solution, called WorldCat Local, on the same architecture and using the same interface principles. Like WorldCat.org, WorldCat Local was designed specifically with the library user, not library staff, in mind; unlike WorldCat.org, it was designed to provide a local-library-specific entry point for the user, providing a unique URL for each library, local library branding for the experience, display of local bibliographic data fields, and sorting of the library's held materials to the top of results sets.

Where WorldCat Local went beyond WorldCat.org was in the introduction of specific discovery-oriented features, most notably access to a central index of discovery metadata, primarily for article e-content. Academic discovery systems quickly evolved into "web-scale" implementations based on a single, pre-index, centralized search of article metadata, in the spirit of the commercial search engines and as opposed to federated searching, which suffered from performance issues, inconsistency, and an inability to reliably do cross-source relevance ranking. OCLC's core competence in building and maintaining WorldCat lent itself to rapidly building a central index of its own and to the new expectations of cloud-based rather than local deployments, and the organization's nonprofit status and neutrality in the industry supported the equally rapid extension of partnership agreements to support loading discovery metadata. WorldCat Local further supplemented the central index with a metasearch component for the broadest possible reach.

The focus on the central index as a complement to WorldCat, integrated under a single search, also signaled a stronger focus on discovery of electronic holdings in addition to print. Shortly after the launch of WorldCat Local, OCLC introduced its own knowledge base to drive electronic fulfillment of materials discovered through the interface. WorldCat Local was built explicitly for patron searches, and it did not include a staff mode; staff users continued to work with the FirstSearch interface. WorldCat Local included integrated reference features for patrons such as a widget allowing users to query the QuestionPoint online reference service. Hundreds of libraries worldwide adopted WorldCat Local as their discovery interface, and it became the public interface for OCLC's WorldShare Management Services (WMS) system.

In January 2014, OCLC announced the launch of WorldCat Discovery, a rebooted platform that would replace the aging FirstSearch interface and eventually both the WorldCat Local and WorldCat.org user interfaces. WorldCat Discovery as a FirstSearch replacement was beta tested with hundreds of libraries during 2013, with the focus split between patron functions and staff functions. The interface was built on the critical principles of responsive design, in which each display and function could size itself to the device being used to access it without degrading the experience, so that the service could be accessed from a single URL from mobile devices, tablets, or laptops, and ensure a consistent quality of experience. As usage continued to shift from desktops to these alternate access methods, OCLC deemed it imperative for any interface expected to reach patrons to natively support these principles.

WorldCat Discovery would also represent the combination of the FirstSearch and WorldCat Local services into a single, multimodal offering that would support the robust patron searching of WorldCat Local, including the Central Index, as well as the focused staff searching experiences of FirstSearch, and would represent a superset of the core functions of those interfaces. Usability testing identified that WorldCat Local and FirstSearch served fundamentally different search needs: WorldCat Local was used by patrons to find what their local library had, or at least what they could fulfill (including copies on the shelf, titles available through holds or interlibrary loan, or through electronic fulfillment links direct to full-text articles online), whereas FirstSearch was mainly used by patrons searching for something they had not found in their local OPAC (in essence, searching for what their library did not have). These two functions had to be reconciled in the combined interface, for example, by introducing different sorting options based on whether the user was looking locally or globally.

OCLC APPROACH TO DISCOVERY

OCLC's approach to discovery begins with the user. Usability testing and interviews involve engaging directly with particular constituencies of the interface, which means working not just with librarians, but also with end users themselves to validate the success of specific workflows.

Users are grouped by their ultimate need rather than simply by role; distinctions such as "staff" or "public" stand in a shorthand for specific needs, but in execution the focus is on more granular workflows that may cross those boundaries. Is the end point of the user session a transaction, such as a check-out, hold, or electronic fulfillment, or is the end point a management function, such as editing a record?

Many of the lessons learned are consistent with larger trends. Users prefer complexity to be transparent and concealed rather than exposed by the application wherever possible, both in terms of calls to action, such as fulfillment links, and in terms of information on the screen. Results screens have moved away from information-rich displays where everything is up front to more economical displays, informed by search engine results. The thinking that users will bounce off a page if all of the options and information are immediately apparent to them has given way to the idea that information can be revealed progressively in subsequent displays; the key is for the interface to let the user know that they are headed in the right direction, and the user will gladly click forward; it is when they are unsure they are going to end up successful that they back out and try afresh. The highly successful deployment of facets in discovery systems bears this out; facets improve upon traditional presearch limiting by telling the user in advance how many matches there are to the presented criteria.

Relevance continues to be both critical and challenging as discovery systems attempt to encompass large and more heterogeneous universes of metadata under a single search box. WorldCat Discovery provides access to WorldCat, including over 300 million titles, and to the central index of over 1.5 billion articles, e-books, and other electronic content. The first screen display, what's "above the fold" on an initial result, has to serve the purpose of letting the user know if they should keep scrolling or drilling in, or whether they should back out and refresh the search. Commercial search engines have trained users that the "best" results are always on top; users do not expect to scroll from poor results to strong ones, and so will try a new search if the first titles they see are out of alignment with their need.

Discovery systems confront the challenge of relevance in support of known item searching. A user enters a title that finds an exact match in the index, but that title is not held by their library. Does the system only show what the library can fulfill, as an OPAC would, and make it look like the title may not have been entered correctly, or should the user be shown the non-locally held material and risk diluting search results with material the library cannot fulfill? A "bird's-eye" view of results, such as WorldCat.org, does not have to reconcile these cases, but locally oriented discovery does. Commercial search engines are bird's-eye views by default and are introducing contextual inputs such as geography or patron history into primary search results to nuance them, but they do not face such a clear distinction between local holdings and global holdings. One solution is to have users self-identify which case they need to support, and the question becomes the best way to set this expectation in the user interface.

One response to these needs is to create multiple access points derived from a single search or expanding query results transparently to users in specific, expected ways. Some such mechanisms are familiar to users, including:

- Type-ahead searches
- Did You Mean . . . ? alternate search suggestions for spelling errors, fuzzy matches
- Disambiguation (is a search for mercury for the substance, the planet, the mythological figure, or the car?)
- Synonyms searching (treating as equivalent words like color or colour)
- Stemming (treating as equivalent words like running, runner, runners)
- A recommendations service for the title or database level, for example, based on aggregate previous usage

A newer mechanism being introduced to search and discovery interfaces is the Knowledge Card, which constructs a brief panel containing information about the topic being searched, for example, about a specific person, place, or thing. Knowledge Card displays can integrate linked data and can include in the display alternate resource links or searches—for example, an author card could display recommended works by that author. Knowledge Cards offered by search engines like Google are creating user expectations to see these displays supplementing search results, which creates an opportunity to use this expected real estate for a variety of the functions described above. Note that unlike a commercial search engine, library discovery would not be presenting this information with the intent of meeting the user need without requiring a click-through; the intent of Knowledge Cards would be to drive more robust usage of the available collections in response to the user's expressed need.

FROM BREADTH TO DEPTH

The arms race within web-scale discovery focused in the early years on the breadth of coverage. How many titles, databases, and providers were represented? How complete a picture of a library's paid content was the service able to access, preferably without resorting to federated searching? As the dominant services have all approached or exceeded a billion or more articles, the focus has shifted from quantity of coverage to quality, from breadth to depth of metadata. The demand is for quality metadata, preferably structured, such as subjects. More metadata can be a two-edged sword, as there is always the risk of diluting results or creating user confusion, and further stress can be placed on relevance algorithms to sort through the noise to find the signal. In some cases, additional metadata may be exempted from the default search and made available only to expert searchers who know how to invoke the option and deal with the results. An extreme case can be found in the growing availability of full-text for articles and for e-books, which due to the volume and relative lack of structure of the data present enormous challenges in term of relevance and setting user expectations. For the majority of use cases, OCLC has found that a separate search option, rather than combining searching of full-text with that of more structured metadata by default, is vastly preferable. The Open Discovery Initiative has attempted to address some of these issues, proposing standard expectations of the level of metadata that could be indexed into discovery services. OCLC welcomes richer metadata in the central index, as this benefits library users and content providers alike by providing more inputs for the index and application to match content with user need.

Discovery and the Digital Reference Desk

Andrew Nagy, ProQuest

As use of discovery services grows, reference librarians are more vital than ever. Web-like search capabilities and student expectations for self-service and immediate access to content might seem to be diminishing the role of reference librarians; however, in our conversations with libraries that have rolled out the Summon discovery service as the digital front door to their libraries' resources, we have found something quite different.

The role of reference librarians is and needs to evolve as the digital nature of library collections continues to increase exponentially and 24/7, anywhere, any device access to research materials becomes the norm. Rather than reducing the roll of reference librarians, discovery services need to allow them to scale their services in innovative ways to help more researchers than ever—and to play a more prominent role in the mission of the academic institution.

JAMES A. CANNAVINO LIBRARY, MARIST COLLEGE

The Summon service allows Marist College to scale to reach more students, improve information literacy skills and build deeper appreciation for the library's information resources. "There are students we see, and students we *never* see," explains Kathryn Silberger, senior librarian/digital content services. "The search logs let us see the distant learning student who never comes into the library. They aren't asking questions at the reference desk, but they are asking questions of the library."

Using Analysis to Improve Information Literacy

Through the logs, the staff is able to determine how students are searching, and they use the analysis to adjust their information literacy teaching. States Silberger, "Every week, I pull the top 50 or top 75 queries that students have entered into Summon. Librarians can see where users have succeeded, if there are consistent errors being made, or if librarians should introduce a better way of searching."

Moreover, she says that during the teaching sessions, "We go into some detail about how Summon is different from the open-web search engines, and why it's a more appropriate source for college research." Freed from spending time teaching how to use a query tool, the librarians focus more on how to conduct proper research, evaluate resources, and use the best content. As Silberger puts it, "I think the difference is that we're giving users a Swiss Army knife as opposed to the toothpick, or the nail file. We're giving them a universal, multidisciplinary skill, because they don't have to contend with all the different interfaces."

A Measureable Impact

"We've been watching numbers, and we've clearly had an impact," Silberger declares. "Students do a lot of searching with Summon, and we see a tremendous amount of linking to full text. If they use Summon to find full text that is relevant to them, that's a successful experience with the library, and we believe that they will feel more comfortable using the library." And while she cannot necessarily point to Summon as the cause, she says, "We've seen the number of people coming into the reference desk go up significantly. It's a pleasant surprise, and here's another one: We had more print books used last semester than we have in the last five years."

KELVIN SMITH LIBRARY, CASE WESTERN RESERVE UNIVERSITY

At Case Western Reserve University, the library used the Summon service to change the reference access model and free the librarians to interact more proactively with students and faculty. Brian Gray, research services team leader, describes the impetus for the change: "It was clear from our statistics that librarians at the reference desk were giving directions and answering other simple questions. Meanwhile, when a librarian wasn't available, other library staff and student helpers were handling the harder questions. Our librarians were only doing about 50% of the hours on the reference desk, and only answering 50% of what we consider hard questions.

He continued, "Using Summon, the main desk started answering first-level reference questions. We figured that by focusing on Summon as the primary search tool—which linked to a lot of the full text anyway—it simplified the process. We have over 200 databases, and that can be intimidating even to a librarian. With Summon, they could focus on listening to the user and figuring out what they need, rather than trying every database until they found an answer."

Freeing Time to Support the Academic Mission

In turn, the move allows librarians to deliver more value to the institution. Declares Gray, "Summon allows us to take the librarians off the desk, to free up time to answer specialized research questions, and to be more directly involved in their assigned academic departments. Librarians are more available to go to departmental meetings and seminars, to hold office hours in their departments, and to be where the faculty and students are—which isn't always in the library."

NEXT STEPS: DEEPER LIBRARIAN INTEGRATION INTO THE DISCOVERY PROCESS

What's next for discovery services? Consider that at a typical university, the library serves thousands and thousands of students, with a relatively small staff. With the discovery service as the primary entrée to the library, there is an opportunity to scale up to meet the needs of more students, and insert librarians into the process where appropriate.

Delivering Rich, Locally Relevant Results

Behind the scenes, a discovery service can make the library's rich academic content more discoverable by leveraging complex relevancy ranking algorithms. Another way is by detecting queries that use common terms and expanding them with specific, academic phrases that are typically used in the controlled vocabularies of the databases. Other features allow librarians to highlight context-specific local resources such as LibGuides, databases with especially relevant content, or a special collection.

Bringing Librarians Front and Center

Along with the search results, context-driven capabilities can also recommend staff librarians who specialize in a specific area of study. Alternatively, online chat functionality built into the interface allows students to immediately engage a librarian, turning the discovery interface into a virtual reference desk. These features can be built into the link resolver as well as the discovery service, so they appear in the search results regardless of the point of entry.

Stewards of the Discovery Process

By embracing discovery services, reference librarians are able to come out from behind the reference desk and become the stewards of the entire discovery process. Meeting student expectations on their own terms and embracing a librarian-assisted self-service model, libraries play a more visible and highly active role in the educational mission of the institution.

U | Reference: An Architect's View

Rayford W. Law, Rayford W. Law Architecture+Planning

The primary focus for this chapter will be focused on the planning and architectural design of the reference service component of the library as a representation of the institutional mission and the community of users of a university campus library. This case study will document two libraries, both of which were a combination new construction and renovation, one on the campus of the Princeton Theological Seminary and the other at Washington University in Saint Louis. In addition to the comparison of the resolution of site-specific issues of building and campus space, project schedule, and budgetary constraints, the discussion will also include universal issues of new technology, new modes of instruction, and the social component of research and learning on campus.

GENERAL PLANNING AND DESIGN CONSIDERATIONS

With the planning of libraries, there is typically the specific challenge of assessing, navigating, and organizing all of the various critical library functions that demand operational and physical solutions. Planning generally starts with the mandatory control point on the entry floor in proximity to circulation, checkout, and any associated help service points, and also extends to those functions that conversely are in demand by users, such as an information or (by any other name) knowledge commons, printing and scanning equipment, info or wayfinding kiosks, catalogs or OPAC stations, current periodicals (digital and print), new publications, or acquisitions. Following from these more strictly library functions are those that complement the research quest or general library experience, such as a café or other streamlined food service, a gallery or curated display, as well as a variety of on-campus learning support or tutorial centers. All of the above represent only the front-of-house or user-transacted components, most of which require some form of back-of-house support, whether that be acquisitions, cataloguing, or reshelving on the one hand or loading dock, processing, and trash/recycling on the other. In many cases, space limitations mean all of these functional requirements may not be accommodated on the same floor level, and through the planning process, they begin to vie for the closest locations on adjacent floors. In any event, this entry floor is a true shared activity space offering.

Somewhere within this mix is reference, with the function marked by any combination of the following: a desk or other furniture-like indication of a service point; a kiosk or other sign of mobile technology; an office or offices; a reference collection (typically dictionaries, encyclopedias, almanacs, atlases, and any number of bibliographic resources) distributed in nearby dedicated shelving; plus user seating either at proper tables or of a softer, more casual variety or both. A small conference room for instruction may also be proximate. Potentially, in an even more expansive scenario, any or all of the above could be housed in a dedicated space or room with or without doors, but generally, not far from the entry sequence into the library.

INSTITUTIONAL PROFILE, PROJECT CHALLENGES, AND DESIGN RESPONSE

Princeton Theological Seminary

New library addition of 79,000 square feet to the renovated North Wing, formerly the Luce Library, including the demolition of the Speer Library (completed September 2014). A small, private seminary in Princeton, New Jersey, of about 500 students, most of which are postbaccalaureate candidates, predominantly master's of divinity, but with 60–80 PhDs.

This library project is the combination of new construction (completed in August 2013) for general collections, and so forth, contiguous to an existing special collections facility (originally finished in 1994, with renovation to be completed in July 2014), the sum of which establishes one of the largest buildings on a small but somewhat fragmented campus. The library is located in a prominent setting, but somewhat tangential, being isolated from other campus buildings by city streets. In terms of the vertical stacking of floors and resulting building volume, the two buildings are each four stories, with one floor below grade and three above.

In this case, while physically integrated into the campus network of outdoor spaces and buildings, going to the library is a deliberate act of intent and not typically a coincident one of merely being in proximity with an impulse to go inside.

As a sister institution to Princeton University, the library serves both the Princeton Theological Seminary and the university, as well as the general public community of Princeton at large, and as importantly the library also views itself in a global context as a theological library of last resort.

The total collections are 1.2 million volumes, making it the second-largest theological collection in the world next to the Vatican Library in Rome.

Reference

In this library, the primary intellectual instrument and armature of the library is the reference librarian, who is the primary provider of reference services and who also manages the accommodations and research assistance for the PhD candidates, faculty, and visiting scholars. To support her there is an assistant librarian whose official title is the web services librarian.

The reference collection has 10,000 print volumes. Per the space constraints stated above, the reference service desk is located on the main floor, while the bulk of the reference collection is one floor down within a dramatically shaped and sunken double height but light-filled reference reading room.

Planning and Design

The basic planning challenges presented by project goals of combining both a new and renovated library facility at the Princeton Theological Seminary are not uncommon. Seamlessly tying together two separate buildings into an easily comprehensible whole means the ground floor (entry level) accommodates a considerable number of public and back-of-house activities and services for both functional necessity and convenience. This includes the main service point designated in the plan as a gently asymmetric curve, which pulls the visitor into the library and also provides checkout and general library information, scanning, and printing. Adjacent is the concourse, with both physical building and collection wayfinding plus OPACs, open reference material, current periodicals in low shelves, study areas, circulation, and gallery display, ultimately leading to a dedicated reference service desk fronting two reference librarian offices and the double doors to the reference reading room.

Other activities on this floor prior to the entry control point include public functions such as a community assembly room for 100 occupants, a small meeting room for 16 people, and a Starbucks-type café, all connected by a gracious foyer with visual connection up into one of the primary user areas in the building, the South Gallery. Other library functions on this floor also include recent acquisitions as well as the IT service desk, current periodicals, another gallery, and back-of-house processing and storage just inside the service dock with adjacent employee entry.

Consequently, in terms of orientation and location, the reference desk is paired opposite the main circulation/service desk, providing an immediate presence just after entry as both service points bracket the casual arrangement and programmatically diverse open planning of the concourse, and all of which fronts onto a dramatic light-filled five-story atrium that spatially organizes the two buildings into one entity.

The insufficient space available on the ground floor to accommodate the reference collection in conjunction with the desire to better utilize the inherited below-grade lower level that now provides the occupiable ground floor of the atrium, led to the reference collection being housed in a distinctive double-height room on the lower level floor, but with the balconied ground floor study overlook and with its own dedicated stair down to the bulk of the collection. In doing so, reference, in terms of both the service point and the collection, is visible from many different places in the building. Moreover, the service point and associated conversations coexist within the vibrancy

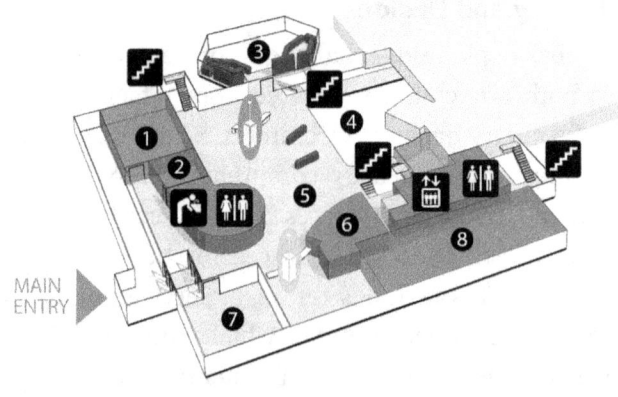

Figure 1. Airline card directory, first floor plan.

and transitional character of the concourse, while the collection and corresponding quiet study space is just beyond through a set of doors in a strongly figural and serenely reflective room.

The architectural treatment of the service point and the reference reading room derives from the emerging character of the building's interior and reinforces the identity of the family of service points within the building. The desk is a long, low, granite work surface supported by simple, variegated cherry millwork that accommodates one or two staff to conduct business with users simultaneously. Laden with power and hardwired data connections (as well as the entire building being wireless), the reference desk was designed to simultaneously acts as a desk, worktable, and instructional display, and correspondingly minimizes any residual institutional gravitas that may inhibit potential customers with research questions.

Signage was also an important consideration, which followed from the general vertical motif also employed at the three other service points in the building: a desktop-to-ceiling mounted pole piercing a vertically elongated lime peel-colored acrylic cube with vertically stacked dark gray capital letters reading REFERENCE. In the context of the cherry and the pale olive flora-like repeating organic pattern of the carpet with the backdrop of the two reference office walls being clear glass, the reference desk becomes an inviting component for fostering an informative exchange.

Assessment

At the Princeton Theological Seminary, the demand for reference service appears to be compliant with the tradition of a qualified reference staff member sitting at a simple piece of furniture, a desk, conspicuously located in the line of site from the entry control point and proximate, if not adjacent, to the hard copy reference collection. At this desk, the presence of technology is minimal as OPACS and other digital search devices are elsewhere, and so, in conjunction with a low and spacious counter, the emphasis is on the direct and

FIRST FLOOR

1   Daniel J Theron Assembly Room
2   Meeting Room
3   Reference Reading Room Mezzanine
4   Iain R Torrance Atrium
5   Concourse
6   Copy/Print/Scan
7   Café
8   Special Collections

Figure 2. First floor key.

personal one-on-one transaction. Thus, the resulting design is a simple, low-key, and understated desk, but in the instance of the overall character of the new library edition, a slightly elongated and clearly immovable piece of millwork, suggesting permanence and inherent flexibility. Furthermore, this freestanding condition confirms the singularity of the reference service in Princeton Theological Seminary Library, which would not otherwise allow for its consolidation into any other service points.

In terms of design fit and appropriate response, the reference librarian has become more comfortable with the millwork as the exaggerated placeholder for the previous furniture, but rarely has more than one user ever been present at the desk at any time. Thus, the anticipated demand, which generated sufficient dimension for multiple transactions with multiple staff to occur, has never been realized. Furthermore, the issue of this desk being remote from the reference collection has been rationalized as a means by which the reference librarian is more proactively "on the floor" in the library. The opinion by many, including the reference librarian, that the reference reading room with its display of the collection is the nicest room in the building evidently provides the motivation for the extensive travel back and forth.

There is one subtle but tangible problem related with the location and size of this desk in the previously described concourse: in the iterations of massaging various program components along with the resultant column spacing, the reference desk is located a bit too far away, maybe 10–15 feet, from the main service point for the direct hand off from this service point to the reference service. Some combination of gesturing and hand signaling sometimes occurs when the direct line of site is not so clear to the new user. This might be seen more as a communication challenge than a design flaw.

WASHINGTON UNIVERSITY IN SAINT LOUIS

John M. Olin Library

A midsized private research institution in suburban St Louis, Missouri, of approximately 14,000 students split evenly between undergraduate and graduate students (expansion and renovation completed 2004).

The library project was the combination of a relatively small expansion of 16,000 square feet at ground floor level as part of a larger comprehensive renovation of the 184,000-square-foot existing facility that serves as the centrally located flagship facility on a campus with 14 libraries.

By virtue of its size, location, and corresponding pedestrian network, the library is essentially unavoidable on the academic hilltop, now called the Danforth Campus, and thereby creates a prominent juncture at the center of campus. The volume of the building as it relates to grade: it is a total of five stories with two below grade and three above.

The total collection is 4.2 million volumes and the facility is a Federal Depository Library; special collections includes various literary collections of Beckett, Nemerov, Gass, Merrill, as well as the Washington University Film and Media Archive.

Reference

The physical planning of reference services included a significant area dedicated to the reference collection as well as the prospect of an intimidating suite of private offices, but in an effort to provide a more visible, user-friendly, and instructive transaction, which also included acting as a liaison with the technical staff on the user's behalf, the dean of libraries collaborated with various interests within and outside of the library to make significant structural changes to the business of reference service. One of the primary changes was with the term reference librarian, which was renamed subject librarian. As a function of the extent and diversity of need, there would be more than a dozen of these subject librarians, but more importantly, these newly named providers would operate with a renewed mission crafted to provide a personalized service, incorporating resources for research, instruction, publishing, and problem solving.

With the requisitely large amount of space needed to individually support and back up the circulation, reserve, reference, and interlibrary loan (ILL) service point, it was determined that all services would be programmed and planned into a combined and shared one-stop help center service point without a freestanding reference desk, and more importantly without, at least in name, reference librarians. The staff at this consolidated service point would be trained in all aspects of the processes and inquiries, including where and to whom the user would next consult. Essentially, this meant there was the logistical possibility to couple reference with circulation/reserve/checkout.

Thus the challenge: how to create anew an inevitable and thereby navigable mix of diverse uses, including a new entrance with functional clarity and a compelling atmosphere. Then for reference, how to streamline the process in order to optimize the service amongst competing activities? Not only how will one organize and design to enhance new behaviors in the presence of new amenities and immediacy of new technology, but also how can a fundamental shift in the organizational structure of reference and corresponding architectural presentation complement the service?

Planning and Design

The project was initiated as a simple planning study for the insertion of a cyber café on the ground floor, but which soon thereafter sponsored a complete rethinking and ultimately the reprogramming and implementation of many library services, and ultimately the complete replanning of the existing facility, with the notable exception that the bulk of the general collection stacks were to be left intact. The ground floor planning also had to recognize the gradual shift in pedestrian traffic on campus over the decades (subsequent to the original 1962 facility) such that the primary entry and attendant control point would need drastic reconsideration as well. Additionally, there was increasing importance being attached to the visibility and integrated curriculum use of special collections, and consequently, the desire for a prominence on the entry floor as well. The specific desire for increased visibility of library use also generated a substantial open reading and study area at grade.

With a new entrance from the south, the visitor immediately sees to the right the cyber café, Whispers, posed at the base of an enclosed three-story atrium capped by an octagonal lantern that, with an existing generous open stair adjacent, provides the visual and spatial focus to organize and orient users within the building. Continuing straight ahead directly into the library is the expansive but welcoming help center, comprised of an undulating wood-trimmed desk in the plan shape of a reverse bell curve so that it reaches out to the user. Moreover, as stated above, this desk was programmed and designed to symmetrically pair reference service with the traditional control point service of circulation and checkout. In this case, reference service is essentially a referral station to filter and categorize the subsequent direction for the user, and in most cases of research queries, forwarding them on to any one of the subject librarians.

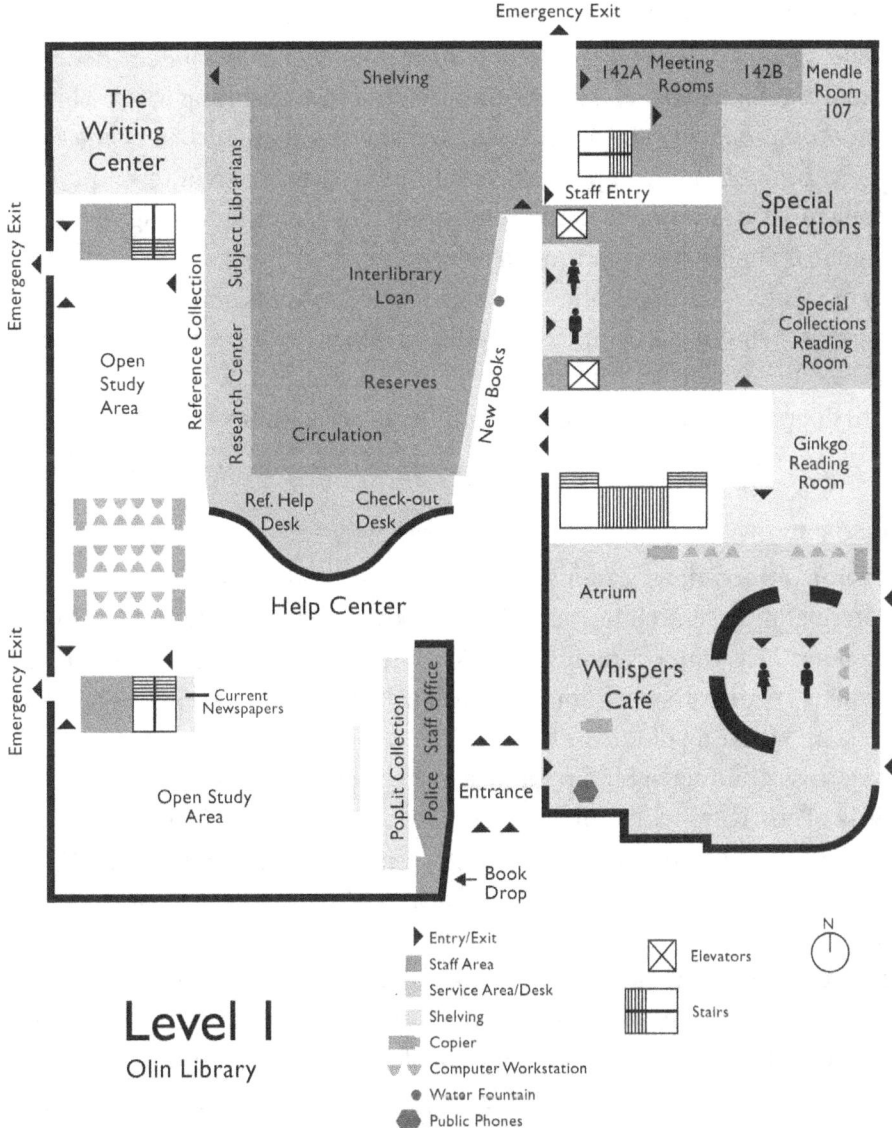

Figure 3. Olin Library level 1 (ground floor) map.

With a few exceptions related to the need of proximity to a specifically related collection, most of the subject librarians are located on the ground floor around the corner to the left from the reference side of the help center. The corresponding original planning concept was leaning toward dedicated private offices, but in the earnest effort to promote the sense of a collaborative consortium of services, each occupant, a subject librarian, would reside in a 140-square-foot office but with two tandem doors—a public one for users and a back-of-house door for consulting with technical staff. Accompanying the physical plan was the development of an open-door policy, promoting a comprehensive and proactive research, teaching, and problem-solving approach. Adjacent within this array are two slightly larger rooms for small group instruction or conferencing. The result is a linear array of faculty-like offices and meeting rooms with walls of a combination of glass for visibility and painted drywall for opacity, where users and librarians would consult and furthermore, whenever occupied by the librarian, both doors would be open for unencumbered accessibility between user and resource, and also symbolic of the customer-friendly service to be offered.

Assessment

Several observations can be offered in the assessment of the general planning and the architecture of the desk to accommodate the pairing of reference help with circulation/checkout, the location of this multipurpose element relative to the subject librarians' offices, as well as the general effect and location of the desk.

Cross-training of both reference and circulation junior staff provides a sense of efficiency in handling any initial queries, regardless of the ultimate nature of the user question. The sense of a seamless, streamlined, multipurpose service point is somewhat compromised by the symmetrical plan of the desk, which continues to reinforce the sense of separation with the "this side reference, that side checkout" feel. This is, in part, due to the initial ground floor planning, which located the checkout function to the east, with its attendant monitoring of the passage of people and books, thereby needing to be visibly proximate to the entry/exit control gates and reference to the west around the corner, but otherwise adjacent to the subject librarians. However, it is also a function of the size of the desk; this piece of double curving millwork is 50 feet in length and visually spans across three column bays, and given that the mirrored double curve creates two welcoming concavities in the plan, it is of no surprise that users are pulled toward the two places in the desk rather than the top of the bell reaching out into the lobby.

The questions of symmetry and dimension of the service desk itself are also tempered by the fact that there is considerable dimension between the entry and the desk. This was partly a response to the painful lack of space in the prerenovation condition and thereby ensuring enough space for self-checkout or general info kiosks, special displays, or any number and variety of activities concurrent with entry and exit to the library. In some fundamental way as perceived by the staff, this distance is seen as creating an intimidating sense of monumentality with the desk and thereby an association of hesitancy in asking for help, although reference and circulation managers have never heard perceptions as such from any users.

The logistical problem of the subject librarians being housed around the corner from the service desk has been exacerbated by the slow but steady, incremental removal of print reference materials adjacent to their offices. Open study areas unrelated to reference or subject librarians replaced this open shelving, thus further diluting their physical presence, although no studies have been made confirming any associated drop in reference traffic. However, a recent service addition to the library, the Campus Writing Center, has been located in the northwest corner of the ground floor, thus filling in an open study cul-de-sac just beyond the subject librarians' offices, not only generating measurable rise in foot traffic past the subject librarians, but also directly feeding to their stated purpose with reference requests coming from users and their advisors at the Campus Writing Center. The unique, but in many ways, fortuitous colocation of these two services in the library has created a vibrant nexus of service activities in this part of the main entry floor quite independent of the consistently vibrant din throughout the rest of this floor.

COMPARISON AND CONCLUSIONS

Even beyond the context of the specific and unique institutional identities of the Princeton Theological Seminary and Washington University, it is quite easy to discern a relatively stark contrast between the functional roles of reference service in each, as well as the planning approach and corresponding accommodation within their respective libraries. It is also indicative of the respective approaches of each library to reference service in the 21st century.

At the Princeton Theological Seminary—the small and intimate community of scholars even within the larger community of Princeton, including the university—the technique for providing reference service is correspondingly simple and personal, without any sense of the user being processed. Both the transaction and the architecture is direct and efficient, but not to the exclusion of utilizing, but not necessarily integrating, currently available digital resources. One might conclude with the attribution that both the service and character evoke a sense of the tradition and timelessness of the pursuit.

At the Olin Library, the operational economics for providing effective reference service in an expanded facility with increased diversity of functions on the main floor, as well as serving the much larger university community, directed a comprehensive integration of distinct and freestanding services into a single one-stop help desk. With the territorial distinction general help/circulation versus reference service assigned to the symmetric form of the desk, the single point of service has not transpired as clearly as originally programmed, although staff training and overall dimension have supported the intent. The personal nature of reference transaction is no less present here than at Princeton, but one of serving greater numbers of users with greater number of librarians, and in this specific case of both of the libraries discussed above, the direct experience is around the corner at Olin rather than across the room at Princeton.

V | Addressing User Intent: Analyzing Usage Logs to Optimize Search Results

Christine Stohn, Ex Libris

INTRODUCTION

Libraries facilitate access to a vast amount of information, be it in their physical or electronic collections or somewhere on the web. The new generation of index-based discovery systems for libraries offers them the tools to effectively expose those collections to their users and at the same time give their users a more personalized search experience than Google. Library patrons use discovery systems to satisfy their information needs for course requirements or their research, to fact-check, or to obtain general information about a topic.

Library discovery systems such as Ex Libris Primo, ProQuest Summon, and EBSCO Discovery Service (EDS) index a large quantity of diverse materials from many publishers and other data providers. Such indexes cover articles, books, and, increasingly, datasets, images, and audiovisual material. The discovery systems usually feature a single search box and present users with one blended result list of items from all of the library's physical and digital collections.

When a discovery system indexes a huge number of items, users can find all—or most—of the material that they need in one system. Features such as filters (for example, to display only items that are available in electronic full text) and facets (for narrowing down results by topic, collection, date, and so on) enable users to focus on a particular item or set of results. However, the more items that a system indexes, the greater the number of results that are retrieved in a single search. Consequently, the process of identifying the relative value of results and ranking them effectively is more difficult for the system. To carry out such a process, discovery systems use ranking algorithms that are designed to determine which results are the best fit for the search query—in other words, to identify the most "relevant" results—and present them at the top of the list. To this end, discovery systems must have an understanding of the user's intent and information-seeking behavior.

One approach to gathering such information is the in-depth analysis of usage logs. Discovery systems such as Ex Libris Primo document every user action in logs (often referred to as transaction logs). The logged data provide a valuable source for the analysis and evaluation of user behavior. This chapter offers some insights into the work that Ex Libris has done on usage log analysis.

USAGE LOG ANALYSIS

Primo is used by millions of people in all types and sizes of organizations—institutions of higher education, research-rich organizations, and more. The diversity of users, of their goals in interacting with the system, and of materials (books, articles, audiovisual materials, and so on) is reflected in the usage logs, which capture millions of user searches. The large-scale analysis of these logs is one of the core tools that Ex Libris employs to gain a deeper understanding of users' search behavior and intent. ProQuest has undertaken similar usage log analyses for its Summon service, as described by Diamond, Price, and Chandrasekar (2013).

The user interactions with the system that are documented in the Primo usage logs include search queries, search refinements, and selection activities, such as full-text requests. Each action is logged separately, with a time stamp and a session identifier, and anonymized to protect the identity of the user. On the basis of the valuable information contained in these logs, adjustments can be made to the Primo searching and ranking technologies so that the search engine will be more likely to identify the material that best matches a user's query and the results can be arranged according to their relevance to the user's context and intent.

Types of Searches

Discovery systems serve a wide variety of users, even within a single institution, and diverse search goals on the part of the users. For example, in an academic environment, undergraduates may seek specific materials recommended by their course instructor, additional material to complete an assignment, or general reference material about a specific topic. Graduate students and other scholars may look for research articles on more specific topics or articles that one of their peers has published or recommended. Whatever their intent, users expect the discovery system to automatically recognize what they are looking for, regardless of how they formulate their search query. The system has to understand not only how users search, but also what their intent is so that it can find the most relevant results and rank them accordingly. To fulfill these requirements, the system must be able to distinguish between the various types of searches and identify their characteristics.

Most of the searches that appear in the Primo usage logs can be divided into known-item searches and exploratory (or topic) searches. In known-item searches, a user wants to find a specific item, such as an article or a book, and expects that item to be at the top of the result list. In a broad topic search, the search engine gives priority to material that provides an overview of the topic, such as review articles and reference works. For more specific topic-based searches, the user is likely to expect more specialized research articles on the subject. By identifying the search type, and thus the user's intent, the search engine can boost the ranking of relevant items. Recognition of common variations in the formulation of search queries provides discovery systems with an additional measure to rank results more effectively.

Known-Item Searches

When conducting a known-item search, users already know what they are looking for. For example, they want to find and retrieve a specific article or book, check whether the item is available from the library, and access it immediately.

A study conducted at the University of Illinois at Urbana-Champaign in 2010 and 2011 found that more than half of the searches captured in the library's log files were for known items (Schlembach, Mischo, & Bishoff, 2013). An analysis of the Primo logs, which reflect usage across more than one thousand institutions, yields a similar result. Effective support for known-item searches is therefore crucial in a library discovery system.

The ability to recognize the patterns and characteristics of known-item searches can help a system automatically identify titles, authors, and citation data. For example, in known-item searches, users often copy and paste entire citations or entire titles into the search box, and many queries combine a title and author. Using such information about query patterns, the search engine can return the exact item that the user expects.

The following examples of known-item searches were culled from the Primo logs:

- Motivating the academically unmotivated: A critical issue for the 21st century
- Sun, J Buys, N, Stewart, D, Shum, D, Farquhar, L, 2011, 'Smoking in Australian university students and its association with socio-demographic factors, stress, health status, coping strategies and attitude, Health Education, Vol. 111 Issue 2, pp.117 132
- Introduction to Special Relativity,rindler
- clark, understanding vulnerability

All four examples exhibit distinct characteristics that together identify the queries as known item searches. Among these characteristics are mixed case, the inclusion of punctuation, phrases that exactly match strings in the system's title index, and complete citation information (including volume, issue, and page number) copied and pasted from a web page. In a study of known-item searches in a library's online catalog, Kan and Poo (2005) identify additional characteristics—for instance, the presence of proper nouns and the inclusion of determiners (such as *a*, *an*, and *the*).

To support known-item searches effectively, the Primo search engine takes apart phrases entered in a search query and distinguishes between words that belong to the title, the author, the year, and so on. For example, in the third search example shown earlier, *Introduction to Special Relativity,rindler*, the system can determine that *Introduction to Special Relativity* is the article title and *rindler* is the author. As a result, the item is retrieved and is presented at the top of the result list.

However, the identification of known-item searches is not always clear-cut. For example, when a two- or three-word search exactly matches an item's title, is the user looking for the item with this title or is the user conducting an exploratory topic search? A query with the phrase *special education*, for instance, matches an exact title but can also be interpreted as an exploratory search.

Exploratory (Topic) Searches

Exploratory (or topic) searches are more difficult to characterize than known-item searches. The Primo logs show that about 50% of search queries contain one to three words. The queries can consist of a phrase that defines a very specific topic—for example, *attachment theory*—or a few key words—for example, *media and marketing*. In addition to matching the words to a specific search index, such as the subject or title index, or to phrases found in the full text of an item, the search engine can use machine learning to extract the characteristics of exploratory searches from the usage logs. Such characteristics include often-used queries of one to three words, phrases that frequently occur together, and queries that commonly trigger the use of facets or the selection of reference material. Upon recognizing an exploratory search, the ranking algorithm can, for example, automatically boost reference material and items that provide a broad topic overview. Some examples of exploratory-search queries from the Primo usage logs are *fracking*, *russian literature*, and *Social Learning Theory*.

Relevance Ranking

"Relevance ranking, whose purpose is to highlight materials that the system deems the most pertinent for a particular query, has become a major factor in satisfying users' information needs" (Sadeh, 2014). According to Saracevic (2007), "relevance is a, if not even *the*, key notion in information science in general and information retrieval in particular" (p. 1915). Saracevic (2007) further notes that relevance is "a thoroughly human notion" (p. 1918). Discovery systems must develop automated calculations of relevance that exploit user-centric factors.

The more effective a result ranking is, the greater the value that the system adds to a user's discovery experience. Because of the widespread familiarity with web search engines such as Google and their excellent ranking reputation, users of library discovery systems tend to look only at the topmost results; the Primo logs show that in most cases, users select one of the first three items. Consequently, items that might be relevant to a user's query remain unnoticed if they are not displayed near the top of the result list.

In 2011, Ex Libris undertook a comprehensive relevance ranking project to better understand search trends and to improve the way in which Primo accommodates the various search practices of end users. This project, well documented by Sadeh (2014), examined usage logs and usage statistics and also monitored real-world Primo users' search behavior. With the project results in hand, the development team enhanced the ranking algorithm and, having established a mechanism for monitoring ranking, now reviews the algorithm on a regular basis.

Prior to the project, the ranking technology focused entirely on traditional ranking methods that had been adapted to the scholarly domain. For example, the occurrence of the query terms in the subject field was given greater weight than their occurrence in the full text of an item. Weightings were similarly applied to other metadata fields.

As a result of the Primo ranking project, built-in mechanisms were leveraged to boost particular item types, such as items of the type *journal article*, and these mechanisms were continuously monitored. Furthermore, a new component was introduced to the ranking algorithm: an item's value score, which is based on usage information from the Ex Libris bX article recommender database; the number of citations for that item; and several other factors. Finally, the ranking algorithm was enriched to take into account aspects of the user's information-seeking behavior—such as the way in which the user phrased the query in question (for example, in an exploratory search)—and certain characteristics of the user, such as his or her academic degree and discipline.

These changes were incorporated into the Primo ScholarRank technology, which was first deployed in 2012. The developers continuously monitor and retune the Primo ranking mechanism.

Measures of Search Success

Search success is a matter of perception and of relevance—that "human notion," as Saracevic puts it (2007, p. 1918). Although an analysis of usage logs can help in the measurement of search success, such a review does not furnish the only measure of success. For example, usage logs do not capture qualitative assessments by users and their quality ratings of the top-ranked results, especially in exploratory searches. Usage logs do, however, provide information about user actions following a search; this information includes search/selection ratios, session duration, search refinements, and more. Selections fall into several categories; for instance, some are related to delivery, such as the clicking of a link that leads to the electronic full text of an item or the placement of a request for a physical book. Other selections documented in the logs express a user's interest in an item, demonstrated by saving the item's citation for future reference, downloading the citation to a citation management tool, and sharing the item's details via email. All of this information from the logs contributes to the assessment of search success.

In a known-item search, the main goal of the user is to find and obtain the desired item, so the selection of the first item presented in the results can be considered a success. However, defining success in exploratory searches is more complicated, especially because many exploratory searches do not result in an immediate selection. Users often undertake a series of searches before arriving at a selection. The first set of search results may help a user formulate a better query for the second and subsequent searches, as seen in the following two (unrelated) examples of exploratory search sessions extracted from the Primo log files. Both sessions show how a user rephrased a search several times to reach the desired result.

Session a:

2014-02-06 14:04:21	*portuguese empire*
2014-02-06 14:06:37	*spanish and portuguese colonialism*
2014-02-06 14:10:41	*a history of portuguese overseas expansion*

Session b:

2014-02-06 21:04:01	*urban culture*
2014-02-06 21:03:48	*urban culture decline*
2014-02-06 20:27:47	*local culture decline*
2014-02-06 20:25:38	*globalization local culture*
2014-02-06 20:27:35	*assimilation local culture*

The success of exploratory searches cannot be assessed simply on the basis of a search/selection ratio and is therefore more difficult to measure than the success of known-item searches; and the majority of exploratory searches result in no selection at all. Log analysis contributes to an understanding of the relationship between searches and selections—for example, which types of searches lead to which selection behavior; how long a user takes, on average, to select an item after a search is completed; and where the selected items are located in the result list. The Primo logs indicate that most selections are made from the first three items in the result list; rarely do users go beyond the first page of results. However, the selection of an item is not the only measure of search success. In exploratory searches, in particular, looking at an abstract, a book description, or metadata may satisfy at least the initial information need of a user and thus can be considered search success.

Log analysis can also provide a variety of key performance indicators (KPIs) that enable developers to monitor how their changes to the search and ranking algorithms affect users' search behavior and how users apply the variety of search features that the system offers. Examples of such KPIs are the amount of time that a user searches before making a selection, the total session time, the number of selections per session, and the number of abandoned searches (sessions without a selection).

CONCLUSIONS

Large-scale usage log analysis is a valuable method for shedding light on information seeking behavior. Applying log data to categorize searches and to analyze user's actions following a search query (such as selecting an item or refining the query), developers of library discovery systems can adjust the search engine and enhance the ranking algorithm to increase the chances of successful search outcomes. In addition, the analysis of usage logs can provide metrics that help with monitoring the discovery system's success in positioning the most relevant results at the top of the list. Thus, usage log analysis offers information that is indispensable in the effort to continuously improve users' experience as they search in a library discovery system that indexes a huge number of diverse materials.

REFERENCES

Diamond, T., Price, S., & Chandrasekar, R. (2013). Actions speak louder than words: Analyzing large-scale query logs to improve the research experience. *The code4lib journal, 21.*

Kan, M.-Y., & Poo, D. C. C. (2005). Detecting and supporting known item queries in online public access catalogs. *JCDL '05. Proceedings of the 5th ACM/IEEE-CS Joint Conference on Digital Libraries*, 91–99. http://dx.doi.org/10.1145/1065385.1065406

Sadeh, T. (2014). Optimizing relevance ranking to enhance the user's discovery experience. In T. Catarci, N. Ferro, & A. Poggi (Eds.), *Bridging between cultural heritage institutions* (pp. 153–164). Berlin: Springer-Verlag. http://dx.doi.org/10.1007/978-3-642-54347-0_17

Saracevic, T. (2007). Relevance: A review of the literature and a framework for thinking on the notion in information science. Part II: Nature and manifestations of relevance. *Journal of the American Society for Information Science and Technology, 58*(13), 1915–1933. http://dx.doi.org/10.1002/asi.20682

Schlembach, M. C., Mischo, W. H., & Bishoff, J. (2013). The use of transaction logs to model user searching behaviours. *Qualitative and Quantitative Methods in Libraries (QQML), 4*, 365–369. Proceedings from the 4th International Conference on Qualitative and Quantitative Methods in Libraries, 22–25 May 2012, Limerick, Ireland.

Educating Reference Librarians for First-Day Success

*Elizabeth Mahoney and Christinger Tomer,
University of Pittsburgh*

This paper discusses the skills that we believe are important for the successful entry-level reference librarian to possess. The paper identifies the skills that seem to be needed by an entry-level reference librarian and provides examples of some methods that we use to train students to become effective reference professionals. While the method of delivering reference service has evolved greatly since Samuel Swett Green's 1876 musings about the personal relations between librarians and readers, the belief that a librarian should be "unwilling to allow an inquirer to leave the library with his question unanswered" (p. 79) is still critical to the goal of the reference process.

It has been suggested by some observers that enhanced search engines and redesigned discovery platforms diminish the value of skilled reference professionals. We disagree and cite the following for our position.

We first examined the American Library Association (ALA) accredited programs to see how many self-identified with reference-focused courses of study. A search of the ALA website found that more than half identify a reference and user services area of concentration (34 of the 58 accredited programs). A further examination of each of the 34 individual school websites showed that 21 locations offered advanced classes in areas such as business, genealogy, medicine, and so forth, and/or reference "tracks" for focused study (http://www.ala.org/CFApps/lisdir/index.cfm). This would indicate an interest in this area of specialization from potential students and programs.

We next looked for evidence that libraries were still seeking reference librarians. Post-degree need was found in a 2010 survey conducted by

Detmering and Sproles, which indicated that students with a reference focus will find a job market in libraries and other information environments. The survey examined entry-level job ads for academic libraries and determined that 49.9% of all those posted were reference positions. Although the number of entry-level reference positions has decreased since a similar study in 2002, it appears that almost half of entry-level positions are in the reference area (Detmering & Sproles, 2012). Another "job ad" study of public service positions found that more than half of the positions required library instruction as a component of the job (Hall, p. 11). These observations confirmed our belief that a need to educate reference professionals is still critical.

More than 100 years ago, Isadore Gilbert Mudge used the phrase "Material, Mind and Method" to describe her approach to teaching reference skills. She edited editions three through six of ALA's *Guide to Reference Books* and recommended the text for self-study and/or use in classrooms such as Columbia's School of Library Service (Richardson, 1992). Some of her strategies continue to be effective and applicable in the teaching of the reference process in today's information environment. Students still need to understand that there *is* a process in reference work—that we have foundations, philosophical and theoretical, which frame the work of the reference librarian. But while basic tenets have remained constant, the skillsets we help students develop are quite different. To prepare a student for first-day success in the reference environment, we still help them clarify thinking about the manner in which they approach a question (the mind and method portion of the Mudge mantra) but we also broaden the scope of materials to which they are exposed.

Prior to the 21st century, we were able to predict the kinds of questions that people might ask with a fairly high degree of accuracy, instruct students in the use of authoritative reference tools, and provide a process to approach the expected questions. This is no longer the case. Technological enhancements have continued to surprise us, such that our approach must now focus less on specific resource titles and more on resource types. We can continue to help the students develop an understanding of the authority of an information source; we can help them develop a personal approach for question negotiation; and we can encourage them to understand their own information-seeking behaviors. By teaching these aspects of the reference process, we are able to help students develop a personal style for the negotiation of information problems—regardless of the information environment. This is a more complicated and challenging way to teach reference skills than efforts in the 20th century. Adding a focused overlay of technology to previously successful teaching methods helps students develop a mastery of the process. The mastery, once internalized, allows for growth and change as new materials and mechanisms appear. What follows are some methods we find helpful in preparing students for their first and subsequent days of reference work in the shifting information environment.

Today, much of what reference librarians do is carried out in distributed computing environments that entail multiple operating systems and an array of relevant computing protocols. The education of reference librarians must necessarily focus, to an unparalleled degree, on aspects of information technology. The principal problem, and it is a problem in varying degrees for every aspect of librarianship, is in determining the fuller scope of what reference librarians need to know about information technology. There is also the corollary problem of the technological skills students bring to the learning process. As Agosto, Rozaklis, MacDonald, and Abels noted in 2010, library and information science (LIS) students bring varying levels of knowledge and skills about information technology to the process, much of it limited and unsophisticated. So care is given to ensure that students emerge from the program able to compose and/or mount HTML pages, create databases, transfer files, use various social media tools, and so forth. Practicing reference librarians must have all of these skills and also be able to embrace and employ the new and relevant developments in information technologies. Such an orientation is empowering for new information professionals. Bronstein reports that reference librarians tend to see new technologies as enhancements, whereas Knibbe-Haanstra had reported previously that technology is a "stressing factor" that adds to and complicates the workloads of reference librarians (Bronstein, 2011; Knibbe-Haanstra, 2008).

A key element in the professional education of librarians and archivists is the availability of a technological infrastructure dedicated to teaching and learning within the LIS domain. In the context of teaching reference sources and services, it is critical to use a variety of resources that provide a glimpse of real life experience. Contributed services such as the Gale/ALISE Bibliographic Instruction Program (http://kb.cengage.com/display/galesupport/Gale+ALISE+Bibliographic+Instruction+Program), Springshare's LibGuides

Sandbox for Library Schools (http://libraryschool.libguidescms.com/), ProQuest's Discover More Corp (http://discovermorecorps.com/), and the ipl2 Librarian Digital Reference Service Student and Volunteer Training (http://training.ipl.org/backroom/refvols/students/) provide valuable resources and experiences. However, there is the question of sufficiency, and it is important that the LIS program meets an acceptable standard. A few programs have developed an extensive technological infrastructure, but even those occasionally fail to provide instruction that enables students to understand how and why key technologies work. For example, almost all librarians work with integrated online library systems (IOLS), but the vast majority of the students who receive degrees today have never seen, much less worked with, the administrative components of an IOLS. Students make extensive use of databases, bibliographic and otherwise, but also need to understand how these databases work. Even better, they should have substantial experience in working with such resources at the design and/or production levels.

Thus, the task of educating reference librarians must include a solid grounding in information technology at a minimum of two levels. First, students must be reasonably adept at working within the framework of a personal computing environment, be it Microsoft Windows, Apple OS X, or Linux, and they must also be able to work effectively in networked, cross-platform environments. They need to understand how operating systems work, the purpose of the applications they use, how to manage files, set permissions, and so forth. Second, students must become familiar with an array of applications and platforms that are specific to the bibliothecal enterprise. In some instances, the elements of the second level at which students need to learn about IT are obvious. For example, in order to provide answers to the questions posed by users, librarians need to efficiently use web search engines such as Google and Bing, proprietary online databases and digital reference resources, online catalogs, and digital repositories. Perhaps somewhat less obvious is that effective use requires a thorough understanding of web navigation, browser functionality, link resolving managers, and data capture capabilities (e.g., bookmark management, screen capture, and screen scraping). LIS students must fully understand the syntax and use of uniform resource locators. They have to use and review Web browsers to fully grasp functional capabilities; they must become skillful in capturing and/or repurposing various types of data taken from the web, discovery platforms, and so forth. These needs identify the skills that LIS students must acquire to be prepared for an entry-level position.

Only slightly less obvious is the fact that skillful reference librarians in the digital age must be familiar with standardized bibliographic and reference formats. They should understand the uses of software platforms that have been developed to support citation management, including EndNote, Mendeley, ReferenceWorks, and Zotero. Students must learn to export, process, and reformat bibliographic information in standardized formats; they must learn to export reference data from publisher platforms, import such data into reference management systems, use those systems to format and/or share data with users, and adapt the systems to more specific requirements of service at the local level.

The need to manage digital documents in the form of Microsoft Word and Open Document Format files, PDFs, HTML files, and e-books creates another layer of complexity. Students must learn how to extract and use metadata from these documents. Compounding the challenges associated with digital documents is the emergence of what Elsevier has dubbed "the article of the future." A composite (or compound) document format, incorporating text, images, data, audio and video, and dynamic processing of content, aimed at making the scholarly paper more expressive and informative. While it is not clear to what extent this "article of the future" will be embraced, it is reasonable to assume that composite documents will soon emerge as a common, if not predominant, form in scholarly and professional publishing. Reference librarians must be prepared to manage the attendant complexities of documents made up of disparate digital objects (http://www.articleofthefuture.com/).

It is increasingly clear that the user is often remote from the library but may still be in need of reference help. Many reference librarians provide screen-to-screen, real-time reference help using chat and/or video conferencing services. This adds another dimension of technical skills for the LIS student to master. At present, the use of videoconferencing systems and services in the reference department is a developing area. However, issues related to complexity of systems, interoperability problems, and bandwidth requirements will be resolved in the next few years. The use of real-time communication services will become more commonplace and will accelerate adoption rates for videoconferencing systems. Examples of easy-to-use systems that nudge along this course of action are Jing and Google+ Hangouts.

Building classes that incorporate information technologies goes hand in hand with developing the critical-thinking and question-negotiation skills for the LIS student. In basic and advanced reference classes, it is effective to continue the past practice in which students answer prepared reference questions (see sidebar for some examples). The exercises allow students to become familiar with reference resources and begin to hone their information retrieval skills. As students supply answers to focused question sets, they are introduced to types of resources for use and exploration. The students have a second activity for question negotiation through participation in the ipl2 Librarian Digital Reference Service Student and Volunteer Training program previously mentioned. Both of these assignments provide students with an opportunity to develop a foundation in the work of reference.

The first instance is a standard approach in which questions are introduced by type (bibliographic, encyclopedia/dictionary, government resources, citation-focused, subject-specific, age-specific, etc.). Students are directed to find answers from specific groups of databases and reference tools. They maintain a record of the steps taken in locating answers, and they are required to explain the appropriateness, accuracy, and authority of the resources they use. In other structured database exercises, students use discovery platforms and vendor products to contrast and compare specific subject focus and content functionality (Credo, EBSCO, Gale Virtual Reference Library, GoGrolier, ProQuest, etc.).

The second opportunity asks that students complete the ipl2 Librarian Digital Reference Service Student and Volunteer Training program. The program provides a training manual that explains the ipl2 mission and offers examples of how to respond to questions using the ipl2 reference philosophies and practices. Students answer practice questions that are reviewed by ipl2 staff volunteers. If acceptable, the student is allowed to answer questions submitted by users (http://www.ipl.org/div/askus/refservice.html). Because they are finding answers in freely available resources rather than subscription databases, the students must weigh issues of accuracy and authority (students use the collection of resources found on ipl2 pages that are taken from the Internet Public Library and the Librarians' Internet Index). They can make appropriate selections and

QUESTION SAMPLES

Please find the best, most authoritative and appropriate source to provide 1) the answer to each question, 2) a screenshot that shows your search strategy, and 3) a citation from the authoritative source used to determine the answer.

1. Please find the formula used to convert Kelvin to Celsius.
2. Please find the history and use of the word bloviate.
3. Provide ISSN, editor, and publisher for the *American Journalism Review*. Where is it indexed?
4. Provide author, title, and ISBN for a 2014 nonfiction children's book about Saturn.
5. Find a pop-up book that features the story of Jonah and the whale. Is there a library in my area that has an available copy?
6. I'm helping my fourth grader with her homework and need a source that shows me examples and illustrations of simple machines; what they are; how they work; and so forth.
7. Please find the name and dates of the 19th-century Spanish artist whose etchings are collected under the title Los Desastres de la Guerra. Please provide images and locations for museum with holdings.
8. Find an obituary for Ezra Stiles, a Connecticut patriot who died in 1795. What was Stiles' birth year? And what publication first printed the obituary?
9. A faculty member is looking for resources on kinship studies. Help identify three books or articles in which *Kinship and Social Organization* (1968) by I. Buchler and H. A. Selby was cited.
10. "Success is not final, failure is not fatal: it is the courage to continue that counts." Please provide the author of the quotation and the occasion upon which this quote occurred (date, location, etc.).

communicate the reasons for their choices to the users. By providing both experiences, one using structured databases and a second using freely available resources, the student learns to use a variety of tools that form the foundation for a personal search process.

An exercise that is used to help students improve their individual communication style is accomplished through the creation of a LibGuide using SpringShare LibGuides Sandbox for Library Schools (http://libraryschool.libguidescms.com/). The assignment lets students observe the LibGuide environment and focus on some of the "best of" LibGuides (http://help.springshare.com/index.php?gid=179). The student must effectively navigate the technology, anticipate the needs of the user in a specific subject (or course) area, communicate with online users, and most importantly, write clearly. Once the LibGuide topic is selected, the student is asked to select and organize core and relevant resources, follow specific preparation guidelines, and include materials in suggested headings (e.g., resources, databases, e-journals, citing and writing, etc.). The student is asked to insert appropriate "bells and whistles," such as embedded media, podcast feeds, Jing videos, survey tools, blogs, and so forth.

While a 15-week class does not allow enough time to help students fully develop their frontline information literacy skills, it is possible to incorporate some of those skills in this assignment. The student must work with multiple platforms, write clearly within a technical environment, and understand the options for selecting appropriate information while providing users with bibliographic choices. In constructing the LibGuide, the student determines the amount of information to provide and considers the manner in which the user absorbs the information. This exercise is designed to discuss the role of instruction in the reference process and encourage students to examine their personal instruction style.

Each term an assignment is developed to help students examine how they function within a group of three or four students. In a more recent version of this exercise, students read an article and replicate research on discovery tool performance. The added benefit of the assignment is that students must utilize assessment and time-management skills. During the data collection part of the assignment, students are exposed to various discovery platforms (Credo, EBSCO, GoGrolier, Google Scholar, ProQuest, Library Discovery platform); in the evaluation portion of the assignment, they build datasets, determine correlation/reliability (using Spearman's rho and intraclass correlation), determine mean performance (ANOVA and Tukey Overall); and in the analysis, writing, and presentation portion of the assignment, they are required to present their findings in an understandable manner. Throughout all, the groups must communicate effectively to be able to provide deliverables in a timely fashion.

The students each have a self-selected group role (coordinator, writer, editor, presenter) and must work together effectively to complete the exercise. On the surface, the exercise will provide a framework should a future employer ask for an evaluation of a reference tool for purchase or weeding purposes. The students are encouraged to reflect on their group roles and think about their success with the assigned tasks. More to the point, the exercise should lead to self-awareness that in the longer term may result in more effective performance within a reference department or a library system.

Reference services begin and end with the questions of users who seek answers. That the conduct of reference services is changing is beyond doubt—the evidence is all around us—but the service itself remains a central function of libraries and archives, and conveying the knowledge and skills needed in order to analyze questions and provide valid answers, with a high degree of efficiency, is still an essential part of the education of information professionals. The reference process is an essential element of the qualitative guarantees on which library services are based, ensuring ready access to authoritative information. Perhaps more to the point, making judgments about the relevance, reliability, and suitability of information resources, and using those resources as a basis for successful service are tasks now more complicated than ever. Given enough time and unlimited resources, any user is capable of finding information to answer a specific question. But in the information economy, as George Gilder noted many years ago, time is the crucial commodity (Gilder, 1996). In that context, reference librarians, who work at the intersection formed by the services such as Google and Microsoft and the needs and wants of library users, continue to provide services that are both effective and efficient. The constant? Users with questions, and not enough time.

REFERENCES

Agosto, D. E., Rozaklis, L., MacDonald, C., & Abels, E.G. (2010). Barriers and challenges to teaching reference in today's electronic information environment. *Journal of Education for Library & Information Science, 51*(3), 177–186.

Bronstein, J. (2011). The role and work perceptions of academic reference librarians: A qualitative inquiry. *portal: Libraries and the Academy, 11*(3), 791–811. http://dx.doi.org/10.1353/pla.2011.0032

Detmering, R., & Sproles, C. (2012). Forget the desk job: Current roles and responsibilities in entry-level reference job advertisements. *College & Research Libraries, 73*(6), 543–555. http://dx.doi.org/10.5860/crl-304

Gilder, G. (1996). Telecosm feasting on the giant peach. *Forbes ASAP, 158,* 84–96.

Green, S. S. (1876). Personal relations between librarians and readers. *Library Journal, 1,* 74–81.

Hall, R. A. (2013). Beyond the job ad: Employers and library instruction. *College & Research Libraries, 74*(1), 24–38. http://dx.doi.org/10.5860/crl-236

Hutchins, M. (1937). Artist-teaching in the field of bibliography; An application of modern educational theories and techniques to the teaching of the first-year library school course in reference. *Library Quarterly, 7,* 99–120. http://dx.doi.org/10.1086/613948

Knibbe-Haanstra, M. (2008). Reference desk dilemmas: The impact of new demands on librarianship. *Reference & User Services Quarterly, 48*(1), 20–25. http://dx.doi.org/10.5860/rusq.48n1.20

Richardson Jr., J. V. (1992). Teaching general reference work: The complete paradigm and competing schools of thought, 1890–1990. *The Library Quarterly, 62,* 55–89. http://dx.doi.org/10.1086/602420

Where Do We Go From Here?

David A. Tyckoson, California State University, Fresno, and John G. Dove, Former CEO of Credo Reference

Anyone who would doubt S. R. Ranganathan's fifth law of library science—*the library is a growing organism* (Ranganathan, 1931)—need only look at the dramatic changes to information production, evaluation, and consumption since April 22, 1993, the date when the decision was made to make the Internet an open public resource. It is that sea change which we are all still absorbing—and the agenda wrought by that decision is still overflowing. For one thing, information, which may be just the right information at just the right time for a particular inquiry, may come not just from resources housed in a particular library, but may instead be satisfied by various resources on the open web. And the misinformation, hidden biases, and even outright scams that sometimes surface from open web searches are a context of which reference librarians need to be aware. Reference librarians and librarianship must include the open web as part of each and every library. In the introduction to this book, we included the short evaluation that Ralph Waldo Emerson made of the Harvard College Library back in 1868:

> Young men go in & then go out of it repelled by the multitude of books which only speak to them of their ignorance,—their very multitude concealing from the gazing youth the one or the few volumes which are there waiting for them with the very information & leading he wants. (Emerson, 1868)

He contrasts that with the goal of making the college library "to be irresistibly attractive" so he can find "the precise author who has written for him alone." This is still the challenge that confronts the implementation of an excellent reference function in today's libraries—finding the right information that meets the specific needs of each user.

If one asks, "Is reference librarianship still a relevant topic?" one only need first to answer the following questions: Are today's libraries more complicated than those of twenty years ago? Or less? Are today's patrons, students, and researchers potentially intimidated or confused about how to make effective use of the libraries to which they have access? The answers are clearly, yes, the library is *more* complicated. The systems we are providing, while more powerful than ever before, are still filled with artificial complexity. The "library" available to everyone is *more* potentially intimidating and confusing than any library in past generations.

Then one might ask, "Is this important?" For that one must answer the question: Do students today (at whatever level) have the information literacy skills that they are going to need in life? If in high school, are they ready for college or to enter the workforce? If in college, are they prepared for what they will need as citizens, employees, or scholars? We challenge you to ask any professor in college or teacher in high school, "Do you think your institution has properly prepared your students for the information literacy skills they are going to need in life?"

The same goes for almost any reference interaction with a new patron or student approaching a reference desk or service. Are they likely to be harboring some fear or intimidation? Are they held back by some misunderstanding that will be a barrier to their getting the information they need and can rely on? Are they harboring a bias that will shut them out from information that could open up a whole new way for them to see the world?

We see several trends important to reference and user services that yield ideas about what lies ahead:

- *21st Century Literacies*: A version of which has been defined by the National Council of Teachers of English (NCTE, 2013) as:
    - Develop proficiency and fluency with the tools of technology;
    - Build intentional cross-cultural connections and relationships with others so to pose and solve problems collaboratively and strengthen independent thought;
    - Design and share information for global communities to meet a variety of purposes;

- Manage, analyze, and synthesize multiple streams of simultaneous information;
- Create, critique, analyze, and evaluate multimedia texts;
- Attend to the ethical responsibilities required by these complex environments.

- *Lifelong Learning*: No longer are the skills you learn before you are twenty defining the skills and knowledge that you will need later in life. As Alvin Toffler asserted in *Future Shock*, "By instructing students how to learn, unlearn, and relearn, a powerful new dimension can be added to education" (1970, p. 271). Toffler goes on to quote psychologist Herbert Gerjuoy, "Tomorrow's illiterate will not be the man who can't read; he will be the man who has not learned how to learn" (p. 271).
- *Filter Failure:* Clay Shirky is famous for having turned the expression "information overload" inside out and asserted that information overload has been with us for centuries—what we are really experiencing is "filter failure" (Shirky, 2008). We flip that question around and posit that the agenda of information science, librarianship, and user-services librarianship in particular is creating a world in which those we have influence over should experience "filter success." It is easy to enumerate a whole set of conditions that are nascent or nonexistent in today's world, but are needed in a world where people experience "filter success," including:
    - Filter transparency, by which people can know what filters are in place, affecting what they see and what they do not see.
    - Filter customization, by which people can change the filters that affect their information lives.
    - Filter standards, by which good principles of "filter success" are established to guide the development of information products.
    - Filter literacy, by which education of our students and citizens gives people the sophistication to be aware of how filters may be helping or hurting their access to knowledge.
- *The Hidden Web:* The open web, a smartphone-enabled, crowdsourced overlay of general information, yellow pages, and geomapping information, now makes ready reference ubiquitous, but this is not true of some of the most important library resources that live behind firewalls. Academic searches have nowhere near the ease of use that basic smartphone access does for general information requests. Inside the academic resources there

- *Inclusivity:* We continue to be challenged by new recognition of the value of inclusion. If the benefits of collaboration and interdisciplinarity are to be gained, we must take on the challenges of inclusion and diversity. Only one out of ten Wikipedia editors are female (NPR, 2014), and many parts of the world have yet to contribute to the collective knowledge of history and development as represented in Wikipedia (let alone the various professional literatures).
- *Changing Technology*: Of course, new technologies are going to spring forward. Some will be what we call "dancing bears" (e.g., Second Life). Others will prove to have value that was not obvious at first, but later will be revealed as astounding (Twitter may be an example).

This last point deserves some emphasis. Because of the very fact that the technology landscape continues to change, there will always be a need for both systems and trained professionals to save time of busy people in the use of these new technologies. Old ways will need to be unlearned and new ways learned.

And this is in no way a new phenomenon. As Ann M. Blair, the respected professor of intellectual history at Harvard University, writes in her book *Too Much to Know,* the problem of finding effective ways to accumulate useful knowledge in one's own lifetime has been with us for centuries, and the use of specialized content, such as reference books, has always been an important strategy followed by learners across many generations. The challenge today, as Blair points out in the conclusion of her book, is that:

> Whereas early modern reference books were criticized for failing to yield material on a topic of interest, an Internet search invariably offers results. Whether those results are good or not depends on our skills in optimizing searches and assessing results. Those skills themselves will require constant honing, in response to changes in the search engines and in the material available for searching. While a savvy user of early modern reference books needed to be familiar with a fairly stable canon of authors quoted and of finding devices, a skilled Internet user must assess an ever-broadening range of materials that can appear on a list of results, from shopping sites to blogs, from government agencies to elaborate scams. (2010, p. 267–268)

It is important to recognize that this is not just a challenge for a person staffing a reference or information desk. It is a challenge to all those who end up creating the learning contexts in which our students, our citizens, and our researchers conduct their information-consuming lives. We need an evolving set of competencies that will make that experience one which is easy, fun, enriching, and devoid of unnecessary impediments.

While thinking of what's going to change, it is useful to predict things that will not change. We do this bravely facing the examples of Gordon Bell, who predicted that the personal computer would never amount to much, and of Bill Gates, who predicted that no one would ever need more than 640K of memory in a personal computer.

In five years there will be another book like this one talking about the future of reference and user services in libraries. We predict that the themes of such a book will continue to include the following:

- The challenge of providing just the right information that will "save the time of busy people" (Hutchins, 1944) will continue to be important.
- The benefits of the Semantic Web will still be described in the future tense, but with many more small examples of things that are working.
- There will continue to be digital and information divides and the imperative to address them.
- The breadth/depth trade-off is solved for books, shelves, rooms, and buildings related to reference information, but not for the mind.
- Library users will still need help—and there will be librarians who provide that help.

The library (writ large—by which we mean the totality of one's available information resources) will continue to be a place of potential intimidation, even as parts of it are successfully transformed into places that are fun, informative, and invigorating. Libraries remain complex institutions, which means that users will continue to need help navigating their resources and their services. Just as Samuel Green suggested at the first ALA conference—and as Ralph Waldo Emerson recommended a decade earlier for the Harvard University Library—there should be a librarian who can work directly with users to teach them how to find resources, to answer their queries, and to recommend useful materials. And by performing those functions, the librarian transforms the user's concept of the library from one of difficulty and incomprehension to one of clarity and understanding.

This is the core of what reference librarians really do—they humanize an otherwise inhuman institution. It is the reference librarian who interacts directly with each library user, finding out her needs, and giving her resources to meet those needs. In a world that continues to become automated and inhuman, this is the true value of the reference librarian. It does not matter if the user is communicating with the librarian in person, through chat, on the phone, or over some as yet undeveloped technology, the reference librarian is and always will be the human interface between the library and the community he serves. And it does not matter if we call them reference librarians, user experience librarians, subject liaisons, or some other new name. The work that they do will continue to advance the traditions of reference librarians of the past.

This is not the first and certainly will not be the last book shedding light on how people in our line of work, whether it is among librarians or the companies that support libraries, take on reimagining reference and reference services. We in no way claim to have exhaustively covered the territory, since there are many topics that time and opportunity have not allowed for inclusion here. But if we have assembled a group of authors who generate just one new idea or one new approach that inspires you to experiment further, then we have fulfilled our mission. We look forward to hearing about it as the world of libraries continues to change.

REFERENCES

Blair, A. M. (2010). *Too much to know: Managing scholarly information before the modern age*. New Haven & London: Yale University Press.

Emerson, R. W. (1868). *Report of the Committee appointed by the Board of Overseers of Harvard College to examine the Library*. Harvard University Archives, USll 10.6.3 Volume XI.

Hutchins, M. (1944). *Introduction to reference work*. Chicago: American Library Association.

National Council of Teachers of English (NCTE). (2013). The NCTE definition of 21st century literacies. Retrieved from http://www.ncte.org/positions/statements/21stcentdefinition

National Public Radio (NPR). (2014). Wikipedia holds an edit-a-thon to draw women editors. Retrieved from http://www.npr.org/2014/03/29/296212010/wikipedia-holds-an-edit-a-thon-to-draw-women-editors

Ranganathan, S. R. (1931). *The five laws of library science*. London: Edward Goldston.

Shirky, C. (2008). It's not information overload. It's filter failure. Retrieved from http://www.youtube.com/watch?v=LabqeJEOQyI

Toffler, A. (1970). *Future shock*. New York: Bantam.

About the Contributors

Martha Adkins is an assistant professor and reference librarian at the Copley Library of the University of San Diego, where she is the theology, religious studies, and classics specialist.

Mary E. Anderson has worked in academic libraries since she was a student assistant in the late 1980s. She loves assisting college students, reading books, and helping patrons solve problems. She is currently the head of circulation services at the University of Missouri-Kansas City Miller Nichols Library.

Phoebe Ayers is a science and engineering reference librarian at the University of California, Davis. She currently serves on the Wikimedia Foundation Board of Trustees, which runs Wikipedia and its sister projects. She is the coauthor of a book about Wikipedia and is a long-time member of the project's community.

Denise Beaubien Bennett is an engineering librarian at the University of Florida's Marston Science Library. She is also the general editor of the ALA's *Guide to Reference* (formerly the *Guide to Reference Books*), the most comprehensive published guide to reference sources and a cornerstone publication of the literature of librarianship.

Ron Burns is the vice president of Global Software Services at EBSCO Information Services. He leads a global team of discovery service engineers and EBSCO's technology customer-outreach initiatives.

Madeline Cohen is an assistant professor and head of reference at Lehman College of the City University of New York (CUNY). She has a BA and MA in history from Hunter College (CUNY), and an MLS from the University of Maryland. She is cochair of the Reference Roundtable of the Library Association of CUNY.

Michael Courtney is the outreach and engagement librarian, distributed education library services coordinator, and liaison to the International Studies Program and the Global Village at Indiana University. He is also an adjunct professor in the Department of Information and Library Science at Indiana University.

Anastasia Diamond-Ortiz is the knowledge manager at the Cleveland Public Library. She is pleased to have been involved in many innovative projects at this institution, especially those focused on community engagement and data visualization. She received her MLIS from Kent State University in 2003.

Kirstin Dougan is an associate professor and music and performing arts librarian at the University of Illinois at Urbana-Champaign. She is also an adjunct professor at the University of Illinois Graduate School of Library and Information Science, where she teaches music librarianship and bibliography.

John G. Dove is best known for his various roles held at Credo Reference, including CEO, president, and senior publisher. He has extensive experience in technology businesses, including electronic publishing and online education extending back to 1968 when he joined a start-up on Wall Street that produced the first end-user accessible online database of stock market information. In the mid-1990s, Dove was president and COO of SilverPlatter, a supplier of electronic and online bibliographic information to research libraries worldwide. In 2000, Dove was COO of GlobaLearn, a company that deployed investigative reporters and photographers to travel the world on behalf of (and wired into) social studies classrooms. Immediately prior to joining Credo Reference in 2003, Dove worked with the E-Government Executive Education program at Harvard's Kennedy School of Government.

Margaret Driscoll is the learning organization librarian at the University of California, Santa Barbara Library. She is also an adjunct instructor at the San Jose State University School of Library and Information Science, where she teaches a course on digital copyright. Her curious and active mind, on top of years of experience in the academic world, keeps her striving to address the brave new world of academic librarianship.

Amanda L. Folk is the reference/public services librarian at the Millstein Library of the University of Pittsburgh at Greensburg and serves as the library liaison to the Humanities Division. She is currently pursuing her PhD at the University of Pittsburgh's School of Education. Her research interests include the curricular integration of information literacy at the undergraduate level and the future of academic libraries as a vital component of the undergraduate experience.

Mandi Goodsett is a reference and instruction librarian working as reference librarian/assistant professor/government documents coordinator at Georgia Southwestern State University. She graduated from the Library and Information Science Program at the University of Illinois at Urbana-Champaign in May 2013 with a special interest in academic libraries and music libraries.

Buffy J. Hamilton is currently a school librarian at Norcross High School in the Gwinnett County Public School District. Prior to coming to Norcross, she was the learning strategist for the Cleveland Public Library in Cleveland, Ohio, and a high school librarian and teacher at the Unquiet Library in Canton, Georgia. She has over twenty years of experience in public education as a high school English teacher, technology integration specialist, and librarian.

Diane Hunter is head of Teaching and Learning Services (formerly head of Reference Services) at the University of Missouri-Kansas City, where she coordinates the library's reference services and information literacy instruction for general education courses. Over more than thirty years in academic library public services, she has experienced numerous changes in the provision of reference services since her first professional library position with a prototype online catalog and perpetual lines of students waiting to ask questions of three librarians at a barrier reference counter. She still enjoys working one-on-one with students, now through online chat and email, as well as face-to-face, and appreciates the more moderate pace of today's reference services.

Joseph Janes is an associate professor and chair of the MLIS Program at the University of Washington Information School. A frequent speaker in the United States and abroad, he is the founding director of the Internet Public Library and coauthor of several books on librarianship, technology, and their interrelations. Janes also writes the "Internet Librarian" column for *American Libraries* magazine.

Rolf Janke founded Mission Bell Media, where he currently serves as CEO. He brings to this new venture over thirty-five years of experience in academic publishing. Prior to MBM, he was the founder and vice president/publisher of SAGE Reference, an imprint of SAGE Publications, Inc.

Kris Johnson works at the Colorado State Library, where since June 2006 she has served as the operations manager for the AskColorado/AskAcademic Virtual Reference Cooperative. Prior to this, she was a tenured information literacy librarian at California State University, Chico.

M. Kathleen Kern is an associate reference librarian at the University of Illinois at Urbana-Champaign. She has written and presented extensively on the topic of the reference interview and management of virtual reference, including the book *Virtual Reference Best Practices: Tailoring Services for Your Library*. She has taught the reference course for Rutgers and for the University of Illinois Graduate School of Library and Information Science, and trained hundreds of graduate students and staff at the University of Illinois Library in the reference interview, database searching, and other reference skills. Kern also is the immediate past president of the ALA's Reference and User Services Association.

Rayford W. Law is the founding principal of Rayford W. Law Architecture+Planning. He is recognized for his broad experience and deep expertise in higher education and library design, and his thirty-year career has been celebrated with numerous awards for design. Law is also thesis faculty in the master's program at Boston Architectural College.

Elizabeth Mahoney is a lecturer at the University of Pittsburgh School of Information Sciences. Her research interests include the design and use of reference resources, digital reference, information retrieval, public librarianship, the history of children's book publishing, and children's literature. She is also past president of the Whitehall Public Library Board of Trustees.

John McCullough is the product manager for discovery at OCLC. Prior to OCLC, he was the vice president for product management at Innovative Interfaces, Inc. McCullough has spent most of his career working with patron-facing interfaces to library data, from text- and Web-based OPACs to the latest generation of discovery layers.

Susan McGlamery is the product manager for QuestionPoint, OCLC's virtual reference service, which includes the 24/7 Reference Cooperative. Prior experience as the coordinator of reference services for the Metropolitan Cooperative Library System (MCLS) in Los Angeles led her to create the 24/7 Reference Cooperative. McGlamery received her MLS from St. John's University in 1987 and her JD from the Emory University School of Law in 1984.

Alesia McManus is director of the library at Howard Community College in Columbia, Maryland. Prior to joining HCC, McManus was head of research and instructional services and head of the Science Library at Binghamton University Libraries; team leader for Science and Technology Services at University of Maryland Libraries (College Park); and science reference librarian at North Carolina State University. McManus has a BS in anthropology from the University of California, Davis, and a master's in library science from UCLA. Her professional interests include information literacy and the digital humanities.

Jessica E. Moyer is an assistant professor in the School of Information Studies at the University of Wisconsin-Milwaukee. She received her PhD from the University of Minnesota, Twin Cities, where her dissertation was "'Teens Today Don't Read Books Anymore!' A Study of differences in Interest and Comprehension Based on Reading Modalities." In addition to the reading habits of teens, Moyer's research interests include adult leisure reading, along with different reading platforms such as audio books and e-books.

Andrew Nagy is a lead product manager at ProQuest. Since joining the company in 2008, he has helped build and launch the Summon service. He currently is the product owner for the Summon service and oversees the search and user experience as well as its API, and works closely with the content operations team. He also is the liaison with the Summon client community, is active in user group meetings, and is a frequent speaker at industry conferences. Nagy has well over a decade of experience in web-based software engineering and product management.

Georgina Parsons gained an MSc in information and library studies, distance learning, from the Robert Gordon University while working at the Open University, United Kingdom, and SirsiDynix, a library management system provider. She is now systems librarian at Brunel University London, and she carries out some additional consultancy. Her interests focus on libraries' use of technology and in particular provisions for mobile devices.

Janet Pinkley is a senior assistant librarian and reference and circulation coordinator at the John Spoor Broome Library at California State University, Channel Islands. She is also a member of the ALA's Reference and User Services Association Dartmouth Committee, which selects the best reference work of the year.

Amanda Clay Powers is an associate professor, coordinator of the Research Services Department, and social media research librarian at Mississippi State University (MSU), where she is the chair of the MSU Libraries' Social Media Program. In addition to giving workshops nationally on managing professional online identity, her research focuses on assessment of reference services and the use of social media in academia. She holds a master's degree from Simmons Graduate School of Library and Information Science and a BA in English from Wellesley College.

Michael Saar is a reference librarian and assistant professor at Lamar University in Beaumont, Texas. He has an MLS degree from the University of Arizona and an MA from the University of Minnesota. He is the appointed library liaison for students with disabilities at Lamar University.

Mara H. Sansolo is the reference librarian at the East Campus of Pasco-Hernando State College, in Dade City, Florida. She earned her MLIS in 2012 from the University of South Florida, and she also holds a BA in women's studies from the University of South Florida.

Kevin Saw is a recent graduate of the Master of Library and Information Science program at St. John's University. As a student at St. John's, Saw completed four internships, including two semesters interning at the Lehman College Library. He is currently employed as a librarian at the St. Paul's School of Nursing and as a substitute facilitator for the Brooklyn Public Library's "Read! Write! Create!" outreach program. He also regularly volunteers with the New York Public Library's Correctional Services, aiding with library service and programming at Rikers Island.

Krista Schmidt is a research and instruction librarian at the Hunter Library of Western Carolina University. She is an information specialist in the disciplines of science, technology, engineering, and mathematics, and assists students and faculty members in learning effective search strategies and using research databases and reference resources. Schmidt was named a "Mover and Shaker" by *Library Journal* in 2013.

Theda Schwing is the continuing resources and database management librarian for OhioLINK. She earned her bachelor's in integrated mathematics education from Miami University and her master's in library science from Kent State University. Before joining OhioLINK, she was the technical services librarian at East Central University in Ada, Oklahoma.

Nicolette Warisse Sosulski has been the business librarian at the Portage District Library since 2005. She was the 2011 winner of the BRASS Gale Cengage Learning Award for Excellence in Business Librarianship. Sosulski was also a QuestionPoint contract librarian for over ten years, where she answered an estimated 15,000 hours of online chat reference questions for people all over the globe.

Christine Stohn is a product manager in the discovery and delivery business unit at Ex Libris. She has over twenty years of experience in the library industry, having worked on the content and data side before joining Ex Libris in 2001. Stohn holds a degree in library sciences from the Free University in Berlin and an information systems degree from the Open University in the United Kingdom.

Ilana Stonebraker is a business information specialist and assistant professor of library science at Purdue University. She teaches an undergraduate information literacy course for management students. Her research interests include building better help systems for libraries and business information literacy.

Christinger Tomer is an associate professor at the University of Pittsburgh School of Information Sciences, where he has been teaching since 1989. Tomer is a graduate of the College of Wooster and Case Western Reserve University. His interests include information technology, digital libraries, and online education.

Michelle Twait is an academic librarian and associate professor at Gustavus Adolphus College in St. Peter, Minnesota. She obtained her MS in library and information science from the University of Illinois at Urbana-Champaign and her MA in educational psychology from the University of Minnesota (Twin Cities). Her research interests include the psychology of decision making, information-seeking behavior, and U.S. women's history.

David Tyckoson is the associate dean of the Henry Madden Library at California State University, Fresno, where he is in charge of all user services for the library. He regularly teaches online courses on reference, including

RUSA's course on the Reference Interview and Infopeople's class on Rethinking Reference Collections. He has published widely on various aspects of libraries and reference services. Tyckoson served as president of RUSA in 2007–2008 and received the Mudge Award for distinguished contributions to reference librarianship in 2005.

Jolanda-Pieta van Arnhem is an instructional design librarian for digital scholarship and services at the College of Charleston Libraries, and is an instructor for the College of Charleston. She obtained her MFA from Vermont College of Fine Arts in 2009 and her MLIS from the University of South Carolina in 2013. She contributes her expertise to the Digital Scholarship and Services Department at the library, providing instruction for faculty, staff, and students regarding information technology utilization and digital scholarship tools for research and classroom use. She authors a regular column, "Mobile Apps in Libraries," on emerging mobile technologies in libraries for *The Charleston Advisor*.

Kaya van Beynen is an associate librarian for library research and instruction at the Nelson Poynter Memorial Library of the University of South Florida, St. Petersburg. As liaison to the College of Education, she provides instruction, research, and collection management support to education students and faculty. Before becoming a librarian, she earned a master's in geography from McMaster University and worked as a researcher at McMaster University, the Smithsonian Institution, and the Hispanic Health Council.

Amanda Viana is the information services librarian and assistant director of the Norton Public Library in Norton, Massachusetts. She is also a library trustee for the Somerset Public Library in Somerset, Massachusetts.

James Williams is the associate dean of public services, administration and technology at the College of Charleston Libraries. He obtained his MLIS from the University of South Carolina in 1997. Williams is responsible for the internal operation of the library, including but not limited to public service, administration, and technology. In his role, Williams often evaluates, recommends, and assists with training staff and students regarding educational technology.

Tao Zhang is the digital user experience specialist and an assistant professor of library science at Purdue University Libraries, where he conducts user experience research to improve the usability of the Purdue University Libraries web presence, including websites and web-facing services and collections. Prior to coming to Purdue, he was a research associate for the Department of Electrical Engineering and Computer Science at Vanderbilt University. He received his PhD in industrial engineering from North Carolina State University in 2009.

Index

ABC-CLIO, 93–94
Abels, E. G., 363
Academic libraries
    course management systems and, 243–252
    crowdsourcing of reference services, 285–293
    OhioLINK consortium, 317–325
    readers' advisory in, 81
    streaming video services, 248–249
    Summon discovery service in, 335–338
Access services desk, 165–170
Active learning, 46
Active listening, 65
Added value
    components of reference works, 98
    to discovery, 126–127
Aggregators, 101–102
Agosto, D. E., 363
ALA Editions, 83
Amazon, 76, 112
American Association of School Librarians (AASL), 41
    information literacy learning outcomes and, 43–45
    Standards for the 21st-Century Learner, 41, 45, 47, 48, 53–57, 151
American Civil War, 93
American Community Survey, 241
American Library Association (ALA), 2, 11, 56
    Guide to Reference Books, 297–301, 362
    on information literacy, 42, 43
    on librarian education, 361
    Reference and User Services Association (RUSA), 134–135, 152

American Library Journal, 2
American Sign Language (ASL), 306
Americans with Disabilities Act, 303
Annotated bibliography, *49*
Anonymity of users, 234
Answerland, 141
Architecture and reference services
    comparison and conclusions, 349–350
    general planning and design considerations, 339–340
    institutional profile, project challenges, and design response in, 340–344
    Princeton Theological Seminary, 340–344, 349–350
    Washington University, St. Louis, 344–349
Argument or debate assignments, *49*
Arp, L., 43, 51
AskAcademic, 133
AskColorado, 8, 133
AskOntario, 136
Assessment
    disabled patrons services, 312–314
    formative, 52–53
    information literacy, 51–53
    LibraryThing for Libraries online catalog, 282–283
    planning and design of libraries for reference services, 343–344, 348–349
    of reference services, 149–150, 157–158
    roving reference, 186–187
    summative, 52–53
Assignment wiki or website, *49*

Association for Educational Communications and Technology (AECT), 42
Association for Information Media and Equipment, et al, vs. The Regents of the University of California, et al., 249
Association of American Colleges and Universities, 53
Association of College and Research Libraries (ACRL)
  Information Literacy Competency Standards for Higher Education, 41, 43, 54–55, 304
  information literacy program learning outcomes and, 43–45
  The Value of Academic Libraries, 10, 153, 155
Auburn University Libraries, 156–157
Audiobooks, 84–85

Backward design
  learning experiences, 45–47
  learning outcomes, 44–45
Baker, Christopher, 33, 34, 35
"Because Student Achievement IS the Bottom Line," 44
Beerbower, Robin, 79
Behrens, B. J., 42
Bell, Gordon, 375
Berger, P., 46, 47, 48
Best practices, 30
"Best Practices in Virtual Reference: Finding Your Virtual References Users Online," 226
"Best Practices in Virtual Reference: Keeping the Virtual Lights On," 225
Bibliography, annotated, 49
Billings, Amy, 33, 34
Blackboard, 50, 243, 244, 252, 328
  course guides, 249–250
  menu options in, 246
  online public access catalog and, 248
  permissions to, 250–251
  student authentication, 245, 249
  textbook costs and, 245–246
Blair, Ann M., 374
Blended learning, 50
Blended librarianship, 50
Blogging, 113
Bloom's Taxonomy of Educational Objectives, 44
Bonnefil, Carol, 231

Book Display Widget, LTFL, 283–284
Bowker, 280
Breeding, Marshall, 125, 127
British Library, 109
British Museum, 109
Bundles, reference work, 100–101
Burgin, Robert, 79, 81
Burns, Vince, 93–94

California State University, 137–138
  Channel Islands, 243–252
Call-Button. *See* On-call reference
Campbell, Jerry, 1
Canino-Fluit, A., 54
Canvas, 50
Case Western Reserve University, 336–337
Casey, Michael, 33, 34, 35
Cassell, K. A., 182
Chandrasekar, R., 352
Change management, 163–171
Channel Islands, CSU. *See* Course management system, CSU Channel Islands
Chat reference services
  anonymity of users of, 234
  global 24/7 virtual, 223–229
  information needs of users, 234
  librarian view of, 231–241
  location of users of, 235–237
  Meebo, 139, 140, 258–259
  misspellings in, 232–233
  patrons of, 232–233
  software, 72, 136, 140
  times patrons use, 237–238
  video, 72
Chelton, Mary K., 81, 82
Chickering, A. W., 46, 48
Children's librarians, 20–22
ChiliFresh platform, 265–270
Circulation desk, 166–168
  single service point with reference services, 207–213
Classroom assessment techniques (CATs), 52
Cleveland Public Library, 20–22, 27
Closed-ended questions, 68–69
Coffman, Steve, 136, 231
Collaboration between libraries and schools, 24, 32–36, 251–252
Collaboration in Libraries and Learning Environments, 144, 145
Collaborative Digital Reference Service (CDRS), 135

Collaborative virtual reference
  24/7 availability, 138, 141, 223–229, 237–238
  benefits of, 143–144
  chat software and, 136, 140
  Colorado Library Research Service (LRS), 142–143
  defined, 134–135
  discovery and, 335–338
  future of, 143–144
  librarian's view of, 231–241
  Library 2.0 movement and, 139–140
  origins of, 133–135
  policies, 228–229
  prevalence of, 142
  strategies for successful, 144–145
  symposia, 138–139
"Collaborative Virtual Reference Service: Lessons from the Past Decade," 137
Collections, reference work, 100–101
  user-generated and curated, 111–112
College of Charleston Libraries. *See* Learning management system, College of Charleston Libraries
Colorado Library Research Service (LRS), 142–143
Commission for Higher Education (CHE), 43
Common Core State Standards (CCSS), 53–54
Communication
  during change management, 165–166
  course management software challenges, 251
  for services to disabled patrons, 311–312
  tools, 8, 14
Communities
  emerging user, 25–26
  identifying needs of, 22–23
  innovation hubs for, 29–30
  libraries role in, 2–6
  museum participatory practices and, 22–23
  reference services support of, 154–155
  using data to connect with needs of, 23–28
Community outreach, 221–222
  community partners for, 216–217
  creating effective library guides for, 217–219
  introduction to, 215–216
  marketing and, 219–221
Conclusion, reference interview, 71–72
Connecting Boys With Books: What Libraries Can Do, 77

Consortium, OhioLINK, 317–325
Construction, library. *See* Architecture and reference services
Convey Systems, Inc., 136, 137
Co-produced experiences, 23
Cords, Sarah Statz, 79
Couros, George, 31, 32
Course management system, CSU Channel Islands. *See also* Learning management system, College of Charleston Libraries
  background, 243
  challenges of, 250–252
  conclusion, 252
  course guides, 249–250
  early implementation, 244–246
  e-reserves, 246–247
  menu options in Blackboard, 246
  print reserves, 248
  streaming video and, 248–249
  student authentication, 245
  textbook costs and, 245–246
  where the students are and, 244–245
Creative Commons Attribution-ShareAlike license, 114
Credo Reference, 7, 102
Crook, L., 143
"Crossing the Aisle: Connecting Fiction and Nonfiction," 79
Cross-training, reference and circulation, 210
CrowdAsk, 285–293
Curated collections, 111–112
Customer service, 64–65
  single point-of-service for, 207–213

Data
  community, 23–28
  usage logs, 351–358
Databases, reference work, 100–101
Dempsey, Lorcan, 121
Dequin, H. C., 304
Design, library. *See* Architecture and reference services
Desire2Learn, 50
DeskTracker, 153
Detmering, R., 362
Diamond, T., 352
Digital Reference Service in the New Millennium: Planning, Management, and Evaluation, 145
Digital reference services. *See* Collaborative virtual reference
"Digital Reference Services Bibliography," 135

Disabled patrons services
  assessment of, 312–314
  communication in, 311–312
  future phases of, 314
  introduction to, 303–305
  project background, 305
  project evaluation, 305–311
Discovery
  adding value to, 126–127
  closing the content gap in, 125–126
  commercial avenues for, 129–131
  deeper librarian integration into process of, 337–338
  defined, 121–123
  digital reference desk and, 335–338
  exploratory (topic) searches, 355
  future directions for, 129–131
  future of libraries in the age of, 131
  integrating traditional tools with, 127–128
  known-item searches, 353–354
  OCLC approach to, 330–332
  OhioLINK, 317–325
  open-source, 126, 129–131
  relevance ranking, 355–356
  Summon service, 335–338
  tool use, 128–129
  types of searches, 352–358
  usage logs, 351–358
  web-scale, 123–125
Diversity and inclusivity, 374
Doan, T., 50
Doll, C. A., 46, 48
Doyle, C. S., 42
Drupal, 131
Duck, Pat, 272

E-books, 82–83, 84, 89
EBSCO
  Academic Search Premier, 81
  Discovery Service, 123, 128, 130, 318–325, 351
Education of librarians, 295–296, 361–369
Education Testing System National Higher Education Information and Communications Technology Initiative (ETS-ICT), 52
EGain, 136
Elsevier, 365
Embedded librarianship, 255–256, 260–261
Emerging user populations, 25–26

Emerson, Ralph Waldo, 3–4, 371, 375
Empathy, 65–66
Empire State Information Fluency Continuum, 54
Encyclopedia Britannica, 99
Encyclopedia of Heavy Metal Music, 93, 94
Encyclopedia of Indie Rock, 93
Encyclopedia of Life (EOL), 111
Encyclopedias, 93–94
Entry-level librarians, 295–296, 361–369
E-reserves
  Blackboard and, 246–247
  migrated to campus LMS, 257
ERIC, 327
Esson, R., 144–145
Ex Libris, 123, 130, 248
  Primo, 351–358
Exploratory (topic) searches, 355
EXtensible Catalog, 131

Facebook, 80, 128, 139, 265, 273
  ChiliFresh platform and, 266–270
  roving reference and, 183
FaceTime, 72
Faculty
  learning management system training for, 256
  reference publishing and, 98–99
Farmer, L. S., 46
Ferriero, David, 109
Filter failure, 373
FirstSearch, 327, 330
Flickr, 111–112
Floyd, Joe, 34
Folk, Amanda, 272
Formative assessment, 52–53
Form-based readers' advisory, 80–81
Framework for Information Literacy for Higher Education, 55–57
Fransen, J., 155
"Future of the Standards, The," 55–56
Future Shock, 373

Gadsby, J., 182
Gale, 7, 363
  Virtual Reference Library, 81, 102
Gamson, Z. F., 46, 48
Gates, Bill, 375
Genreflecting: A Guide to Popular Reading Interests, 77
GeoCommons, 26

Georgia Southwestern State University, 216, 221–222
    community partners, 216–217
    creating effective library guides for, 217–219
    introduction to, 215–216
    marketing by, 219–221
Gerjuoy, Herbert, 373
Gibson, Craig, 54
Gilder, George, 369
Gimlet, 153
Gladwell, Malcolm, 231
Global Voices, 113
"Going Where the Students Are: A Symposium on Live Reference in the CSU," 137–138
Google, 9, 76, 265, 328, 332. *See also* Discovery; Internet, the
    Chromebook, 35
    as discovery tool, 128, 129
    + hangouts, 366
    knowledge graph, 115
    learning experiences using, 46
    Meebo, 139, 140, 258–259
    (r)evolution, 150–153
    Voice, 183
Graham-Smith, S., 304
Gray, Brian, 336–337
Green, Samuel, 2, 11, 361, 375
Guidelines for Behavioral Performance of Reference and Information Services Providers, The, 63–64, 72
"Guidelines for Cooperative Reference Services," 135
"Guidelines for Implementing and Maintaining Virtual Reference Services," 134
Guide to Reference Books, 297–301, 362
Gustavus Adolphus College, 199. *See also* Peer reference tutoring
Gwinnett County Public Library (GCPL), 32–36

Hamilton, Buffy J., 33, 34
Harvard University, 3–4
HBO, 76
Hidden web, 373–374
Higher order thinking skills (HOTS), 44, *45*
High stakes assessment, 52
Huang, S., 304
Hufford, J. R., 150
Hulu Plus, 76
Human Click, 136

Hunter Library, Western Carolina University, 191. *See also* On-call reference
Hurricane Katrina, 28

ICQ, 140
Imposed query, 67
Inclusivity and diversity, 374
"Increase Awareness for Virtual Reference Services," 226
Information Industry Association (IIA), 41
Information literacy
    assessment, 51–53
    concept of, 41
    defined, 41–42
    developing learning experiences for, 45–47
    developing learning outcomes for, 43–45
    digital discovery and, 335–336
    filter failure, 373
    lifelong learning and, 373
    program components, *51*
    standards development, 42–45
    for the 21st century, 53–57, 372–373
    technology and pedagogy in, 48
Information Literacy Competency Standards for Higher Education (ACRL), 10, 43, 54–55, 304
"Information Power," 42
"Information Power: Building Partnerships for Learning," 44
"Information Power II," 43
Information Skills for an Information Society: A Review of Research, 42
Innovation
    hubs, 29–30
    practices of, 31, *32*
Inquiry models, 47, 54
Instant messaging (IM), 139, 140, 193–194, 258–259
Institute and Museum Library Services (IMLS), 53
Interlibrary loan (ILL), 5, 141, 142, 321
Internet, *See also* Google; Technology; Twitter; Wikipedia
    ChiliFresh platform, 265–270
    crowdsourcing of reference services, 285–293
    hidden web, 373–374
    information resources on, 5–6, 7, 14–15
    learning experiences using, 46
    reference interviews and, 9
    web-scale discovery, 123–125
    YouTube, 113, 260

Interviews, reference, 9
  art and strategy of, 63–64
  building rapport and reflecting empathy in, 65–66
  closed-ended questions, 68–69
  concluding, 71–72
  introduction to, 61
  open-ended questions in, 66–68
  reflection and change, 72–73
  searching after, 69–71
  starting with customer service, 64–65
  understanding user information needs and contexts using, 61–63
iPad, 183
Ipl2 Librarian Digital Reference Service Student and Volunteer Training program, 364, 366
iSkills, 52–53
Ithaka S + R, 155, 156

James A. Cannavino Library, Marist College, 335–336
Janes, Joseph, 141, 145, 231
Jing, 366, 368
John, Joanne, 226
John M. Olin Library, Washington University, 344–349
Johnson-Varney, Suzanne, 322–324
John Spoor Broome Library, CSU Channel Islands. *See* Course management system, CSU Channel Islands
Journals, *49*
"Just-in-time" model, 163, 195

Kaspusniak, Renee, 82
Kelvin Smith Library, Case Western Reserve University, 336–337
Kern, K. M., 133
Kirkwood, H., 50
Knibbe-Haanstra, M., 363
KnowItNow24x7, 8
Knowledge Card, 332
Known-item searches, 353–354
Krannert Center for the Performing Arts (KCPA), 216
Kuali OLE, 130
Kuhlthau, Carol, 42, 62
K-W-L, 52

Lafayette, S., 304
Lamar University. *See* Mary and John Gray Library, Lamar University

Lancaster, Frederick Wilfrid, 131
Land, Ray, 55
Lankes, David, 19, 231
"Leaders as readers: What happens when directors choose reading as core initiative," 78
Lean In, 79
Learning
  blended, 50
  commons, 50
  information literacy programs
    activities and assignments design, 47–48
    environments, 48–50
    experiences, 45–47
    outcomes, 43–45
    technology in, 48
  logs, *49*
  outcomes, 43–45, *51*
  physical environments, 50, *51*
Learning management systems, *See also* Course management system,
  conclusion, 260–261
  connecting library resources and services to campus LMS redux, 256–260
  death of Meebo and, 258–259
  determining needs and creating plan for, 254–255
  embedded librarianship and, 255–256
  introduction, 253–254
  launch, 256
  LMS upgrades and, 259–260
  migrating electronic reserves to LMS, 257
  reference desk changes and, 257–258
  tutorials and training for faculty and students, 256
Lehman College Leonard Lief Library, 181–182, 188.
Lesson planning, 46–47
Levitin, Daniel, 231
LibAnalytics, 153
LibChat, 258
LibGuides, 127, 128, 215–216, 217, 258, 259, 262, 337
  creating effective, 217–219
  for disabled patrons, 311
  marketing, 219–221
  Sandbox for Library Schools, 363–364, 368
LibQual+, 155, 156

Librarians
  blended, 50
  children's, 20–22
  reference
    active listening by, 65
    challenges of teaching sources in LIS programs for, 295–296
    communication tools, 8
    direct assistance provided by, 2
    entry-level, 295–296, 361–369
    factual questions asked of, 6
    finding out what users need, 9
    as library counselor, 3–4
    management of change by, 163–171
    on-call, 191–197
    on-the-job training tools for, 296–297
    Personal Librarian program, 173–180
    perspective on peer reference tutoring, 204–205
    reader's advisory by, 8–9
    relevance of today's, 371–376
    role of, 5
    roving, 181–188
    teaching information literacy skills, 9–10
    training in reader's advisory, 77–78
Librarianship
  blended, 50
  embedded, 255–256, 260–261
  training, 295–296, 361–369
Libraries
  in the age of discovery, 131
  collaborations with schools, 24, 32–36
  as complex and mystifying, 3–4
  as growing organisms, 371
  as innovation hubs, 29–30
  multi-directional content experiences in, 22–23
  online catalogs, 248, 279–284
  planning and architecture of, 339–350
  as responsive organizations, 23–28
  role in communities, 2–6
  sharing of collections by, 5
  types of, 4
Libraries Unlimited, 77, 83
Library á la Carte, 249–250
Library H3lp, 140
Library Journal, 2
  on readers' advisory, 75, 77, 78, 79, 81, 83, 84
Library 2.0 movement, 139–140
Library of Congress, 109, 135, 136
Library Services and Technology Act (LSTA), 138
LibraryThing for Libraries, 280–284
LibStats, 153
Licensing, open, 114–115
Lifelong learning, 373
Lindauer, B. G., 51
Lipow, Anne, 231
Listening, active, 65
LivePerson, 136
LMS. *See* Learning management system, College of Charleston Libraries
Local Facility Survey, 155, 156
Logs
  learning, 49
  usage, 351–358
Lower order thinking skills (LOTS), 44
Lund, Jennifer, 33, 34
Luo, L., 137
Lynch, Clifford A., 122

MacDonald, C., 363
Makerbot printers, 35
Manifesto for Agile Software Development, 24
Marist College, 335–336
Marketing and community outreach, 219–221
Mary and John Gray Library, Lamar University
  assessment of, 312–314
  communication with disabled patrons at, 311–312
  disabled patrons project background, 305
  future phases of service at, 314
  introduction to, 303–305
  project evaluation, 305–311
Maryland AskUsNow!, 8
Mastel, K., 155
Mastery, subject, 231
Mathews, Brian, 29
McGlamery, Susan, 136, 231
MediaWiki, 104
MEDLINE, 327
Meebo, 139, 140, 258–259
Metacognition, 55
Metadata, 332–333
MetaFilter, 113
Metaliteracy, 55–56
Metropolitan New York Library Council (METRO), 181
Meyer, Jan, 55
Miller, Bill, 1

Miller Nichols Library, University of Missouri-Kansas City, 207–213
Millstein Library, University of Pittsburgh at Greensburg, 271–278
Monitoring of student learning, 52
Moodle, 50
Mudge, Isadore Gilbert, 362
Multi-directional content experiences, 22–23
Mun, Lorri M., 149
Murawski, Mike, 30
Museum participatory practices, 22–23, 30
Music and Performing Arts Library, University of Illinois at Urbana-Champaign, 216, 221–222
   community partners, 216–217
   creating effective library guides for, 217–219
   introduction to, 215–216
   marketing by, 219–221

Nackerud, S., 155
National Archives and Records Administration (NARA), 109
National Art Education Conference, 30
National Center for Education Statistics, 241
National Commission on Libraries and Information Science (NCLIS), 41
National Council of Teachers of English (NCTE), 372–373
National Information Standards Organization, 126
Needham, W. L., 304
Needs, community, 22–23
Netflix, 76
Neutral point of view (NPOV), 105
Neutral questioning, 67
New York Public Library, 109
Nicol, E. C., 143
Nonfiction Readers' Advisory, 79
Norcross High School (NHS) Media Center, 32–36
Norton Public Library, 279–284
NoveList K-8, 79
NoveList Plus, 79, 84
Nunn, B., 182

Oakleaf, Megan, 153–154
OCLC, 123, 130, 135
   approach to discovery, 330–332
   FirstSearch, 327, 328, 330
   history of, 327–330
   Knowledge Card, 332
   metadata depth, 332–333
   Open WorldCat Initiative, 327–329

QuestionPoint, 8, 136, 137, 138, 139, 144, 223–229, 231
O'Connor, L., 50, 52
Ohio Library and Information Network (OhioLINK)
   background, 317–319
   challenges and customization, 320–321
   implementation, 319–320
   preliminary results and feedback, 321–325
Ohio Library Council, 63
On-call reference
   background and history, 191–192
   from idea to solution, 194
   measuring success and looking forward with, 196–197
   pilot project and full integration of, 194–196
   temporary fixes and major changes leading to, 192–193
O'Neill, Thomas P. "Tip," 4
One-minute papers, 52
Online public access catalog (OPAC), 327
Online public access catalogs (OPACs)
   CSU Channel Islands, 248
   Norton Public Library, 279–284
On-the-job training tools for librarians, 296–297
Open access to information, 99–100
   user-generated content and, 114–115
   web-discovery and, 126, 129–131
OpenBib, 131
Open Discovery Initiative, 126
Open-ended questions, 66–68
OpenStreetMap (OSM), 26, 111
Open WorldCat Initiative, 327–328, 327–329
Oxford University Press, 91–92

Pandora, 8
Pardue, Bill, 226
Participatory design
   children's librarians and, 20–22
   defined, 19–20
   future of, 28–32
   guideposts for, 20–22
   learning and participatory playbook, 31
   museums and, 22–23, 30
   participatory learning and, 20
   practices of innovation and, 31, 32
   present-day practices, 32–36
   reflections on, 37
   using data to connect with community needs, 23–28
Participatory Museum, The, 20

Passive learning, 46
Patrons. *See* Users, library
Pearl, Nancy, 77–78
Pedagogy, 30
  technology and, 48
Peer reference tutoring
  activities during shifts, 203
  background, 199
  conclusion, 205
  introduction to, 199–201
  librarians' perspectives on, 204–205
  peer tutors' perspectives on, 203–204
  scheduling, 202–203
  selection process, 201
  training, 201–202
Peer review, 49
Penner, K., 182
Personal Librarian program (University of San Diego)
  conclusion, 179–180
  future of, 178–179
  implementation, 176–177
  overview and vision, 173–175
  planning, 176
  research on, 175
  results to date, 177–178
Peterson, K., 155
Pew Internet and American Life Project, 24
Piderit, S. K., 164
Planning and design, library. *See* Architecture and reference services
Poole's Index to Periodical Literature, 5
Portfolios, 49
Portland Art Museum, 30
Poudre River Public Library, 28
Practices of innovation, 31, 32
Presidential Committee on Information Literacy (ALA), 42, 43
Price, S., 352
Princeton Theological Seminary, 340–344, 349–350
Print reserves and course management systems, 248
"Progress Report on Information Literacy: An Update on the American Library Association Presidential Committee on Information Literacy: Final Report, A," 43
ProjectSAILS, 52–53
ProQuest, 123, 364
  Summon, 335–338, 351–358
Public Library Association (PLA), 77, 79
Public library coordination with schools, 24, 32–36

Publishing, reference, 7
  added value in, 98
  aggregators, 101–102
  collections, bundles, and databases in, 100–101
  currency in reference works and, 97–98
  faculty and, 98–99
  free and open access and, 99–100
  introduction to, 89–90
  shift in sustainable growth equation for, 90–102
  spotlight on Damon Zucca, Oxford University Press, 91–92
  spotlight on Vince Burns, ABC-CLIO, 93–94
  strategy for successful, 102
  technology and, 90–95
  textbooks, 101
  topic selection, 96
  usage of reference works and, 96–97

Qian, S., 182
QuestionPoint (OCLC), 8, 136, 137, 138, 139, 144, 223–229, 231
Questions
  closed-ended, 68–69
  open-ended, 66–68
Quora, 112

Radford, Marie L., 65, 149
Ranganathan, S. R., 13, 121, 371
Rapport building, 65–66
"Readers' Advisory 101," 81
Readers' advisory (RA), 8–9
  in academic libraries, 81
  challenges, 82–83
  e-books and, 82–83, 84
  face-to-face versus traditional, 78–79
  form-based, 80–81
  future of, 83–85
  versus Google and Amazon, 76
  improvement in services, 81–82
  innovations in, 80–81
  librarian's reading habits and, 83
  for nonfiction, 79
  relation to reference, 75
  rise of, 77–78
Readers' Advisory Handbook, The, 77
Readers' Advisory Services in the Public Library, 77, 79
Reading Refresh, 80
Read On, 77
Real Story, The, 79

Reference and Information Services: An Introduction, 77
Reference and User Services Association (RUSA), 63, 134–135, 152
Reference and User Services Quarterly, 80
Reference interviews, 9
    art and strategy of, 63–64
    building rapport and reflecting empathy in, 65–66
    closed-ended questions, 68–69
    concluding, 71–72
    introduction to, 61
    open-ended questions in, 66–68
    reflection and change, 72–73
    searching after, 69–71
    starting with customer service, 64–65
    understanding user information needs and contexts using, 61–63
Reference Librarian, The, 240
Reference publishing, 7
    added value in, 98
    aggregators, 101–102
    collections, bundles, and databases in, 100–101
    currency in reference works and, 97–98
    faculty and, 98–99
    free and open access and, 99–100
    introduction to, 89–90
    shift in sustainable growth equation for, 90–102
    spotlight on Damon Zucca, Oxford University Press, 91–92
    spotlight on Vince Burns, ABC-CLIO, 93–94
    strategy for successful, 102
    technology and, 90–95
    textbooks, 101
    topic selection, 96
    usage of reference works and, 96–97
Reference Reborn: Breathing New Life into Public Services Librarianship, 145
Reference services. *See also* Collaborative virtual reference; User-generated content
    access services and, 165–170
    adaptation to change, 168–169
    assessment of, 149–150, 157–158
    community support by, 154–155
    contribution measurements, 154
    crowdsourcing, 285–293
    death of, 77–78
    encyclopedias, 93–94
    equity and tiered, 167–168
    Google and, 150–153
    Guide to Reference and, 297–301
    hidden web, 373–374
    historical perspective on, 2
    information availability, 6–7
    "just-in-time" model of, 163
    learning management systems and, 257–258
    line ups, transfers, and service quality, 166–167
    managing change of, 163–171
    on-call, 191–197
    to patrons with disabilities, 303–314
    peer reference tutoring, 199–205
    Personal Librarian program, 173–180
    perspectives on problems with, 1
    planning and architectural design for, 339–350
    public satisfaction with, 155–156
    publishers, 7
    reimagining, 11–16, 371–376
    relevance of today's, 371–376
    roving, 181–188
    single service point with circulation services, 207–213
    for "Somewhere Out There Patron," 229–241
    teaching sources in LIS programs, 295–296
    tiered services, 166–167
    toward a new valuation of, 153–158
    transaction data, 156–157
    transcripts, 156
    24/7 virtual, 138, 141, 223–229
    uniqueness of, 10–11
"Reference Services in Face-to-Face and Virtual Environments," 149
Reimagined reference, 11–16, 371–376
    future of, 13–16
    resources on, 12–13
"Reinventing Undergraduate Education," 43
Relevance ranking, 355–356
Report of the Committee appointed by the Board of Overseers of Harvard College to examine the Library, 3
Research-Based Readers' Advisory, 81
Responsive organizations, libraries as, 23–28
Rethinking Reference movement, 1
Roberts, S., 144–145
Ross, Catherine, 81

Roving reference, 181
  assessment of, 186–187
  background, 181–182
  conclusions, 188
  data collection, 183–184
  findings, 184–186
  literature review, 182–183
  methodology, 183
  recommendations for, 187–188
Rozaklis, L., 363
Ruane, E., 182
Rubric Assessment of Information Literacy Skills (RAILS), 53
Rubrics, assignment, 53

Sadeh, T., 356
Sandberg, Sheryl, 79
San José Public Library, 78
Saracevic, T., 355, 356
Saricks, Joyce G., 77
Sawn, Kevin, 181
Schilling, I., 304
Schools
  collaborations with public libraries, 24, 32–36
  information literacy programs learning outcomes for, 43–45
Searching, 69–71. *See also* Discovery
  Boolean, 129
  measures of success, 356–358
  relevance ranking, 355–356
  types of, 352–358
Serials Solutions, 127, 130–131
Shadowing, 193
Sharkey, J., 50, 52
Shea, Erin, 79
Shearer, Kenneth, 81
Shirky, Clay, 373
Silberger, Kathryn, 335–336
Silins, Venta, 81
Simon, Nina, 20
Single point-of-service desk, 207–213
SirsiDynix catalog, 279–280
"6 Pieces of Evidence, The," 63, 67
Skype, 14
Sloan, B., 135, 137
Social media, 15. *See also* Internet, the
  discussion and sharing sites, 112–113
  learning experiences using, 46
  online social tools for libraries, 265–270
  reader's advisory services and, 80
  roving reference and, 183

"Somewhere Out There Patron" (SOTP). *See also* Collaborative virtual reference
  defined, 231
  how users access services as, 238–241
  librarian's chat experience with, 231–241
  location of, 235–237
  times for accessing services, 237–238
  what are the information needs of, 234
  who is the, 232–233
SOPAC, 131
Southeastern Automated Information Library System (SAILS), 279–284
Springshare, 127, 363. *See also* LibGuides
Sproles, C., 362
StackExchange, 112
"Stalking the Wild Appeal Factor: Readers' Advisory and Social Networking Sites," 80
Standards for the 21st-Century Learner (AASL), 41, 45, 47, 48, 57
  Google and, 151
  information literacy and, 53–57
Stanford Encyclopedia of Philosophy, 100
"State of Readers Advisory, The," 83
Stover, Kaite, 80
Streaming video, 248–249
Stripling Model of Inquiry, 47, 54
Students. *See also* Users, library
  authentication, 245, 249
  with disabilities, 303–314
  learning experiences, 45–47
  learning management system training for, 256
  learning outcomes (SLOs), 44–45, *51*
  library and information science, 295–296
  peer reference tutoring by, 199–205
Subject mastery, 231
Summative assessment, 52–53
Summer MakerCamp, 34–35
Summon discovery service, 335–338
  usage logs, 351–358

Taylor, R., 61, 63
Technology. *See also* Internet, the; Social media
  audiobooks, 84–85
  changing, 374
  communications, 8, 14
  course management systems (*See* Course management system, CSU Channel Islands)

for disabled patrons services, 312–314
discovery tools, 128–129, 368–369
e-books, 82–83, 84
innovations and reader's advisory, 80–81
instant messaging, 139, 140. 193–194, 258–259
learning for entry-level librarians, 363–364
learning management systems (*See* Learning management system, College of Charleston Libraries)
on-call reference and, 193–197
online catalogs, 248, 279–284
pedagogy and, 48
reference publishing and, 90–95
roving reference and, 183
24/7 virtual reference cooperation and, 138, 141, 223–229
Twitter reference and, 271–278
used by chat reference patrons, 238–241
Teen Tech Week 2014, 33–34
Textbooks, 101
  costs, 245–246
Thiele, Jennifer, 82
Thingiverse, 34
Thomas, Steve, 33, 34
Thomsett-Scott, B. C., 133
Threshold concepts, 55–56
Tiered reference services, 166–167
Tinkercad, 34, *35*
"Tips for the Reluctant Readers' Advisor," 83
Tobias, Christine, 240
Toffler, Alvin, 373
Too Much to Know, 374
Tucker, Spencer, 93
Tucker-Raymond, Caleb, 141
Tutor.com, 137
Tutoring, peer reference, 199–205
21st century literacies, 53–57, 372–373
24/7 global virtual reference cooperation, 138, 141, 223–229, 237–238. *See also* Collaborative virtual reference
"Twenty Years of Virtual Reference," 137
Twitter, 35, 113, 128, 139, 152, 265
  community outreach using, 220
  as reference medium, 271–273
  roving reference and, 183
Tyckoson, David, 1

University of Phoenix, 101
University of San Diego (USD), 173. *See also* Personal Librarian program
University Pittsburgh at Greensburg (UPG), 271–278
Usage logs
  analysis, 352–358
  introduction to, 351–352
  measures of search success, 356–358
  relevance ranking and, 355–356
User-generated content. *See also* Wikipedia
  curated collections, 111–112
  evaluating, 113–115
  openness of, 114–115
  question-answering, education, and how-to sites, 112
  reference works, 111
  social media and, 112–113
  user expectations and, 115–117
Users, library. *See also* Students
  anonymity of, 234
  building rapport with, 65–66
  chat reference needs, 231–241
  with disabilities, 303–314
  emerging populations of, 25–26
  generated sites, 110–113
  information literacy skills, 9–10
  reference interviews of, 9
  understanding information needs and contexts of, 61–63

Valuation of reference 7, 153–158
Value of Academic Libraries, The, 10, 153, 155
VALUE Rubrics, 53
Vaughn, Jason, 123
Victorian Women Writers Project, 126
Video
  as added-value component to works, 98
  chat, 72
  streaming, 248–249
"Virtual Reference Bibliography," 133
Virtual Reference Desk (VRD) Conference, 138–139
Virtual reference services. *See* Collaborative virtual reference
Vnuk, R., 84

Washington University, St. Louis, 344–349
Weak, E., 137
Web-scale discovery tools, 123–125
Weiner, S., 50
WikiHow, 112
Wikimedia Commons, 104, 111–112
  sharing collections via, 109
Wikimedia Foundation, 104

Wikipedia, 7, 9, 99, 328. *See also* User-generated content
  contributing to, 107–110
  core editorial policies, 105
  editors, 374
  evaluating articles on, 106–107
  future of, 115–117
  GLAM and Wikipedians-in-Residence, 109–110
  Loves Libraries, 109
  openness of, 114–115
  in other languages, 106
  popularity and scope of, 103
  structure and editing of, 103–105
  user-generated and open content, 110–113
Wiki Project Med, 115
Wikisource, 104
Wikivoyage, 104
Wiktionary, 104
Williamsburg Regional Library, 80
Williford, Anna Mary, 272
Woodard, B. S., 43, 51
WorldCat Discovery, 329–330, 331
WorldCat.org, 328–329
Wyatt, Liam, 109–110

Xerxes, 131

Yahoo, 328
  IM, 140
Yale University, 175
Young, Courtney, 240
YouTube, 113, 260

Zucca, Damon, 91–92
Zurkowski, Paul, 41

www.ingramcontent.com/pod-product-compliance
Lightning Source LLC
Chambersburg PA
CBHW052123230426
43671CB00009B/1097